M.F.K. FISHER'S

TRANSLATION OF

THE
PHYSIOLOGY
OF TASTE

OR

MEDITATIONS ON
TRANSCENDENTAL
GASTRONOMY

BY

Jean Anthelme Brillat-Savarin

NORTH POINT PRESS

San Francisco

1986

North Point Press
850 Talbot Avenue
Berkeley, California
94706

THE TRANSLATOR'S PREFACE

I made this translation by myself, and can therefore thank none for it but perhaps my first teacher, who helped me learn to read. I have put it into the simplest words I know, since I feel that it is a singularly straightforward and unornamented piece of prose to have been written in a flowery literary period. I have kept as far as possible its measured rhythm, and have changed into colons only a few overburdened commas and semicolons. As I have more than once pointed out along the way, the Professor's idiosyncrasies of spelling foreign words I have accentuated with SPACED SMALL CAPS, to differentiate them from his own stressed words. I emerge from the real ordeal of translation with an even realer humility.

As for the numerous glosses which I have added to the text, I can give thanks, but not enough, to several friends who have helped me. Lawrence Clark Powell and Robert Vosper of the Library of the University of California at Los Angeles let me call upon them for anything I wanted from their prodigious stacks, and H. Richard Archer of the William Andrews Clark Memorial Library in Los Angeles did the same from his more limited and perhaps more precious shelves. The three of them added hours of their own and their staffs' time to track down abstruse, possibly unimportant, but interesting notes for me. Miss Althea Warren, then head of the Los Angeles Public Libraries, and one of her witty and seemingly tireless assistants named Armine Mackenzie, were unreasonably generous of their time and advice. I could use the rare and often fantastic gastronomical library of Harold H. Price of San Francisco. I could call on the energetic and profound knowledge of Dr. Henry B. Bieler of Pasadena, for not only biological but spiritual data connected with the miracle of hunger and its perils and pleasures. I could depend upon the conscience of Frances Wolf to plunge dauntlessly into batch after batch of finicky transcribing of my two-finger type. In countless moments of despair, chagrin, exasperation (but never boredom), I could turn to the ruthless editorial eye of Donald Friede.

For all this I hold myself blessed among translators, and I end my honest labor with the hope that what I have done will find more favor than blame among the four (and more) categories of gastronomers that Brillat-Savarin wrote of in 1825. It has taken me only some two years to translate what he spent perhaps twenty-five or thirty years writing.

That is as it should be.

M.F.K. FISHER
1949

The need for simplicity which Brillat-Savarin helped to strengthen in me is even stronger than it was in 1949 and I see no need to add to what I wrote then, except perhaps to avow that my love for the old lawyer burns as brightly now as ever.

M.F.K. FISHER
1971

A TABLE
OF THE CONTENTS

Meditation 2: On Taste

Meditation 3: On Gastronomy

Meditation 4: On Appetite

Meditation 5: On Food in General

Meditation 8: On Thirst

Meditation 9: On Drinks

Meditation 10: The End of the World

Meditation 11: On Gourmandism

Meditation 12: On Gourmands

Meditation 13: On Gastronomical Tests

Meditation 14: On the Pleasures of the Table

Meditation 15: On Hunting-Luncheons

Meditation 16: On Digestion

Meditation 17: On Rest

Meditation 18: On Sleep

Meditation 19: On Dreams

Meditation 20: On the Influence of Diet

Meditation 21: On Obesity

Meditation 22: On the Treatment of Obesity

Meditation 23: On Thinness

Meditation 24: On Fasting

Meditation 25: On Exhaustion

Meditation 26: On Death

Meditation 27: On Cooking

Meditation 28: On Restaurateurs

PART I

APHORISMS

OF THE PROFESSOR

TO SERVE AS A PREAMBLE TO HIS WORK

AND AS A LASTING FOUNDATION FOR

THE SCIENCE OF GASTRONOMY

I. The Universe is nothing without the things that live in it, and everything that lives, eats.

II: Animals feed themselves; men eat; but only wise men know the art of eating.

III: The destiny of nations depends on how they nourish themselves.[1]

IV: Tell me what you eat, and I shall tell you what you are.[2, 3]

V: The Creator, while forcing men to eat in order to live, tempts him to do so with appetite and then rewards him with pleasure.

VI: Good living is an act of intelligence, by which we choose things which have an agreeable taste rather than those which do not.

VII: The pleasures of the table are for every man, of every land, and no matter of what place in history or society; they can be a part of all his other pleasures, and they last the longest, to console him when he has outlived the rest.

VIII: The table is the only place where a man is never bored for the first hour.

IX: The discovery of a new dish does more for human happiness than the discovery of a star.[4]

X: Men who stuff themselves and grow tipsy know neither how to eat nor how to drink.

XI: The proper progression of courses in a dinner is from the most substantial to the lightest.

XII: The proper progression of wines or spirits is from the mildest to the headiest and most aromatic.

XIII: It is heresy to insist that we must not mix wines: a man's palate can grow numb and react dully to even the best bottle, after the third glass from it.

XIV: A dinner which ends without cheese is like a beautiful woman with only one eye.

XV: We can learn to be cooks, but we must be born knowing how to roast.

XVI: The most indispensable quality of a cook is promptness, and it should be that of the diner as well.

XVII: A host who makes all his guests wait for one late-comer is careless of their well-being.[5]

XVIII: He who plays host without giving his personal care to the repast is unworthy of having friends to invite to it.

XIX: The mistress of the house should always make sure that the coffee is good, and the master that the wines are of the best.

XX: To invite people to dine with us is to make ourselves responsible for their well-being for as long as they are under our roofs.

THE TRANSLATOR'S GLOSSES

1. Here it is hard not to quote almost anyone in the world who has thought more than three thoughts, since one of them is bound to be about his nourishment. To tease myself I like to remember what a man said who has perhaps most puzzled and astonished the other thinkers. It was Albert Einstein. "An empty stomach is not a good political adviser," he decided quite early

in his life, as simply as if he were chalking one more equation on the world's blackboard.

2.   More than two decades after these Aphorisms first appeared, the German philosopher of materialism, Ludwig Andreas Feuerbach, stated with an air of belligerent discovery, *Der Mensch ist was er isst* . . . "Potato blood can make no revolution," he said disgustedly, and he recommended that the hungry weaklings who had failed to bring off the 1848 Revolution in his country change their diet to one of beans! His theory, though not original with him as he believed, was kept alive in the Teutonic mind long enough to have Hitler's humanitarians apply it to many a nation made hungry so systematically that not even potato blood flowed through its veins. It would be difficult for the Professor, I think, to preserve his philosophical calm in the face of such murderous application of his Aphorism . . .

3.   See page 154 and my note on page 158.

4.   This most quoted of the Professor's rules of conduct came, he writes with such candor that it cannot be a confession ("Varieties," XXV, page 411), from his old friend Henrion de Pansey, a well-known French lawyer whose first names were Pierre-Paul and whose four-line eulogy was not needed until four years after Brillat-Savarin published it in 1825. They seem to have been without mutual jealousy or suspicion, unusual in any old men but especially those who must weave their way together through the courts of law.

5.   One of the great English gourmets of the nineteenth century set his dinner hour at five in the afternoon, which was the proper time in those days, and at five minutes past five he locked his door and firmly hid the key. Latecomers were not only turned away, but were never asked again.

DIALOGUE
BETWEEN THE
AUTHOR AND
HIS FRIEND

[THE FIRST COMPLIMENTS HAVING BEEN PAID]

FRIEND—This morning my wife and I decided, at breakfast, that you really ought to have your GASTRONOMICAL MEDITATIONS published, and as soon as possible.[1]

AUTHOR—*What woman wants, God wants.* There, in five words, you have the whole guide to Parisian life! But I myself am not a Parisian, and anyway as a bachelor . . .[2]

FRIEND—Good Lord, bachelors are as much victims of the rule as the rest of us, and sometimes to our great disadvantage! But in this case even celibacy can't save you: my wife is convinced that she has the right to dictate to you about the book, since it was at her country house that you wrote the first pages of it.

AUTHOR—You know, my dear Doctor, my deference for the ladies. More than once you've complimented me on my submission to their orders. You were even among those who once said that I would make an excellent husband! Nevertheless, I refuse to publish my book.[3]

FRIEND—And why?

AUTHOR—Because, since I am committed to a life of serious professional studies, I am afraid that people who might know the book only by its title would think that I wrote nothing but fiddle-faddle.

FRIEND—Pure panic! Aren't thirty-six years of continuous public service enough to have established the opposite reputation? Anyway, my wife and I believe that everyone will want to read you.

AUTHOR—Really?

FRIEND—Learned men will read you to learn more from you, and to fill out for themselves what you have only sketched.

AUTHOR—That might well be . . .

FRIEND—The ladies will read you because they will see very plainly that . . .

AUTHOR—My dear friend, I am old! I've acquired wisdom, at least: *miserere mei!* [4]

FRIEND—Gourmands will read you because you do justice to them, because at long last you give them the place they merit in society.

AUTHOR—This one time you're right! It is incredible that they have been misunderstood for so long, the poor fellows! I suffer for them like their own father . . . they are so charming, and have such twinkling little eyes!

FRIEND—Moreover, have you not often told us that our libraries definitely lack a book like yours?

AUTHOR—I've said so . . . I admit that, and would choke myself rather than take it back!

FRIEND—Now you are talking like a man completely convinced! Come along home with me and . . .

AUTHOR—Not at all! If an author's life has its little pleasures, it also has plenty of stings in it. I'll leave all that to my heirs.

FRIEND—But you disinherit your friends then . . . your acquaintances, your contemporaries. Have you enough courage for that?

AUTHOR—Heirs! Heirs! I've heard it said that ghosts are deeply flattered by the compliments of the living. That is a divine blessing which I'll gladly reserve for the next world.

FRIEND—But are you quite sure that these compliments will reach the right ghost? Are you equally sure of the trustworthiness of your heirs?

AUTHOR—I haven't any reason to believe that they will neglect one such duty, since for it I shall excuse them from a great many others!

FRIEND—But will they, can they, give to your book that fatherly love, those paternal attentions without which a published work seems always a little awkward on its first appearance?

AUTHOR—My manuscript will be corrected, neatly copied, polished in every way. There will be nothing more to do but print it.

FRIEND—And the chances of fate? Alas, similar plans have caused the loss of plenty of priceless works! Among them, for instance, there was that of the famous Lecat, on the state of the soul during sleep . . . his life work . . .

AUTHOR—That was, undoubtedly, a great loss. I am far from aspiring to any such regrets.

FRIEND—Believe me, your heirs will have plenty to cope with, what with the church, the law courts, the doctors themselves!

Even if they do not lack willingness, they'll have little time for the various worries that precede, accompany, and follow the publication of a book, no matter how long or short it may be.

AUTHOR—But my title! My subject! And my mocking friends!

FRIEND—The single word *gastronomy* makes everyone prick up his ears. The subject is always fashionable. And mockers like to eat, as well as the rest. And there's something else: can you ignore the fact that the most solemn personages have occasionally produced light works? There is President Montesquieu, for instance.†

AUTHOR—By Jove, that's so! He wrote THE TEMPLE OF GNIDUS . . . and one might do well to remember that there is more real point in meditating on what is at once necessary, pleasant, and a daily occupation, than in learning what was said and done more than two thousand years ago by a couple of little brats in the woods of Greece, one chasing, the other pretending to flee . . .

FRIEND—Then you give up, finally?

AUTHOR—Me? I should say not! I simply showed myself as an author for a minute. And that reminds me of a high-comedy scene from an English play, which really amused me. I think it's in a thing called THE NATURAL DAUGHTER. See what you think of it.‡

The play is about Quakers. You know that members of this sect thee-and-thou everyone, dress very simply, frown on war, never preach sermons, act with deliberation, and above all never let themselves be angry.

† *M. de Montucla, known for an excellent* HISTORY OF MATHEMATICS, *also wrote a* DICTIONARY OF GASTRONOMICAL GEOGRAPHY.
‡ *The reader in French must have noticed by now that my friend lets himself be thee-and-thou'd without reciprocating. This is because I am old enough to be his father, and because he would be very much upset if I changed, in spite of his having become a figure of considerable reputation in his own right.*

Well, the hero is a handsome young Quaker, who comes on the scene in a severe brown suit, a big flat-brimmed hat, uncurled hair . . . none of which facts prevents him from being normally amorous!

A stupid lout, finding himself the Quaker's rival in love, and emboldened by this ascetic exterior and the nature it apparently hides, teases and taunts and ridicules him, so that the young hero grows increasingly furious and finally gives the fool a good beating.

Once having done it, though, he suddenly reassumes his Quakerish manners. He falls back, and cries out in his shame, "Alas! I believe that the flesh has triumphed over the spirit!"

I feel the same way. After a reaction which is certainly pardonable, I go back to my first opinion.

FRIEND—It simply can't be done. You admit that you have shown yourself as an author for a second or two. I've got you now, and I'm taking you to the publisher's. I'll even tell you that more than one friend has already guessed your secret.

AUTHOR—Don't leave yourself open! I'll talk about you in return . . . and who knows what I may say?

FRIEND—What could you possibly say about me? Don't get the idea you can scare me off!

AUTHOR—What I shan't say is that our native land † prides itself on having produced you; that at twenty-four you had already published a textbook which has since become a classic; that your deserved reputation inspires great confidence in you; that your general appearance reassures the sick; that your dexterity astounds them; that your sympathy comforts them. All this is common knowledge. But I shall reveal to the whole of Paris (*here I draw myself up*), to all of France (*I swell with oratorical rage*), to the Universe itself, your only fault!

† *Belley, capital of the district of Bugey, a charming countryside with high mountains, hills, rivers, limpid brooks, waterfalls, chasms . . . a true "English garden" of a hundred square leagues, and where, before the Revolution, the Third Estate held, by the local constitution, the power of veto over the other two orders.*

FRIEND (*gravely*)—And what is that, may I ask?

AUTHOR—An habitual vice, which all my exhortations have not corrected.

FRIEND (*horrified*)—Tell me! Don't torture me like this!

AUTHOR—You eat too fast! †

[HERE THE FRIEND PICKS UP HIS HAT, AND EXITS SMILING, FAIRLY WELL CONVINCED THAT HE HAD MADE A CONVERT.]

THE TRANSLATOR'S GLOSSES

1. Dr. Richerand, although younger than the Professor by many years, was probably his closest friend, and is most often mentioned in this book. It was he who wrote the introduction to the second edition, which appeared soon after Brillat-Savarin's death, and which is plainly a tender eulogium rather than a dispassionate preface. He began by saying, "The fine man who wrote this book has portrayed himself in it with such charm, and has told of the main happenings of his life so pleasantly and with such truth, that few words will suffice to finish his story . . ." After an obviously emotional résumé of the Professor's career (". . . recalled to the Court of Appeals by the choice of the Senate, for twenty-five years he held the respect of his inferiors, the friendship of his equals, and the affection of everyone who knew him . . ."), Dr. Richerand wrote, "A man of great wit, a most agreeable dinner companion, and one endowed

† *Historical.*

with measureless gaiety, he was the center of attraction in any gatherings fortunate enough to have his company, for he gave himself up willingly to the seductions of worldly society, and only spurned them when he could delight in the more intimate pleasures of true friendship." It was of himself that the grieving Richerand spoke, here, and of the many gay fine hours he had known with Brillat-Savarin at Villecrêne, where they tasted quietly those "intimate pleasures of true friendship."

2. The only contradiction I know of to this plain statement, made early in the book by the man best qualified to say, is in a preface to THE PHYSIOLOGY OF TASTE written in Paris in 1879 by Charles Monselet, after talking with many people who still remembered Brillat-Savarin: "His widow lived long after him," Monselet said flatly. "M. Lefeuve affirms that she was still living in 1859, in the Rue Vivienne." This is the one mention I have ever found of a marriage in the Professor's life, and although it is pointless of me to quarrel with a man so much nearer the scene and the period than I, I think it possible that the French critic referred to the widow of one of Brillat-Savarin's brothers, who is said to have died in Paris in 1836, leaving a family behind him.

3. When Brillat-Savarin finally published his book, a few months before his death in February, 1826, he did it at his own expense and anonymously. It was the astonishment of his friends, who had never suspected his worldly classicism, that gave THE PHYSIOLOGY OF TASTE its first literary push. Everyone from Dr. Richerand to his somewhat unsuspected admirer Honoré de Balzac (who later tried the first imitation of it in his PHYSIOLOGY OF MARRIAGE) was eager to write some kind of preface to the flood of pirated editions that followed, and the eager tricks that publishers have resorted to since 1826 to get it into print would amuse none more than the Professor himself, who could not but pay from his own pocket for its first appearance. The title page from the editions through 1838 reads as follows: THE PHYSIOLOGY OF TASTE, or *Meditations On Transcendental Gastronomy, An historical, theoretical, and timely Work, Dedicated to Parisian Gastronomers,* BY A PROFESSOR, *Member of Numerous Scholarly Societies.*

4. When Brillat-Savarin used Latin words or phrases he sometimes italicized them and as often not. The comparatively few people who could read, in his day, knew this so-called "dead"

language almost as well as their own living ones. It was when he blithely sprinkled his pages with words from any of the four or five "living" languages he professed to be familiar with that his italics became a necessity. Then a double-type became even more necessary for me, to show, for instance, that when a pretty American girl sang YANKEE DUDDE it was not a printer's error but the Professor's! That holds true throughout this translation: whatever is in simple italics is as Brillat-Savarin so accentuated it; whatever is placed in S P A C E D S M A L L C A P S represents a typographical way of showing that here Gallic enthusiasm triumphed over erudition, and led the old lawyer down a misspelled but always delightful path bordered by linguistic lilies.

A BIOGRAPHY
OF DR. RICHERAND

The doctor introduced in the preceding Dialogue is far from being some such creature of fantasy as a mythical Chloris, but is rather a living, breathing, handsome man; and whoever knows me will already have recognized in him my friend Dr. Richerand.

As I was writing about him, my mind went back to men who came before his time, and I realized with pride that the district around Belley, my birthplace in the Department of the Ain, has for a long time given to Paris, the capital of the world, some doctors of great distinction. I could not resist the temptation of raising a modest monument to them, here in this short sketch.

During the Regency, Genin and Civoct were physicians of the highest standing, and poured an honestly acquired fortune back into their native soil. The first was completely hippocratic, ethical in the extreme; the second, whose patients included a large number of beautiful ladies, was much milder and more accommodating . . . *res novas molientem,* as Tacitus put it.

Toward 1750, Dr. La Chapelle distinguished himself in the dangerous career of military medicine. He left several useful books on the subject, and we owe to him the introduction of the treatment of inflammations of the chest with fresh butter, a method which works miracles when it is employed within the first thirty-six hours of the attack.[1]

About 1760, Dr. Dubois[2] had great success in the treatment of the vapors, a disorder very fashionable at that time, quite as popular as the nervous breakdowns which have replaced it! His stylish reputation is all the more astonishing when I recall that he was far from handsome . . .

Unhappily, he accumulated a fat fortune too early in life. He fell into the clutches of his own laziness, and seemed quite content to devote himself to being a charming dinner guest and a wholly amusing conversationalist. He was a sturdy fellow, and lived more than eighty-eight years, in spite of, or rather because of, the dinner parties of both the old and the new *régimes*.†

Toward the end of the reign of Louis XV, Dr. Coste, a native of Châtillon, came to Paris. He brought with him a letter of introduction from Voltaire to the Duke of Choiseul, whose patronage he was lucky enough to win from his very first visit.

Coste rose fast, thanks to the Duke's protection and that of his sister the Duchess of Grammont, and within a few years Paris counted the doctor among its most promising physicians.

The same protection which had so helped his climb dragged him away from his easy, profitable career, to put him at the head of the health service in the army which France sent to the United States, which were then fighting for their freedom.

Dr. Coste returned to France, having fulfilled his duties. He passed almost unharmed through the bad days of 1793, and was elected Mayor of Versailles, where he is still remembered for his active and yet paternal and kindly administration.

Before long the Directory recalled him to military medicine: Bonaparte appointed him one of three general inspectors of the armies' medical services. There Coste was unfailingly the

---

† *I smiled when I wrote this, for it reminded me of a renowned and lofty academician, whose funeral oration was delivered by Fontenelle. The departed had never done any more than play skilfully at the serious pursuits of life, but nevertheless the permanent secretary managed to deliver with great talent an impressive and even a lengthy panegyric. (See, further, the Meditation on the pleasures of the table, in which Dr. Dubois appears in action.)*

friend, protector, and father of younger men who prepared for the same career as his. Finally he was named royal physician at the Invalides, and he practiced there until his death.

Such faithful services could not go unrewarded under the government of the Bourbons, and Louis XVIII did no more than his just duty in conferring on M. Coste the order of Saint-Michel.

The doctor died a few years ago, leaving an honored memory, a fortune largely philosophical in content, and a single child, wife of that M. de Lalot whose colorful and profound eloquence in the Chamber of Deputies still did not prevent his political shipwreck.

One day when we were dining with M. Favre, the priest of Saint-Laurent, our compatriot Dr. Coste told me of his lively quarrel, that same morning, with Count de Cessac, at that time minister and director of the War Department, over some economizing the count wanted to do to curry favor with Napoleon.

This penny pinching was to consist of withholding from sick soldiers half their daily allotments of bread-and-water gruel, and of washing the lint packing from their bandages so that it could be used a second or third time.

The doctor had protested with violence against these plans, which he qualified as *abominable,* and he was still so full of the quarrel at dinner that he fell into another rage, exactly as if the object of his wrath were there before him.

I never knew whether the count was really dissuaded from carrying out his little plan, or simply left it hidden in his brief case, but what is certain is that the sick soldiers continued to drink all the gruel they wanted, and that their bandages once used were thrown away.

About 1780 Dr. Bordier, born near Ambérieux, came to practice medicine in Paris. His technique was pleasant, and he had a sure sense of diagnosis and an optimistic approach.

He was named professor in the College of Medicine. His manner was simple, but his lectures were fatherly and rewarding. Honors sought him out when he thought least of them, and he was made doctor to the Empress Marie-Louise. But he enjoyed himself only a short time in this position: the Empire dissolved, and the doctor himself was carried off by a disease of the leg which he had fought all his life.

Dr. Bordier was a contented man, with a trustworthy and benevolent nature.

Toward the end of the eighteenth century appeared Dr. Bichat . . . Bichat whose every written word carries the sign of genius, who used up his life to advance science, who united in himself a vital enthusiasm with a deep patience for more limited souls, and who, dead at thirty, deserved great public memorials to his name.

Later, Dr. Montègre brought into the clinics of Paris his philosopher's spirit. He directed with skill the publication of THE HEALTH GAZETTE, and died when he was forty, in the West Indies, where he had gone to complete his projected works on yellow fever and the *vomito negro*.

At this moment (1825), Dr. Richerand stands on the top rung of the ladder of surgical medicine, and his ELEMENTS OF PHYSIOLOGY has been translated into every tongue. He is invested with the highest possible confidence, named as he was at an early age professor in the Paris College of Medicine. No man has a more comforting manner than he, nor a gentler hand . . . nor a surer scalpel.

Dr. Récamier,[3] professor in the same school, sits at the side of his compatriot.

The present thus cared for, the future looks bright. Under the direction of such teachers, youths from the same countryside of Belley study to follow their distinguished examples.

Already the Drs. Janin and Manjot burn up the sidewalks of the capital. Dr. Manjot (39, Rue du Bac) devotes himself particularly to childhood illnesses; his theories are excellent, and before long he will surely become well known to the public because of them.

I hope that any courteous reader I may have will forgive the meanderings of this oldster, whose thirty-five years in Paris have not yet made him forget either his own country or his compatriots. It has been hard indeed for me to stay silent about many doctors whose names are still venerated in Belley, and who, although they did not have the chance to shine on the great stage of the capital, still had no less training, no less worth, than these others.

*   *   *

THE TRANSLATOR'S GLOSSES

1.   This treatment is interesting if only for its simplicity, today when sesquipedalian sulfas rule our distintegration. It is comforting to remember that Dr. Oliver Wendell Holmes used to carry a horse chestnut in one pocket and a potato in another to ward off rheumatism. That was in 1875 or thereabouts, but even today thoughtful doctors say that Holmes knew as much as any physician needs to. The same may be true of La Chapelle.

2.   For more about this genial old fellow see page 187 and the story of the longest repast the Professor, who was a connoisseur of them, ever made in his life. In my opinion there are too few ancients like Dr. Dubois, or perhaps that is but a sentimentalized theory of mine which would totter if I had to spend my days with some lip-smacking patriarch. One normally tolerant woman I know found herself tight-mouthed and Puritanical when a local grocery store complained that her venerable uncle was pinching the salesgirls, and when she asked him why, he thought for a time and then said impersonally, "They are pinchable." Perhaps she should have insinuated a few busts of Madame Récamier into her uncle's surroundings . . .

3.   In the earliest edition I have, 1838, there is a footnote here which reads, "Godson of the author; he it was who cared for Brillat-Savarin during his last brief illness." There is no sign of who added this note, but obviously it could not have been the Professor, who as far as is known wrote all the others in the book. Dr. Récamier, probably a cousin of Brillat-Savarin as well as of the beautiful Juliette (see page 346), had a simple case of pneumonia on his hands at the end of January, 1826. His old relative had gone rather grudgingly to the cold chapel of Saint-Dénis, on January 21, to a mass for the repose of the soul of Louis XVI to which he had been peremptorily invited by his superior, the president of the French bar. His serious view of his responsibilities as a judge outweighed the fact that he had a touch of *la grippe*, and he stood dutifully through the long

prayers for the beheaded monarch, prayers which managed to kill off three of the wisest old men of Paris. All of them sickened quickly, and on February 2 Brillat-Savarin was the last of the trio to die. He had seemed, it was noted, to have a presentiment that his end was upon him, and he waited for it without regret or weakness, for he had long contemplated Death with the same philosophical detachment he felt toward Life. (See page 410, for instance.) One of his admirers wrote, "He left the world like a satisfied diner leaving the banquet-room . . ."

THE AUTHOR'S
PREFACE

It has not meant a great deal of work for me to prepare this book which I now offer to the public's kindness. I had only to put in order the material I had spent so long in collecting: it was an entertaining task, and one which I did well to save for my old age.[1]

I soon saw, as I considered every aspect of the pleasures of the table, that something better than a cook book should be written about them; and there is a great deal to say about those functions which are so ever-present and so necessary, and which have such a direct influence on our health, our happiness, and even on our occupations.

Once I realized this basic fact, all the rest swung into focus. I looked about me. I made notes. Often, in the midst of the most luxurious festivities, the pleasure of observing my fellow banqueters saved me from my own possible boredom.

Of course, in order to carry out my plans, I needed to be doctor, chemist, physiologist, and even something of a scholar. But I became all these without the slightest pretensions to being a writer as well. I was carried along by a laudable curiosity, by a fear of lagging behind the times, and by a desire to be able to hold my own with the men of science with whom I have always loved to associate.†

I am above all a lover of doctors. It is almost a mania with me, and one of the happiest moments of my life was when, as a guest, I entered the amphitheatre with the judges to listen to Dr. Cloquet's presentation of his prize thesis, and heard a murmur of curiosity run through the audience. The students had mistaken me for a distinguished foreign scientist, honoring the gathering with his presence!

There is another memory almost as dear to me, of the day when I demonstrated to the administrative board of the Society for the Encouragement of National Industry my IRRORATOR,[4] an instrument of my invention which is nothing more nor less than a compression pump for perfuming the air.

I had brought, in my pocket, one of the well-primed machines. I turned the cock. With a hissing whistle there rose, straight to the ceiling, an odorous vapor which rained down in tiny drops upon the scientists and their papers.

Then I saw, to my inexpressible delight, the most learned heads in all Paris bow under my IRRORATION, and I complimented myself wholeheartedly when I noticed that the most thoroughly besprinkled were also the most pleased . . .

Sometimes as I have considered the solemn meditations into which the breadth of my subject has drawn me, I have sincerely feared becoming boresome, for I myself have yawned, now and then, over other men's works.

I have done everything in my power to avoid this danger: I have barely touched on the many subjects which might have become dull; I have sown my book with anecdotes, some of them personal; I have left out various unusual and fantastic details which an unprejudiced critic could rightly have frowned upon; I have tried to keep interest awake by making clear to the average mind certain facts which until now have been intelligible only to the most erudite. If, in spite of all these efforts, I have not presented to my readers some easily digested science,

† *"Come to dinner with me next Thursday," M. Greffuhle[2] said to me one day. "You may choose for yourself whether it will be with scientists or men of letters." "My choice is made," I replied. "Let us dine twice!" Thus it was, and the meal with the men of letters was notably subtler and more delicate. (See "Meditation 10.")*[3]

I shall still comfort myself with the reassurance that the majority will forgive me, suspecting my good intentions.

I could be accused, I know, of letting my pen run away with me occasionally, and of garrulity in my storytelling. But is it my fault that I am old? Is it my fault that, like Ulysses, I have known the manners and the towns of many nations? Can I be blamed for writing a little of my own life story? The reader must at least be grateful to me for sparing him my *Political Memoirs*, which might as well be published as any other man's, since for thirty-six years I have watched the drama of history from a front seat.

Above all I beg not to be thought of as a compiler. If I had been reduced to that, I would have pushed aside my pen long since, and not been any the unhappier for it!

I say, like Juvenal:

Semper ego auditor tantum? numquamne reponam! and those who know will easily see that since I am accustomed in equal parts to the uproar of society and the silence of my workroom, I have done well to profit by both these extremes.

Finally, I have given myself much private satisfaction in this book. I have mentioned several of my friends, who hardly expected such a thing; I have called up some pleasant memories, and clarified others that were on the point of fading; as the saying goes, *I have taken my coffee:* humored myself.

There may perhaps be one reader, less amiable than the rest, who will complain, "What I really wanted to know was . . . What is he thinking of, to say that . . . etc., etc.?" But I am sure that all the others will call him to order, and that an imposing majority will accept with kind understanding these well-intentioned outpourings.

There is still something I must say about my style, for *The style's the man himself*, according to Buffon.

But do not think that I am going to claim an indulgence which is never granted to those who most need it. I shall make a simple statement, that is all.

By rights I should write wondrously well, for Voltaire, Jean-Jacques, Fénélon, Buffon, and later Cochin and d'Aquesseau have been my favorite authors: I know them by heart.

But perhaps the gods have ordered otherwise; and if they have, here is the reason why:

I know, more or less well, five living languages,[5] a fact which has given me an enormous stock of words of every hue and connotation.

When I need a certain expression, and I do not find it anywhere in my French pigeon-hole, I take it from a neighboring one, and therein for the reader lies the necessity either to translate me or to guess my meaning. He has no other choice!

I could easily do otherwise, but I am kept from it by a belief in my own theory to which I cling invincibly.

I am completely persuaded that the French language, my own, is comparatively thin. And what can be done to strengthen it? Borrow or steal!

I do both, since such borrowings are not subject to repayment, and the theft of words is not punishable by law.

The reader will have a faint idea of my daring when I tell him that I call a man who does any kind of errand for me a VOLANTE (from the Spanish), and that I was once determined to make a French word from the English verb *to sip*, which means *boire à petites reprises*, until I unburied the old *siroter*, which used to have much the same meaning.

I well know that the classicists will call up the names of Bossuet and Fénélon to shame me, of Racine and Boileau and Pascal and others of the time of Louis XIV. I can already hear them, making a frightful fuss about it!

To all of which I reply calmly that I am far from denying the merits of any of those writers, whether I named them or merely implied their existence. But what does that prove? Nothing at all, unless it is that although they did the best they could with an inadequate tool, they would have done incomparably better with a superior one. It is the same as saying that Tartini would have played even better on the violin if his bow had been as long as Baillot's.

I am, apparently, on the side of the neologists and even of the romanticists; the latter discover hidden treasures in our language, and the former are like mariners who sail to far lands to seek out what we need.

Northern people, especially in England, have an immense advantage over us in this respect: there, genius is never hampered in its expression, but creates or borrows freely as it wills. One result is that our translators, especially of works of great depth and vitality, never make more than pale and twisted copies of the originals.†

I once heard at the Institute a most expert discourse on the danger of neologism, the need to protect our language from inventions and to preserve it as it was when the writers of the Golden Age marked out its heights and depths.

As a chemist would, I passed this opinion through the crucible of my logic. Here is what was left in the ashes: *We have done so well that there is no way to do better, nor to do otherwise.*

However, I have lived long enough to know that each generation says the same thing, and is inevitably laughed at by the men who live in the next one.

Besides, how can words rest unchanged when morals and ideas show a continuous flux? Even if we do what our forefathers did, we cannot do it in the same way: there are whole pages in some of the old French texts that could never be translated into either Latin or Greek.

Every tongue has had its birth, its apogee, its fading, and not a single one, from Sesostris to Philip Augustus, exists now except in the monuments of its antiquity. It will happen thus to French: in 2825 A.D. I shall be read only with a dictionary, if at all . . .

I once had a furious argument about this with the agreeable M. Andrieux, of the Academy.

I made my attack in good form. I charged vigorously. And I would have taken him, if he had not made an immediate retreat before which I did not place too much of an obstacle, since I had suddenly recalled, fortunately for him, that he was one of the editors of the new Dictionary!

I shall end now, with an observation so important that I have saved it for the last one.

When I write and speak of myself as *I*, in the singular, it presupposes a collaboration with my reader: he can examine what I say, question it, argue, even laugh. But when I arm my-

---

† *The excellent translation of Lord Byron, by M. Benjamin Laroche, is an exception to this rule but does not destroy it. His is a feat of skill, an accident which cannot be repeated.*

self with the redoubtable *we*, I am The Professor: he must bow down!

I am Sir Oracle,
And when I ope my lips, let no dog bark.

SHAKESPEARE, *The Merchant of Venice*, ACT I, SCENE 1.

THE TRANSLATOR'S GLOSSES

1. Jean Anthelme Brillat-Savarin was born in Belley, in the Ain, in France, on the first day of April, 1755. He lived and died a lawyer, like the other men of his family. As Mayor of Belley he resisted the bloody revolutionists in 1793, and was forced to flee his country, first to Switzerland and then to America. He spent some two years in New York, giving language lessons and playing his violin in a theatre orchestra. In 1796 he returned to France, and although he had lost almost everything, including his fine little vineyard, he was reinstated as an honorable citizen. He was appointed judge in the Court of Appeal in Paris, after a few years of service as secretary to the General Staff of the French Army in Germany and as Commissioner to the Tribunal of the Seine-et-Oise, and he spent the last twenty-five years of his life peacefully and unobtrusively as a conservative royalist, unmoved by political upheaval and the feverish social changes of life in Paris at the beginning of the nineteenth century. In 1825 he published at his own expense THE PHYSIOLOGY OF TASTE, on which he had been working with amusement and pleasure for some three decades. He died on February 2, 1826.
2. See page 248 for more about this opinionated and admirable gentleman, who in the manner of the day chose to live fast and well, rather than at the more sedate pace of his admittedly more intelligent Professor.
3. I hesitate to quarrel with what is apparently Brillat-Savarin's own advice, but I feel that "Meditation 12" is more connected

with this footnote than the tenth one. Certainly a discussion of the various kinds of gourmands seems more linked with this little anecdote of the two dinner parties than does one which details with such quirkish dispassion as Number 10 the possible last days of our planet and ourselves!

4.   Here is the first of uncounted (at least by me) inventions in language, by the lively-minded old Professor. Some of them are "barbaric," as one translator has bluntly stated, but always they are amusing as sidelights on the writer's character, if for no other reason. Anyone with a basic knowledge of Latin can understand most of them, and in this translation they have been set in S P A C E D S M A L L C A P S, along with Brillat-Savarin's unconscious boners in his use of English and other "living" languages, to differentiate them from the simple italics which he himself used for emphasis in his text or, occasionally, for foreign phrases.

5.   It will easily be seen throughout this book that the Professor's statement, even though he qualified it by saying "more or less well," was somewhat ingenuous. His American, for instance, is more French than his French, and presented with disarming trust and self-confidence. There is a little Italian in a footnote or two. There are a handful of Spanish words. There is a modicum of Gallicized German, which he may have spoken with some fluency because of his service with the army in Germany and because of the many titled exiles from that country who flocked to the salons and dining rooms of such people as his cousin Madame Récamier. But there is a pleasing smugness in his assumption that five living languages were "more or less" at his command.

MEDITATION 1

ON THE SENSES

The senses are the organs by which man communicates with the world outside himself.

Number of Senses

1: There are at least six of them:

Sight, which embraces space itself, and tells us by means of light of the existence of the objects which surround us, and of their colors.

Hearing, which absorbs through the air the vibrations caused by agreeably resonant *or* merely noisy bodies.

Smell, by means of which we savor all odorous things.

Taste, by which we appreciate whatever is palatable or only edible.

Touch, by which we are made aware of the surfaces and the textures of objects.

Finally *physical desire*, which draws the two sexes together so that they may procreate.

It is astonishing that, almost to the time of Buffon, so important a sense as this last one was misunderstood, and confused with or rather linked with the sense of touch.

However, the two have nothing in common: the sixth sense has its own organism, as much so as the mouth or the eyes, and the strange part of it is that although each sex possesses everything necessary to produce this reaction of desire, male and female must be together before they can attain the end for which it was created. If *taste*, whose purpose is to enable a man to exist, is indisputably one of his senses, then how much more reasonable it is to call a sense that part of him destined to make mankind itself survive.

Let us therefore give to *physical desire* the *sensual* position it is entitled to, and then depend on our offspring to keep it there.

The Use of the Senses

2: If it is permissible to travel back, in one's imagination, to the dawn of humanity, it is equally permissible to believe that man's first sensations were purely direct; that is to say that he saw but vaguely, that he heard dimly, that he chose without thought the food he ate without tasting, and that he copulated with brutality instead of pleasure.

But because all these senses sprang from the soul, that special attribute of human beings, that ever-active cause of perfectibility, they were thought about, compared, judged. Soon one sense came to the aid of another and another, for the use and the well-being of the sentient *ego*, or, what is the same thing, the individual.

Thus, touch corrected the errors of sight; sound, by means of the spoken word, became the interpreter of all emotions; taste helped itself through sight and smell; hearing compared the noises that came to it, and was able to judge distances; and desire invaded the precincts of all the other senses.

The flood of time, rolling over centuries of mankind, brought endless new perfections whose genesis, always active although almost unperceived, is found in the progress of our senses, which, over and over, demand their satisfaction.

Thus, sight gives birth to painting, sculpture, every kind of spectacle;

From sound come melody and harmony, music and the dance, with all their ramifications;

From smell springs the discovery of perfumes, and their culture and use;

Taste develops the production, the selection, the preparation of everything that can nourish us;

Touch brings us skill in all the arts and industries;

Physical desire develops whatever can induce or embellish the union of the two sexes and, since the time of Francis I, it also nurtures romantic love, coquetry, and fashion, and above all coquetry, which was born in France, which has no other name than its French one, and which the world's choicest souls come every day to study in Paris, their spiritual capital.

This theory, strange as it may sound, is nevertheless easy to prove, since in no other language can we express ourselves clearly on these three prime motives of modern society.

I once wrote on this subject a dialogue which had its good points, but which I decided to leave out of my book so that each reader might have the pleasure of creating one according to his own tastes: there is room in it for a whole evening's display of fancy, and even of knowledge.

We said before that physical desire had invaded the workings of all the other senses; no less strongly has it influenced all our sciences, and on looking at them closely it will be seen that everything subtle and ingenious about them is due to this sixth sense, to the desire, the hope, the gratitude that spring from sexual union.

Such is, then, in good truth, the genesis of even the most abstract sciences: they are nothing more than the immediate result of our continuous attempt to gratify the senses we have developed.

The Improvement of the Senses

3:   These senses to which we owe so much are still far from perfection, as I need not take time to prove. I shall simply observe that both sight, so ethereal, and touch, at the other end of the scale, have gradually acquired an additional power which is most remarkable.

By means of *lenses*, eyes can escape, as it were, a senile weakening which triumphs over most of the other senses.

The *telescope*, for another instance, has discovered stars hitherto unknown to us and inaccessible to our native means of measurement. It has seen such distances that luminous bodies, in spite of their immense size, have appeared to us as no more than cloudy and almost invisible spots.

The *microscope* has initiated us into the knowledge of the inner configurations of things; it has shown us forms of life which we never even suspected before. Through it we have seen creatures a hundred thousand times smaller than the tiniest ones visible to our naked eyes, animalcules which move and feed and multiply, so that our imagination is confounded by the presupposition of the minute size of their various organs.

On the other hand, mechanical skills have added to our various powers; man has carried out every plan he has been capable of making, and has thrown off burdens which in the beginning he seemed powerless to fight against.

By means of weapons and the lever he has made all nature submit to him; he has bent it to his pleasures, his needs, his whims; he has turned it upside down, and a puny biped has become lord of creation.

Sight and touch thus fortified could well belong to more superior beings than we are; or, better yet, mankind would be quite different if all the other senses had been equally developed.

It must be noted, however, that although touch has made great progress as a muscular power, civilization has done almost nothing with it as a sensitive apparatus; but we must not despair, remembering that mankind is still very young, and that it is only after a long series of centuries that the senses can enlarge their domains.

For instance, it is but some four hundred years ago that *harmony* was discovered, that celestial science, which is to sound what painting is to colors.†

---

† *We know that some people maintain the contrary; but this fact is beyond argument.*
If the ancients had understood harmony their writings would have

Doubtless the ancients knew how to sing to instruments played in unison; but their knowledge stopped there: they could neither separate one sound from another nor appreciate what they might thus hear.

It is only since the fifteenth century that the tonal scale has been established and the arrangement of chords determined, to accompany the human voice and strengthen its range of expression.

This discovery, so late in coming and yet so natural, doubled our sense of hearing, which was now shown to include two more or less independent faculties, one to receive sounds and the other to appreciate their tones.

German scholars even assert that those men who can hear harmony have one more sense than their fellows.

As for people to whom music is but a welter of confused noises, it can be noticed that they usually sing out of tune, which leads me to believe that their hearing apparatus is made so that it receives only waveless short vibrations, or, more likely, that because their two ears are not tuned to the same pitch, the differences in wave lengths and in sensitivity can only transmit to their brains a vague and indeterminate sensation, like two instruments playing in different keys and in different rhythms, without even a common melody to follow.

The last few centuries have also brought important enlargements to the sphere of taste: the discoveries of sugar and its many uses, of alcohol, of ices, vanilla, tea, and coffee, have transmitted previously unknown pleasure to our palates.

Who can say if the sense of touch will not be next, and if some lucky accident will not open up to us a new source of happiness through it? Such a thing is more than likely, since the tactile sense exists on every surface of the body, and as a result can be excited everywhere.

---

preserved some precise mention of it, instead of a few vague phrases on the subject, to which almost any interpretation can be given.

Moreover, it is impossible to trace the beginning and the progress of harmony in the classical monuments which have come down to us; this is a debt we owe to the Arabs, who gave us the organ, which, producing several sustained notes simultaneously, gave birth to the first conception of harmony.

The Power of Taste

4: We have seen that physical desire is a part of all the sciences; it asserts itself in them with that tyranny which always characterizes it.

Taste, a more cautious and prudent faculty although no less active a one, has arrived at the same goal with a slowness which guarantees the lasting quality of its triumphs.

We shall devote ourselves later to the consideration of this progress; but at this point we can remark that any man who has enjoyed a sumptuous meal, in a room decorated with mirrors and paintings, sculptures and flowers, a room drenched with perfumes, enriched with lovely women, filled with the strains of soft music . . . that man, we say, will not need to make too great an affort to convince himself that every science has taken part in the scheme to heighten and enhance properly for him the pleasures of taste.

Reasons for the Action of the Senses

5: Let us now look at the general working of all our senses, and we shall see that the Creator has had two ends in view, one of which is the result of the other, namely, the preservation of the individual and the continuation of the species.

Such is the destiny of man, considered as a sentient being: it is to this double end that all his actions lead.

His eyes perceive exterior objects, reveal to him the wonders that surround him, and teach him that he is but part of a great whole.

His hearing catches the sounds about him, not only as a pleasant sensation, but also as an intimation of the movements of other bodies which may mean danger to him.

Feeling stands guard to warn him, by means of pain, that he has been hurt.

His hands, those faithful servants, not only help him to protect himself and to stand upright, but by preference they curve themselves around those objects which his instinct tells him are the right ones to repair the damages which have been caused him by his struggle to survive.

His sense of smell next explores these objects, for harmful substances almost always have a stench.

Finally taste asserts itself, man's teeth come into action, his tongue and palate unite to enjoy the flavor of what he eats, and soon his stomach begins to assimilate the meal.

In this state an unfamiliar languor creeps over him, objects fade, his body grows limp, his eyes close; everything disappears, and his senses fall into a complete repose.

When he awakens, he sees that nothing around him has changed; however, a secret fire burns in his breast, a new organ has been developed; he feels that now he must share his life with someone.

This active, troubling, imperious sentiment is common to both sexes; it brings them together and unites them, and when the germ of a new life has been fertilized, the two people can sleep again in peace; they have fulfilled the most sacred of their duties in thus making sure that mankind will continue.†

Such are the conclusions, general and philosophical, which I have felt I should offer to my readers, to lead them easily into the more detailed examination of the sense of taste.

---

† *M. de Buffon has painted, with all the charms of the most brilliant eloquence, the first moments in the life of Eve. We can only pretend, having been called to discuss a similar subject, to sketch it lightly with pencil; our readers will know how to add the colors to the canvas.*

MEDITATION 2

ON TASTE

Definition of Taste

6: Taste is the sense which puts us in contact with savorous or sapid bodies, by means of the sensation which they cause in the organ destined to appreciate them.

This sense, which can be excited by appetite, hunger, and thirst, is the basis for several operations which result in a man's growth and development, in his self-preservation, and in the general repairs to his body of the losses caused by elimination and evaporation.

All organized species of existence do not nourish themselves in the same way; the Creator, as varied in his methods as he is sure in his results, has given to each form of life a different way of conserving itself.

Plants, at the bottom of the scale, feed themselves through their roots, which, embedded in the earth, choose by means of their own peculiar mechanism the various substances which will make them grow and flourish.

A little higher up the scale we find those creatures which, although they are blessed with animal life, are still deprived of the power of moving about. They are born into surroundings which favor their existence, and from which their special organs extract whatever they need to last their apportioned spans of life. They do not look for their nourishment, but rather it seeks them out.

Another way has been arranged for the creatures who roam the world, of whom man is without doubt the most highly developed. An instinct peculiar to him warns him when he must eat; he looks for food; he seizes whatever he suspects will satisfy him; then he eats, feels strong again, and goes on through his whole life in this pattern which has been set.

Taste can be considered under three different headings:

In physical man it is the apparatus by which he distinguishes various flavors.

In moral man it is the sensation which stimulates that organ in the center of his feeling which is influenced by any savorous body.

Lastly, in its own material significance, taste is the property possessed by any given substance which can influence the organ and give birth to sensation.

Taste seems to possess two main functions.

(1) It invites us, by arousing our pleasure, to repair the constant losses which we suffer through our physical existence.

(2) It helps us to choose from the variety of substances which Nature presents to us those which are best adapted to nourish us.

In this choice, taste is greatly helped by the sense of smell, as we shall see later; it can be established as a general maxim that nourishing things are not repulsive to either sense.

The Operation of Taste

7: It is not easy to determine precisely what parts make up the organ of taste. It is more complicated than it seems.

Certainly, the tongue plays an important role in the mechanics of tasting: endowed as it is with a fairly powerful muscular force, it helps to moisten, mash, churn about, and swallow the food.

Moreover, by means of the varying numbers of papillae which protude like tiny buds from its surface, it saturates itself with the tasteful and soluble particles of whatever body it is in contact with; this, however, is not enough, and several other adjacent parts of the mouth work together to complete the sensation: the insides of the cheeks, the roof of the mouth, and above all the nasal channel, upon whose importance the physiologists have perhaps not insisted strongly enough.

The inside cheeks furnish saliva, which is equally necessary to the act of chewing and to making the food of such a consistency as can be swallowed; they are, like the palate or roof of the mouth, gifted with their share of enjoyment, and I do not even know whether, in certain cases, the gums themselves may not share somewhat in this appreciation; while without that final savoring which takes place at the back of the tongue, the whole sensation of taste would be obscure and quite incomplete.

Anyone who has been born without a tongue, or whose tongue has been cut out, still has a moderately strong sense of taste. The first instance can often be found in literature; the second has been fairly well described to me by a poor devil whose tongue had been amputated by the Algerians, to punish him for having plotted with one of his fellow prisoners to break out and flee.

This man, whom I met in Amsterdam, where he made his living by running errands, had had some education, and it was easy to communicate with him by writing.

After I had observed that the forepart of his tongue had been cut off clear to the ligament, I asked him if he still found any flavor in what he ate, and if his sense of taste had survived the cruelty to which he had been subjected.

He replied that what tired him most was to swallow (which he could not do without some difficulty); that he still possessed the ability to taste fairly well; that he could tell, with other more normal men, what was pleasant or unappetizing; but that very sour or bitter things caused him unbearable pain.

He also told me that the amputation of tongues was common in African kingdoms, that it was performed especially on men believed to be the ringleaders in any plots, and that there were appropriate instruments for it. I should have liked him to describe the operation to me, but he showed at this point such misery and revulsion that I did not insist on it.

I thought about what he had told me; and turning back to the days of ignorance when we used to pierce and cut out the tongues of religious blasphemers, and to the period in history when such laws were made, I felt that I was right in concluding that they were of African origin, brought back to Europe by the Crusaders.

I have already stated that the sense of taste resides mainly in the papillae of the tongue. Now the study of anatomy teaches us that all tongues are not equally endowed with these taste buds, so that some may possess even three times as many of them as others. This circumstance explains why, of two diners seated at the same feast, one is delightfully affected by it, while the other seems almost to force himself to eat: the latter has a tongue but thinly provided with papillae, which proves that the empire of taste may also have its blind and its deaf subjects.

The Sensation of Taste

8:   Five or six opinions have been broached by now on the way in which the sensation of taste functions; I have my own personal one, and here it is:

This sensation is a chemical operation which is accomplished, as we have already remarked, by moisture. That is to say, the sapid molecules must be dissolved in no matter what kind of fluid, so that they may then be absorbed by the sensitive projections, buds, or suckers which line the interior of the apparatus for tasting.

This theory, whether new or not, is supported by physical and almost palpable proofs.[1]

Pure water awakens no sensation of taste, because it contains no sapid bodies. But dissolve a pinch of salt in it, or add a few drops of vinegar, and the sensation will occur.

Other drinks, however, impress our taste sense because they are nothing more nor less than solutions charged in varying degrees with appreciable particles.

In vain might the mouth be filled with separate morsels of an insoluble body: the tongue would experience the sensation of touch, but never of taste.

As for flavorsome and solid bodies, the teeth must cut them up, saliva and the other taste fluids must soak them, and the tongue must roll them against the palate so that they exude a juice which, by now sufficiently sapid, is appreciated by the taste buds which in turn give to the mashed food that passport it needs to be admitted to the human stomach.

This theory, which will be developed even further, easily answers the main questions that can arise.

If it is asked what I mean by the word sapid, I reply that it is anything which is soluble and which can be absorbed by the taste buds.

And if it is asked how a sapid body acts, I reply that it acts whenever it finds itself in such a state of dissolution that it can penetrate the cavities meant to receive and transmit taste.

In a word, nothing is sapid which is not either already dissolved, or easily soluble.

The Tastes

9:   The number of tastes is infinite, since every soluble body has a special flavor which does not wholly resemble any other.

Tastes are modified, moreover, by their combinations with one, two, or a dozen others, so that it is impossible to draw up a correct chart, listing them from the most attractive to the most repellent, from the strawberry to the griping bitter apple. Anyone who has ever attempted this has of course failed.

This is not astonishing, for given the fact that there exists an indefinite series of simple tastes which can change according to the number and variety of their combinations, we should need a whole new language to describe all these effects, and mountains of folio foolscap to define them, and unknown numerical characters for their classification.

Up to the present time there is not a single circumstance in which a given taste has been analyzed with stern exactitude, so that we have been forced to depend on a small number of generalizations such as *sweet, sugary, sour, bitter,* and other like ones which express, in the end, no more than the words *agreeable* or *disagreeable,* and are enough to make themselves understood and to indicate, more or less, the taste properties of the sapid body which they describe.

Men who will come after us will know much more than we of this subject; and it cannot be disputed that it is chemistry which will reveal the causes or the basic elements of taste.

Influence of Smell on Taste

10: The pattern which I have set for myself has unwittingly led me to the point where I must concede all due rights to the sense of smell, and must recognize the important services which it renders to us in our appreciation of tastes; for, among the authors whose books I have read, I have found not one who seems to me to have paid it full and complete justice.

For myself, I am not only convinced that there is no full act of tasting without the participation of the sense of smell, but I am also tempted to believe that smell and taste form a single sense, of which the mouth is the laboratory and the nose is the chimney; or, to speak more exactly, of which one serves for the tasting of actual bodies and the other for the savoring of their gases.

This theory can be strikingly supported; however, since I have no desire to set up my own school, I mention it only to give my readers food for thought, and to show that I have studied my subject at first hand. Therefore I shall now continue my exposition of the importance of smell, at least as a necessary aid to taste if not as an integral part of it.

Any sapid body is perforce odorous, which places it in the realm of the sense of smell as well as in that of taste.

A man eats nothing without smelling it more or less consciously, while with unknown foods his nose acts always as the first sentinel, crying out *Who goes there?*

When the sense of smell is cut off, taste itself is paralyzed, as can be proved by three experiments which anyone may perform with equal success.

First experiment: When the nasal membrane is irritated by a violent *coryza* (head cold), taste is completely wiped out: there is absolutely no flavor in anything one swallows, in spite of the fact that the tongue continues to be in its normal state.

Second experiment: If one eats while pinching shut his nostrils, he is astonished to find his sense of taste imperfect and faint; by this means, the nastiest dosage can be swallowed quite easily.

Third experiment: The same effect is produced if, at the moment of swallowing, one continues to leave his tongue pressed against the roof of his mouth instead of letting it return to its natural place; in this case the circulation of air has been stopped, the sense of smell is not aroused, and the act of tasting has not taken place.

These various effects all stem from the same cause, the lack of cooperation of the sense of smell, with the result that a sapid body is appreciated only for its own juice and not for the fumes which emanate from it.

Analysis of the Sensation of Tasting

11: I feel, having thus set forth the principles of my theory, that it is certain that taste causes sensations of three different kinds: *direct*, *complete*, and *reflective*.

The *direct* sensation is the first one felt, produced from the immediate operations of the organs of the mouth, while the body under consideration is still on the fore part of the tongue.

The *complete* sensation is the one made up of this first perception plus the impression which arises when the food leaves its original position, passes to the back of the mouth, and attacks the whole organ with its taste and its aroma.

Finally, the *reflective* sensation is the opinion which one's spirit forms from the impressions which have been transmitted to it by the mouth.

Let us put this theory into action, by seeing what happens to a man who is eating or drinking.

He who eats a peach, for instance, is first of all agreeably struck by the perfume which it exhales; he puts a piece of it into his mouth, and enjoys a sensation of tart freshness which invites him to continue; but it is not until the instant of swallowing, when the mouthful passes under his nasal channel, that the full aroma is revealed to him; and this completes the sensation which a peach can cause. Finally, it is not until it has been swallowed that the man, considering what he has just experienced, will say to himself, "Now there is something really delicious!"

In the same way, in drinking: while the wine is in the mouth, one is agreeably but not completely appreciative of it; it is not until the moment when he has finished swallowing it that a man can truly taste, consider, and discover the bouquet peculiar to each variety; and there must still be a little lapse of time before a real connoisseur can say, "It is good, or passable, or bad. By Jove, here is a Chambertin! Confound it, this is only a Suresnes!"

It can thus be seen that it is in following certain well-studied principles that the true amateurs SIP their wine (*ils le sirotent*), for, as they hesitate after each taste of it, they enjoy the same full pleasure that they might have had if they had drunk the whole glass in one gulp.

The same thing happens, but much more obviously, when the sense of taste must be disagreeably assaulted.

Take, for example, an invalid whose doctor prescribes an enormous glass of that old-fashioned black medicine which was drunk during the reign of Louis XIV.

His sense of smell, faithful guide, warns him of the revolting taste of the horrible fluid; his eyes pop out as if he recognizes real danger; disgust is plainly written on his face; already his stomach heaves. But he is begged to drink, and he stiffens with resolve; he gargles first with a little brandy, holds his nose, and swallows . . .

While the foul brew fills his mouth and coats it, the sensation is confused and tolerable; but, with the last swallow, the after-tastes develop, the nauseating odors become clear, and the patient's every feature expresses a horror which only the fear of death itself could make him endure.

If, on the other hand, it is a matter of some such insipid drink as a glass of water, there is neither taste nor aftertaste; one feels nothing, cares nothing; one has drunk, and that is all there is to it.

Order of the Various Impressions of Taste

12: Taste is not as richly endowed as hearing, which can listen to and compare several sounds at the same time: taste is simple in its action, which is to say that it cannot receive impressions from two flavors at once.

But taste can be double, and even multiple, in succession, so that in a single mouthful a second and sometimes a third sensation can be realized; they fade gradually, and are called aftertaste, perfume, or aroma. It is the same way as, when a basic note is sounded, an attentive ear distinguishes in it one or more series of other consonant tones, whose number has not yet been correctly estimated.

Men who eat quickly and without thought do not perceive the taste impressions of this second level, which are the exclusive perquisite of a small number of the chosen few; and it is by means of these impressions that gastronomers can classify, in the order of their excellence, the various substances submitted to their approval.

These fleeting nuances vibrate for a long time in the organ of taste: students of them assume without even realizing it a proper stance for the pronouncement of their verdicts, always with necks stretched and noses twisted up and to the left, as it were to larboard.

Pleasures Caused by Taste

13: Let us now look philosophically for a moment at the joy or sadness which can result from the sense of taste.

First of all we are confronted with the application of that truism unfortunately too well known, that man is much more sensitive to pain than to pleasure.

Obviously our reactions to extremely bitter, acid, or sour substances cause us to suffer deeply painful or grievous sensations. It is even held that hydrocyanic acid kills so quickly only because it causes such intense agony that our vital forces cannot long endure it.

On the other hand, agreeable sensations extend over only a small scale, and if there is a fairly appreciable difference between an insipid flavor and one that stimulates the taste, the space between something called good and something reputed to be excellent is not very great. This is made clearer by the following comparisons: first or positive, a dry hard piece of boiled meat; second or comparative, a slice of veal; third or superlative, a pheasant cooked to perfection.

However, taste as Nature has endowed us with it is still that one of our senses which gives us the greatest joy:

(1) Because the pleasure of eating is the only one which, indulged in moderately, is not followed by regret;

(2) Because it is common to all periods in history, all ages of man, and all social conditions;

(3)   Because it recurs of necessity at least once every day, and can be repeated without inconvenience two or three times in that space of hours;

(4)   Because it can mingle with all the other pleasures, and even console us for their absence;

(5)   Because its sensations are at once more lasting than others and more subject to our will;

(6)   Because, finally, in eating we experience a certain special and indefinable well-being, which arises from our instinctive realization that by the very act we perform we are repairing our bodily losses and prolonging our lives.

This will be more thoroughly developed in the chapter which we shall devote especially to *the pleasures of the table*, considered from the point to which our modern civilization has brought them.

The Supremacy of Man

14:   We have been reared with the agreeable belief that, of all the creatures who walk, swim, climb, or fly, man is the one whose sense of taste is the most perfect.

This belief threatens to be overthrown.

Dr. Gall [2] states, backed by I do not know what investigations, that there are animals whose tasting apparatus is more developed and even more perfect than ours.

This doctrine is shocking to hear, and smacks of heresy.

Man, king of all nature by divine right, and for whose benefit the earth has been covered and peopled, must perforce be armed with an organ which can put him in contact with all that is toothsome among his subjects.

The tongue of an animal is comparable in its sensitivity to his intelligence: among fish it is but a movable bone; among birds in general it is a membranous cartilage; in the four-legged world it is often sheathed with scales or roughnesses, and moreover has no power of circular movement.

Man's tongue, on the other hand, by the delicacy of its surfaces and of the various membranes which surround it, proves clearly enough the sublimity of the operations for which it is destined.

What is more, I have discovered at least three movements

in it which are unknown to animals, and which I describe as movements of SPICATION, ROTATION, and VERRITION (from the Latin *verro*, I sweep). The first takes place when the tip of the tongue protrudes between the lips which squeeze it; the second, when it rolls around in the pace between the cheeks and the palate; the third, when it catches, by curving itself now up and now down, the particles of food which have stuck in the semicircular moat between the lips and the gums.

Animals are limited in their tastes; some live only upon plants, and others eat nothing but meat; still others nourish themselves solely upon seeds; none of them knows combinations of flavors.

Man, on the other hand, is *omnivorous*; everything edible is prey to his vast hunger, and this brings out, as its immediate result, tasting powers proportionate to the general use which he must make of them. That is to say, man's apparatus of the sense of taste has been brought to a state of rare perfection; and, to convince ourselves thoroughly, let us watch it work.

As soon as an edible body has been put into the mouth, it is seized upon, gases, moisture, and all, without possibility of retreat.

Lips stop whatever might try to escape; the teeth bite and break it; saliva drenches it; the tongue mashes and churns it; a breathlike sucking pushes it toward the gullet; the tongue lifts up to make it slide and slip; the sense of smell appreciates it as it passes the nasal channel, and it is pulled down into the stomach to be submitted to sundry baser transformations without, in this whole metamorphosis, a single atom or drop or particle having been missed by the powers of appreciation of the taste sense.

It is, then, because of this perfection that the real enjoyment of eating is a special prerogative of man.

This pleasure is even contagious; and we transmit it quickly enough to the animals which we have tamed and which in one way or another make up a part of our society, like elephants, dogs, cats, and even parrots.

If some animals have a larger tongue that others, a more developed roof to their mouths, an ampler throat, it is because this tongue, acting as a muscle, must move bulky food; this palate must press and this throat must swallow larger portions than average; but all analogy is opposed to the inference that their sense of taste is proportionately greater than that of other animals.

Moreover, since taste must not be weighed except by the nature of the sensation which it arouses in the center of life, an impression received by an animal cannot be compared with one felt by a man: the latter sensation, at once clearer and more precise, presupposes of necessity a superior quality in the organ which transmits it.

Finally, what is left to be desired of a faculty sensitive to such a degree of perfection that the gourmands of Rome could tell by the flavor whether fish was caught between the city bridges or lower down the river?

And do we not have, in our own days, those gastronomers who pretend to have discovered the special flavor of the leg upon which a sleeping pheasant rests his weight? [3]

And are we not surrounded by gourmets who can tell the latitude under which a wine has ripened just as surely as a pupil of Biot or Arago[4] knows how to predict an eclipse?

What follows from there? Simply that what is Caesar's must be rendered unto him, that man must be proclaimed *the great gourmand of Nature*, and that it must not seem too astonishing that the good doctor Gall does as Homer did, and drowses now and then:

Auch zuweiler schalffert der guter G (all) .[5]

Plan Adopted by the Author

15: Thus far we have only considered taste in the aspects of its physical make-up, and, with the exception of some anatomical details which would be missed by few people, we have held ourselves strictly to the scientific level. But the task which we have set ourselves does not end there, for it is mainly because of its moral history that this restorative sense retains its importance and its glory.

We have therefore followed, according to an analytical plan, the theories and facts which make up this history, in such a way that instruction can result without boredom.

It is thus that, in the following chapters, we shall show how sensations, by force of repetition and consideration, have perfected the organ of taste and enlarged the sphere of its power; how the need to eat, which was nothing but instinct at first, has become a powerful passion which has a marked influence on everything connected with society.

We shall tell too how all sciences which are concerned with physical composition have exerted themselves to classify and segregate those bodies which can be recognized by taste, and how travellers have aimed at the same goal, in enabling us to experiment with exotic substances which Nature itself seems never to have intended to come together.

We shall follow chemistry up to the very moment when it invades our kitchens, those subterranean laboratories of gastronomy, to enlighten our assistants, pose certain principles, create new methods, and unveil natural laws which, until then, have remained a mystery.

Finally we shall see how, by the combined influences of time and experience, a new science is suddenly revealed to us, which nourishes, restores, conserves, entices, consoles and, not content to cover with flowers the path of each individual's progress, contributes powerfully to the strength and prosperity of empires themselves.

If, in the midst of these solemn meditations, a piquant anecdote, a pleasant memory, or some adventure of an active life forms itself at the tip of our pen, we shall let it take shape, to divert for a little while the close attention of our readers, whose numbers do not alarm us and with whom, on the contrary, we love to gossip, for if they are men we are sure that they are as charitable as they are learned, and if they are ladies they must of necessity be charming.

Here the professor, full of his subject, lets his pen drop, and mounts into other higher planes. He swims up the flood of the centuries, and seeks out in their cradle the sciences which have for their purpose the gratification of taste; he follows the progress of this sense through the black night of history; and then seeing that the first years have always been less rich than those that follow, insofar as the pleasures they offer us may go, he seizes his lyre, and sings in Dorian mood the historical Elegy which will be found among the Varieties. Look for it at the end of the book.

THE TRANSLATOR'S GLOSSES

1.   According to a report made in THE NEW YORKER in 1947 about a chemist whose avocation was taste, many people (including the chemist) are nontasters. Tests are made with para-ethoxyphenyl thio-carbamide, more nonchalantly referred to as PTC, a very bitter brew. The ability to taste PTC is inherited, and two nontasters who marry have nontasting children. Arabs are 33 per cent nontasters, and, in a way that for some reason is surprising, American Indians are 94 per cent tasters.

2.   Franz Joseph Gall (1758–1828) was a German physician who after many years of unrecognized labors in Vienna settled in Paris. His RECHERCHES SUR LE SYSTEME NERVEUX EN GENERAL, which he wrote with his pupil Spurzheim, also a refugee in France, was an important part of nineteenth century medical literature, but his founding of the science of phrenology is what makes him still remembered, if but dimly.

He believed, and preached successfully, that the human mind consists of a group of separate localized faculties, each seated in its particular "organ" or locality, and that the development of these faculties may be judged by the shape of the skull. Phrenology fell into disrepute, to put it mildly, when country-fair fakirs assumed its basically honest mantle, but endocrinologists have lately found, somewhat to their embarrassment, that old Dr. Gall suspected a great many things they are now trying hard to prove about the physical appearance of various glandular "types."

3.   This gentle bit of teasing is an offshoot of the ageless joke in any rural community that a porker's right hind leg makes a tenderer ham than the left (or is it the opposite?) because he toughens the left one by using it to scratch himself . . .

4.   These two men, obviously, were astronomers in high repute

when the Professor wrote. Arago's four-volume ASTRONOMI POPULAIRE, which was published after his death in 1853, is still read by physicists, although no more by the college kind.

5. This is a fine example of the Professor's rather pedantic sense of humor, in which he translated a line of Latin, ". . . *aliquando bonus dormitat Homerus*," into Dr. Gall's native German, in order to make a mild little joke.

MEDITATION 3

ON GASTRONOMY

The Origin of Sciences

16:   The sciences are not like Minerva, who sprang fully armed from the brain of Jupiter; they are the daughters of time, and take shape very gradually, at first by the assembling of methods developed through experience, and then later by the discovery of principles which have been deduced from the combining of these methods.

Thus the old men of ancient tribes, whose wisdom called them to the bedsides of the sick, whose human pity drew them to succor the wounded, were the first doctors.

The Egyptian shepherds who observed that certain stars, after set periods, swung back to the same places in the sky, were the first astronomers.

The man who first expressed by symbols the very simple proposition that *two plus two equals four* created mathematics, that most powerful of sciences, which has truly elevated mankind to the throne of the universe.

In the course of the past sixty years several new sciences have come to take their places in our system of knowledge, among them stereotomy or the geometry of solids, descriptive geometry, and the chemistry of gases.

All these, nurtured during an infinite number of generations, will make a progress doubly assured by the art of printing, which releases them from the danger of retrogression. Who knows, for instance, that the chemistry of gases may not finish by conquering those elements which until now have been so unruly; may not succeed in combining them, mixing them in proportions never before attempted, and obtaining from them new substances and new effects which will enormously enlarge our powers?

Origin of Gastronomy

17: The science of gastronomy appeared like the others in her turn, and all her sisters drew near to cede a proper place to her.

Naturally! How could anything be refused to one who succors us from our birth to our burial, who adds to the delights of love and the strength of friendship, who disarms hatred, makes business easier, and offers us in our short span of life the sole pleasure which, since it is not followed by fatigue, remains to comfort us when the others no longer can?

Obviously while cooking was practiced solely by paid servants, while its secrets stayed below ground in the kitchens, while the cooks kept their knowledge to themselves and wrote only books of directions, the results of their labors could be no more than the products of an art.

At last, however, and perhaps even too late, scientists lent themselves to a study of gastronomy.

They examined, analyzed, and classified the alimentary substances, and reduced them to their simplest elements.

They studied the mysteries of assimilation, and, considering inert matter in all its changes, they saw how it could come to life.

They watched the passing or permanent effects of diet, over periods of days or months or a lifetime.

They studied its effect on human thought, whether it be that the soul finds itself influenced by the senses or that it feels without depending on those organs; and from all these labors they evolved a lofty theory which concerns man himself and every living thing capable of being assimilated.

While all this happened in the scientists' private workrooms, it was being said aloud in the world's drawing rooms that a science which nourishes men is worth at least as much as one which teaches them to kill each other; poets sang of the pleasures of the table, and books which had good living for their subject began to show a more profound view of it than heretofore, and to set forth maxims for it of a more thoughtful tenor.[1]

Such, then, are the events which preceded the coming of Gastronomy.

Definition of Gastronomy

18: Gastronomy is the intelligent knowledge of whatever concerns man's nourishment.

Its purpose is to watch over his conservation by suggesting the best possible sustenance for him.

It arrives at this goal by directing, according to certain principles, all men who hunt, supply, or prepare whatever can be made into food.

Thus it is Gastronomy, to tell the truth, which motivates the farmers, vineyardists, fishermen, hunters, and the great family of cooks, no matter under what names or qualifications they may disguise their part in the preparation of foods.

Gastronomy is a part of:

Natural history, by its classification of alimentary substances;

Physics, because of the examination of the composition and quality of these substances;

Chemistry, by the various analyses and catalyses to which it subjects them;

Cookery, because of the art of adapting dishes and making them pleasant to the taste;

Business, by the seeking out of methods of buying as cheaply as possible what is needed, and of selling most advantageously what can be produced for sale;

Finally, political economy, because of the sources of revenue which gastronomy creates and the means of exchange which it establishes between nations.

It rules over our whole life; for the cries of the newborn babe beg for his wet nurse's breast; and the dying man still receives with some pleasure his final potion, which, alas, it is too late for him ever to digest!

It concerns also every state of society, for just as it directs the banquets of assembled kings, it dictates the number of minutes needed to make a perfectly boiled egg.

The subject matter of gastronomy is whatever can be eaten; its direct end is the conservation of individuals; and its means of execution are the culture which produces, the commerce which exchanges, the industry which prepares, and the experience which invents means to dispose of everything to the best advantage.

Various Concerns of Gastronomy

19: Gastronomy considers taste in its pleasant as well as its unfortunate aspects; it has uncovered the gradual excitation of which taste is capable; it has regulated that activity, and has set certain limits to it which any man who respects his own dignity will never pass.

It has also considered the action of foods on man's morale, on his imagination, his spirit, his judgment, his courage and perceptions, whether he be awake, asleep, active, or resting.

It is gastronomy which decides the point of fitness of every nourishing substance; for not all of them are desirable in the same way.

Some of them must be used before having reached their final stage of development, like capers, asparagus, suckling pigs, squabs, and other creatures which are eaten in their early days; others must be enjoyed at the moment when they have attained the peak of their growth, like melons, most fruits, mutton, beef, and all adult animals; still others when they begin to decompose, like medlars, woodcocks, and above all pheasants; others, finally, when all the arts of gastronomy have removed their noxious qualities, as with potatoes, the cassava plant, and others.

It is gastronomy which classifies these things according to their different qualities, which indicates those agreeable in combination, and which, by measuring their various degrees of edibility, separates those which can form the basis of our meals from those which are no more than accessories; that is, those which, without being really necessary, are nonetheless a pleasant distraction, and which become the obligatory accompaniment of any convivial celebration.

Gastronomy takes an equal interest in the liquids we consume, following the time, the place, and the weather. She teaches us how to prepare them, to keep them, and above all to present them in a pattern so well calculated that the enjoyment which results grows steadily deeper, to the moment where true pleasure ends and its abuse begins.

It is gastronomy which so studies men and things that everything worth being known is carried from one country to another, so that an intelligently planned feast is like a summing-up of the whole world, where each part is represented by its envoys.

Advantages of Gastronomical Knowledge

20: Gastronomical knowledge is necessary to every man, because it tends to add to the sum of his predestined pleasure; its usefulness increases in proportion to the social rank of the individual; and in the end it becomes indispensable to those men who, blessed with enormous fortunes, entertain a great deal, whether for reasons of political protocol, their own inclinations, or their obedience to fashion.

There is this special advantage in their gastronomical knowledge, that they attain through it a completely personal note in the way their table is maintained; they are able to supervise up to a certain point the arrangements which they must then entrust to others, and they may even direct them occasionally.

The Prince of Soubise planned to give a great party one time; it was to end with a supper, and he asked for the menu.

His steward appeared at his morning conference with a handsomely decorated sheet of paper, and the first notation the prince's eyes fell upon was this: *fifty hams.*

"Look here, Bertrand," he said, "it seems to me you are dreaming! Fifty hams! Are you trying to treat my whole regiment?"

"Not at all, sir! Only one ham will appear on the table, but the rest are essential for my *sauce espagnole,* my white sauces, my garnishes, my . . ."

"Bertrand, you're thieving from me, and I shan't let you get away with it."

"Ah, my lord," the artist said, hardly able to hold back his wrath, "you know very little of our resources! Command me, and I can put these fifty hams which seem to bother you into a glass bottle no bigger than your thumb!"

What was there to say to such a positive assertion? The prince smiled, nodded his head, and the menu was approved.

Influence of Gastronomy on Business

21: It is well known that among men who are still somewhat primitive any affair of importance is settled at the table; it is in this atmosphere of feasting that savages decide to make either war or peace; and even without going so far away from home we see that our own villagers carry on most of their business in their taverns.

This observation has never been ignored by men with great interests at stake; they have observed that a well-fed man is not at all the same as a hungry one; that the table constitutes a kind of tie between the bargainer and the bargained-with, and makes the diners more willing to receive certain impressions, to submit to certain influences: from this is born political gastronomy.[2] Meals have become a means of governing, and the fate of whole peoples is decided at a banquet. This is neither a paradox nor even real news, but a simple observation of the facts. Let one open any book of history, from Herodotus to our own days, and he will see that, without even excepting conspiracies, not a single great event has occurred which has not been conceived, prepared, and carried out at a feast.[3]

An Academy of Gastronomers

22: Such is, at first glance, the kingdom of gastronomy, a domain fertile in every kind of results, which can only grow mightier by the discoveries and the labors of the wise men who till it; for it is inconceivable that gastronomy, before too many years, will not have its own academicians, its professors, its yearly courses and its contests for scholarships.

First of all a rich and zealous enthusiast must organize in his own home a series of periodical gatherings, where the best-trained theoreticians will meet with the finest practitioners, to discuss and penetrate the different branches of alimentary science.

Then (and this is the story of all such schools) the government will step in, to regulate, protect, subsidize, and finally to seize one more chance to give back to the people some compensation for all the orphans its cannons have made, and all the women who have wept because of them.

How happy will be the man of might who gives his name to this essential institution! It will be repeated from century to century with those of Noah, of Bacchus, of Triptolemus[4] and of other benefactors of the human race; he will be among ministers what Henry IV is among the kings, and his eulogy will be on every *tongue*,[5] without any law to force putting it there.

THE TRANSLATOR'S GLOSSES

1. In MAN, BREAD, AND DESTINY, J. C. Furnas wrote cynically, "Books which suggest simplicity in the kitchen never sell well." His, which did suggest just that, has gone into many editions since it first appeared in 1937.
2. In an unsigned article in ST. JAMES'S MAGAZINE, published in London in 1868, a reviewer of the Professor's book said with what might almost be called enthusiasm, "Speaking of Brillat-Savarin, it is no exaggeration to declare, that every statesman, as well as every physician, ought to make a pocket companion of his PHYSIOLOGIE DU GOUT."
3. The Professor's enthusiasm for his subject sometimes overpowered his innate sense of detachment, and he permitted himself a fine extravagance like this, as if to prove himself reassuringly human. It is said that more than once, during the twenty-five or thirty years he worked on THE PHYSIOLOGY OF TASTE, he could not bear to leave the manuscript at home and tucked it into his hip pocket to carry to the law courts so that he might make a few revisions as the spirit moved him. At least once it

was lost. Fortunately it turned up: it is hard to imagine either French or English letters without it.

4. Triptolemus, one of the principal figures in Greek religion, is said to be the inventor of the plow and of agriculture, and therefore the real father of what we call civilization.

5. This pardonable play on words must have pleased Brillat-Savarin, in a quiet but thorough way. In spite of his surface flippancy, he felt strongly about the social importance of gastronomy, and the chance to imply that full mouths would be praiseful mouths was one that he could not let slip by him.

MEDITATION 4

ON APPETITE

Definition of Appetite

23: Movement and life cause a steady loss of substance in any living being; and the human body, that highly complicated machine, would soon be useless if Providence had not placed in it a sentinel which sounds warning the moment its resources are no longer in perfect balance with its needs.

This guardian is appetite, by which is meant the first warning of the need to eat.

Appetite declares itself by a vague languor in one's stomach and a slight feeling of fatigue.

At the same time one's soul concerns itself with things connected with its own needs; memory recalls dishes that have pleased the taste; imagination pretends to see them; there is something dreamlike about the whole process. This state is not without its charms, and a thousand times we have heard its devotees exclaim with a full heart: "How wonderful to have a good appetite, when we are sure of enjoying an excellent dinner before long!"

However, one's whole digestive machine soon takes part in

the action: the stomach becomes sensitive to the touch; gastric juices flow freely; interior gases move about noisily; one's mouth waters, and every part of the machine stands at attention, like soldiers waiting only for the order to attack. A few minutes more, and spasmodic movements will begin: one will yawn, feel uncomfortable, and in short be hungry.

It is easy to watch all the nuances of these various states in any drawing room when dinner has been delayed.

They are as much a part of instinct that the most exquisite politeness cannot hide their symptoms, from which fact I have coined the following aphorism: Of all the qualities of a good cook, punctuality is the most indispensable.

Anecdote

24:   I shall illustrate this important maxim by the details of what I once observed at a gathering I attended,

Quorum pars magna fui,

where my enjoyment in watching saved me from miserable discomfort.

I was invited, this day, to the home of an important official.[1] The card read five thirty, and at that precise hour all the guests had arrived, because it was common knowledge that the host loved punctuality and sometimes scolded his lazier friends.

I was struck, on my arrival, by an air of alarm which I saw everywhere: the guests whispered among themselves, or peeked through the windowpanes into the courtyard, and some of their faces showed plain stupefaction. Obviously something extraordinary had occurred.

I went up to the one of the guests I felt would be best able to satisfy my curiosity, and asked him what had happened. "Alas!" he answered in a voice of the deepest suffering, "his lordship has been summoned to a conference of state. He just this moment left for it, and who knows when he will be back again?"

"Is that all?" I replied, in an insouciant way which was far from genuine. "It's a question of a quarter-hour at the most; some information they needed; everyone knows that an official banquet is taking place here today; there is absolutely no reason to make us fast at it." I continued to talk this way; but in the bottom of my heart I was not without anxiety, and I should have loved to be safely out of the whole business.

The first hour passed well enough, with the guests seated next to their preferred friends; conversational banalities were soon exhausted, and we amused ourselves by guessing the reasons why our good host had been thus summoned to the Tuileries.

During the second hour a few signs of impatience began to show themselves: the guests looked at each other worriedly, and the first ones who complained aloud were three or four of the company who, not having found places to sit down and wait, were especially uncomfortable.

By the third hour, discontent was general, and everyone complained. "When will he be back?" one of them asked. "What can he be thinking of?" another said. "This is murderous!" said a third, and everywhere it was demanded, with never a satisfactory reply, "Should we go? Should we not go?"

By the fourth hour all the symptoms had grown worse: the guests stretched themselves, at the risk of knocking into their neighbors; the room was filled with the singsong of helpless yawns; every face was flushed with concentration; and not a soul listened to me when I risked remarking that our host was without doubt the most miserable of any of us.

At one point our attention was riveted by a ghostly sight. One of the guests, more familiar to the house than some of us, roamed as far as the kitchens; he came back completely out of breath; his face looking as if the end of the world were upon us, and he burst out in an almost unintelligible voice, in that heavy tone which betrays both a fear of being heard and a wish to be listened to: "His lordship left without giving any orders, and no matter how long he is gone, nothing will be served until he comes back!" He had spoken: the horror which his announcement roused could not possibly be outdone by the trumpet of the last judgment.

Among all these martyrs, the unhappiest was the good d'Aigrefeuille, well-known to all of Paris in those days; his body was the personification of misery, and the agony of a Laocoön showed in his face. Pale, distracted, sightless, he hunched himself into a chair, crossed his little hands over his generous belly, and closed his eyes, not to sleep, but to wait for his own death.

It was not Death, however, who came. About ten o'clock there was the sound of carriage-wheels in the courtyard. Everyone jumped to his feet. Gaiety took the place of sadness, and five minutes later we were seated at the table.

But the time of appetite had passed. There was a feeling of astonishment at beginning a dinner at this unfamiliar hour; our jaws could not attain that synchronized chewing which is a guarantee of perfect digestion, and I learned later that several of the guests were inconvenienced by it.[2]

The procedure indicated in such a situation is not to eat immediately after the enforced fast has ended, but to drink a glass of sugared water, or a cup of broth, to comfort the stomach; and then to wait another twelve or fifteen minutes, since otherwise the abused organ will find too oppressive the weight of the foods with which it has been overstuffed.

Mighty Appetites

25: When we read, in earlier writings, of the preparations which were made to entertain two or three people, as well as the enormous portions which were served to a single man, it is hard not to believe that our ancestors who lived nearer than we to the beginnings of the world must have been endowed with a much greater appetite than ours.

This appetite was held to increase in direct ratio to the importance of the person; and that man to whom was served no less than the whole back of a five-year-old bull was served his drink in a cup almost too enormous to lift.

There are still a few living witnesses of what happened in the old days, and written memoirs are full of examples of an almost incredible voracity, one which covered every kind of edible thing, down to the most unclean.

I shall spare my readers these somewhat disgusting details, and I prefer to tell them of two special feats which I myself witnessed, and which will not demand blind faith in order to be believed.

Some forty years ago I paid a flying visit to the vicar of Bregnier, a man of great stature, whose appetite was renowned throughout the district.

Although it was hardly noon, I found him already eating. The soup and boiled beef had been served, and after these two traditional dishes came a leg of mutton *à la royale*,[3] a handsome capon, and a generous salad.

As soon as he saw me arriving, he ordered a place set for me, which I very wisely refused; for, alone and without help from me, he easily got rid of the whole course, which is to say, the mutton down to its bone, the capon down to its several bones, and the salad down to the bottom of the bowl.

Next came a good-sized white cheese, from which he cut a wedge-shaped piece of precisely ninety degrees; and he washed down the whole with a bottle of wine and a carafe of water, after which he rested.

What delighted me about it was that, during this entire operation which lasted about three quarters of an hour, the good priest seemed completely at his ease. The generous-sized chunks he tossed into his great mouth did not keep him from either talking or laughing; and he polished off everything that was served to him with no more fuss than if he were nibbling at three little larks.

In the same way General Bisson, who drank eight bottles of wine every day with his breakfast, had an air of not even touching them; he used a larger glass than his guests', and emptied it oftener; but you would have said that he did it without paying any attention to it, and while he thus absorbed some sixteen pints of wine he was no more kept from joking and giving his daily orders than if he had drunk only a tumblerful.

This feat reminds me of the brave General P. Sibuet, from my own part of the country, who was for a long time first aide-de-camp to General Masséna,[4] and who died on the field of honor at the passage of the Bober in 1813.

Prosper, when he was eighteen years old, and had that happy appetite which is Nature's way of saying that she is busy finishing off the creation of a fine sturdy man, went one evening into the kitchen of Genin's inn, where the old men of Belley were used to meet together to eat chestnuts and drink the newly fermented white wine which is called *bourru* in that district.

Genin had just taken off the spit a magnificent turkey, a fine well-shaped bird, golden brown, cooked to perfection, whose aroma would have tempted a saint.

The old men, who were no longer hungry, paid little attention to it; but the digestive powers of young Prosper were violently aroused by it; his mouth began to water, and he exclaimed, "I just got up from the dinner table, but I'll still bet that I can eat this big turkey singlehanded." "*Sez vosu mezé, z'u payo,*" replied Bouvier du Bouchet, a fat farmer who was there, "*è sez vos caca en rotaz, i-zet vo ket pairé et may ket mezerai la restaz.*" †

The contest started immediately. The young athlete took off a wing very nicely, and swallowed it in two mouthfuls, after which he cleared his teeth by munching the neck of the bird, and drank a glass of wine by way of interlude.

Then he attacked the leg, ate it with the same poise, and dispatched a second glass of wine, to prepare a passageway for what was still to come.

Soon the second wing followed the same path: it disappeared, and the contestant, more and more active, seized upon the last of the four members, when the unhappy farmer cried out mournfully: "*Hai! ze vaie* PRAOU *qu'i-zet fotu; m'ez, monche Chibouet, poez kaet zu daive paiet, lessé m'en a m'en mesiet on mocho.*" ‡

Prosper was as decent a young fellow as he was later to be a good soldier; he not only agreed to the request of his antagonist, who drew as his share the carcass of the still appetizing bird, but with a very good grace he paid both for the turkey and the drinks that went with it.

General Sibuet enjoyed telling of this prowess of his younger days; he said that what he did in sharing the bird with the

---

† "*If you eat it, I'll pay for it; but if you falter on the road, it's you who who will pay, and I who will finish it off.*"

‡ "*Alas! I can see that you've won; but, Monsieur Sibuet, since I'm to pay for it, at least leave me a bit of it to eat.*"

I am happy to cite this example of the dialect of Bugey, in which can be found the TH *of the Greeks and the English, and, in the word* PRAOU *and ones like it, a diphthong which exists in no other language, and whose sound cannot be indicated by any known symbol. (See the third volume of* MEMOIRS OF THE ANTIQUARIAN SOCIETY OF FRANCE.)

farmer was nothing but politeness; he insisted that without this he was confident he could have won the bet; and judging by what was left of his appetite when he was forty, there can be no doubt of his boast.

THE TRANSLATOR'S GLOSSES

1.   It is amusing to think that this personage was probably Talleyrand himself. Brillat-Savarin was a good friend of his, a trusted adviser on things gastronomical as well as legal, and the man who became known as a prince among diners owed much to the quiet judge, even to the point of shamelessly paraphrasing one of his aphorisms by writing that the first duty of a statesman is to look well after his own liver. He should know if should any man in the world, but thanks to THE PHYSIOLOGY OF TASTE we see that at least once he did not take care of either his own liver or his guests'!

2.   Digestion is one of the most delicately balanced of all human and perhaps angelic functions. Anyone who has ever had a disturbing telephone call, for instance, after a peaceful perfect meal, and has felt his finer nerves start up in outrage at the shock, will agree with this minor profundity of mine and with the neater statement of an American Professor, Charles Townsend Copeland, who once said, "To eat is human, to digest divine."

It takes divinity of both body and soul to have a human mechanism accept food and assimilate it as willingly as the palate has given it the first password. Any medical textbook can present the clinical outlines of digestion, but not the most prescient psychiatrist has yet been able to pin down the moment at which an honest morsel of beef changes from a young boy's meat to a madman's poison. If good digestion be even the outer fringes of divinity, let every mortal strive to reach it . . .

3.   In cook books written within fifty years of Brillat-Savarin's day there is no mention of this way of serving mutton.

Anything *à la royale* would, or at least *could*, be made into a kind of delicate custard and poached, but it is hard to imagine mutton that way. However, it is equally hard to imagine eating mutton before a capon . . .

4. André Masséna (1758–1817) was Italian Marshal of France. His worst enemies could say nothing really bad about him, and Napoleon used him as a tactician even though he was avowedly republican in sentiment. It is said that Masséna's complete lack of ambition is what saved his neck.

MEDITATION 5

ON FOOD
IN GENERAL

SECTION I

Definitions

26:   What is meant by food? *Popular reply:* Food is everything that nourishes.

Scientific reply: Food is all those substances which, submitted to the action of the stomach, can be assimilated or changed into life by digestion, and can thus repair the losses which the human body suffers through the act of living.

Thus, the distinctive quality of food consists in its ability to submit to animal assimilation.

Analytical Process

27:   The animal and vegetable kingdoms are the ones which, up until now, have furnished food to humanity. The only things drawn from minerals have been remedies or poisons.

Since analytical chemistry became an exact science, great progress has been made in deciding the double nature of the elements which make up our bodies, and of the substances which nature seems to have destined to repair our bodily losses.

The most praiseworthy and at the same time most painstaking labors have been performed, following this double path, and scholars have studied both the human body and the foods by which it restores itself, first in their secondary aspects and then in their basic elements, further than which it has not yet been permitted to us to penetrate.

Here I meant to insert a little essay on food chemistry, and to have my readers learn into how many thousandths of carbon, hydrogen, and so forth, both they and their favorite dishes could be reduced; but I was stopped by the observation that I could hardly accomplish this except by copying the excellent chemistry books which are already in good circulation. I was also fearful of becoming very dull, and I have limited myself to the use of systematic terms, except now and then for giving a few chemical results in less dusty and more intelligible phraseology.

Osmazome

28:   The greatest service rendered by chemistry to alimentary science is the discovery or even more the exact comprehension of osmazome.

Osmazome is that preeminently sapid part of meat which is soluble in cold water, and which differs completely from the extractive part of the meat, which is soluble only in water that is boiling.

It is osmazome which gives all their value to good soups; it is osmazome which, as it browns, makes the savory reddish tinge in sauces and the crisp coating on roasted meat; finally it is from the osmazome that come the special tangy juices of venison and game.

This property is found mainly in mature animals with red flesh, blackish flesh, or whatever is meant by well-hung meat, the kind that is never or almost never found in lambs, suckling pigs, pullets, or even in the white meat of the largest fowls. It is for this reason that lovers of poultry have always preferred the second joint: in them the instinct for flavor came long before science confirmed it.

It is also the infallible goodness of osmazome which has caused the dismissal of so many cooks, destined as they were to ruin their basic soup stock; it is osmazome which has made the reputation of the richest consommés, which once made toast soaked in bouillon a favorite restorative during weakening curative baths, and which inspired Canon Chevrier to invent a soup pot which locked with a key. (It is this same holy Father who never used to serve spinach on a Friday unless it had been cooking since the Sunday before, and put back each day on the stove with a new lump of fresh butter.)[1]

Finally, it is to husband this substance, as yet largely unrecognized, that the maxim has been propounded that in order to make a good bouillon the pot must only *smile* with heat, a truly worthy expression considering the country from which it came.

Osmazome, discovered at last after having for so long delighted our forebears, can be compared with alcohol, which tipsified many generations of men before any of them knew how to strip it naked in the analytical process of distillation in a laboratory.

During the action of boiling water osmazome gives place to what is understood more especially by extractive matter: this last product, reunited with the osmazome, makes up the juice of meat.

Elements of Food

Fiber makes up the tissue of meat and is what we see after it has been cooked. It is resistant to boiling water, and holds its shape in spite of having been stripped of a part of its coverings. To carve meat well, care must be taken to have the flesh make a right angle, as nearly as possible, with the knife blade: the meat thus carved will look nicer, will taste better, and will be more easily chewed.[2]

Bones are composed mainly of a kind of gelatin and of phosphate of chalk.

The quantity of gelatin in them decreases with the advance of age. At seventy years, a man's bones are no more than flawed marble; this is what makes them so breakable, and dictates a law of caution in old people to avoid all possible falls.[3]

Albumen is found equally in flesh and in blood; it coagulates at a heat of less than 40 degrees: it is what makes up the scum of a soup pot.

Gelatin is found equally in both the soft and cartilaginous parts of the bones; its distinctive quality is to coagulate at room temperatures, and two and a half parts to one hundred of hot water are enough for this experiment.

Gelatin is the base for jellies both rich and meager, for puddings, like *blancs-mangers*, and for all similar preparations.

Grease is a solid oil which forms in the interstices of cellular tissue, and collects in masses in those animals predisposed to it by art or nature, like pigs, poultry, ortolans, and figpeckers; in a few of these creatures it loses its insipidity and takes on a faint aroma which makes it most agreeable.

Blood is made up of an albuminous serum, fibrin, a little gelatin, and a little osmazome; it coagulates in warm water, and becomes a most nourishing food (for instance, black pudding).[4]

All these principles which we have passed in review are common to mankind and to the animals upon which he nourishes himself. Therefore it is not too astonishing that a meat diet is above all strengthening and restorative; for the particles of which it is composed, possessing the same characteristics as our own and yet having been made assimilable, can easily be absorbed once more when they have been submitted to the vital action of our digestive organs.

Vegetable World

29: However, the vegetable world presents no less variety to our nourishment, no fewer resources.

Starch is a perfect food, especially when it is least mixed with foreign matter.

By this starch is meant the flour or dust which comes from cereal grains, from legumes such as beans, and from many root vegetables, among which the potato at this moment holds first place.

Starch is the base of bread, of cakes, and of thick soups of all kinds, and for this reason forms a very great part of almost every person's nourishment.

It has been observed that such a diet softens a man's flesh and even his courage. For proof one can cite the Indians, who live almost exclusively on rice and who are the prey of almost anyone who wishes to conquer them.

Almost all domestic animals will eat starch with avidity, and they are, in contrast, unusually strengthened by it, because it is a more substantial nourishment than the fresh or dry leaves which are their habitual fodder.

Sugar is no less negligible, either as a food or as a medicine.

This substance, exclusive to the Indies and our colonies in the old days, became a native of Europe at the beginning of this the nineteenth century. It was discovered and developed in grapes, turnips, chestnuts, and above all beets; to such an end that, frankly speaking, Europe could in this regard take care of itself and do without either America or the Indies. This is a praiseworthy service which science has rendered to the world, and an example which may well have far-reaching results. (See later, the section entitled Sugar.)

Sugar, whether in a solid state or in the various plants where nature has placed it, is extremely nourishing; animals love it, and the English, who give a great deal of it to their thoroughbred horses, have observed that these creatures fare better than others in tests to which they are submitted.

Sugar, which in the time of Louis XIV was found only in apothecary shops, has given birth to various lucrative activities, such as the making of little frosted cakes, of candies, of heavy liqueurs, and of other dainties.

Sweet oils also have their origin in the vegetable kingdom; they are not pleasant to the taste, except as they may be blended with other substances, and they must above all be considered as seasoning.

Gluten, which is found especially in the residue of wheat flour, helps enormously in the fermentation of the bread of which it forms a part; chemists have gone so far as to ascribe an active animal nature to it.

In Paris one can buy, for children, birds, and even for men in certain districts, cakes in which gluten predominates, thanks to the fact that a part of the starch has been washed out with water.

Mucilage owes its nutritive quality to the various substances which it has collected in a whole.

Sap can become, if need be, a food; this is not too astonishing, since it contains very nearly the same elements as sugar.

The vegetable gelatins which are extracted from many kinds

of fruits, notably apples, gooseberries, quinces, and some others, can also serve as a food: they do very well, combined with sugar, but always less so than the animal jellies which are extracted from the bones, the horns, and the feet of calves and from the essence of fish. This nourishment is in general light, soothing, and wholesome. Thus both kitchen and pantry seize upon it and claim it.

Difference Between Fasting and Feasting

30: There are in fish most of the substances which we have already pointed out as part of land animals, like fibrin, gelatin, and albumen, except for the natural gravy, which is composed of osmazome and extracted essence. For this reason it is reasonable to say that gravy is what differentiates ordinary dishes from a meager Lenten diet.

This last point is still further strengthened by another peculiarity, that fish also contain a large amount of both phosphorus and hydrogen, those most combustible elements in nature. From this it follows that a fish diet is a very heating one, a theory which may well support certain old-fashioned speculations about various religious orders whose supposedly meager regimen was thus directly contrary to the one of their ascetic vows most often broken.

Specific Instance

I shall say no more about this physiological question, except to give one instance which can easily be verified:

A few years ago I went to look at a country house near Paris on the banks of the Seine opposite the island of Saint-Denis, in a little hamlet which consisted mainly of eight fishermen's huts. I was struck by the number of children who swarmed along the road.

I mentioned my astonishment to the boatman with whom I was crossing the river. "Sir," he said, "there are only eight families of us here, and we have fifty-three children, forty-nine of them girls and only four boys, one of them my own." As he spoke, he straightened himself triumphantly, and pointed out to me a little rascal five or six years old, stretched out on the bow of the boat, crunching away happily on some raw crayfish. This little hamlet was called . . .

From this incident, which happened more than ten years ago, and from various others which I cannot very well recount with discretion, I have been led to think that the reproductive activity induced by a fish diet may well be more exciting than it is full-bodied and substantial; I am even more inclined to believe this since, quite recently, Doctor Bailly has proved, by a series of facts observed during almost a full century, that every time the birth of girls greatly outnumbers that of boys in an annual census, the overabundance of females is directly due to debilitating circumstances. This may well indicate to us the origin of the pleasantries which have always been made to the man whose wife has just presented him with a daughter.

There is much more that could be said about foods in general, and about the various changes they undergo when combined, but I hope that the preceding discussion will more than suffice for most of my readers. The rest I must refer to the professional treatises, while I finish my Meditation with two observations which are not without interest.

The first is that the processes of animal life are carried out in much the same way as those of the vegetable, which is to say that the restorative current formed by digestion is absorbed in various manners by the sieves or suckers with which our organs are provided, and then becomes flesh, nails, bone, hair, just as the same bit of earth sprinkled with the same water will produce a radish, a lettuce, or a dandelion according to which seeds the gardener has planted in it.

My second observation is that we never obtain in living organisms the same results as in abstract chemistry, because organs which are meant to create life and movement act powerfully upon the elements which are subjected to them.

But Nature, who loves to bring us to a dead halt in our attempts to unveil her, has hidden the laboratory where she performs her miracles; and it is truly difficult to understand, once granted that the human body is made up of lime, sulphur, phosphorus, iron and ten other substances, how all this can continue to maintain its balance and renew itself over many years on nothing, say, but bread and water.

THE TRANSLATOR'S GLOSSES

1. I have tasted spinach prepared almost as fastuously, and must admit that it is delicious. I also like spinach *à la mode de pressure cooker* 1947: take three cellophane packages of washed or frozen spinach, put in cooker, cook two minutes according to directions, drain, stir lightly with lump of sweet butter and salt, and serve very hot. This would seem barbaric and probably inedible to Canon Chevrier.

2. The reassuring simplicity of this direction must have been of great comfort to many a carver discouraged by the usual elaborate instructions. It is not strange, of course, that the act of cutting meat should be invested with much significance and pomp: from the time of the first stone knives, the first raw or roasted carcasses, it is the man of skill and virile prowess who has been the one to dole out what meat was mete for his dependents. But the art of carving is one that, when learned at all, must be practiced faithfully, and few families now have either the ovens or the appetites (given the incomes) for haunches and hams big enough to work on.

My father is one of the four or five men I know who still make a little show, a kind of precise ballet, of carving, and since our family has shrunk with the passage of time and peace and war he has few chances in a year to stand up to a bird or a great roast of beef. When he does, it is a noble performance, and one that rightly should be done to the sound of trumpets.

What makes his ritual even more impressive is the legend that when he was courting my mother, her father, who felt that although mine-to-be was obviously a gentleman he seemed somewhat unpolished, announced that if he could carve a duck he would do for marriage. Father was warned, he practiced at night in the kitchen of a saloon, and the next Sunday he cut his way through a brace of canvasbacks with a surgeon's finesse and aplomb, so artfully that he was given not only my mother's hand but the family whetstone and carving knives. Or so I have been told.

At least he had no need for what is described in Soyer's GASTRONOMIC REGENERATOR as a Tendon Separator. In the 1847 edition of the great chef's (and inventor's!) book he wrote, in a long sales talk about his gadget, "To a clever carver, sitting at a homely table or public banquet, it matters little whether all eyes are fixed upon him or a fidgety footman is at his elbow. He quietly distributes the several dainties according to the fancies of the guests, and everything goes on in comfort. But to a person inexperienced, the notion of being placed at either end of the table, to stay the ravenous appetites of some of the guests, causes such a nervous excitement, that it is not an uncommon thing to see the splashing of sauce and gravy on those around—perchance the sudden appearance of an unfortunate limb flying with terrific velocity on a lady's dress, the whole of the company being thus thrown into confusion—the poor carver's apologies received with black looks, and the harmony of the party placed in jeopardy.

"It is with a view to extricate society from such an awkward position that the inventor . . ." and so on, wrote the dashing chef of the Reform Club. Perhaps there are still English gentlemen who "boldly take the carving knife in hand, delighted to comply with the invitation of the Amphytrion," thanks to Soyer's Separator, but my good father, amorous and earnest, managed very well without it in an Iowa village in 1902, and I for one am indeed glad.

3. This is a good example of the Professor's candid view of life, of man, of the world. In it he discusses without any change of spiritual expression, in the same breath really, the aspect of boiled beef and the fragility of old men's bones, just as in "Meditation 6" he includes in his essay on the uses of sugar in preserving fruit a speculation as to its possible success in embalming cadavers. There is nothing repulsive about these juxtapositions. They are dispassionate and thoughtful, the attitude of a good doctor which Brillat-Savarin would have liked to be, a good lawyer which he was.

4. In Paris spicy *boudin* used to be served on Christmas Eve. It seems to me that a little earlier in the year it was brought

around, sizzling and rich and *free*, in the larger cafés of Burgundy. And I remember that the prostitutes would snatch at it, daintily of course but with avidity, as if it could give them some magic strength. If the waiter liked them they could have two or three pieces, and for once there would be no joking about the bulls it had been drawn from. Each fashionably thin pale woman would eat-eat-eat, in a silence straight from THE GOLDEN BOUGH.

MEDITATION 6

ON FOOD IN GENERAL

SECTION II

Special Foods

31: My list of subjects has been made and my whole book has been well-formed in my head since the moment I started to write; however, I have gone forward but slowly, since part of my time must be devoted to more serious labors.

During this period, then, some parts of the material which I believed was my special property have been stripped bare by other writers; elementary books on chemistry and medicine have been widely circulated; and things which I meant to be the first to disclose are now popular knowledge: for instance, I devoted to the chemistry of soup stock several pages which in their substance can now be found in two or three recently published works.

The result is that I have had to edit this part of my book, and I have cut it down so drastically that it is reduced to a few basic principles, to a few theories which it is impossible to propound too often, and to a few observations, the fruit of long experience, which I hope will be new to the great part of my readers.

I. Pot-au-feu, Soup, etc.

32:   A piece of beef destined to being treated with lightly salted boiling water, in order to draw out its soluble parts, is called *pot-au-feu*.

Bouillon is the liquid which is left after this operation.

The meat which has thus been drained of its solubles is called the *bouilli*.

The water first of all dissolves part of the osmazome; then the albumen, which coagulates at about 104 degrees Fahrenheit, forms a scum which is usually skimmed off; then the rest of the osmazome dissolves with the juice or extractive part; and so finally do portions of the outer coating of the fibers, which are pulled off by the continuous movement of the boiling liquid.

To make a good bouillon, the water must heat gradually, so that the albumen will not coagulate inside the meat before it can be extracted; and the boiling must be kept at a simmer, so that the various parts which are successively dissolved may mix together easily.

Vegetables and roots are added to the bouillon to enhance its flavor, and bread or flour pastes to make it more nourishing: the result is called soup.

Soup is a healthy, light, sustaining food which is food for everyone; it soothes the stomach and encourages it to receive and digest more nourishment. People threatened with overweight should eat only plain bouillon.

It is generally agreed that nowhere can be found soup as good as that of France, and I have found this to be very true during my wanderings. This is not too surprising: soup is the basis of our national diet, and centuries of experience have brought it to its present perfection.

II. Bouilli

33:   The boiled beef, bouilli, is a healthy food, which quickly appeases hunger and which is fairly easily digested, but which by itself does not restore any too well the bodily losses, since it has lost a good part of its digestible juices while being boiled.

It is held as a general rule of cookery that boiled beef has lost one-half of its original weight.

We can place in four categories the people who eat bouilli:

(1) Creatures of habit, who eat it because their parents did, and who, following this example with implicit faith, hope devoutly to be so imitated by their own children;

(2) The impatient souls, who, loathing inaction at the dinner table, have formed the habit of hurling themselves immediately at the first thing which is served (*materiam subjectam*);

(3) The uninterested, who, never having received from heaven the sacred fire, look on meals as a duty to be performed, place on the same level everything which can nourish them, and sit at table like oysters in an oyster bed;

(4) The gluttons, who, endowed with a hunger whose immensity they try to hide, hurry to pile into their stomachs a first sacrificial victim, to appease the gastric blaze which devours them and to serve as a kind of cushion for the succession of foods which they intend to send down to the same destination.

Real professors of the science of gastronomy never touch bouilli, both out of respect for its principles and because they have preached from their pulpits this incontestable truth: Bouilli is flesh without its blood.†

III. Poultry

34: I am a great lover of secondary causes, and I believe firmly that the whole gallinaceous race was created for the sole purpose of filling our larders and enriching our banquets.

Certainly wherever you meet a member of this numerous family, from the quail to the turkey cock, you can be sure of finding a delicate food and a flavorful one, equally good for the convalescent and the sturdiest healthy man; for what one of us, condemned by his doctors to the diet of a desert hermit, has not beamed at the sight of a nicely carved chicken wing, which informed him in its own way that he was about to be given back to polite society?

We do not seem able to satisfy ourselves with the qualities

---

† *This truth begins to be appreciated, and boiled beef has disappeared from truly well-planned dinners; it is replaced by a fine roast, a turbot, or a stew of fish and wine called a* MATELOTE.[1]

which nature has given to the roosterish clan; art has stepped in; and with the pretext of bettering them we have made them into martyrs. Not only do we deprive them of their means of reproduction, but we condemn them to solitary confinement and darkness, we force them to eat, and by doing so we make them much heavier than they were ever meant to be.

It is true that this unnatural weight of fat is also completely delicious and that it is by means of these damnable practices that we give our capons the finesse and delicacy which make them preferred on the finest tables.

Thus bettered, poultry is for the cook what canvas is for a painter, or the cap of Fortunatus[2] for a conjurer; it is served to us boiled, roasted, fried, hot or cold, whole or cut up, with or without sauce, boned, skinned, stuffed, and always with equal success.

Three districts of the old prerevolutionary France can quarrel over the honor of providing the best poultry, namely Caux, Mans, and Bresse.

As far as capons are concerned, there is some question, and whatever is immediately on the tip of the fork will seem the best; but for fat pullets, the preference goes to those of Bresse, which are called *poulardes fines* and which are round as apples; it is a great pity that they are so scarce in Paris, where they never are found except in hampers from the country.

IV. *Turkeys*

35: The turkey is certainly one of the most delightful presents which the New World has made to the Old.

People who love to know more than their fellows say that turkeys were known to the Romans, that one was cooked for the wedding of Charlemagne, and that it is therefore stupid to attribute this flavorsome innovation to the Jesuits.

To these contradictions one can but submit two facts:

(1) The name of the bird, *coq d'Inde*, which bears out its origin, since in the old days America was known as Western India;[3]

(2) The shape of the turkey, which is obviously a foreign one.

These facts could not possibly lead any scholar astray.

However, although already thoroughly convinced, I have made fairly thorough investigations on this subject, which I pass on gladly to the reader, and which have resulted in the following conclusions:

(1)   The turkey appeared in Europe toward the end of the seventeenth century;

(2)   It was brought here by the Jesuit fathers, who raised a great quantity, especially on a farm which they owned on the outskirts of Bourges;

(3)   It is from there that turkeys have spread little by little over the whole of France; it is because of this that in many places, and in the common language, turkeys used to be called *jesuits* and still are;

(4)   America is the only place where the wild turkey has been found in its native state (it does not exist in Africa);

(5)   On the farms of North America, where turkeys are very common, they are supplied either from eggs which have been found and hatched, or from young birds which have been trapped in the woods and domesticated: for this reason they are more nearly in their primitive state there, and still keep their original plumage.

Vanquished by these arguments, I must pay double homage to the good Fathers, for they have also brought home with them *quinine*, which is called in English *Jesuit's bark*.

This same train of research has taught me that turkeys gradually grow used to life in France. Knowing observers have told me that toward the middle of the last century barely ten out of every twenty domesticated birds would flourish, whereas now, all things being equal, twenty of them will yield fifteen. Rainstorms have always been the worst disaster for them: heavy raindrops, beaten against them by the wind, hurt their tender unprotected skulls and cause their death.

Turkey Lovers

36:   The turkey is the largest and, if not the most delicate, at least the most flavorful of our domestic birds.

It also enjoys the unique advantage of attracting to it every class of society.

When the vine tenders and the plowmen of our countryside want to treat themselves to a party on a long winter night, what do you see roasting over the bright kitchen fire where the table is laid? A turkey.

When the practical mechanic or the artisan brings a few of his friends together to celebrate some relaxation all the sweeter for being so rare, what is the traditional main dish of the dinner he offers? A turkey stuffed with sausages or with Lyons chestnuts.

And in our most renowned gastronomical circles, in those exclusive gatherings where politics must yield place to dissertations on the sense of taste, what do the guests wait for? What is it that they want? What is served up in the place of honor? A truffled turkey! . . . And my secret diary[4] notes that its restorative juices have more than once lighted up a face until then preeminently and discreetly diplomatic.

Financial Influence of the Turkey

37: The importation of turkeys has made an important addition to our national wealth, and has become a fairly large trade.

Farmers can more easily pay their land rents by raising turkeys, and young ladies pile up respectable fortunes for their marriages; town dwellers who want to treat themselves to a feast of this outlandish meat must give up their gold in return.

From this purely financial consideration of my subject, turkeys which are truffled are of especial interest.

I have some reason to believe that from the first of November until the end of February, three hundred truffled turkeys a day are consumed in Paris: in all, that makes thirty-six thousand birds.

The average price of each one, thus prepared, is at least 20 francs, or 720,000 francs in all; all of which adds up to a very pretty little financial transaction. And to this must be added a like sum for poultry, pheasants, chickens and partridges, truffled in the same way, which can be seen every day spread out on the shelves of the provision shops, to the agony of those people too short of cash to buy them.

*　　*　　*

Exploit of the Professor

38:   While I was in Hartford, in Connecticut, I had the good luck to kill a wild turkey. This deed deserves to go down in history, and I shall recount it all the more eagerly since I myself am its hero.

A worthy old landowner (AMERICAN FARMER) had invited me to come hunt on his property; he lived in the backwoods of the State (BACK GROUNDS), promised me partridges, grey squirrels, and wild turkeys (WILD COCKS), and gave me the privilege of bringing with me one or two of my chosen friends.

As a result, one fine day of October 1794 we set out, Monsieur King and I, mounted on two hired nags, with the hope of arriving by nightfall at Monsieur Bulow's farm, situated five whole ungodly leagues from Hartford.

M. King was a hunter of an extraordinary kind: he loved the sport passionately, but when he had killed any game he looked on himself as a murderer, and delivered himself of sensitive moral speculations and elegies on the final passing of his victims, which of course did not in the least keep him from starting the hunt all over again.

Although our road was hardly more than a track, we arrived without accident, and were received with that kind of cordial and wordless hospitality which expresses itself by its actions, which is to say that in a very few minutes all of us had been looked after, refreshed, and lodged—men, horses, and dogs according to their particular needs.

We spent some two hours in looking over the farm and its dependencies. I could describe all of that if I wished to, but I much prefer picturing to the reader M. Bulow's four fine daughters (BUXUM LASSES), for whom our visit was a great event.

Their ages ranged from sixteen to twenty; they were radiant with freshness and good health, and there was about all of them such simplicity, such graceful naturalness, that their most ordinary actions endowed them with a thousand charms.

Shortly after we returned from our walk we sat down around a plentifully laden table: a handsome piece of CORN'D BEEF, a STEW'D goose, and a magnificent leg of mutton, then root-vegetables of all kinds (PLENTY), and at the two ends of the table two enormous jugs of an excellent cider, of which I could not drink enough.

When we had proved to our host that we were genuine hunters, at least in our appetite, he began to talk of the real purpose of our visit: he described to the best of his ability the places where we would find our game, the landmarks which we must watch for to guide us safely back again, and above all the farms where we could find refreshment.

During this conversation the ladies had prepared some excellent tea, of which we drank several cups; then they showed us to a room with two beds in it, where the day's exercise and the good food soon sent us off into a delicious sleep.

The next morning we set out for the hunt a little late, and soon coming to the edge of the clearings made by M. Bulow's workmen, I found myself for the first time in my life in virgin forest, where the sound of the axe had never been heard.

I wandered through it with delight, observing the benefits and the ravages of time, which both creates and destroys, and I amused myself by following every period in the life of an oak tree, from the moment it emerges two-leaved from the earth until that one when nothing is left of it but a long black smudge which is its heart's dust.

M. King chided me for my wandering attention, and we took up the hunt more seriously. First of all we killed some of those pretty little grey partridges which are so plump and so tender. Then we knocked down six or seven grey squirrels, highly thought of in that country; and finally our lucky start led us into the midst of a flock of wild turkeys.

They arose, one after another, in quick noisy flight, screaming loudly. M. King fired first, and ran ahead: the others were by now out of range; then the laziest of them rose from the earth not ten paces from me; I fired at it through a break in the woods, and it fell, stone dead.

Only a hunter will understand the bliss such a lucky shot gave me. I picked up the superb winged creature,[5] and stood admiring it from every angle for a good quarter-hour, when I heard M. King cry out for help; I ran to him, and found that he was only calling me to aid him in the search for a turkey which he declared he had killed, but which had nonetheless completely disappeared.

I put my dog on the scent, but he led us into thickets so dense and thorny that a serpent could not have gone through them, and we were forced to give up, which threw my companion into a temper which lasted until we returned to the farm.

The rest of our hunt is hardly worth describing. On the way back, we lost ourselves in the boundless woods, and were in great danger of having to spend the night in them, had it not been for the silvery voices of the young Bulows and the deep bass of their father, who had been kind enough to come in search of us, and who helped lead us out of the forest.

The four sisters had put on their full battle dress; freshly laundered frocks, new sashes, pretty hats and neatly shining shoes told that they had gone to some expense for our benefits; and as for me, I was willing enough to be my most agreeable to the one of these young ladies who took my arm with as much a proprietary air as any wife.

When we got back to the farm we found supper ready for us; but, before starting to eat, we sat down for a few minutes before a lively blazing fire which had been lighted, even though the weather would not have seemed to call for it. We found it very comforting indeed, and were refreshed by it almost magically.

This custom doubtless came from the Indians, who always have a fire burning in their wigwams. Perhaps it is also a custom given to us by Saint Francis of Sales, who once said that a fire is good twelve months of the year. (*Non liquet.*)

We ate as if we were starved; a generous bowl of punch helped us to finish off the evening, and a discussion in which our host talked much more freely than the day before held us late into the night.

We talked of the War of Independence, in which M. Bulow had served as a ranking officer; of M. de La Fayette, steadily greater in the minds of the Americans, who always spoke of him familiarly by his title (THE MARQUIS); of agriculture, which during that period was enriching the United States, and finally of my own dear France, which I loved much more since I had been forced to leave it.

From time to time, as an interlude in our conversation, M. Bulow would say to his oldest daughter: "Mariah! Give us a song." And she sang to us without more urging, and with a charming shyness, the national air YANKEE DUDDE, and the lament of Queen Mary and the one of Major Andrew, both of them very popular in this country. Mariah had taken a few lessons, and there in the backwoods was thought to be something of an artist; but her singing was praiseworthy mainly because of the quality of her voice, which was at once sweet, fresh, and unaffected.

The next day we left, in spite of the friendliest protests, for even in America I had certain duties to perform. While the horses were being saddled, M. Bulow, having drawn me to one side, spoke in the following profoundly interesting way:

"You see in me, my dear sir, a happy man, if such there be on earth: everything around you and all that you have so far observed is a product of what I own. These stockings I wear were knitted by my daughters; my shoes and my clothes come from my own sheep; they help also, with my gardens and barnyards, to furnish me with simple nourishing food; and what makes our government so admirable is that here in Connecticut there are thousands of farmers just as happy as I am, and whose doors, like mine, are never bolted.

"Taxes here are almost nothing; and as long as they are paid we can sleep in peace. Congress does everything in its power to help our newborn industry; agents come from every direction to buy up whatever we have to sell; and I have cash on hand for a long time, for I have just sold for twenty-four dollars a barrel the wheat I usually get eight for.

"All this is the result of the liberty which we have fought for and founded on good laws. I am master in my own house, and you will not be astonished to know that we never hear the sound of the drum here, nor, except for the fourth of July, the glorious anniversary of our independence, do we ever see soldiers, or uniforms, or bayonets."

During the whole of our trip homeward I was plunged in profound thought. It may be believed that I was pondering the parting speech of M. Bulow, but I had something quite different on my mind: I was considering how best I should cook my turkey, and I was not without some worries, for I feared that in Hartford I might not find all the ingredients I would need—

and I was determined to raise a worthy monument to the spoils of my skill.

I inflict on myself a painful sacrifice in leaving out the details of the elaborate preparations I made for the fitting and distinguished way I planned to entertain my American dinner guests. It is enough to say that the partridge wings were served *en papillote*, and the grey squirrels simmered in Madeira.

As for the turkey, which was our only roast, it was charming to look at, flattering to the sense of smell, and delicious to the taste.[6] And as the last morsel of it disappeared, there arose from the whole table the words: "VERY GOOD! EXCEEDINGLY GOOD! OH! DEAR SIR, WHAT A GLORIOUS BIT!" †

V. Game

39:   By game we mean those animals which live in the woods and fields in a state of natural freedom, and which are still good to eat.

We say *good to eat,* because some of these creatures are not properly covered by the title of game, like the foxes, badgers, crows, magpies, screech owls, and others: they are called vermin, *bêtes puantes.*

We classify game in three divisions:

The first begins with the thrush, and continues down through all the diminishing sizes of what are called the little birds.

The second begins with the corncrake and goes on up through the snipe, the partridge, the pheasant, to the rabbit and the hare; it is properly called field game, marsh game, furred game, and feathered game.

The third is best known under the name of venison; it in-

---

† *The flesh of the wild turkey is darker and with a stronger flavor than that of the domestic bird.*

I have learned with pleasure that my estimable colleague, M. Bosc, has shot them in Carolina, and that he found them delicious and much better than the ones we raise in Europe. He advises anyone who plans to grow them to give them the greatest possible liberty, and to take them out into the fields and even the woods, there to add to their flavor and bring them as nearly as possible to the state of the truly wild species. (ANNALES D'AGRICULTURE, *pamphlet issued February 28, 1821.*)

cludes the wild boar, the roebuck, and all the other cloven-hooved animals.

Game is one of our favorite delicacies; it is a food at once healthy, warming, savorous, and stimulating to the taste, and is easily assimilated by anyone with a youthful digestive apparatus.

But these qualities are not so inherent that they can be independent of the skill of whoever tampers with them. If you throw some salt, some water, and a piece of beef together into a pot you will have some boiled beef and some soup. For beef substitute some wild boar or roebuck, and you will have absolutely nothing edible; all credit, in this case, must go to the domesticated provender of the butcher shop.

But game, under the command of a knowing chef, undergoes a great number of cunning modifications and transformations, and supplies the main body of those highly flavored dishes which make up truly gastronomical cookery.

Game also draws a great deal of its value from the nature of the country where it has matured: the flavor of a red partridge from Périgord is not that of one from Sologne; and while a hare killed on the plains outside of Paris makes but an insipid dish, a young one born on the sunburned slopes of Valromey or the upper Dauphiné is perhaps the tastiest of all four-legged game.

By far the most important of the small birds, because of its excellence, is the figpecker.

It grows at least as fat as the redbreast or the ortolan, and nature has moreover given it a slight bitterness and a unique flavor so exquisite that they seize upon, flood, and beautify every possible avenue of taste. If a figpecker could grow as big as a pheasant, it would be worth the price of an acre of land.

It is a great pity that this remarkable bird is found so seldom in Paris; true, a few arrive now and then, but they are completely lacking in the fat which constitutes their especial merit, and it can truthfully be said that they resemble but faintly those which are found in the east or southern parts of France.†

---

† *When I was young in Belley, I used to hear talk of the Jesuit Father Fabi who had been born in that diocese, and of the special predilection he had for figpeckers.*

As soon as they could be heard singing in their annual migratory flight, people would say, "There are the figpeckers, so Father Fabi must be on his way." And sure enough, he never missed arriving on the first

Few people know how to eat small feathered game; here is the best way, as it was told me confidentially by Canon Charcot, a born gourmand, and a true gastronomer thirty years before the word was known:

Take by the beak a fine fat little bird, salt him lightly, pull out his gizzard, stuff him deftly into your mouth, bite him off sharply close to your fingertips, and chew with vigor: there will flow from him enough juice to fill your whole mouth, and you will enjoy a taste experience unknown to the common herd.

Odi profanum vulgis, et arceo. HORACE.[7]

The quail is, among game as it is properly labelled, everything that is most delightful and tempting. One of these really plump little birds is pleasing equally for its taste, its shape, and its color. It is unfortunate to serve it any way but roasted or *en papillote*, because its aroma is extremely fleeting, and whenever the bird comes in contact with a liquid this perfume dissolves, evaporates, and is lost.[8]

Snipe is still another distinguished bird, but few people know all its charms. It is never at its peak of desirability unless it has been roasted under the very eyes of a hunter, above all the hunter who has killed it; then the process is carried out according to his personal prejudices, and his mouth waters in a regular flood of anticipation.

Above all other feathered game should come the pheasant, but once again few mortal men know how to present it at its best.

A pheasant eaten within a week after its death is more worthless than a partridge or a pullet, because its real merit consists in its heightening flavor.

---

of September with a friend: they came expressly to feast themselves during the whole flight; all of us took turns delightedly in asking them to dinner, and they left Belley about the 25th.

As long as he was in France, Father Fabi never missed his annual ornithological pilgrimage, and he did not stop until he was sent to Rome, where he died as a penitentiary in 1688.

Father Fabi (Honoré) was a man of great learning; he wrote several works on theology and on physics, in one of which he tried to prove that he had discovered the circulation of the blood before Harvey or at least at about the same time.

Science has studied the expansion of that flavor, experience has put knowledge into action, and a pheasant taken at the peak of its ripening is something worthy of the greatest of gourmands.[9]

Later on in the Varieties I shall give the method of roasting a pheasant *à la sainte alliance*.[10] The time has come when this method, until now known only to a little group of friends, must spread outside that circle, for the good of mankind. A truffled pheasant is less good than one would believe; the bird is too dry to permeate the fungus; and moreover the gaminess of the one and the delicate odor of the other are self-contradictory as they merge, or rather it can be said that they are unsuitable together.

VI. Fish

40: Certain scholars, and they none too orthodox, have argued that the ocean was the cradle of everything that exists; that mankind itself was born in the sea, and that it owes its present state to the influence of the air and of the habits it has been forced to form in this element comparatively new to it.

However this may be, it is at least certain that the watery kingdoms hold an immense number of beings of every form and of every size, who are endowed with vital properties in extremely differing proportions, and according to a system which is not at all that of warm-blooded creatures.

It is no less true that these sea animals offer to us, everywhere and at all times, a vast world of edibles, and that, in the present state of science, they bring to our tables a most agreeable variety.

Fish, less nourishing than red meat, more appetizing than vegetables, are a compromise, a *mezzo termine* which agrees with almost every temperament and which can even be permitted to invalids.

The Greeks and Romans, although less advanced than are we in the art of seasoning fish, nonetheless were great lovers of it, and carried their appreciation of it to the point of being able to tell by its taste from what waters it had been taken.

They stored it in special tanks; and everyone knows of the cruelty of Vadius Pollio, who fed his sea eels on the flesh of slaves which he had killed expressly, a crime which the Emperor Domitian disapproved of highly, but without doing anything to punish it.

There has always been a heated argument as to which fish is best, fresh-water or salt-water.

The problem will probably never be settled, which is one more confirmation of the Spanish proverb, *Sobre los gustos, no hai disputa*. Every man reacts differently to a thing: his fleeting sensations cannot be expressed in any known symbols, and there is no scale for determining whether a cod, a sole, or a turbot is better than a salmon trout, a fine fat pike, or even a six- or seven-pound tench.

It is agreed that fish is much less nourishing than red meat, whether it is because it contains no osmazome or because, being much lighter in weight for the same bulk, it has less substance. Shellfish, especially oysters, furnish very little real nourishment, which is what makes it possible to eat a great many of them without spoiling one's appetite for the meal which will follow right after them.

I remember that in the old days any banquet of importance began with oysters, and that there were always a good number of the guests who did not hesitate to down *one gross* apiece (twelve dozen, a hundred and forty-four). I always wondered what the weight of this little appetizer would be, and finally I confirmed the fact that one dozen oysters (including their juice) weigh *four ounces*, which makes the gross amount to *three pounds*. I feel quite sure, then, that these same guests, who were not at all deterred from dining well after their oysters, would have been completely surfeited if they had eaten the same weight of meat, even if it had been the delicate flesh of a chicken.

Anecdote

In 1798 I was in Versailles as commissary of the Directory, and was often in contact with a gentleman called Laperte, who was registrar of the tribunal of that province; he was a great lover of oysters and was forever complaining that he had never had enough of them, "a real bellyful" as I told him he should put it.

I resolved to give him this satisfaction for once, and with just such a plan in mind I invited him to dine with me the next day.

He came: I kept him company through the third dozen, and then let him go on alone. He managed very well without me, and by the end of the next hour was in his thirty-second dozen, eating slowly because the maid who opened them for him was none too skilful.

All this time I was unoccupied, and since it is at table that this is especially painful, I finally interrupted my companion at the moment when he seemed going at his best speed, by saying, "My dear fellow, it's your fate today not to have that bellyful! Let us begin our dinner." We did so, and he enjoyed it with the vigor and polish of a man finishing a long fast.[11]

Muria—Garum

41: The ancients produced from fish two extremely strong seasonings, *muria* and *garum*.

The first was nothing but the brine of the tunny, or rather the juice which flowed from it when it was salted.

Garum, which was more costly, is much less well known to us. It is believed that it was made by pressing the seasoned entrails of the scomber or mackerel, but if that were so its high price would not be justified. There is reason to believe that it was an imported sauce, perhaps that *soy* which comes to us from India and which is known to be the result of letting certain fishes ferment with mushrooms.

Some peoples, because of their differing conditions, are forced to live almost solely on fish; they nourish their animals as they do themselves, and habit soon accustoms these creatures to their unnatural diet; they even fertilize the land on fish, and still the sea which surrounds them continues to supply them with a never-varying amount of it.

It has been observed that these peoples are less brave than others who live on meat: they are pale, which in itself is not surprising, since the elements of which fish is composed must perforce add more to the lymphatic content of the blood than to its replenishing forces.

Many examples of longevity have also been noted among fish-eating nations, whether because their light and unsubstantial diet saves them from the inconveniences of high blood pressure, or because the essences of this food, which are supposed to form light fishbones and cartilages which are not meant to last very long, act in human beings to hold back that general hardening of all parts of their bodies which is the natural cause of death.

However that may be, fish in the hands of a skilled cook can become an inexhaustible source of gustatory pleasures; it is served whole, cut in fillets, or sliced, boiled in water, fried, simmered in wine, cold, hot, and always equally acceptable; but there can be no praise more justly given to it than when it appears as a matelotte.

This stew, although it is a customary bargemen's dish and is at its best as cooked by the tavern keepers who feed them along our river banks, nonetheless owes a matchless delicacy to this rough origin; and fish lovers never see it appear without crying out with delight, either because of its clean wholesome taste, or because it combines several good qualities, or because it can be eaten almost indefinitely without any fear of either satiety or indigestion.[12]

Analytical gastronomy has long tried to determine what effects a fish diet has on animal economy and the opinion is unanimous that they are strongly sexual and awaken in both sexes the instinct of reproduction.

Once this result was admitted, it was found that there are two causes of it so obvious that they can be understod by anyone: (1) various ways of preparing fish in which the seasonings are plainly excitant, such as with caviar, pickled herrings, marinated tunny, salted cod, stockfish, and the like; (2) the various essences with which the fish is imbued, which are above all inflammable and which are converted into oxygen and turned sour by the processes of digestion.

A still profounder analysis has discovered a third and even more active cause of the sexual effects of a fish diet: the presence of phosphorus, which occurs already formed in the milt, and which always appears in decomposition.

These physical truths were without doubt unknown to the ecclesiastical law makers who imposed a Lenten diet on various priestly orders, such as the Carthusians, the Franciscans, the Trappists, and the barefoot Carmelites as reformed by Saint

Theresa; for it is impossible to believe that they could deliberately have wished to make even more difficult that vow of chastity already so antisocial in its observances.

Doubtless, in this state of affairs, a great many astounding victories have been won, and thoroughly rebellious instincts have been overthrown; but also how many defeats! How many falls from grace! These latter seem to have been well attested to, since they have succeeded in giving to more than one order of monks a reputation comparable only to that of Hercules among the Danaïdes, or of Marshal Saxe with Mademoiselle Lecouvreur.[13]

This theory of the heating effects of fish can be clarified by an anecdote which must be old enough, since it has come down to us from the Crusades.

The Sultan Saladin, wishing to prove to what point he could push the continence of the dervishes of his country, took two of them into his palace, and for a certain period of time fed them upon the most delicious meats.

Very soon the signs of their self-denials began to melt away, and they regained some of their normal weight.

When they reached this state, the Sultan had two odalisks of an overpowering beauty given to them as companions; but the women failed in their most skilful attacks upon the dervishes' continence, and the two saints emerged from their subtle trial as unsullied as the Visapur diamond.

The Sultan still kept them in his palace, and seemingly to celebrate their triumph he submitted them for several weeks to a diet equally as luxurious as the first one, but made up exclusively of fish.

Finally the dervishes were submitted once again to the combined forces of youth and beauty; but this time nature won, and the too-happy ascetics succumbed . . . most magnificently, it must be added.

It is probable that, if the course of events brought about a resurgence of monastic foundations, the superiors who in these present days would be charged with organizing them would adopt a diet much better aimed at the accomplishment of monkish duties.[14]

*   *   *

Philosophical Reflection

42:   Fish, by which I indicate all species of it considered as a whole, is for a philosopher an endless source of meditation and of astonishment.[15]

The varied forms of these strange creatures, the senses which they lack and the restrictions of those which they possess, their different means of existence, the influence upon this of the places in which they must live and breathe and move about: all these things extend the world of our ideas and the limitless modifications which spring from matter, from movement, from life itself.

As for myself, I feel something like a real respect for fish, which comes from my profound persuasion that they are plainly antediluvian creatures; for the great Flood, which drowned our granduncles toward the eighteenth century of the creation of the world, was for the fishes no more nor less than a period of joy, conquest, and festivity.

VII. Truffles

43:   Whosoever pronounces the word *truffle* gives voice to one which awakens erotic and gastronomical dreams equally in the sex that wears skirts and the one that sprouts a beard.

This most honest sharing of emotions springs from the fact that the renowned tuber is not only delicious to the taste, but is believed to rouse certain powers whose tests of strength are accompanied by the deepest pleasure.

The beginnings of the truffle are not known: it can be found, but none understands how it is born or how it develops. The cleverest men have devoted themselves to it: they have believed that the seeds were found, and that they could be sown at will. Useless efforts! Lying promises! Never yet has such a planting been followed by a harvest, and this is perhaps not too unfortunate; for, since the price of truffles depends largely on public whim, perhaps they would be less highly valued if they were abundant and inexpensive.

"Good news, my dear friend!" I said one time to Madame de V . . . ; "we have just been presented in the Society for the Encouragement of Industry with a new method by which the most exquisite lace can be produced, and at practically no cost!"

"Heavens!" that beautiful lady answered with a bored look. "If lace were cheap, do you suppose that I would bother to wear such ragged-looking stuff?"

The Erotic Properties of Truffles

44: The Romans had a kind of truffle; but it does not seem probable that the French variety got as far as their tables. The ones which were so highly prized by them came from Greece, from Africa, and above all from Lybia; their flesh was white or reddish, and the Lybian truffles were at once the most sought after and the most delicate and odorous.

Gustus elementa per omnia quaerunt. JUVENAL.

It is a long time from the Romans until now, and the renewal of a taste for truffles is fairly recent, for I have read several old pharmacy manuals where no mention of them was made: it could almost be said that the generation which lives and breathes at this moment of writing has witnessed that renaissance.

Truffles were rare in Paris as near ago as 1780; they could be found only at the *Hôtel des Américains* and the *Hôtel de Provence*, and then in but small amounts; and a truffled turkey was a luxurious item which could be seen only on the tables of the highest nobility or the best-paid whores.

We owe their increasing presence to the merchants of fine edibles, whose number also has increased greatly, and who, seeing that this certain article was in high favor, have bought it up all over the kingdom and who, paying high prices and ordering it to be shipped to Paris by messenger and by fast coach express, have caused a general widespread hunt for truffles (this last being necessary since, impossible as they are to cultivate, it is only by careful search that the supply of them can be added to).

It can be stated that at this moment the glory of the truffle is at its peak. No man would dare assert that he had dined at a table where at least one truffled dish was wanting. The intrinsic excellence of an *entrée* counts for nothing if it is not enriched with truffles. And who has not felt his mouth water at the mention of *truffes à la provençale?*

A *sauté* of truffles is a plate which is concocted and served by the mistress of the house herself; in short, the truffle is the diamond of the art of cookery.

I have looked for a reason for this preference, for it has seemed to me that many other foods had an equal right to it, and I have found it in the general conviction that the truffle contributes to sexual pleasures; moreover, I have been led to conclude that the greatest part of our perfections, our predilections, and our admirations spring from the same cause, in so powerful and general an homage do we hold this tyrannical, capricious sense!

This discovery of mine led me on to wonder if the truffle's amorous effects were real, and the opinion of it based on fact.

Such a research is doubtless shocking and could be snickered at by the sly; but evil be to him who thinks it! Any truth is good to know. First of all I talked with the ladies, because they possess both a clear eye and a delicate sense of tact; but it was soon plain to me that I should have begun this project some forty years earlier, and I could draw out only ironical or evasive answers.

A single friend took me in good faith, and I shall let her speak for herself: she is a sensitive unaffected woman, virtuous without being smug, and for whom passion is by now no more than a memory.

"Monsieur," she said to me, "in the days when we still served early suppers, I once served one to my husband and a friend. Verseuil (which was the latter's name) was a good-looking fellow, far from dull, who often came to our house; but he had never said a word to me which might infer that he was my suitor: and if he flirted a little with me, it was in such a discreet way that only a fool could have misunderstood it. He seemed fated, that day, to keep me company, for my husband had a business appointment and soon left us. Our supper, although light enough, had however for its main dish a superb truffled fowl. The subdelegate of Périgueux had sent it to us. In those days that was truly a treat; and, knowing its origin, you can imagine how near perfection it came. The truffles above all were delicious, and you know how much I love them; still, I restrained myself; and I drank but one glass of wine; I had a flash of feminine intuition that the evening would not come to an end without some sort of disturbance. Soon after supper my husband left, and I was alone with Verseuil, whom he looked upon as quite without menace to our ménage. For a time the conversation flówed along without much excitement. Then it seemed to become more restricted and more absorbing. Verseuil showed himself successively as flattering, expansive, affectionate, caressing, and finally realizing that I did no more than lightly turn aside his prettiest phrases, he became so insistent that I could no longer hide from myself what he hoped would result. I awoke, then, as from a dream, and repulsed him all the more easily since I felt no real attraction to him. He persisted with an activity which could have become really offensive; I was hard put to it to bring him to his senses; and I admit to my shame that I succeeded in doing it only by pretending to him that there might still be some hope for him, another time. Finally he left me; I went to bed and slept like a babe. But the next morning was Judgment Day for me; I thought over my behavior of the night before, and I found it infamous. I ought to have stopped Verseuil at his first protestations and not have lent myself to a conversation which from the beginning promised ill. My pride ought to have awakened sooner, and my eyes should have frowned severely on him; I should have rung for help, cried out, become angry, done, in other words, everything that I did not do. What can I say to you, Monsieur? I blame the whole thing on the truffles; I am truly convinced that they had given to me a dangerous inclination; and if I did not renounce them completely (which would have been too stern a punishment for me), at least I never eat them, now, that the pleasure they give me is not mixed with a little mistrust." [16]

One avowal, no matter how frank it may be, cannot form a whole doctrine. Therefore I continued my investigations; I searched through my own memories; I consulted the men who through their worth share most completely my confidence in them as individuals; I brought them together in a committee, in a tribunal, in a senate, in a sanhedrin, in an Areopagus, and we have rendered the following decision, to be commented upon by writers of the twenty-fifth century:

"The truffle is not a positive aphrodisiac; but it can, in certain situations, make women tenderer and men more agreeable."

White truffles are found in Piedmont which are highly thought of; they have a little taste of garlic which does nothing to flaw their perfection, since it leaves no disagreeable aftertaste.

The best truffles of France come from Périgord and from upper Provence; it is toward the month of January that they hold all their flavor.

They grow in Bugey, as well, and of the highest quality; but this variety has the great fault of being hard to keep. I have tried four times to bring them in good shape to the people who would most appreciate them in Paris, and have succeeded but once; but at least my friends understood my good intentions and the merit of a difficulty nobly met.

The truffles of Burgundy and the Dauphiné are of an inferior quality; they are hard and lack flavor; thus it is that there are truffles and truffles, as with everything else.[17]

Dogs and pigs which have been especially trained are most often used for truffle hunting; but there are men too whose glance is so keen that they can tell with some certainty by looking at a piece of land whether any truffles are to be found in it, and what will be their size and quality.

Are Truffles Indigestible?

It remains for us only to investigate whether the truffle is hard to digest.

Our answer is no.

This official and final decision is founded on the following facts:

(1) The nature of the object itself (the truffle is a food which is easy to chew, and light in weight, and which contains nothing hard or leathery);

(2) Our observations during the past fifty years, which have unrolled without our ever having seen a truffle eater with indigestion;

(3) The testimony of the most famous physicians of Paris, a notably gourmand city and preeminently truffle loving;

(4) Finally, the daily behavior of the doctors of law, who, all things being equal, eat more truffles than any other class of

citizens; witness, among others, Dr. Malouet, who absorbed enough of them to give indigestion to an elephant, and still lived to be eighty-six.

Therefore it can be regarded as a certainty that truffles as a food are as healthy as they are pleasant, and that if they are eaten in moderation they will be assimilated as smoothly as a letter falls into a mailbox.

This does not mean that it is impossible to be indisposed after a big meal where, among many other things, truffles were eaten; but such accidents happen only to those unfortunates who stuff themselves at the first course as if they are ramming heavy artillery, and then cram in still more at the second, for fear of letting any of the good things pass them by.

This is plainly not the fault of the truffles; and it is certain that there would be many more sufferers if, in the same circumstances, they had gobbled a like quantity of potatoes.

Let us end with a story which shows how easy it is to be mistaken when we do not watch carefully.

One day I had invited to dine with me a Monsieur S . . . , a most charming old gentleman, and a highly developed gourmand. Whether it was because I did not know his personal idiosyncrasies or simply because I wished to prove to all my guests that their satisfaction was my chief concern, I had not spared the use of truffles, which appeared in this case in the guise of a generously stuffed young turkey hen.

M. S . . . ate of it energetically; and since I knew that he had lived at least until that moment without dying from it, I let him continue, at the same time begging him not to hurry, since nobody had designs on the property legated in his will.

Everything went off very well indeed, and the party broke up rather late; but as soon as old M. S . . . reached his home he was seized with violent cramps in his stomach, a feeling of nausea, a convulsive cough, and a general illness.

This condition lasted for some time and gave rise to much anxiety. It was of course believed to be an indigestion from the truffles he had eaten. Then nature came to the aid of the victim. M. S . . . opened his capacious mouth, and violently belched out a single fragment of truffle, which flew against the wall hangings and bounced back with such force that it was not without danger to the people who were trying to make him more comfortable.

At the same instant all the unpleasant symptoms ceased, peace reigned again, digestion took up its interrupted duties, and the sick man fell asleep and awoke the next morning in good health and quite without resentment toward me.

The cause of this illness was soon known. M. S . . . had eaten for a great many years; his teeth had not been able to withstand the hard usage he had given them; several of these priceless little bones had fallen out, and the ones left in his mouth did not bite together as they should.

In this state of affairs a truffle had missed being chewed, and, almost whole, had been precipitated into the chasm of his throat; digestive action had carried it as far as the pyloris, where it stuck; it was this mechanical action which caused the unpleasantness, just as the expulsion of the morsel was the remedy.

Thus it was that he never had indigestion at all, but simply the presence of a foreign body in his system.

This at least was what was decided by the committee of investigation which examined the chief bit of evidence, and which was good enough to name me as scribe of the whole event.

M. S . . . , nothing daunted, has remained faithfully enthusiastic about truffles: he attacks them always with the same courage; but now he takes care to chew them more carefully, and to swallow them with more prudence; and he is grateful to God, in the joy of his heart, that this wise precaution has prolonged the years of his enjoyment of them.

VIII. Sugar

45: So far has science advanced at the present time that the word *sugar* means a sweet tasting substance which can be crystallized and which, by fermentation, yields carbonic acid and alcohol.

In bygone days *sugar* meant only the thickened and crytallized juice of the cane (*arundo saccharifera*).

This reed is a native of the Indies; moreover, it is certain that the Romans did not know sugar as an ordinary plant nor in its crystallized form.

A few notations in old books make it easy to believe, however, that the Romans knew that a sweet juice could be extracted from certain reeds. Thus Lucan wrote:

Quique bibunt tenera dulces ab arundine succos.

But it is a long gap between a watery syrup flavored with cane juice to the sugar that we now enjoy; and science in the days of the Romans was not advanced enough to bridge it.

It is in the colonies of the New World that sugar was really born; the cane was imported there about two hundred years ago; and there it thrives. Experiments were made with the sweet juice which flows from it, and little by little they succeeded in producing cane syrup, then refined syrup, then raw sugar, and then molasses and various refinements of sugar itself.

The cultivation of sugar cane has become singularly important, for it is a source of great wealth, for those who grow the cane as well as those who sell its products and refine them, and finally for the governments which collect the taxes on it.

Indigenous Sugar

It was believed for a long time that true sugar could develop only in a tropical climate; but toward 1740 Margraff discovered it in several plants of the temperate zones, among others in the beetroot; and this discovery was brought to the point of proof by the experiments which Professor Achard carried out in Berlin.

At the beginning of the nineteenth century our government helped several scholars continue this research, since events had made cane sugar scarce and resultingly expensive in France.

This project was highly successful: it was assured that sugar was fairly abundantly present in much of the vegetable kingdom; it was found in grapes, in chestnuts, in potatoes, and above all in beets.

This last plant became the object of extensive culture and of a mass of experiments which made it very clear that if need be the Old World could, in respect to sugar, get along quite well without the New. France sprouted with factories which operated with varying success, and sugar refining became a national industry: a new art, and one which events may revive, one of these days.

Among these factories the best was established at Passy, near Paris, by M. Benjamin Delessert, a respectable citizen whose name is always connected with whatever is good and useful.

He succeeded, thanks to a series of well-planned experiments, in ridding the manufacturing process of many questionable steps, made no mystery of his discoveries even to other men who might have been tempted to become his rivals in business, was visited by the head of our government, and finally was charged with furnishing his sugar to the royal palace itself.

New events, the Restoration and the Peace Treaty, brought down the price of colonial sugar, and the manufacturers of beet sugar have now lost much of their industrial importance. However, there are still a few who prosper, and M. Delessert produces several thousand pounds of sugar every year, on which he does not lose any money, and by which he is able to keep up with new methods which may once again prove useful.

When beet sugar was plentiful on the market, some prejudiced people, creatures of habit, or merely stupid ones, found that it tasted queer and that it did not sweeten properly; some even insisted that it was unhealthy to use.†

Countless precise experiments have proved the contrary; and Count Chaptal has described their results in his excellent book: APPLIED CHEMISTRY IN AGRICULTURE, Volume II, page 12, the first edition.

"Sugars which come from these various plants," the distinguished chemist writes, "are definitely of the same structure and do not differ in any way, once they have been brought by refining to the same degree of purity. Their taste, crystallization, color, and weight are absolutely identical, and any man who is well used to judging or eating these products can be defied to tell one of them from another."

---

† *It can be added here that at the general meeting of the Society for the Encouragement of National Industry a gold medal was presented to M. Crespel, manufacturer of Arras, who produces more than one hundred fifty thousand loaves of beet sugar annually, from which he makes a tidy profit, even with prices for cane sugar as low as two francs twenty centimes the kilogram: a direct result of his selling his waste material for distillation purposes and then using its by-products for cattle feed.*

It is a striking example of the strength of human prejudice and the difficulty there is in overcoming it to learn that among one hundred natives of Great Britain chosen without discrimination there are not ten of them who believe that sugar can be produced from beetroots.

Various Uses of Sugar

Sugar was introduced to the European world through the apothecary shop. It must have played an important role there, since it used to be a common saying when describing a person who had some essential lack: *He's like an apothecary without sugar.*

Its origin was enough to put it in disfavor: some said that it was heating to the blood; others that it weakened the chest; still others even held that it led toward apoplexy: but calumny was forced to yield to the truth, and it is more than eighty years ago that this memorable adage was first heard: *Sugar harms only the pocketbook.*

Protected by this uncontrovertible statement, the use of sugar has daily become more widespread and more general, and there is not a single article of food which has undergone more changes and more combinations.

Many people like to eat it in its pure state, and members of the medical profession often prescribe it in this form, especially in hopeless cases, as a remedy that can do no harm and that moreover is not repulsive.

Mixed with water it produces sugar water, a refreshing, healthy, pleasant drink which is sometimes a salutary tonic.

Mixed in larger quantities with water, and then concentrated by heat, it produces syrups which can be combined with any flavor and served at any time of day as refreshing beverages which everyone enjoys for their variety.

Mixed with water which has been skilfully frozen, it produces sherbets, which are Italian in origin, and whose importation into France seems owed to Catherine de' Medici.

Mixed with wine, it produces cordials, a restorative so well known that in certain countries they are soaked into the toast which is served to young couples on their wedding nights, just as in Persia sheep's trotters soused in vinegar are served on like occasions.

Mixed with flour and eggs, it produces sponge cakes, macaroons, cracknels, muffins, and that multitude of delicate pastries which make up the fairly new art of baking little cakes.

Mixed with milk it produces the creams, custards, and other dainty preparations which end a meal so pleasantly, by substituting for the substantial taste of the meats their own more refined and ethereal flavors.

Mixed with coffee, sugar accentuates the aroma.

Mixed with *café au lait*, it produces a food which is light, enjoyable, easy to make, and admirably suited to people who must go to their businesses immediately after breakfasting. *Café au lait* is also supremely popular among the ladies; but the cold eye of science has discovered that too frequent a use of it can prove harmful to that which they hold most dear.[18]

Mixed with fruit and flowers, sugar produces jams, marmalades, preserves, pastes, and candied fruits in a conserving process which lets us enjoy their flavors long after the time which nature had meant them to last.

It is possible that sugar, considering it in this last mentioned capacity, might be useful in the art of embalming, which is still but poorly understood in this country.

Finally sugar, mixed with alcohol, produces those spirituous liqueurs which, as is well known, were invented to comfort the old age of Louis XIV, and which, conquering the palate by their strength and the sense of smell by the odorous gases which are united in them, still form one of our greatest gastronomical treats.

The uses of sugar do not stop there, however. It can be said that it is the universal flavoring, and that it ruins nothing. Some people put it in meat dishes, some with vegetables, and it is often eaten with fresh fruit. It is a requisite in the currently stylish mixed drinks such as punch, negus, syllabub, and others of an exotic origin; and its applications have an infinite variety, since they adapt themselves to both nations and individuals.

Such, then, is the substance which Frenchmen in the reign of Louis XIII hardly knew by name, and which for those of the nineteenth century has become a staple food of the first necessity; there is not a woman, especially if she be well-to-do, who does not spend more for her sugar than for her bread.

M. Delacroix, a writer as charming as he is prolific, complained once to me at Versailles about the price of sugar, which at that time cost more than five francs a pound. "Ah," he said in a wistful, tender voice, "if it can ever again be bought for thirty cents, I'll never more touch water unless it's sweetened!" His wish was granted: he is still living, and I hope that he has kept his word.

IX. Origin of Coffee

46: The first coffee plant was found in Arabia, and in spite of the many transplantings to which this bush has been subjected, the best coffee still comes to us from there.

An ancient legend tells us that coffee was discovered by a shepherd, who noticed that his flock was in a state of agitation and even gaiety whenever it browsed on the berries of the coffee plant. Whatever the truth of this old story,[19] only half of the honor of the discovery must go to the observant shepherd; the rest unquestionably belongs to whoever was the first man to decide to roast the coffee beans.

The beverage brewed from raw beans is truly insignificant; but roasting develops in them an aroma and forms an oil which characterizes coffee as we know it today, and which would have remained eternally unsuspected without the intervention of heat.

The Turks, who are our masters in this instance, do not use a mill for grinding the bean; they break it up in mortars with wooden pestles, and when these implements have been used a long time they become highly prized and are sold at staggering figures.

It occurred to me to verify, for several reasons, if as a result of this there were any differences in the flavor of the ground coffee, and which of the two methods was preferable.

Therefore I roasted with great care a pound of good mocha; I separated it into two equal portions, one of which I had ground in a mill and the other I pounded with a pestle according to the Turkish manner.

I made coffee with first one and then the other of the powders; I took a similar weight of each, and then poured the same quantity of water on each one, and stirred each with exactly the same force.

I myself tasted this coffee, and then had it sampled by the most devout connoisseurs. The unanimous opinion was that the beverage made from the pounded bean was obviously superior to that which came from the milled coffee.

Anyone can perform the same experiment. Meanwhile I shall cite this rather unusual example of the influence of such-and-such a method of procedure.

"Monsieur," Napoleon said one day to Senator Laplace, "why is it that a glass of water in which I let a bit of sugar loaf melt seems much better to me than one in which I put the same quantity of crushed sugar?"

"Sire," the scientist replied, "there are in existence three substances, of which the principles are exactly the same: sugar, sap, and starch; they differ only in certain respects, which are still a secret of nature; and I believe that it is possible, in the friction which is set up by the pestle, that certain amounts of sugar become changed into sap or starch, and cause the difference which occurs in this case."

This statement was given some publicity, and later observations have confirmed its value.

Different Ways of Making Coffee

A few years ago it seemed as if everyone was trying at the same moment to discover the best way to make coffee; this was a result, almost certainly, of the fact that the chief of state drank a great deal of it.

It was suggested that it be made unroasted, unground, with cold water, boiled for three-quarters of an hour, made in a steam cooker, and so on.

I have tried, in my time, all these methods and all that have been proposed up until today, and I have settled for obvious reasons upon the one which is called *à la Dubelloy*,[20] which consists of pouring boiling water upon coffee placed in a receptacle of porcelain or silver pierced with little holes. This first essence is taken out, heated gently to boiling point, put once more through its sieve,[21] and the result is coffee as clear and as good as is possible in this world.

I have tried among many other methods to make coffee in a high-pressure pot; but the result was a drink bursting with oils and bitterness, good at its best for scraping out the gullet of a Cossack.

Effects of Coffee

Doctors have propounded various opinions on the healthful properties of coffee, and have not always been able to agree; we can pass to one side of this argument, in order to save ourselves for the most important point, which is its influence upon the organs of thought.

It is beyond doubt that coffee greatly excites the cerebral powers; also any man who drinks it for the first time is bound to be kept from a good share of his natural sleep.

Sometimes this effect is softened or modified by habit; but there are many people in whom this excitation always occurs, and who because of it are forced to give up drinking coffee at all.

I have said that this effect can be modified by habit, which in itself does not keep it from appearing in another form, since I have observed that people who are not made insomniac by it at night have an especial need to drink it during the day in order to stay awake, and often fall asleep after dinners at which they have not drunk it. There are also those who are drowsy all day if they have not had their morning cup of it.

Voltaire and Buffon drank a great deal of coffee; perhaps the former owed to this habit the admirable clarity which one senses in his works, and the latter the enthusiastic harmony which is found in his literary style. It is plain enough that many pages of Essays on Man, about the *dog*, the *tiger*, the *lion*, and the *horse*, were written in a state of extraordinary cerebral exaltation.

Insomnia caused by coffee is not painful; a sufferer from it is very clear-thinking and has no wish to go to sleep: that is all. He is not nervous and unhappy as he would be if insomniac from any other cause, all of which does not mean that this form of tempestuous excitation cannot be extremely harmful if it lasts too long.

Long ago it was only the fairly old people who drank coffee; now everyone takes it, and perhaps that is the spiritual lash that drives such a mob up all the roads toward Olympus, and toward the temple of Memory.

The shoemaker who wrote the tragedy THE QUEEN OF PALMYRA, which all Paris listened to a few years ago, drank a great deal of coffee: in this at least he rose higher than the *joiner of Nevers*, who was only a drunkard.[22]

Coffee is a much more powerful stimulant than is believed. A strong man can live a long time and still drink two bottles of wine every day. The same man could not long support a like quantity of coffee; he would become imbecilic, or would die of consumption.

I once saw in London, in Leicester Square, a man whom the immoderate use of coffee had reduced to a wretch (CRIPPLE); he no longer suffered, was used to his condition, and had cut himself down to five or six cups a day.

It is a sacred duty for all the fathers and mothers of the world to forbid coffee to their children with great severity, if they do not wish to produce dried-up little monsters, stunted and old before they are twenty. This warning is above all applicable to the parents of Paris, whose children are not always as strong and healthy as if they had been born in certain country districts, such as the Ain for instance.

I am among those who must shun coffee, and I shall end this essay by telling *how* I was one day roughly subjected to its power.

The Duke of Massa, at that time Minister of Justice, had asked me for a piece of work which I wished to edit carefully, and for which he had left me very little time: he wished it the next day.

I resigned myself to spending the night on it; and to protect myself from the desire to sleep, I fortified my dinner with two large cups of coffee, as strong as they were odorous.

I went to my rooms at seven o'clock to pick up the papers which had been announced as on their way to me; but I found only a letter which informed me that because of some sort of bureaucratic protocol I should not receive them until the following morning.

Thoroughly disappointed in every sense of the word, I went

back to the house where I had dined, and took a hand at the card game without feeling any of that absent-mindedness which usually bothers me.

I could lay this to the coffee; but, even while paying homage to this reaction, I was not without some worry as to how I should pass the night.

Nevertheless I went to bed at my usual hour, thinking that even if I did not sleep tranquilly, at least I should drowse for four or five hours and thus ease myself gently into the next day's activities.

I was mistaken: two hours after I went to bed I was more awake than ever; I was in a state of extremely active mental excitement, and my brain felt like a mill grinding madly, with nothing to grind upon.

I suspected that I should profit by this activity, or otherwise sleep would never come; and I occupied myself by putting into verse form a little story which I had read lately in an English book.

I finished it with ease; and since I still felt neither more nor less sleepy, I tried a second poem, but it was useless. A dozen couplets had exhausted my poetic verve, and I had to give up.

I spent the night, then, without sleep and without feeling drowsy for a single instant; I got up and spent the whole day in the same state, without either meals or occupations bringing about a change in it. Finally, when I once more went to bed at my usual hour, I figured that for the past forty I had not closed my eyes.

X. *Chocolate and Its Origins*

47: The men who first assaulted the frontiers of America were driven there by the hunger for gold. At that time, almost all the known values were in terms of minerals; agriculture and commerce were in their infancy, and political economy had not yet been born. The Spaniards, therefore, hunted in the New World for precious metals, since found to be almost sterile in that they depreciate as they multiply, and in that we have discovered many other more active means of adding to the main body of wealth.

But those far countries, where sunshine of every degree makes the fields burst with richness, were found perfect for the cultivation of sugar and coffee; they also hid, it was disclosed, the first potatoes, indigo plants, vanilla, quinine, cocoa, and so forth; and it is these which were the true treasures.

If these discoveries have taken place in spite of the barriers erected by a suspicious nation, it is reasonable to hope they will be multiplied in the years to come, and that the researches carried on by the scholars of old Europe will enrich the Three Powers with a multitude of substances which will give us entirely new sensations, just as vanilla has already done, or which will add to our alimentary resources, like cocoa.

We have come to think of *chocolate* as the mixture which results from roasting together the cacao bean with sugar and cinnamon: such is the classic definition. Sugar is an integral part of it; for with cacao alone we can only make a cocoa paste and not chocolate. And when we add the delicious perfume of vanilla to this mixture of sugar, cacao, and cinnamon, we achieve the *ne plus ultra* of perfection to which such a concoction may be carried.

It is thus to a small number of ingredients that taste and experience have reduced the things which have been mixed with cacao, such as pepper, pimento, anis, ginger, and so on, each of which has been tried out successively.

The cacao plant is native to South America; it is found both on the islands and on the continent; but by now it is agreed that the trees which give the best fruit are those which flourish along the shores near Maracaibo, in the valleys of Caracas, and in the rich province of Soconusco. There the pod is larger, the sugar less bitter, and the aroma more refined. Since the time when these lands became less inaccessible, such comparisons have been made whenever wished, and skilled palates have not been misled by them.

The Spanish ladies of the New World are madly addicted to chocolate, to such a point that, not content to drink it several times each day, they even have it served to them in church. This sensuality has often brought down upon them the wrath of their bishops; but the latter have ended by closing their eyes to the sin, and the Reverend Father Escobar, whose spiritual reasoning was as subtle as his moral doctrine was accommodating, issued a formal declaration that chocolate made with water was not contrary to the rules of fast days, even evoking (to the profit of his penitents), the time-worn adage, *Liquidum non frangit jejunium.*

Chocolate was brought into Spain during the seventeenth century, and it immediately became popular because of its extremely strong flavor, which was appreciated by women and especially by monks. Fashion has not changed in this respect; and even today, on the Peninsula, chocolate is served whenever there is any reason for offering refreshments.

It was carried over the mountain frontiers with Anne of Austria, daughter of Philip III and wife of Louis XIII. Spanish monks, too, made it known by the presents which they sent to their French brothers. The various ambassadors from Spain to Paris also helped make chocolate fashionable, and at the beginning of the Regency it was more commonly known than coffee, since it was drunk as a pleasant aliment, while coffee was still thought of as a luxurious and rare beverage.

It is common knowledge that Linnaeus[23] called cocoa *cacao theobroma* (drink of the gods). It has always been wondered why he gave it such a strong title: some people have attributed it to his own passionate love for the drink; others to his wish to please his confessor; still others to his gallantry, since it was his queen who was the first to introduce it to common usage. (*Incertum.*)

Properties of Chocolate

Chocolate has given rise to profound dissertations whose purpose was to determine its nature and its properties and to place it properly in the category of hot, cold, or temperate foods; and it must be admitted that these written documents have done little to set forth the truth.

But with time and experience, those two sublime teachers, it has been shown as proof positive that carefully prepared chocolate is as healthful a food as it is pleasant; that it is nourishing and easily digested; that it does not cause the same harmful effects to feminine beauty which are blamed on coffee, but is on the contrary a remedy for them; that it is above all helpful to people who must do a great deal of mental work, to those who labor in the pulpit or the courtroom, and especially to travellers; that it has produced good results in cases of chronic illness, and that it has even been used as the last resource in diseases of the pylorus.

Chocolate owes these different properties to the fact that, being in truth no more than *eleosaccharum*, there are few substances that contain more nourishing particles for a like weight: all of which makes it almost completely assimilable.

During the last war cacao was scarce, and above all very expensive: we busied ourselves in finding a substitute for it; but all our efforts were fruitless, and one of the blessings of peace has been to rid us of the various brews which we were forced to taste out of politeness, and which had no more to do with chocolate than chicory has to do with real mocha coffee.

Some people complain that they cannot digest chocolate; some, on the other hand, insist that it does not satisfy them and that it digests too quickly.

It is quite possible that the first have only themselves to blame, and that the chocolate they use is either of inferior quality or badly prepared; for good well-made chocolate can be assimilated by any stomach which can still digest even feebly.

As to the others, the remedy is easy: they should fortify themselves at breakfast with a little meat pie, a cutlet, or a skewered kidney; then they should drink down a good bowl of the best Soconusco chocolate, and they would find themselves thanking God for their supraperfect digestive systems.

This gives me a chance here to put down an observation the correctness of which may be counted on:

When you have breakfasted well and fully, if you will drink a big cup of chocolate at the end you will have digested the whole perfectly three hours later, and you will still be able to dine . . . Because of my scientific enthusiasm and the sheer force of my eloquence I have persuaded a number of ladies to try this, although they were convinced it would kill them; they have always found themselves in fine shape indeed, and have not forgotten to give the Professor his rightful due.

People who habitually drink chocolate enjoy unvarying health, and are least attacked by a host of little illnesses which can destroy the true joy of living; their physical weight is almost stationary: these are two advantages which anyone can verify among his acquaintanceship and especially among his friends who follow this diet.[24]

Here is the proper place to speak of the properties of chocolate drunk with amber, which I myself have checked over a long period of time, and the result of which experiments I am proud to offer to my readers.†

Very well then: if any man has drunk a little too deeply from the cup of physical pleasure; if he has spent too much time at his desk that should have been spent asleep; if his fine spirits have temporarily become dulled; if he finds the air too damp, the minutes too slow, and the atmosphere too heavy to withstand; if he is obsessed by a fixed idea which bars him from any freedom of thought: if he is any of these poor creatures, we say, let him be given a good pint of amber-flavored chocolate, in the proportions of sixty to seventy-two grains of amber to a pound, and marvels will be performed.

In my own particular way of designating things I call ambered chocolate *chocolate of the unhappy*, since, in each one of the various physical or mental states which I have outlined, there is a common but indefinable ground of suffering, which is like unhappiness.[25]

Difficulties in Making Good Chocolate

In Spain, chocolate is excellently made; but we have almost given up importing it because it is not uniform in quality and when inferior material is imported we are forced to use it as it comes to us.

Italian chocolates are not at all to the French taste; in general the cacao is over-roasted, which makes the beverage bitter and without nourishment, since a part of the nut itself has been turned into ash.

Since chocolate has come into common usage in France, everyone has been taught how to make it; but few people have really mastered the art, which is far from an easy one.

First of all it is necessary to be able to tell good cacao from bad, and to be *determined* to use it in its purest form, for there are inferior samples in even the best boxes of it, and a careless

† *See in the Varieties.*

merchant often lets bruised kernels slip by, which his conscience should make him reject. Then the roasting of the cacao is still another delicate operation; it demands a certain feeling for it which must border on inspiration. There are roasters who are born with this instinct, and are infallible.

Then a special talent is needed for the proper regulation of the amount of sugar which must enter into the mixture; it cannot be fixed in routine and inflexible proportions, but varies according to the intensity of flavor of each lot of cacao beans and the point at which the roasting is stopped.

Pounding and mixing both demand special care, as well, since upon them depends the digestibility of the chocolate.

Other considerations must govern the choice and amount of flavoring, which cannot be the same for chocolates meant to be used as food and those meant to be eaten as delicacies. This flavoring must also be adjusted to whether or not vanilla has been added to the mixture. The net result is that, in order to make a truly exquisite chocolate, countless subtle equations must be solved, from which we benefit without even having been conscious of them.

For some time now machines have been used for the making of chocolate; we do not feel that this method adds anything to the quality of the product, but certainly it lessens the hand-work, and those manufacturers who have adopted it should be able to sell their product at much lower prices. Nevertheless they manage to dispose of it at even higher ones, a fact which makes it only too clear that the true commercial spirit has not yet appeared in France; for, rightly applied, the facility of production realized by machinery ought to prove profitable to both merchant and buyer.

As a lover of chocolate I have fairly well run the gamut of local purveyors, and have finally chosen M. Debauve, Rue des Saints-Pères 26, chocolatemaker to the king, thanking heaven meanwhile that such regal favor has fallen so rightly.

It is not too astonishing: M. Debauve, a highly distinguished pharmacist, brings to the manufacture of his chocolates the skills which he acquired through long study in a much wider sphere.

People who have not worked at a certain subject, no matter what it may be, have no conception of the difficulties which must be overcome to attain perfection in it, nor how much attention, instinct, and experience are necessary to produce, for instance, a chocolate which is sweet without being insipid, strong but not bitter, aromatic but not unwholesome, and thick but not grainy.

Such are the chocolates of M. Debauve: they owe their supremacy to a good choice of materials, to a stern vow that nothing inferior ever come from his factory, and to the master's eye which sees to every detail in production.

M. Debauve, moreover, as an enlightened pharmacist, has succeeded in offering to his numerous clients some pleasant remedies for certain sickly tendencies.

Thus, to those who are too thin he suggests the use of a restorative chocolate with salep;[26] to highly nervous people, antispasmodic chocolate flavored with orange-flower water; to irritable souls, chocolate with milk of almond; to which list he will undoubtedly add my *chocolate of the unhappy*, well prepared with amber *secundum artem*.

But his main merit is to offer to us, at a moderate price, an excellent average-priced chocolate, from which we can make a good breakfast; which will delight us, at dinner, in custards; and which will still please us, at the end of the evening, in the ices and little cakes and other delicacies of the drawing room, without even mentioning the amusing distraction of pastilles and crackers, with or without mottoes.

We know M. Debauve only by his products; we have never seen him; but we do know that he helps mightily to free France from the tribute which she used to pay to Spain, in that he provides both Paris and the provinces with a chocolate whose reputation does not cease to grow. We also know that every day he receives more orders from beyond our borders; it is therefore because of this fact, and as a charter member of the Society for the Encouragement of National Industry, that we make here this mention and this recommendation of him, of which it will soon be seen that we are not too generous.

Official Way of Making Chocolate

Americans make their chocolate without sugar. When they wish to drink it, they have boiling water brought to them;

then each person grates into his cup the amount of cacao he wishes, pours the hot water over it, and adds sugar and flavoring according to his own tastes.

This method appeals neither to our manners nor to our preferences, and here in France we like to have chocolate served to us all prepared.

Transcendental chemistry has taught us that it should neither be grated with a scraper nor ground with a pestle, since the dry friction which results in either case turns part of the sugar into starch, and makes the beverage less flavorsome.

Therefore, to make chocolate, that is to say to make it ready for immediate use, about an ounce and a half should be taken for each cup, and then dissolved slowly in water as it heats, stirring the whole meanwhile with a wooden spatula; it should boil then for fifteen minutes, so that the solution takes on a certain thickness, and then be served very hot.

"Monsieur," Madame d'Arestel, Superior of the convent of the Visitation at Belley, once said to me more than fifty years ago, "whenever you want to have a really good cup of chocolate, make it the day before, in a porcelain coffeepot, and let it set. The night's rest will concentrate it and give it a velvety quality which will make it better. Our good God cannot possibly take offense at this little refinement, since he himself is everything that is most perfect." [27]

THE TRANSLATOR'S GLOSSES

1. In the text on page 91 the Professor spells this word with two *t*s. Perhaps this footnote was added after his death? Certainly it is one of the rare inconsistencies in his precise and finicky style.

2. In an old tale, Fortunatus had in his pocket an inexhaustible purse, and on his head a magic cap that could transport him anywhere at all. (In the end he was undone . . .)

3. For a man who interested himself as passionately as did the

Professor in the subject of turkeys, he was both vague and illogical. It is true that turkey cocks were called *coqs d'Inde* in France in his time, but they had been called turkeys and recognized as natives of Africa since 1555 in England, albeit they were really guinea fowl. But at about the same time our presently known turkeys were found by Europeans in Mexico. As for Brillat-Savarin's next sentence, about "the shape," it is a strangely unlegal sentence for a cautious old lawyer: does the shape of a thing prove it to be of this land or that?

4.   These secret-diary references are a plague, at least to anyone who is as curious as I have come to be about the Professor. It is astonishing that any man living in his period could leave so little behind him. He and most of his friends were at one time or another political refugees, salving themselves with the unguent of continual letter writing, journal keeping. But not only is there no mention of any titillating and tight-locked memoirs of Brillat-Savarin: there is almost no mention of the man himself, although he moved discreetly through a dozen concentric social circles touching the Chaussée d'Antin. I think that his occasional waggish references to his secret diary are waggish, and no more: he was plainly a desirable companion, which meant that the ladies liked him, and in a man of the years he bore when he polished this book for the printer, sly humorous references would be much more *de rigueur* than any more direct approach to their feminine attributes. I have known professors past their virile prime who made themselves welcome indeed for the things they managed not to say, rather than the things they were unable to do. There was always a note, a hint, of possibility, past or even present, which Brillat-Savarin sounded often with his preeminently ungossipy hints of gossip.

5.   The Professor uses the pretty word *volatile* here. It was still heard as an adjective in English in the nineteenth century, when "volatile insects" flitted through novels and text books alike, and directions for carving, as in Soyer's GASTRONOMIC REGENERATOR, referred ponderously to feathered game as "the volatile species." But as a noun few writers since Brillat-Savarin have used it. "*J'empoignai le superbe volatile,*" he said, and the picture of him standing proud and alone in the virgin American forest with his wild catch in his fist is as good as any for an honest Latinism's obit.

6.   It is too bad, indeed it is a pity, that the Professor suppressed the details of his solemn labor. How was his "superb volatile" prepared? It was roasted, and it was good, and that is all we know. Did he baste it often? Half sweet butter and half olive oil, kept mixed and hot, are good for that. Did he stuff the bird?

The only living human being I have known who could speak casually of hunting, cleaning, and then roasting a wild turkey, and all that in the state of Arkansas, told me that in general the birds are stuffed lightly with cold cornbread and plenty of butter. In general, this woman said to me, histing blue denim pants over her flat hip-bones and looking Chinese-like over her straight lower lids, in general wild turkeys isn't thought highly of and people who cook them at all slice off the two breast-meat pieces and fry them in good hog fat (*Filets de coq d'Inde sauvage*, I thought), and they sure enough taste damn near as good as steak, she said. But if they are roasted they take a lot of basting to keep from being dry, and yes they should be stuffed.

I thought, as she spoke, of all the stuffings in the world, especially of the one in which fresh shelled oysters and then melted butter and then fresh oysters are poured into the dark hollow until it can hold no more and must be stiched shut. I thought of what Morton Thompson once wrote at the end of a recipe on How To Cook A Turkey: "No pen, unless it were filled with Thompson's gravy, can describe Thompson's dressing and there is not paper enough in the world to contain the thoughts and adjectives it would set down, and not marble enough to serve for its monuments."

7.   This brutishly refined recipe has made me search through every book I own, without success, and at the end I must admit that the puzzling part of it is what Canon Charcot did with the feathers. Did he pull them from the little live bird? This seems likely, from what the Professor writes in "Meditation 27" (on page 281). Or did he dip it still peeping into a pot of boiling water? Or did he choke down the whole musty mouthful without a single refinement?

I prefer to think that the tiny fat carcass was plucked with finicky care by a lay brother, and then rubbed artfully with a bit of sweet butter so that the powdering of salt would stick, when hunger finally pushed the Canon to devour it. I can see him tuck the wee thing into his ample mouth, snip off the two curled claws with his strong teeth, and flick them over his shoulder as he champs and chews and holds back with his sensitive lips the juice that leaps forth from his tongue and his gums and his "inner cheeks." I hear the mighty ecclesiastical crunching. It is good.

8.   Not all gastronomers agree with this didactic statement, as the recipe for Quails Richelieu with its poaching in veal stock can prove, but it is true that any man who has once eaten the little birds roasted in the ashes of a sleeping log fire will never again much care for other methods.

The main things being to hand, that is the quails and the ashy hearth, the rest is simple. The birds are happiest stuffed with "a smooth truffled game forcemeat," to quote Escoffier, but this is really not necessary. Then each is well wrapped in a buttered grape leaf, in a slice of bacon, and finally in two sheets of sturdy buttered parchment paper. These little packages are tucked deeply into the hot cinders on the hearth for thirty-five minutes, and the laziest of the hunters can be appointed watchman beside them, to keep the ashes and himself just below a glow. When they are served, the outer charred layer of paper is removed, and they wait on the hot plates for the first prick of the fork, the first ecstatic puff of delicately gamy perfume from their pierced wrappings. They will be ambrosia on earth. They will, like the "pigeons so finely roasted" that Dean Swift wrote about, cry "Come eat me!"

9.   This is what the chef of a small famed restaurant near Cassis-sur-Mer once told me: tie the ankles of a snipe or woodcock together, and hang him head down in an airy place until he is so far gone that the weight of his body pulls him off the hook! He is then ready, at his peak . . .

10.   This recipe is to be found on page 375, and is also almost unchanged in the American edition of Escoffier.

11.   It is easy to find incredible stories of great oyster-eating, from Roman times until today (or at least yesterday). The emperor Vitellius, for example, ate the "breedy creatures" four times a day, exactly 1200 of them at each meal . . . and even if they were as small as the little metallic Olympias of the Pacific Coast, that would make a fair sized bulk. And in THE OYSTER, published anonymously in London in 1863, it says: "I once

heard of an individual who made a bet that he would eat twelve dozen oysters, washed down by twelve glasses of Champagne, while the cathedral clock . . . was striking twelve. He won his bet by placing a dozen fresh oysters in twelve wine glasses, and having swallowed the oysters, he washed down each dozen with a glass of Champagne. I should not have mentioned this disgusting feat, but to add that he felt no evil effects . . . , proving incontestably the digestive and sanitary properties of this mollusk."

12. There are as many recipes for this fish stew as there are good cook books, of course. Given the basic facts that a matelote (Brillat-Savarin spelled it here with two *ts*) can be made with either red or white wine, and with any kinds of fish from eels to guppies, the tendency among chefs has apparently been to remove the ways of preparing it as far as possible from the waterside taverns where the Professor says it tasted the best. By the time it got to Queen Victoria's table, for instance, her good Francatelli had turned this simple fisherman's dish into a revoltingly luxurious mess of forcemeat dumplings, truffles, cream, and such like.

The recipe that to me seems nearest the Professor's ideal is from a paper-bound "Treatise on Home Cooking in Bordeaux," which looks unassuming enough for the lowliest inn kitchen, and is in truth larded with more than its fair share of things to make gastronomers sigh aloud.

Take a good carp (or whatever fish you have) and cut it into slices the thickness of two fingers, after having cleaned it properly.

Put a tablespoonful of butter and a chopped onion into a casserole. When it is golden add a tablespoonful of flour, which you will let brown; moisten with a generous pint of red wine and a tablespoonful of strong meat stock. Add a *bouquet garni*, a clove of garlic, 12 good-sized mushrooms, salt, pepper, and 24 little onions which you have peeled and browned lightly but thoroughly in butter.

Let the sauce cook ten minutes. Add the slices of fish to it and let it simmer very gently for 20 minutes. Take out the *bouquet* and the garlic, and then serve with the edges of the casserole encircled with slices of crusty bread fried in the best butter. Eat with spoons, like a *cioppino*.

A *bouquet garni*, it is perhaps useless to explain in this age of oversubscribed gastronomical monthlies and quarterlies, is, according to André Simon, "a fagot of herbs, chiefly parsley, thyme, and bay leaf, also celery, leeks, and so on." (A fagot, which I myself write with two *g*s, as the Professor wrote matelote with two *t*s, is a bundle of herbs tied together.)

13.   Maurice, Count of Saxe (1696–1750), was a natural son of Augustus II of Saxony and Poland, Marshal of France and one of the most brilliant generals in its history, and the all-demanding lover of many beautiful women. Chief among them was Adrienne Lecouvreur (1692–1730), for many years the idol of Paris at the Comédie Française, where she did much to bring more naturalness and spontaneity to the over-stylized acting of the period. Her life was made tragic by her passion for Saxe, and when she died mysteriously, it was believed to be from poison in a bouquet sent her by the Duchess of Bouillon, her rival for his ruthless and insatiable attentions. He lived many years more, and in his latter ones wrote an extraordinary book on military tactics with the dreamy title, MES REVERIES.

14.   "God walks among the pots and pipkins," Saint Theresa is said to have said. And Brillat-Savarin manages to make plain, with typically nineteenth-century mockery, that Venus too enjoys strolling through even the most monastic kitchens (see, for instance, the incident of the dish of eel on page 359), dipping the tip of her finger into this ascetic matelote, that treacherously innocent fish pie, confounding the holy fathers' vows with what gastronomical chemists may call phosphorus but ordinary men more rightly know as hell-fire.

15.   The most meditative statement I have ever read about Fish, not a fish or the fish but Fish, is a poem from the Japanese. In Japan the seventeen-syllable exercise known as a haiku is considered proper for kings as well as philosophers, and the one I have always remembered, sometimes in spite of myself, could almost as well have been written by an emperor as a thinker. It is, in its own restrained way, full of passion:

Young leaves ev'rywhere;
The mountain cuckoo singing;
My first Bonito!

It is perhaps easier to slide from the sublime to the ridiculous gastronomically than any other way, so I do not hesitate to add here that a bonito is a striped tunny about three feet long, found in tropical waters. It is contraband in California. I have often eaten fillets of it in a restaurant in Hollywood, where it is served grilled almost black on one side and doused with lemon and melted butter. I have always thought that I would like a chance to cook it myself, and not do it so thoroughly (I feel the same way about every shad roe I have ever tasted), but rather than forego its delicate flesh I would eat it always in a public place and in solid charcoal form.

16.   The truffle problem (are they or are they not restorative, aphrodisiac, enervating, aperitive, what you will?) can be called moot. It is especially hard for Americans to decide, since there are no native truffles in any of their uncountable kinds of country. (My grandmother claimed to have found *morilles*, most trufflish of mushrooms, in both New York State and Iowa.) The gritty tubers that come in high priced tins or bottles from France are but poor shadows of what they may once have been. Thin slices of them in restaurant *pâtés* are impressive but tasteless. Thin slices of them warmed in white wine, cooled, then drained and used at home are passable. Whole, they remain gritty tubers, less succulent than the war diet of tulip bulbs in Holland, much less so than what Thackeray described in MEMORIALS OF GORMANDISING: "Presently, we were aware of an odour gradually coming towards us, something musky, fiery, savoury, mysterious,—a hot drowsy smell, that lulls the senses, and yet enflames them,—the *truffles* were coming."

The discreet French lady who relented long enough to talk to Brillat-Savarin was at least honest enough to make it plain that her senses *were* enflamed . . . which is more than could be claimed by any of us Yankee ladies who had indulged in even the highest priced tin of them, I am afraid.

17.   Here Brillat-Savarin said, ". . . as there are fagots and fagots," quoting from Molière's LE MEDECIN MALGRE LUI, in which Sganarelle wants to show that his fagots are better than any others, and says, "Il y a fagots et fagots . . ."

18.   Here is one of the Professor's sly ambiguities: just what do the ladies hold most dear? Is it their beauty, their smooth skins, their chastity . . . ? The answer, pretty clearly, is on page 110, but it need not put an end to all speculation.

19.   Once on a Dutch freighter in 1939 there was a man who lay back in his deck chair sipping tonic water and gin, talking of the old days before he settled down in Surabaya. He had been a planter; now he was full of regrets and wrenching chills.

Hunting had been good then, he said: there were even boys who followed along with baskets to pick up the wild tiger droppings, to let them dry and then screen them and bring them to the masters' houses . . . handfuls of the best Java coffee in the world, the beans that had emerged whole from the crucible of digestion, the magically ripe, flavorsome berries that had escaped the long savage bowels to be ground up for the planters' pleasure.

What? Had we never tasted this most exquisite of coffees? The Dutchman lay back, shaking with fever, laughing into his glass.

20.   Francatelli, *maître d'hôtel* and chief cook to Her Majesty Queen Victoria, said in the twenty-sixth edition of his *Modern Cook*, which was first published in 1846: "The Cafetière à la Dubelloy . . . is best adapted for making good coffee." Here is a straightforward statement, surely, and one made at least twenty years after Brillat-Savarin said the same.

Francatelli on the subject of coffee is interesting, especially since he was writing for Englishmen, those men of ill repute as far as mocha is concerned. His rival Soyer could say as much on the other side of the page, for he admitted in his 1847 edition of the Gastronomic Regenerator that he had bribed his cook with the promise of a new silk frock to tell him her recipe for coffee . . . and that she said, proud soul of Albion, ". . . as soon as I have poured the coffee from the pot, I put another quart of boiling water over it. This I find saves me an ounce of coffee by boiling it instead of water, and pouring it over as before."

I've been to London, but never to see the Queen . . . yet even so I think that I've drunk of this regal coffee, this twice-boiled British brew. (An outraged amateur in Cornwall once swore to me that the coffee in his hotel was made from very old charwomen, dried brown in a slow oven and then crumbled and steeped in water.) It is comforting to know that Victoria's own chef preferred *café à la Dubelloy.*

Francatelli wrote: ". . . if you have done reasonable honour to some of the good things which I will suppose your table to have been supplied with, pray let the wine alone for the present, and order up the coffee—*hot, strong,* and *bright!* Let it be made with pure—picked overland Mocha,—fresh roasted pale—coarsely ground,—and pray do forbid your housekeeper to clarify it with egg; but tell her to use a bit of genuine Russian isinglass, not the spurious filth made from all sorts of abominations, and sold at most Italian warehouses under the name of isinglass."

The best isinglass (genuine Russian, of course!) is made from sturgeon; this is logical if it is logical that the best caviar (also genuine Russian!) is made from or by sturgeon too. It is a kind of gelatin, "very pure in form" the Oxford Dictionary says, which would most probably apply to Francatelli's reference, although unfortunately I can find no other mention of this usage.

The word itself comes from an obsolete Dutch one, *huisenblas*, sturgeon's bladder. There may be some connection between this word and the fact that when an old woman who made the most famous sparkling ruddy beef broth in all Delaware, the kind that was served at weddings and baptisms and such, was asked the secret of her diamond-clear elixir, she held off for a long time and then confessed as delicately as possible that to each gallon of consommé she added at the last one cup of the best bull piss.

21. It is basically distressing to have to admit that the Professor used his coffee grounds twice, but at least he did it with no fuss about economy! The best use I have ever read about is one I found in a manual of "Helpful household hints" compiled near the turn of the twentieth century by a group of church women in a small American town: "Dried coffee grounds will make good filling for pincushions, and will not pack down nor rust the needles . . ."

22. It would probably be an entertaining sortie into the jungle of possible footnotes to find out who the two drunkards were, the one on caffeine and the other, banal soul, on mere alcohol. Like the Professor at least three times in this book, I leave it to those who may come after me.

23. Karl von Linné, as Linnaeus called himself after he was given a grant of the patent of nobility, was a Swedish botanist, and probably one of the world's greatest. He lived from 1707

to 1778, and in that time wrote 180 books, most of them important to other botanists and a few of them, like his GENERA PLANTARUM, which introduced the use of specific names of plants, still in common use.

24. One thing the Professor was perhaps too kind to mention: many people who are fighting the foul coils of alcoholism have discovered or been rightly told that chocolate and liquor do not in general marry well. They go serenely to the obligatory cocktail routs, fortified by a cup of hot, if un-ambered, cocoa, or a bar or two of that childhood favorite, Hershey's. And if, when they feel that they must drink or die, they are still strong enough to fill their mouths instead with chocolate, they survive a little longer.

25. It sometimes seems that Brillat-Savarin was unduly interested in his own set of restoratives and stimulants, especially for a man as sturdy as he is said to have been. But he lived in a time when, much more than now, the fittest were the ones to survive. Malnourishment sat on every lowly doorstep, and plague still flitted over the gutters of crowded towns. Rich people, if they avoided the sicknesses of venery, lived much longer than poor ones, but even their life span was short compared with ours, and they suffered abominably from gout and gall- and kidney-stones. Most of all, perhaps, well-fed lassitude weighed them down, and where today the fat people of the world can tickle themselves with nembutal and Seconal and various soothing "neutralizers," and even the poor can down their daily or hourly cokes, there was nothing in the Professor's day but to sip tea, grow red-faced over punch, or grasp in desperation for a cup of his famous restorative broth. He was a man with true compassion for his weaker brothers—perhaps because even in his strength he had endured the same faint moments as had they—and he felt with the instinct of a good physician that physical sustenance is of the spirit too.

26. This is a nourishing flour made from the dried and powdered roots of various orchids, and first devised by the Turks as a restorative drug.

27. The good Mother Superior's small innocent bit of Jesuitical quibbling is less important, in this anecdote of the Professor's, than her too-fleeting hint about the night's repose for a pot of

chocolate. It reminds me of what a man in New York once told me about the hot cocoa, as it was called, that could be bought in the Horn and Hardart's, those exciting frightening eating places which may last long after such literary master-pieces as this one are forgotten, because of their pure autom-atism.

The man said, as we sat at the bar in the Colony Restaurant, which in 1945 was the antithesis of an automat, that the reason the best hot chocolate in all America could be bought at Horn and Hardart's was that their chief drink-cook was a Dutchman, and as such knew the prime secret for it. What is that? We drank another glass of champagne. "It is that chocolate," the man said happily, proud of his private knowledge, "should be made at least twenty-four hours before it is to be served, and preferably forty-eight, so that it may take on the lightest pos-sible hint of fermentation. Then it should be beaten again, heated, and served!"

This secret is a good one, especially if the drink be made, as Brillat-Savarin advises, of the best possible ingredients. The liquid should be mixed as if it were to be drunk the next mo-ment, and then allowed to rest two nights, not one, in a warmish place and in a porcelain or enamel pot, to thwart the acids. It should be stirred up once the next day after making, and the following day beaten lightly, heated but not boiled, and poured foaming into its pitcher again.

Mexican chocolate, which is the grandmother of the kind the Professor used to order from Spain or buy from the pharmacist M. Debauve, comes from any Mexican store, in Paris or Lon-don or Chicago, or even Cuernavaca, still in flat rounds marked off in quarters as it was for the Aztecs in the sixteenth century, as it was in the nineteenth when William Prescott wrote about them and their passion for hot chocolate in his HISTORY OF THE CONQUEST OF MEXICO. The sections should be melted in hot milk, one for each cupful, and then the whole beaten in its pot until it foams and sends out a fine gas of cinnamon, orange-peel, and honest-to-god *cacao*.

And on the other hand, there is a brew made in an obliquely similar way by the Russians: a heavy syrup of bitter chocolate, sugar, and vanilla, cooled and then blended with its weight of rich cream, whipped. Gobbets of this fastuous dark thick sauce are put in cups which have been heated, and hot milk is poured over (from a *silver* pot. Amateurs of chocolate are invariably finicky about the pots. Perhaps a china one would do . . .), and there you are, all at once, in the nursery and a Viennese coffee house and . . . Russia?

MEDITATION 7

THEORY OF FRYING †

48:   It was a beautiful day in May: the sun shed his gentlest rays on the begrimed roofs of the City of Pleasure, and the streets were free of both mud and dust (a rare thing).

The heavy mail coaches had long since ceased to thunder over the pavement; the rubbish carts were still at rest, and all that one saw were those open carriages from which our own and foreign beauties, shaded by the most elegant of hats, are in the habit of shedding such disdainful glances upon the lowly, and such coquettish ones upon the handsomer fellows.

It was, in other words, three o'clock in the afternoon, when the Professor sat himself down in his easy chair.

His right leg was pressed vertically down upon the floor; the left, as it stuck out, formed a diagonal line; his back was comfortably supported deep in the chair, and his hands rested on the lions' heads which capped the arms of this venerable piece of furniture.

His lofty forehead betrayed a love of serious studies, and his mouth a taste for pleasant distractions. His air was contempla-

---

† *This word* FRYING *applies equally, in French, to the* ACTION, *to the means employed to* FRY, *and to the thing which is* FRIED.

tive, and his manner such that any man who saw him would certainly say, "This Ancient of Days must be a sage." [1]

Thus ensconced, the Professor called for his chief cook, [2] and soon the servant arrived, ready to receive suggestions, lessons, or commands.

Sermon

"Maître la Planche," said the Professor, in a tone grave enough to pierce the hardest heart, "everyone who has sat at my table proclaims you as a *soup-cook* of the highest order, which is indeed a fine thing, for soup is of primary concern to any hungry stomach; but I observe with chagrin that so far you are but an *uncertain fryer*.

"Yesterday I heard you moan over that magnificent sole, when you served it to us pale, flabby, and bleached. My friend R . . .† threw a disapproving look at you; Monsieur H. R . . . averted his gnomonic nose, and President S . . . deplored the accident as if it were a public calamity.

"This misfortune happened because you have neglected the theory of frying, whose importance you do not recognize. You are somewhat opinionated, and I have had a little trouble in making you understand that the phenomena which occur in your laboratory are nothing more than the execution of the eternal laws of nature, and that certain things which you do inattentively, and only because you have seen others do them, are nonetheless based on the highest and most abstruse scientific principles.

"Listen to me with attention, then, and learn, so that you will have no more reason to blush for your creations."

I. Chemistry

"Liquids which you expose to the action of fire cannot all absorb an equal quantity of heat; nature has made them receptive to it in varying degrees: it is a system whose secret rests with her, and which we call *caloric capacity*.

† M. R . . . *was born at Seyssel, near Belley, about 1757. An elector of the grand college, he can be thought of as the happiest combination of prudent behavior joined to the most inflexible honesty.*

"For instance, you could dip your finger with impunity into boiling spirits-of-wine, but you would pull it out as fast as you could from boiling brandy, faster yet if it was water, and a rapid immersion in boiling oil would give you a cruel injury, for oil can become at least three times as hot as plain water.

"It is because of this fact that hot liquids react in differing ways upon the edible bodies which are plunged into them. Food which is treated in water becomes softer, and then dissolves and is reduced to a *bouilli*; from it comes soup-stock or various essences: whereas food which is treated in oil grows more solid, takes on a more or less deep color, and ends by burning.

"In the first case, the water dissolves and pulls out the inner juices of the food which is plunged into it; in the second, these juices are saved, since the oil cannot dissolve them; and if the food becomes dry, it is only because the continuation of the heat ends in vaporizing their moistness.

"These two methods also have different names, and *frying* is the one for boiling in oil or grease something which is meant to be eaten. I believe that I have already explained that, in the culinary definition, *oil* and *grease* are almost synonymous, grease being nothing more than solid oil, while oil is liquid grease."

II. Application of Theory

"Fried things are highly popular at any celebration: they add a piquant variety to the menu; they are nice to look at, possess all of their original flavor, and can be eaten with the fingers, which is always pleasing to the ladies.

"Frying also furnishes cooks with many ways of hiding what has already been served the day before, and comes to their aid in emergencies; for it takes no longer to fry a four-pound carp than it does to boil an egg.[3]

"The whole secret of good frying comes from the *surprise*; for such is called the action of the boiling liquid which chars or browns, at the very instant of immersion, the outside surfaces of whatever is being fried.

"By means of this *surprise*, a kind of glove is formed, which contains the body of food, keeps the grease from penetrating, and concentrates the inner juices, which themselves undergo an interior cooking which gives to the food all the flavor it is capable of producing.

"In order to assure that the *surprise* will occur, the burning liquid must be hot enough to make its action rapid and instantaneous; but it cannot arrive at this point until it has been exposed for a considerable time to a high and lively fire.

"The following method will always tell you when the fat is at a proper heat: Cut a finger of bread, and dip it into the pot for five or six seconds; if it comes out crisp and browned do your frying immediately, and if not you must add to the fire and make the test again.

"Once the *surprise* has occurred, moderate the fire, so that the cooking will not be too rapid and the juices which you have imprisoned will undergo, by means of a prolonged heating, the changes which unite them and thus heighten the flavor.

"You have doubtless noticed that the surface of well-fried foods will not melt either salt or sugar, which they still call for according to their different natures. Therefore you must not neglect to reduce these two substances to the finest powder, so that they will be as easy as possible to make adhere to the food, and so that by means of a shaker you can properly season what you have prepared.

"I shall not speak to you of the choice of oils and greases; the various manuals which I have provided for your pantry bookshelf have already shed sufficient light for you on this subject.

"However, do not forget, when you are confronted with one of those trout weighing barely a quarter-pound, the kind which come from murmuring brooks far from our capital, do not forget, I say, to fry it in your very finest olive oil: this simple dish, properly sprinkled with salt and decorated with slices of lemon, is worthy to be served to a Personage.†

† M. Aulissin, a highly trained lawyer from Naples, and a delightful amateur violoncellist, dined one day at my home and, eating something which pleased him especially, said to me, "Questo è un vero boccone di cardinale!"

"Why," I asked him in the same language, "don't you say as we do in France: fit for a king?"

"Monsieur," the amateur replied, "we Italians feel that kings cannot possibly be gourmands, because their meals are too short and too solemn; but cardinals? Eh?!!" And he chuckled in his own well-known little way: hou, hou, hou, hou, hou, hou!

"In the same way treat smelts, which are so highly prized by the gastronomers. The smelt is the figpecker of the seas: the same tiny size, the same delicate flavor, the same subtle superiority.

"My two prescriptions are founded, again, on the nature of things. Experience has taught us that olive oil must be used only for operations which take very little time or which do not demand great heat, because prolonged boiling of it develops a choking and disagreeable taste which comes from certain particles of olive tissue which it is very difficult to get rid of, and which are easily burned.

"You have charge of my domestic regions, and you were the first to have the glory of producing for an astonished gathering an immense turbot. There was, on that occasion, great rejoicing among the chosen few.

"Get along with you: continue to make everything with the greatest possible care, and never forget that from the instant when my guests have set foot in my house, it is *we* who are responsible for their well-being."

THE TRANSLATOR'S GLOSSES

1.   The Professor lived much longer than most men of his day, and was in robust health and gay vigorous spirits until the time of his death, a walking proof of many of his own gastronomical theories. (See page 160, for instance.)

2.   It is reported (by Graham Robertson in LIFE WAS WORTH LIVING) that James A. McNeill Whistler once said in his customarily iconoclastic way, "I don't see why people make such a to-do about choosing a new cook. There is only one thing that is absolutely essential. I always ask at once, 'Do you drink?', and if she says 'No!' I bow politely and say that I am very sorry but I fear that she will not suit. All *good* cooks drink."

If Whistler meant that all good cooks drink to excess, his quip is only superficially amusing, and is part of the grim picture drawn by statistics which show that in many great prisons there are more cooks than there are representatives of any other one profession. Most cooks, it would seem, are misunderstood wretches, ill-housed, dyspeptic, with aching broken arches. They turn more eagerly than any other artists to the bottle, the needle, and more vicious pleasures; they grow irritable; finally they seize upon the nearest weapon, which if they are worth their salt is a long knife kept sharp as lightning . . . and they are in San Quentin.

On the other hand, some of the best cups I have ever downed were in the company of good cooks, men (and a few women) who were peaceful and self-assured, confident that they were artists among their sincere admirers.

3.   It is interesting that here, as on page 52, the Professor betrays a characteristic of every good amateur cook I have known (using the word amateur as the opposite of professional): "a perfectly boiled egg" is in his mind all that the word perfection can mean. It is unsullied, and pure in form. It is a challenge to any human being's sense of balance, of time, and of taste. It has submitted to none of man's gastronomical caprices (a Mr. Robert Fudge reported in London in Mid-Victorian days that Paris had 686 ways of preparing an egg), and the most capricious gastronomer will feel respect for it, if indeed it be "perfectly boiled."

MEDITATION 8

ON THIRST

49:   Thirst is the inner consciousness of the need to drink.
Since a bodily heat of about 104 degrees Fahrenheit causes a
steady evaporation of the various fluids whose circulation main-
tains life, the resulting losses would very quickly make these
fluids inadequate to carry out their functions if they were not
often renewed and refreshed: it is this need which gives rise
to the feeling of thirst.

It is my belief that the seat of thirst is found in the whole
digestive system. When a man is thirsty (and as a hunter I have
often been so), he distinctly feels that all the absorbent parts
of his mouth, throat, and stomach are involved in a parched
craving; and if now and then he assuages his thirst by an outside application of moisture, for instance as when he takes a
bath, the liquid is carried to the seat of his discomfort as soon
as it is absorbed into his circulation, and acts as a remedy for
his desiccated organs.

*   *   *

Differing Kinds of Thirst

When this need is examined in its fullest scope, it can be seen that there are three kinds of thirst: latent, artificial, and burning.

Latent or habitual thirst is the unconscious balance which is established between bodily evaporation and the need to replenish the vaporized moisture; it is this which leads us, without our feeling any misery because of it, to drink during our meals, and makes us able also to drink at almost any time of the day. The thirst is always with us and in its way is part of our very existence.

Artificial thirst, which is peculiar to the human race, comes from an inborn instinct which we possess to want in our drink a strength which nature has not put there, and which is made only by fermentation. This thirst constitutes a factitious enjoyment rather than a natural need: it is in truth unappeasable, because the drinks which we take to ease it have the inevitable effect of making it worse; this thirst, which ends by becoming habitual, is what makes drunkards in every country of the world, and it almost always happens that their drinking will not cease either until there is nothing more to be drunk or until their thirst has got the better of them and destroyed them.

When, on the other hand, one's thirst is appeased only by pure water, which seems to be the natural antidote for it, one never drinks a swallow more than is needed.

Burning thirst is the kind which is caused by an increasing need to drink and the impossibility of satisfying one's latent thirst.

It is called *burning* because it is accompanied by a hot sensation of the tongue, dryness of the palate, and a consuming heat throughout the whole body.

The feeling is so strong that the word thirst is synonymous, in almost every language, with extreme covetousness and with imperious desire, as for instance a thirst for gold, for wealth, for power, for revenge, and so on, expressions which would not become current if any man who had felt actual thirst once in his life did not admit their rightness.

Hunger is accompanied by a pleasant sensation, so long as it does not become too strong; thirst on the other hand has no gentle dawning, and from the instant it begins it causes discomfort, and an anxiety which is horrible if there is no hope of relieving it.

In compensation, the act of drinking can, according to circumstances, give us extremely poignant delight; and when we appease a consuming thirst or satisfy a moderate one with a delicious drink, our whole papillary apparatus is titillated, from the tip of the tongue to the depths of the stomach.

One can die much more quickly from thirst than from hunger, too. There are examples of men who, given a supply of water, have lived more than eight days without eating, whereas those who are quite without anything to drink never survive the fifth day.

This is because the former are attacked only by exhaustion and weakness, where the latter are consumed by a burning and mounting fever.

Men do not always survive even five days of thirst, and in 1787 one of the Swiss Guard of Louis XVI died after staying only twenty-four hours without anything to drink.

He was in a tavern with some of his comrades: there, as he held out his glass, one of them teased him for drinking more than the rest of them and for not being able to wait his turn.

At this he bet that he could go a whole day without a drink, and they took him up on the wager, which was to be ten bottles of wine.

From this moment the soldier stopped drinking, even though he stayed some two hours longer watching his friends enjoy themselves.

The night passed well, naturally; but at sunrise he found it very hard not to have his usual little nip of brandy, which he had never missed taking.

All morning he was nervous and uneasy; he came and went, stood up and sat down without purpose, and had the air of not knowing what to do with himself.

At one o'clock he lay down, feeling that he might be more peaceful in bed: he suffered, and was really ill, but his friends entreated him in vain to take a drink; he insisted that he would hold out easily until nightfall; he wanted to win his bet, and undoubtedly felt a little soldierly pride, also, in being able to withstand suffering.

He endured it until seven o'clock: but at seven-thirty he felt very ill, began to die, and expired without being able even to sip at a glass of wine which was held out to him.

I was told all these details the same evening by M. Schneider, worthy fifer of the Swiss Guard, in whose home I lived at Versailles.

Causes of Thirst

50: Various circumstances, either alone or combined, can help to increase thirst. We shall outline a few which have not been without influences on our manners.

Heat augments thirst; from this springs the penchant men have always had for settling along the banks of rivers.

Physical labor augments thirst; thus men who employ workers never hesitate to encourage them with drinks; and from that springs the proverb that the wine which is given to them is always cheap at any price.

Dancing augments thirst; and from that comes the long list of invigorating and refreshing drinks which are always found at balls and parties.

Oratory augments thirst; therefore we have the glass of water which all speakers practice drinking gracefully, and which will soon be seen on the edge of every pulpit, beside the customary white handkerchief. †

Sexual delights augment thirst; this must be why, in the poetical descriptions of Cyprus, Amathontes, Gnidos and other places inhabited by Venus, they are never without their bosky shades and their little winding, murmuring, flowing brooks.

Singing augments thirst; and from this springs the universal belief that musicians are indefatigable drinkers. As a musician myself, I must protest against this reputation, which is neither justified nor truthful.

The artists who perform in our drawing rooms drink with

† *Canon Delestra, a most agreeable preacher, never missed swallowing a candied nut at the end of each division in his sermons, so that his listeners would have time to cough, spit, and blow their noses.*

both discretion and wisdom; but what they must deny themselves on one hand they make up on the other; and even if they are not topers, they are consummate trenchermen, so much so that it is rumored that the annual banquet in celebration of Saint Cecilia's Day at the Society of Transcendental Harmony has sometimes lasted more than twenty-four hours.

Example

51: Exposure to a brisk wind is a very strong cause of mounting thirst, and I think that the following example of this will be read with enjoyment, especially by hunters.

It is well known that quail thrive in the high mountains, where they are surest of hatching all their eggs because of the later harvests.

When the rye is cut, they retreat into the barley and the oats; and when these last are reaped, they migrate to the fields where the ripening is less advanced.

This then is the time to hunt them, because all the birds which a month before were scattered over a whole parish are now gathered into a few little fields, and it being the end of the season they are marvellously big and plump.

It is for this reason that I found myself one day, with a few friends on a hillside near the little town of Nantua, in the county known as "Plan d'Hotonne," and we were on the point of starting our hunt, on one of the most beautiful days of the month of September, under a brilliant sun unknown to COCK-NEYS.†

However, while we breakfasted, a really violent north wind arose, contrary to all our hopes but still not keeping us from heading for the open country.

We had hunted for a quarter-hour at most when the softest of our band began to complain that he was thirsty; we would undoubtedly have teased him about it, if each of us had not already felt the same need.

We all drank, since the donkey bearing our supplies had come along with us, but our relief did not last long. Our thirst

---

† *It is by this term that one designates the inhabitants of London who have never left their city; it is the same as the French word* BADAUD.

returned, and in such intensity that some of us believed ourselves to be ill, and others on the verge of it, and we spoke of heading back, which would have meant a ten-league journey all for nothing.

I had had time to assemble my thoughts, and I had uncovered the reason for this extraordinary need. I called all my comrades together, therefore, and told them that we were under the influence of four distinct things which had united to undo us: the marked decrease of the atmospheric pressure at that altitude, which perforce made our circulation more rapid; the direct action of the sun which beat down upon us; the walking which made us breathe more heavily; and, more than anything else, the action of the wind, which, piercing us through and through, undid the good work of the perspiration we might have raised, absorbed its fluids, and prevented it from forming on our skins.

I added that, in spite of this situation, there was no real danger; having recognized the enemy we must resist it; and it would be held back if we drank every half-hour.

This precaution, however, was insufficient, for our thirst was unquenchable: neither wine, nor brandy, nor wine and water mixed, nor even brandy mixed with water, could help us. We were thirsty even as we drank, and felt uneasy for the whole day.

It finished, though, as will any other day: the owner of the Latour estate opened his doors to us, and we added our supplies to his.

We dined in a marvellous fashion, and not much later went to bury ourselves in the hay, to fall into a delicious sleep.

The next day my theory received the sanction of experience. The wind died completely away during the night; and although the sun was as beautiful as the day before, and even hotter, we hunted for a good part of the day without feeling any inconvenient thirst.

But the worst damage had already been done: our flasks, although we had filled them at the beginning of the hunt with wise forethought, had not been able to stand up under the repeated assaults of the day before; they were nothing more than soulless bodies by now, and we were forced to fall back on the kegs of the country tavern keepers.

There was no help for it, but we could not restrain our plaints; and I hurled toward that desiccating north wind an invective oration when I was confronted with a dish fit for any king's table, a plate of fresh spinach cooked with quail fat, to be enjoyed with a wine barely as decent as one from Suresnes.†

† *Suresnes, a charming little village, about two leagues from Paris, is noted for its bad wines. One proverb says that in order to drink a glass of Suresnes wine you must have three people, the drinker and two people to support him and give him courage. The same is said of the Périeux wine, which still does not keep it from being drunk.*

MEDITATION 9

ON DRINKS †

52: By *drinks* we must understand any liquid which can be mixed with our food.

Water seems to be the most natural one. It is found wherever there are animals, takes the place of milk for adults, and is as necessary to us as the air itself.

Water

Water is the only liquid which truly appeases thirst, and it is for this reason that only a small quantity of it is drunk. The main body of other liquids which man consumes are no more than palliatives, and if he were limited to water, it would never have been said of him that one of his privileges was to drink without being thirsty.

Prompt Effect of Drinks

Drinks are absorbed by the animal system with facility; their

† *This chapter is purely philosophical: the listing of various recognized beverages could not possibly be contained in the plan which I am following in this work: there would be no end to it.*

On Drinks | 141

effect is immediate, and the relief which they give is in a way instantaneous. Give to a tired man the most substantial foods, and he will eat them but painfully and without feeling any appreciable benefit. Give him a glass of wine or brandy, and in an instant he feels better and you will see him come to life again.

I can add weight to this theory with a rather remarkable fact which I learned from my nephew, Colonel Guigard, no story-teller by nature, but whose veracity is flawless.

He was in command of a detachment returning from the siege of Jaffa, and was not more than a few hundred paces from the place where they were to stop and find water, when his men began to come across the bodies of soldiers who should have been one day's march ahead of them, all dead of the heat.

Among the victims of this searing climate was one who was known by several soldiers of my nephew's detachment.

He had been dead for more than twenty-four hours, and the sun which had been beating down on him all day had turned his face as black as a crow's.

Some of his comrades drew near him, perhaps to take one last look at him or more likely to strip him if there was any-thing of value left upon him, and they were amazed to find that his limbs were still limp and that he even seemed to have a little bodily warmth around his heart.

"Give him a drop of the real stuff," said the clown of the group, "and I'll bet that if he's not too far gone into the next world he'll come back to taste it."

And sure enough, at the first spoonful of the spirits the corpse opened his eyes. His friends cried out, and began to rub his temples and gave him still a little more to drink, and at the end of a quarter of an hour he could, with a little help, stand up.

He was led thus to the oasis; the soldiers cared for him dur-ing that night, gave him a few dates to eat and fed him care-fully, and the next day, mounted on an ass, he rode into Cairo with the other men.

Strong Drinks

53:   A thing most worthy of note is that instinct, as general as it is imperious, which leads us to seek out strong drinks.

Wine, the most agreeable of beverages, whether we owe it to

Noah who planted the first vine or Bacchus who pressed the first grapes, dates from the beginning of the world; and beer, which is credited to Osiris, goes back to those days beyond which nothing is certain.

All men, even the ones we have agreed to call savages, have been so tortured by this thirst for strong liquors, which they are impelled to procure for themselves, that they have been pushed beyond their known capacities to satisfy it.

They have soured the milk of their domestic animals; they have extracted the juices of various fruits and roots where they have suspected there might be the elements of fermentation; and wherever men have gathered together they have been armed with strong drinks, which they employed during their feastings, their sacrificial ceremonies, their marriages, their funerals, and in fact whenever anything happened which had for them an air of celebration and of solemnity.

Wine was drunk and sung to for centuries before it was suspected that the spirit in it which gave it strength could be extracted; but the Arabs taught us the art of distilling, which they had invented in order to concentrate the odor of flowers, and above all that of roses, so celebrated in their writings; and then we began to think that it would be possible to uncover in wine the cause of that exaltation of flavor which gives to its taste such a special excitement; and, from one hesitant trial to another, alcohol was developed, and then spirits-of-wine, and then brandy.

Alcohol is the king of potables, and carries to the *nth* degree the excitation of our palates: its diverse preparations have opened up to us many new sources of pleasure;† it gives to certain medicaments‡ a strength which they would not have without it; it has even become in our hands a powerful weapon, for the nations of the New World have been almost as much conquered and destroyed by brandy as by firearms.

The method by which we discovered alcohol has led to other important results; for, since it consists in separating and stripping down to their essentials the parts which constitute a body and distinguish it from all others, it has served as a model for

† *Liqueurs.*
‡ *Elixirs.*

scholars devoting themselves to like research, who have disclosed to us completely unknown substances, such as quinine, morphine, strychnine and the like, already or still to be discovered.

However it may be, this thirst for a kind of liquid which nature has sheathed in veils, this extraordinary need which acts on every race of mankind, in every climate and in every kind of human creature, is well worth the attention of the philosophical observer.

I have thought on it, as has many another, and I am tempted to put the desire for fermented liquors, which is unknown to animals, beside that fear of the future which is equally foreign to them, and to regard both these manifestations as distinctive attributes of man, that masterpiece of the last sublunary revolution.

MEDITATION 10

THE END OF THE

WORLD [1]

54:   I said: *the last sublunary revolution,* and this thought, expressed as it was, has led me far afield, very far indeed.

Indubitable signs teach us that this globe had already undergone several complete changes, which have been in effect *ends of the world;* and I do not know what instinct it is which warns us that there will be still more of them.

Often before now we have believed these revolutions ready to happen, and there are many people still living who once hurried to confess their sins because of the watery comet predicted by the good Jerome Lalande.

According to what has been written on the subject, we seem only too eager to surround such a catastrophe with avenging fury, with destructive angels and the sound of trumpets, and other no less horrifying accompaniments.

Alas, we do not need such histrionics to be destroyed; we are not worth such a funereal display, and if God wishes it he can change the whole surface of the globe without such exertion on his part.

Let us suppose, for instance, that one of those wandering stars, whose paths and purposes are unknown to any of us, and whose appearance is always accompanied by a legendary fear, let us suppose, I say, that such a comet flies near enough to the sun to be charged with a terrible excess of heat, and that it then comes near enough to us to cause a six-month period of a general temperature of about 170 degrees Fahrenheit (twice as hot as that of the comet of 1811).

At the end of this murderous period, all animal and vegetable life will have perished, and all sounds have died away; the earth will turn silently until other circumstances have developed other germs of creation on it; and still the cause of our disaster will lie lost in the vast halls of outer space, and we shall have passed no nearer to it than a few million leagues.

This happening is as possible as any other, and it has always been for me a tempting thing to dream upon, and one I have never shunned.

It is a strange experience to follow, in spirit, this unearthly heat, to try to predict the effects of it and its development and the way it acts, and then to ask:

What happens during the first day of it, and the second, and so on until the last one?

What about the air, the earth, the waters on the earth, and the forming and mixing and exploding of all the gases?

What happens to mankind, according to age, sex, and strength or weakness?

What about man's obedience to law, his submission to authority, his respect of other people and the property of his fellows?

What does he do about trying to escape from the situation?

What happens to the ties of love, of friendship and of kinship, of selfishness and devotion to others?

What about religious sentiments, faith, resignation, hope, et cetera, et cetera?

History can supply us with a few facts about the moral reactions; for the end of the world has already been predicted more than once, and even fixed on a certain date.

I really feel ashamed about not telling my readers how I myself have decided all these questions; but I do not wish to deprive them of the pleasure of doing it for themselves. It can eliminate a few insomniac hours for them, and even pave the way for some daytime *siestas*.

Real danger tears down all social ties. For instance, in the epidemic of yellow fever which struck Philadelphia in 1792 or thereabouts, husbands closed doors against the wives who shared their homes, children abandoned their fathers, and other such phenomena were common.

Quod a nobis Deus avertat!

THE TRANSLATOR'S GLOSSES

1.   There is a book by C. F. Ramuz, PRESENCE DE LA MORT, called in English THE END OF ALL MEN, which is more like this Meditation than anything I know of. There are many such books, of course: speculations on the end of the world are irresistible, and most of the speculators manage to put pen to paper, always with a horrendous and sadistic chill of discovery, as if the discussion of mass catastrophe makes easier in some way the realization that they, too, will die. Brillat-Savarin's orderly chapter, which has about it an impersonal rhythm, a kind of jauntily philosophical brutality, must surely have slept somewhere in the stern brain of Ramuz, for he wrote it again in his END OF ALL MEN, and there seems nothing strange about finding the two men so alike.

The French judge in 1825 and the Swiss author a hundred years later, the one writing with easy graceful restraint and the other with obscure passionate harshness: they have discussed in their own ways the possible death of life, and have arrived, in a miracle of time and space, a kind of artistic collusion, at the same place. The Frenchman asks the questions; the Swiss answers them: the dialogue is good.

"Meditation 10" should always be printed as a foreword to Ramuz' book. Or perhaps THE END OF ALL MEN should in some way be used as a footnote here in THE PHYSIOLOGY OF TASTE!

MEDITATION 11

ON GOURMANDISM

55: I have thumbed every dictionary for the word *gourmandism*, without ever being satisfied with the definitions I have found. There is a perpetual confusion of *gourmandism* in its proper connotation with *gluttony* and *voracity*: from which I have concluded that lexicographers, no matter how knowing otherwise, are not numbered among those agreeable scholars who can munch pleasurably at a partridge wing *au suprême* and then top it off, little finger quirked, with a glass of Lafitte or Clos Vougeot.

They have completely, utterly forgotten that social gourmandism which unites an Attic elegance with Roman luxury and French subtlety, the kind which chooses wisely, asks for an exacting and knowing preparation, savors with vigor, and sums up the whole with profundity: it is a rare quality, which might easily be named a virtue, and which is at least one of our surest sources of pure pleasure.

Definitions

Let us make a few definitions, for a clearer understanding of this subject.

Gourmandism is an impassioned, considered, and habitual preference for whatever pleases the taste.

It is the enemy of overindulgence; any man who eats too much or grows drunk risks being expelled from its army of disciples.

Gourmandism includes the love of delicacies, which is nothing more than a ramification of this passion for light elegant dishes of little real sustenance, such as jams, pastries, and so on. This is a modification introduced into the scheme of things for the benefit of the ladies, and of such men as are like them.

No matter how gourmandism is considered, it deserves praise and encouragement.

Physically, it is the result as well as the proof of the perfect state of health of our digestive organs.

Morally, it is an implicit obedience of the rules of the Creator, who, having ordered us to eat in order to live, invites us to do so with appetite, encourages us with flavor, and rewards us with pleasure.

Advantages of Gourmandism

Gourmandism, considered as a part of political economy, is a common tie which binds nations together by the reciprocal exchange of objects which are part of their daily food.

It is something which makes wines, brandies, sugars, spices, vinegars and pickles, and provisions of every kind, travel from one end of the world to the other.

It gives a corresponding price to mediocre or good or excellent supplies, whether these qualities come to them artificially or by nature.

It sustains the hopes and ambitions and performances of that mass of fishermen, hunters, gardeners and such, who each day fill the most luxurious pantries with the results of their labors and their discoveries.

It is, finally, the means of livelihood of an industrious multitude of cooks, bakers, candymakers and other preparers of food with varying titles who, in their own ways, employ still more workers of every kind to help them, all of which causes a flow of capital whose movement and volume could not be estimated by the keenest of calculators.

And note well that any industry which has gourmandism for its object is but the more fortunate since it both has the fattest fortunes behind it and depends on the commonest daily human needs.

In the social state to which we have come today, it is hard to imagine a nation which would live solely on bread and vegetables. This nation, if it existed, would inevitably be conquered by a meat-eating enemy, as with the Hindus, who have fallen time after time before any armies that wished to attack them; or on the other hand it would be subjugated by the cooking of its neighbors, like the Boeotians of long ago, who became gourmands after the battle of Leuctra.

More Advantages

56: Gourmandism offers great resources to the government: it adds to taxes, to duties, and to indirect fiscal returns. Everything that we swallow must be paid for, and there is not a single treasury which does not owe part of its real strength to our gourmandizing.

What shall we say of the hundreds of cooks who, for several centuries now, leave France every year to exploit the appetites of other lands? Most of them are successful men, and bring back to their own country the fruits of their labors, in obedience to an instinct which never dies in a true Frenchman's heart. This importation of wealth is more than might be guessed, and its bearers will influence posterity.

What could be fairer, if nations honored their great men, than a temple with altars raised to gourmandism by the natives of our own France?

Powers of Gourmandism

57: In 1815, the treaty of the month of November imposed on France the condition of paying seven hundred and fifty million francs in three years to the Allies.

To this duty was added the one of making good the reclamations of inhabitants of the different countries, whose united rulers had set forth the amounts, coming altogether to more than three hundred million.

And finally to all this must be added the requisitions of every possible kind made by the enemy generals, who heaped wagons with goods which they headed for the frontiers, and which the public was later forced to pay for; all this came to more than fifteen hundred millions.

It was possible, and in fact rightful, to fear that such considerable payments, which moreover were made every day in bullion, would put a fearful strain on the treasury, and would cause a depreciation in all paper values and be followed by that misery which hovers over a penniless and helpless nation.

"Alas!" cried the moneyed fellows who watched the ominous wagon going to be loaded at the bank in the Rue Vivienne, "alas, there is our silver, flowing out of the country in a flood. By next year we'll kneel before a crownpiece if we ever see one; we'll be living like beggars; business will be dead; there will be nothing left to borrow; we'll have famine, plague, a civil death."

What actually happened gave the lie to all these fears, and to the great astonishment of everyone who was connected with finance, the national payments were easily met, credit increased, people borrowed eagerly, and during the whole period of this SUPERPURGATION the exchange, that infallible measure of the circulation of money, was in our favor: that is to say, we had the arithmetical proof that more money came in to France than left it.

What power is it that came to our aid? What godlike thing was it that caused this miracle? It was gourmandism.

When the Britons, Germans, Huns, Cimmerians, and Scythians poured into France, they brought with them a rare voracity, and stomachs of uncommon capacity.

They were not long satisfied with the official fare which was offered to them by an enforced hospitality; they hungered for rarer delicacies, and before long the Queen of Cities was no more than an immense mess hall. These invaders ate in the restaurants, in the cook shops, in the taverns and the bars, in the stores, and even in the streets.

They stuffed themselves with meat, fish, game, truffles, cakes, and above all with our fruits.

They drank with a thirst as abysmal as their hunger, and always demanded the best wines, hoping to discover unknown pleasures in them, which they were inevitably astonished not to recognize.

Superficial observers did not know what to think of this endless, meaningless eating; but the real Frenchmen chuckled and rubbed their hands together as they said: "Look at them, under our spell! They have spent more crowns tonight than the Government paid them this morning!"

It was a happy period for everyone who catered to the pleasures of the palate. Véry built up his fortune; Achard began his; Beauvilliers made a third lucky one, and Madame Sullot, whose shop in the Palais-Royal was not more than ten feet square, sold as many as twelve thousand little tarts a day.†

This still lasts: foreigners flood into our country from every part of Europe, to carry on in peacetime the pleasant habits they formed during the war; they feel helplessly drawn to Paris, and once there they must enjoy themselves at any price. And if our public stock is high, it is less because of the good rate of interest it carries than because of the innate confidence which is felt in a country where gourmands are made happy.‡

Portrait of a Pretty Gourmande

58: Gourmandism is far from unbecoming to the ladies:[1] it agrees with the delicacy of their organs, and acts as compensation for certain pleasures which they must deny themselves, and certain ills to which nature seems to have condemned them.

Nothing is more agreeable to look at than a pretty gourmande in full battle-dress:[2] her napkin is tucked in most sensibly; one of her hands lies on the table; the other carries elegantly carved

---

† *When the army of invasion went through Champagne, it took six hundred thousand bottles of wine from the renowned cellars of M. Moët of Epernay.*

He felt repaid for this enormous loss when he discovered that the scavengers did not forget their taste for his wine, and that the orders which he received from the northern countries were more than doubled after the war.

‡ *The facts on which this section is based were given to me by Monsieur M. B . . . , an aspiring gastronomer who is worthy of his aspirations, since he is both a banker and a musician.*

little morsels to her mouth, or perhaps a partridge wing on which she nibbles; her eyes shine, her lips are soft and moist, her conversation is pleasant, and all her gestures are full of grace; she does not hide that vein of coquetry which women show in everything they do. With so much in her favor, she is utterly irresistible, and Cato the Censor himself would be moved by her.[3]

Anecdote

Here, however, I must recall a bitter memory.

One day I found myself seated at the dinner table next to the lovely Mme. M . . . d, and I was silently congratulating myself on such a delightful accident when she turned suddenly to me and said, "To your health!" At once I began a compliment to her in my prettiest phrases; but I never finished it, for the little flirt had already turned to the man on her left, with another toast. They clicked glasses, and this abrupt desertion seemed to me a real betrayal, and one that made a scar in my heart which many years have not healed over.

Women Are Gourmandes

The leanings of the fair sex toward gourmandism are in a way instinctive, for it is basically favorable to their beauty.

A series of precise and exhaustive observations has proved beyond doubt that a tempting diet, dainty and well prepared, holds off for a long time the exterior signs of old age.

It adds brilliancy to the eyes, freshness to the skin, and more firmness to all the muscles; and just as it is certain, in physiology, that it is the sagging of these muscles which causes wrinkles, beauty's fiercest enemy, so it is equally correct to say that, other things being equal, the ladies who know how to eat are comparatively ten years younger than those to whom this science is a stranger.

Painters and sculptors have long recognized this truth, and they never portray subjects who, through choice or duty, practice abstinence, such as anchorites or misers, without giving them the pallor of illness, the wasted scrawniness of poverty, and the deep wrinkles of enfeebled senility.

Effects of Gourmandism on Sociability

59: Gourmandism is one of the most important influences in our social life; it gradually spreads that spirit of conviviality which brings together from day to day differing kinds of people, melts them into a whole, animates their conversation, and softens the sharp corners of the conventional inequalities of position and breeding.

It is gourmandism, too, which motivates the effort any host must make to take good care of his guests, as well as their own gratitude when they perceive that he has employed all his knowledge and tact to please them; and it is fitting at this very place to point out with scorn those stupid diners who gulp down in disgraceful indifference the most nobly prepared dishes, or who inhale with impious inattention the bouquet of a limpid nectar.

General rule. Any preparation which springs from a high intelligence demands explicit praise, and a tactful expression of appreciation must always be made whenever it is plain that there is any attempt to please.

Influence of Gourmandism on Wedded Happiness[4]

Finally, when gourmandism is shared, it has the most marked influence on the happiness which can be found in marriage.[5]

A married couple who enjoy the pleasures of the table have, at least once a day, a pleasant opportunity to be together; for even those who do not sleep in the same bed (and there are many such) at least eat at the same table; they have a subject of conversation which is ever new; they can talk not only of what they are eating, but also of what they have eaten, what they will eat, and what they have noticed at other tables; they can discuss fashionable dishes, new recipes, and so on and so on; and of course it is well known that intimate table talk [CHITCHAT] is full of its own charm.

Doubtless music too holds a strong attraction for those who love it; but it demands work and constant practice.

Moreover, it can be interrupted by a cold in the nose, or the music may be lost, the instruments out of tune; one of the musicians may have a headache, or feel lackadaisical.

On the other hand, a shared necessity summons a conjugal pair to the table, and the same thing keeps them there; they feel as a matter of course countless little wishes to please each other, and the way in which meals are enjoyed is very important to the happiness of life.[6]

This observation, rather new in France, did not escape the English moralist Fielding,[7] and he developed it by depicting, in his novel PAMELA, the different ways two married couples might bring their day to a close.

The first husband is a nobleman, the older son, and for that reason possessor of all the family wealth.

The second is his younger brother, married to Pamela: he has been disinherited because of this union, and is living on half pay, in circumstances so straitened that they border on abject poverty.

The peer and his wife enter the dining room from opposite directions, and greet each other coldly in spite of not having been together at all during the day. They sit down to a magnificently appointed table, surrounded by gold-braided footmen, serve themselves in silence, and eat without pleasure. As soon as the servants have withdrawn, however, a kind of conversation begins between them: bitterness creeps into it; it becomes a quarrel, and they get up in fury, each one to go alone to his apartment, to meditate on the delights of widowhood.

The nobleman's brother, on the contrary, is welcomed with the tenderest warmth and the sweetest caresses as he comes to his modest dining room. He seats himself at a frugal table; but need that mean that the dishes served to him are not excellent? It is Pamela herself who has prepared them! They eat with joy, while they chat of their projects, of their day's happenings, of their affection. A half bottle of Madeira helps them to prolong both the meal and the companionship; soon the same bed welcomes them, and after the ecstasies of well-shared love, a sweet sleep makes them forget the present and dream of an even better future.

All praise then to gourmandism, as we thus present it to our readers, and for as long as it does not distract mankind from either his honest labors or his duties! Even as the excesses of

Sardanapalus could not make women a thing of horror, so the excesses of Vitellius have not succeeded in forcing anyone to turn his back on a well-ordered banquet.

When gourmandism turns into gluttony, voracity, or perversion, it loses its name, its attributes, and all its meaning, and becomes fit subject either for the moralist who can preach upon it or the doctor who can cure it with his prescriptions.

Gourmandism as the Professor has discussed it in this Meditation has no true name except the French one, *la gourmandise*; it cannot be designated by the Latin word *gula*, any more than by the English *gluttony* or the German *lusternheit*; therefore I advise whoever is tempted to translate this instructive book to use the noun as I have, and simply to change the article, which is what everyone has done with *la coquetterie* and everything connected with it.

NOTE
OF A PATRIOTIC
GASTRONOMER

I notice with pride

that *La Coquetterie* and *La Gourmandise,*

those two great virtues which our social existence

has evolved from our most imperious needs,

are both of them of French origin.

THE TRANSLATOR'S GLOSSES

1.   This is a view not held by either the ladies or their critics in
Victorian days. It is a long time since I read CHROME YELLOW,
by Aldous Huxley, but I am sure I remember two sisters who

languished at table in it, and had heavily laden trays delivered surreptitiously to them in their tower? And Disraeli said, coldly and to the dismay of many a female reader, "If a woman eats she may destroy her spell, and if she will not eat, she destroys our dinner."

2.   In a literary flight dated "Reform Club, May 14, 1846," and called DIALOGUE CULINAIRE ENTRE LORD M. H. ET A. SOYER, the dashing Victorian chef set down a series of noble platitudes, and ended with this bit of fast-talk:

"SOYER. Permit me to point out to you, Mylord, that a gastronomical reunion without ladies is in my eyes a garden without flowers, the ocean without its waves, a flotilla without sails.

"LORD M. True enough, such gatherings are the cradle of joviality and good morals, just as debauchery is the tomb of decency itself."

3.   Byron, who loathed seeing women eat, still wrote ironically, if in a somewhat roundabout style:

"Happiness for man—the hungry sinner!
   Since Eve ate apples, much depends on dinner."

This is a comparatively elegant way of saying, the way to a man's heart is through his stomach. (See page 153.) A Frenchman named Berjane said it more nicely in a book published in London in 1931, called FRENCH DISHES FOR ENGLISH TABLES: "A woman who knows how to compose a soup or a salad that is perfectly harmonious in flavour ought to be clever at mixing together the sweet and harsh elements of a man's character, and she will understand how to charm and keep forever her husband's heart and soul."

4.   In spite of the fact (or perhaps because of it!) that according to his own word Brillat-Savarin never married, he obviously spent much thought upon the eternal problem of conjugal life. It was plain to his friends, as it is now to me, that he would have made a good husband: in the opening dialogue with Dr. Richerand he says as much. He was tall as a drum major, Balzac reported. He was thickset, with more than a hint of a paunch . . . but with handsome legs, he admitted blandly of himself. He could be a tender and sensitive lover, as his sad little story of Louise makes clear. He was the confidant of many attractive women, on every subject from the relative value of lace to the erotic influence of truffles. He was an amiable dinner com-

panion, and at times a witty one, according to almost all of the surprisingly few people who wrote memoirs of him in a period distinguished by the flood of them which flowed from countless voluble minds. His own references to the ladies, no matter how late in years he made them nor how veiled they were in his peculiarly Gallic elegance, are full of gaiety, a sense of real pleasure, and an appreciation as healthy as it was refined. He liked to eat with pretty women, sing to them, tease them. Above all, perhaps, he liked to look at them, no matter whether his eye was purely voluptuous or was tempered by a physician's appraisal or a confessor's pity. It may be that his years of exile gave him a fear of too much domestic stability, a hesitation to put down emotional roots when he knew too well how easily they could be torn up. It may be that the death of Louise, so early in his life (see page 253), broke his dream of what marriage must be for him. Nothing prevented him, however, from thinking deeply on the subject of what it should be for others, and from reaching certain conclusions which, while not new, have seldom been more simply set forth, directly in this section, and indirectly in many others.

5. The notes on page 151 are appropriate to this section, if it be granted that conjugal happiness consists in shared pleasures. It is as impossible to enjoy a meal with a dour-faced, sourvoiced husband, for any woman, as it is for a man to lie happily with a stiff stick of a wife . . . and the other way about. One good thing leads to another, as the Professor points out with customary discretion.

6. Nothing is easier than to paraphrase one of the Professor's aphorisms, and here it is inevitable to observe, "Tell me *how* you eat, and I shall tell you what you are." (IV, page 3.) Shakespeare said, in his COMEDY OF ERRORS, "Unquiet meals make ill digestion," and any man alive can remember a meal eaten glumly, irascibly, and in the end dyspeptically. Acid words lead to acidity in the guts, and that in turn makes any soul a sourish thing.

7. It was Samuel Richardson, not Fielding, who wrote PAMELA; OR VIRTUE REWARDED, in 1740. This novel in letter form was as popular in its French translation as in English, and it is surprising that the Professor ascribed it to the wrong author.

MEDITATION 12

ON GOURMANDS

60: No man is a gourmand simply because he wishes to be one. There are certain people to whom Nature has denied either an organic delicacy or a power of concentration, without which the most delicious dishes can pass them by unnoticed.

Physiology has already recognized the first of these abnormalities, and has showed us that the tongues of such wretches are so sparsely provided with the sensitive taste buds meant to absorb and appreciate flavors that they can awaken but vague sensations: indeed, such people are as blind to taste as true blind men are to light.

The second class of unfortunates is made up of the inattentive, the flighty, the overly ambitious and all those who try to do two things at once, and eat only to fill their bellies.

Napoleon

Such was, among many others, Napoleon: he was irregular with his meals, and ate quickly and untidily; but there was also in this characteristic that absolute determination which he felt about everything. As soon as he sensed the first twinge of hunger it must be satisfied, and his personal equipment was so arranged that at no matter what hour, no matter where, it was possible to serve him at his first word with poultry, some cutlets, and coffee.

Predestined Gourmands

But there is a privileged class of men whom a materialistic and organic predestination summons to the full enjoyment of taste.

I have always been a follower of Lavater and Gall:[1] I believe in inborn tendencies.

Since there are people who have obviously been put into the world to see badly, walk badly, hear badly, because they are born myopic, limping, or deaf, why can it not be that there are others who are meant to enjoy more deeply certain series of sensations?

Moreover, no matter how unobservant one may be, he is bound to recognize on every side of him faces which bear the uncontradictable imprint of this or that dominant trait, such as impertinent disdain, self-complacency, misanthropy, sensuality, etc., etc. The truth is that anyone with an insignificant make-up can be all of these things unsuspected; but when a man's aspect has strongly defined characteristics, it rarely gives itself the lie.

Human passions act on the muscles, and very often, no matter how much someone may hold his tongue, the various sentiments that surge in him can be read plainly on his face. This self-control, even if not habitual, will finish by leaving obvious traces, and give to the face a recognizable cast.

Sensual Predestination

61: People predestined to gourmandism are in general of medium height;[2] they have round or square faces, bright eyes, small foreheads, short noses, full lips and rounded chins. The women so predisposed are plump, more likely to be pretty than beautiful, and have a tendency toward corpulence.

The ones who are most fond of tidbits and delicacies are finer featured, with a daintier air; they are more attractive, and above all are distinguished by a way of speaking which is all their own.

It is by these outer traits that the most agreeable dinner companions must be judged and chosen: they accept everything that is served to them, eat slowly, and enjoy reflectively what they have swallowed. They never hurry away from any place where they have been offered an unusually pleasant hospitality; they stay for the rest of the evening, since they know all the games and pastimes which are the ordinary accompaniment of any gastronomical gathering.

People to whom Nature has denied the capacity for such enjoyment, on the other hand, have long faces, noses, and eyes; no matter what their height, they seem to have a general air of elongation about them. They have flat dark hair, and above all lack healthy weight; it is undoubtedly they who invented trousers, to hide their thin shanks.

Women whom Nature has afflicted in the same miserable way are scrawny, and bored at table, and exist only for cards and sly gossip.

This physiological theory will not, I hope, find many readers to contradict it, for each one can verify it by looking around him: however, I shall add wcight to it with some cold fact.

I was seated one day at a very important banquet, and saw across from me an exquisite girl whose face was completely sensual. I leaned toward my neighbor, and murmured to him that it was impossible that this young lady be anything but *gourmande*, given such physical characteristics.

"Ridiculous!" he answered me. "She is at most fifteen, and that is hardly the age for gourmandism. What is more, just let us watch her . . ."

The beginnings were not at all favorable for me, and I began to fear that I had made a foolish wager, for during the first two courses the girl ate so lightly that I was astonished and began to believe that I had fallen this time upon an exception, there being one, of course, to every rule. But finally the dessert arrived, a dessert as impressive as it was generous, and I felt more hopeful. I was not deceived: not only did she eat everything that was offered to her, but she even asked for portions from those plates which were farthest from her. Finally she had tasted every one; and my neighbor confessed his astonishment that this little belly could hold so many things. Thus my diagnosis was confirmed; thus science once more triumphed.

Some two years later, I met the same lady once again. It was eight days after her marriage. She had developed in the best possible way; she permitted herself more than a trace of coquetry; and in unveiling her charms to the last permissible limits of fashion, she was truly ravishing. Her husband was a study: he resembled a certain ventriloquist who knew how to laugh with one side of his face and weep with the other, which is to say that he seemed delighted to have his wife admired, but that as soon as he felt the admiration too pressing he was wracked with a shudder of very obvious jealousy. The latter sentiment conquered; he took his wife off to a distant province, and as far as I know that is the end of the story.

Another time I made much the same kind of observation about the Duke Decrès, who was for so long Minister of the Marine.

It will be remembered that he was fat, short, dark, curlyheaded and square-cut; that he had a round face, to put it mildly, with a prominent chin, fleshy lips, and the mouth of a giant; therefore I immediately designated him as a predestined lover of good food and beautiful women.

This physiological comment I slipped gently and in a low murmur into the ear of a very pretty lady who was, I believed, equally discreet. Alas, I was mistaken! She was a true daughter of Eve, and it would have stifled her to keep my secret. Thus it was that, the same evening, the Duke was fully informed of the scientific deduction I had made from his physical outlines.

I learned this the next day in a very amiable letter he wrote me, in which he modestly disclaimed possessing the two traits which I had credited to him, no matter how desirable both of them might be. I still did not feel defeated. I replied that Nature creates nothing in vain; that she had evidently shaped him to perform certain missions which, if he did not carry them out, simply contradicted his own destiny; and that, moreover, I had no right to be entrusted with such confidences from him, etc., etc.

Anecdote

Our correspondence ended there; but, a short time after, all Paris was told by means of the newspapers of the memorable battle between the Minister and his cook, a battle which was long and noisy, and in which the Duke was not always on top. Well, since after such a fracas the cook was not sent packing (as indeed he was not), I can, I believe, draw the conclusion that the Duke was completely dominated by the talents of this artist, and that he despaired of ever finding another who would know so well how to flatter his palate; otherwise he would never have been able to endure his very natural distaste for being served by such a belligerent rascal.

As I was writing this little incident, one fine winter evening, Monsieur Cartier, formerly first violin at the Opera and an adept teacher, came in and sat down by my fire. I was full of my subject, and looking at him with great attention, "My dear fellow," I asked him, "how does it happen that you are not a gourmand, when you have all the signs of being one?" "I was one of the first rank, once," he replied, "but I gave it up." "From common sense?" I asked him. He said nothing more, but gave a real Walter-Scott sigh, which is to say that it sounded much more like a dismal groan.

Gourmands by Profession

62: If there are gourmands by predestination, there are also those by profession; and here I must point out four great categories of them: the bankers, the doctors, the writers, and the men of faith—the *devout*.

The Bankers

Bankers are the real heroes of gourmandism. In this case *hero* is the proper word, for there was at one time a state of war: the landed nobility would have crushed the financiers under the weight of its titles and escutcheons, if the latter had not fought back with their sumptuous larders and their money boxes. Cooks fought genealogists, and even though the dukes did not wait to leave the banquet halls before they mocked their hosts, at least they had accepted the invitations, and their very presence attested to their defeat.

What is more, anyone who can pile up a great deal of money easily is almost forced, willynilly, to be a gourmand.

Inequality of conditions leads to inequality of wealth, but inequality of wealth does not necessarily lead to a corresponding inequality of needs! He who can pay each day for a dinner big enough to serve a hundred people is often stuffed from eating no more than the leg of a chicken. It is necessary then that art summon all its resources, to enliven this feeble shadow of an appetite by dishes which will nourish without damaging, excite without exhausting. It is thus that Mondor[3] became a gourmand, and that fellow devotees from every walk of life have since imitated him.

And in all the series of recipes which the books of elementary cooking present to us, there are one or more which are labeled *à la financière*. It is well known, moreover, that it was not the king, but the bankers who collected his rents for him, who in the old days enjoyed the first dish of little green Spring peas, for which they always paid a good eight hundred francs.

Things are no different today: the bankers' tables continue to offer everything that is most perfect in nature, that is earliest in the hothouses, that is most subtle in culinary art.

The Doctors

63:   Causes of another order, although no less powerful, act on the doctors: they have gourmandism thrust upon them, and would have to be made of bronze to resist its seduction.

Our dear doctors are all the more welcome among us because health, which is under their special patronage, is the most precious of all our attributes; thus do they become spoiled children in the full force of the term.

Always waited for with impatience, they are welcomed with ceremony. It is a pretty invalid who summons them; it is a charming girl who greets them tenderly; it is a father, or a husband, who entrusts them with everything held most dear. Hope tugs at them from the right, and gratitude from the left; they are stuffed with dainties as if they were pet doves; they let themselves accept, and in six months they are used to it, and are hopeless gourmands [PAST REDEMPTION].

This is what I dared explain one day at a dinner party with eight others, under the chairmanship of Dr. Corvisart.[4] It was about 1806:

"You are," I cried in the inspired voice of a Puritan preacher, "the last remaining members of a corporation which in the old days took in the whole of France. Alas, the others have been destroyed or scattered: no more royal rent collectors, no more abbés, chevaliers, white monks; the whole gastronomical responsibility rests on you alone! Bear up bravely under this great responsibility, even if it means for you the fate of the three hundred Spartans at Thermopylae!"

I had spoken, and there was not a word of contradiction: we acted accordingly, and there the truth rests.

I made at this dinner an observation which is worth being made known.

Dr. Corvisart, who could be very agreeable when he wished, drank nothing but champagne chilled with ice. Thus, from the very beginning of the repast and while the other guests were eating, he was jolly, talkative, reminiscent. By the time for dessert, on the contrary, and when the general conversation began to grow more lively, he became solemn, taciturn, and even somewhat morose.

From this observation and from others like it I have deduced the following maxim: *Champagne, which is stimulating in its first effects* (ab initio), *is stupefying in those which follow* (in recessu); this is moreover a notorious effect of the carbonic acid gas which such wine contains.

Admonition

64: While I have the doctors here at my mercy, I do not wish to leave off without reproaching them for the extreme severity which they use toward their patients.

From the minute that one has the misfortune to fall into their hands, they submit him to a procession of prohibitions, and make him renounce everything enjoyable in his daily habits.

I protest against most of these interdictions as useless.

I say *useless*, because sick people almost never benefit from what is unpleasant to them.

A sensible doctor must never lose sight of the natural tendency of our preferences, nor forget that if painful sensations are depressing by their very nature, those which are agreeable lead perforce toward our well-being. It has often been seen how a little wine, a sip of coffee, or a few drops of liqueur will bring back a smile to the face of the most hopeless invalid.

What is more, they must surely understand, these stern tyrants, that their prescriptions are almost always futile; the patient does what he can to avoid them; his relatives are never at a loss for excuses to humor him, and he does not die any the sooner or later for it.

The daily liquor ration of a sick Russian soldier in 1815 would have knocked out a bully from the Paris markets, and that of the English would have set even a Limousin[5] back on his heels. And it was impossible for anyone to avoid his full portion, since military inspectors bustled ceaselessly through our hospitals, keeping an eye on both the issue and the consumption of such rations.

I stick to my opinion about this system of prescribing with all the more confidence since it is bolstered by numerous facts, and since the most successful doctors are inclined to agree with it.

Canon Rollet, who died about fifty years ago, was a real drinker, as was the custom in those bygone days. He once fell ill, and the first words the doctor spoke to him were to forbid him to touch any more wine. However, at the physician's next visit he found the patient in bed, and beside it an almost perfect example of incriminating evidence: a table covered with a fine white cloth, a crystal goblet, a handsome wine bottle, and a napkin for drying the culprit's lips.

At this sight he fell into a violent fit of anger, and was threatening to wash his hands of the case, when the unhappy canon cried out in a mournful voice, "But, Doctor! Remember, please, that when you forbade me to drink, you at least did not forbid me the pleasure of looking at the bottle!"

The physician who treated Monsieur de Montlucin, of Pont-de-Veyle, was even harsher in his methods, for not only did he prohibit the use of wine to his patient, but he told him to drink plain water in large doses.

A short while after the departure of the tyrant, Madame de Montlucin, eager to carry out the orders and to hasten the recovery of her husband, presented him with a large glass of the most limpidly pure water.

The invalid took it docilely, and set himself with resignation to drinking it; but after the first swallow he stopped, and handed the glass back to his wife: "Take it, my dear," he said, "and keep it for some other time: I've always heard it said that one must never run the risk of an overdose of any kind of medicine."

The Writers

65: In the gastronomical empire, the position of men of letters is very close to that of the doctors.

During the reign of Louis XIV, writers were drunkards; they but followed the fashion, and the memoirs of that period are very edifying on the subject. Today writers are gourmands, which is a great improvement.

I am far from being of the opinion of the cynic Geoffroy,[6] who once said that if modern literature lacks force it is because the authors drink only sugar water.

I believe, on the contrary, that he has done a double injustice, and is mistaken both in the fact itself and in its results.

This present period is rich in talents; they perhaps do themselves harm by their very numbers; but posterity, looking at it more dispassionately, will find much to admire in it: thus it is that we ourselves have recognized the masterpieces of Racine and Molière, which were coldly received by their contemporaries.

Never has the social position of men of letters been pleasanter than now. They no longer live in the remote garrets which used to embarrass them; the fields of literature have grown more fertile for them, and even the Hippocrenic stream flows over gold dust; the equals of anyone, they no longer need cringe to the voice of patronage; and, to crown it all, gourmandism overwhelms them with her finest favors.

We associate with men of letters because of our respect for their talents, because in general their conversation has something piquant about it, and also because it has been fashionable for some time now for each social set to have its own author.

These gentlemen always arrive a little late; the result is that they are welcomed all the more heartily, having been waited for; they are tempted with the daintiest tidbits so that they will return some other time for more, and they are plied with the best wines so that they will sparkle while they are there: since they accept all this as their due, they soon grow used to it, and become gourmands forever.

In fact, this state of affairs has advanced almost to the point of becoming a little scandalous. More than one ferrety gossip has whispered that certain literary lions have been seduced at the dinner table, that certain advancements are the result of this or that truffled pâté, in short that the lock of the temple of immortality has been picked with a fork. But this is nothing but mischievous slander; these rumors have died away with all the others: what has been done has been well done, and naturally the only reason I mention it here at all is to show that I keep abreast of whatever is connected with my subject.[7]

The Devout

66: Last of all, gourmandism counts many of the devout among its most faithful followers.

We give to this word *devout* the same meaning as did Louis XIV and Molière, that is as it is applied to the men of the cloth whose whole religion consists of outward observances; people of true piety and charity have no part of it.

Let us see, then, how they have come to join the church. Among those who wish to make this move, most choose the easiest way to do it; the ones who shun their fellowmen, sleep upon stone, and drape themselves with haircloth, have always been exceptions and will always be so.

There are, of course, some things in life which are unequivocably damned, and which can nevermore be enjoyed once the vows are taken, like dancing, the theatre, gambling, and other such pastimes.

But while all these things as well as the people who practice them are abominated, gourmandism appears and insinuates itself with a completely theological reasonableness into the monkish picture.

By divine right man is the king of nature, it is argued, and everything that the earth produces has been created for his use. It is for him that the quail fattens, for him that mocha has so sweet a perfume, for him that sugar is beneficial to the health.

Why not, then, take advantage, at least with a proper moderation, of the good things that Providence offers to him, especially if he continues to think of them as fleeting and perishable, and even more especially if they intensify his gratitude toward the author of all beings!

And even stronger reasons serve to strengthen these first ones. How can anyone do too much to welcome the men who direct our souls and keep us on the straight and narrow path? Should we not make any such admirably intended meetings as pleasant as possible, and more frequent?

Sometimes, too, the gifts of Comus arrive without being solicited: it may be a souvenir of old school days, it may be a present from a faithful friend or from a penitent in apology, it may be something in payment of a bargain already made, or an offering from a debtor. How can such boons be spurned? And how can we ignore the rules of reciprocity, and not return their worth? It is a matter of pure necessity.

What is more, things have always been like this:

Nunneries in the old days were veritable storehouses of the most delectable tidbits, which is why some connoisseurs feel so bitterly about the edicts closing their doors.†

Several monastic orders, the Bernardine especially, made a profession of good living. Cooks employed by the cloth surpassed the limits of their own art; and when Monsieur de Pressigny (who died archbishop of Besançon) returned from the conclave which elected Pius VI in 1775, he said that the best dinner offered to him in all Rome was at the table of the head of the Capuchins.

Chevaliers and Abbés

67: There can be no better way for us to finish this Meditation than to make honorable mention of two classes of gourmands which we have watched in all their glory, and which the Revolution has wiped out: the chevaliers and the abbés.

And what gourmands they were, those good old friends! It

† *The best liqueurs of France used to be made at La Côte by the Visitandines; the sisters of Niort invented sugared angelica; the cakes made with orange-flower water by the nuns of Château-Thierry are still praised; and the Ursulines of Belley owned a recipe for candied nuts which was a treasure of sensual delight. It is to be feared, alas, that it has been lost.*

was impossible to ignore the evidence of their flaring nostrils, their popping eyes, their glistening lips and their licking tongue-tips; and yet each class had a way of eating which was peculiar to it.

The chevaliers showed something military in the way they sat; they apportioned their mouthfuls with dignity, and chewed them with great calm, the while they looked tranquilly about the table, from host to hostess, with a horizontal and approving gaze.

The abbés, on the contrary, hunched themselves to be nearer their plates; their right hands curved around their forks like the paw of a cat who flicks hot chestnuts from a fire; their faces shone with pleasure, and their glance had something about it of pure concentration which is easier to imagine than to paint.

Since three-quarters of the present generation have never seen anything to resemble the chevaliers and the abbés whom I have just described, and since it is nevertheless necessary to be able to recognize them in order to understand many books written during the eighteenth century, we shall borrow from the author of AN HISTORICAL TREATISE ON DUELLING a few pages which can leave nothing to be desired on this subject. (See the "Varieties," number XX.)

Inevitable Longevity of Gourmands

68:   As a result of my preceding lectures, I am happier than I imagined possible to be able to give to my readers a wonderful bit of news, which is that good living is far from being destructive to good health and that, all things being equal, gourmands live much longer than other folk. This has been mathematically proven in a very well-constructed essay which was read just lately at the Academy of Sciences by Dr. Villermet.

In it he compared the various levels of well-nourished society with those that are badly fed, and ran their gamut in his study. In this scale of comparisons he noted those parts of Paris where the standard of living is generally high and, in the same category, those which are completely opposite, as for example the suburb of Saint-Marceau and the Chaussée-d'Antin.

In conclusion the doctor extended his researches to the outer fringes of France and compared, under the same subject heading, those which are more and less fertile: without fail he discerned that human mortality diminishes in direct proportion to the ability to nourish the population properly, and also that those people who are condemned by fate to be malnourished may at least comfort themselves with the assurance that they will be released by death sooner than their fat brothers.

The two extremes of this situation are that only one man in fifty who lives well dies in a single year, whereas among those who are most exposed to misery one out of four dies in the same period of time.

This is not because men who live an easy life can not fall ill! Alas, they do wander at times into the domain of the doctors, who have the habit of classifying them as *good patients*; but since they have a greater reserve of vitality, and since every part of their organism is better cared for, Nature itself has more resources, and their bodies are incomparably better prepared to resist disintegration.

This physiological truth has all the more weight when we remember that every time some imperious circumstance like a war, or a siege, or a violent change in weather, has lessened our means of survival, the resulting state of distressful malnutrition has always been accompanied by epidemics of contagious diseases and a great increase in mortality.

The Lafarge insurance company, so well-known to Parisians, would without doubt have flourished if those who established it had let Dr. Villermet's truths enter into their calculations.

They figured the mortality rate according to the tables established by Buffon, Parcieux, and others, all of them fixed on numbers drawn from all classes and all ages of a certain population. But since men who are able to place their capital according to its probable revenue are in general able as well to escape the dangers of childhood, and are used to a well-ordered, proper, and even enjoyable existence, *death passed them by*, the speculators' hopes were deceived, and the whole scheme fell through.

This was, of course, not the only reason for the failure, but it was a basic one, and it was told to me by my friend Professor Pardessus.

Monsieur de Belloy, archbishop of Paris, who lived nearly a hundred years, had a fairly hearty appetite; he loved good living, and more than once I have seen his patriarchal figure come to life at the arrival of a plate of distinction. Napoleon never failed, on every occasion, to show him deference.

THE TRANSLATOR'S GLOSSES

1.   There is a note about Dr. Gall on page 47. As for Johann Kaspar Lavater, he was a Swiss preacher and writer who was born in 1741 and died in 1801. His main work was a series of treatises and essays on physiognomy, or the art of judging character from facial characteristics.

2.   Balzac wrote that Brillat-Savarin was as tall as a drum major, of "almost colossal stature," and on page 384 the Professor says, "I am thickset, very tall . . ."

3.   Mondor was a pompous, ridiculous, rich man, formerly a liveried flunky, the hero of a once-fashionable poem called L'Art de Diner en Ville, which was published in 1810. Its author Colnet died of the cholera in 1832, after many stormy years as a royalist writer, but his brilliant letters in the Gazette de France were not remembered as long as his cynical witty exposure of the art of cadging a good dinner in Paris . . . then and now, too, in Paris and everywhere. Find a wealthy snob, he counselled . . . and then flattery, unlimited insensate flattery! Malice, and gossip! Servility!

4.   Jean Nicolas Corvisart-Desmarest, a fashionable physician who was put in personal charge of Napoleon's well-being, died in 1821 at the age of 66, a fairly ripe one for those days.

5.   This reference goes back to Rabelais, who quoted a supposition as prevalent in his day as in Brillat-Savarin's that the natives of Limôges were powerful tosspots. It may have been the famous porcelain factories with their glowing kilns that gave the Limousins such a mighty thirst.

6.   Julien Louis Geoffroy (1743–1814) was a well-known man of letters who was feared for his wittily damning theatrical criticisms in the Journal des Debats.

7.   Oh! Oh fie, Professor! And perhaps ouch!

MEDITATION 13

ON

GASTRONOMICAL

TESTS

69:   It has been seen in the preceding chapter that the distinguishing characteristic of those who have more pretension than right to the title of gourmands consists in the fact that when confronted by the most delicious viands, their eyes stay dull and flat and their faces remain unanimated.

Such people do not deserve to have wasted on them treasures whose value they cannot appreciate: therefore it has seemed especially important to us to be able to recognize them, and we have sought out every means of attaining this knowledge, important as it is to the classification of men and the understanding of our guests.

We have plunged into this research with the ardor that spells success, and it is to our perseverance that we owe the privilege of presenting to the noble body of amphitryons our discovery of *gastronomical tests*, a discovery which will bring honor to the nineteenth century.

By *gastronomical tests* we designate dishes of recognized savor and of such acknowledged excellence that nothing more than the sight of them will awaken, in a well-balanced man, all his gustatory powers; as a result, anyone who in the same situation shows neither the flash of desire nor the glow of ecstasy can rightly be set down as unworthy of the honors of the gathering and all its accompanying delights.

The method of the tests, duly examined and weighed in grand council, has been inscribed in its golden book in the following terms, couched in a tongue which remains changeless.

Utcumque ferculum, eximii et bene noti saporis, appositum fuerit, fiat autopsia convivae; et nisi facies ejus ac oculi vertantur ad ecstasim, notetur ut indignus.

This has been translated by the sworn translator of the grand council as follows:

Whenever a dish of distinguished and well-known savor is served, the host will observe his guests attentively, and will condemn as unworthy all those whose faces do not express their rapture.

The power of the tests is relative, and must be adapted to the natures and habits of various classes of society. All these things having been properly weighed, a test must be planned so as to arouse admiration and surprise: it is a kind of dynamometer whose force increases as we mount higher in the social scale. Thus the test to be given to a man of humble means living on the Rue Coquenard would have no effect on a well-to-do shopkeeper, and would be ignored completely at a dinner of the gastronomical elect (SELECT FEW) given by a banker or a diplomat.

In the enumeration which we are about to make of the dishes which have been judged worthy of being called tests, we shall begin with those of the lowest dynamometric pressure and gradually increase it, to clarify the whole system in such a way that not only can it be used by everyone with profit, but it can be imitated and augmented along the same lines, called by its user's own name, and employed by him in whatever walk of life he chances to occupy.

For a moment or two we considered giving here, as concrete proofs, the recipes for the various dishes which we have selected as tests, but we have refrained; we believe that this would do an injustice to the various collections which have already appeared, including the one by Beauvilliers and the recently published COOK OF COOKS. We must content ourself with recommending these books to the reader, as well as those by Viard and Appert, and observing that in the latter he will discover various scientific facts never before found in works of this kind.

It is regrettable that the public cannot enjoy a shorthand reporting of all that was discussed in the grand council, while the tests were being determined. What went on will remain forever lost in secrecy, but at least there is one incident which I have been permitted to reveal.

A certain member† proposed that there be negative tests, and tests by privation.

For instance, some accident has destroyed a dish of special delicacy, or a hamper of game which should arrive by a certain post has been delayed: no matter whether this be actual or only a supposition, the host, on announcing the unhappy news, will watch and take note of the misery which deepens on the faces of his guests, and will thus be able to formulate a clear scale of their gastric sensitivity.

But this proposition, although tempting at first mention, did not stand up under a more considered examination. The president very rightly observed that such occurrences, which would have but a superficial effect upon the dulled organs of unappreciative diners, could easily have a deadly influence on true gastronomers, even to the point of causing a mortal seizure. Therefore, in spite of some insistence on the part of its author, the proposition was unanimously rejected.

We continue now, by giving the lists of dishes which we have decided worthy to be used as tests; we have divided them into three sections of gradually increasing strength, following the plan and method already outlined:

Gastronomical Tests

FIRST SERIES
Presumed Income: 5,000 Francs (Mediocrity)

A big fillet of veal larded with fat bacon and cooked in its own juices;

A domestic turkey stuffed with Lyons chestnuts;

† M. F . . . S . . . , *who, because of his classic features, the refinement of his palate, and his administrative talents, has everything needed to become a perfect financier.*[1]

Fattened pigeons covered with bacon and well cooked;

Eggs *à la neige;*

A dish of sauerkraut (SAUR-KRAUT) bristling with sausages and crowned with smoked bacon from Strasbourg.

Comment: "Say, now! That looks damned good! Come on, let's do it justice! . . ."

SECOND SERIES

Presumed Income: 15,000 *Francs* (*Ease*)

A fillet of beef, pink inside, larded and cooked in its own juices;

A haunch of venison, with sauce of chopped gherkins;

A boiled turbot;

A choice leg of mutton *à la provençale;*

A truffled turkey;

Early green peas.

Comment: "Ah, my dear fellow! What a delightful sight! It's a veritable wedding feast!" †

THIRD SERIES

Presumed Income: 30,000 *Francs and More* (*Wealth*)

A seven-pound fowl, stuffed round as a ball with Périgord truffles;

An enormous *pâté de foie gras* from Strasbourg, in the shape of a bastion;

A large carp from the Rhine, *à la Chambord,* richly dressed and decorated;

Truffled quails *à la moelle,* on canapés of toast spread with butter flavored with sweet basil;

A stuffed and basted river pike, covered with a cream of shrimps, *secundum artem;*

A well-hung pheasant, served roasted *à la sainte alliance* and dressed in his tail feathers;

One hundred stalks of early asparagus, of the thickness of a pencil, with sauce *à l'osmazome;*

Two dozen ortolans *à la provençale,* following the recipe given in THE SECRETARY AND THE COOK;

† *In order to articulate this phrase with properly fashionable diction, each letter must be sounded to the full.*[2]

A pyramid of meringues flavored with vanilla and rose water. (This test is useful only on the ladies, on men with well-rounded feminine calves, and so on.)

Comment: "Ah, Sir (or My lord), what an admirable chef you have! It is only at your banquets that we can enjoy such delicacies!" [3]

GENERAL SURVEY

In order to produce the full effect of any test, it should be served generously: experience, founded on a knowledge of human nature, has taught us that the most delicious rarity loses its influence when its quantity is stingy; the first delightful emotion it arouses in the diners is rightly discouraged by their fear that they will receive but a thin share of the dish, or even be forced, in some cases, to refuse it out of politeness. This often happens at the table of pretentious misers.

I have had many a chance to verify the effects of gastronomical tests; the one I shall recount will suffice.

I was guest at a dinner of gourmands of the fourth category, the clergy, where there were only two of us who belonged among the unconsecrated, my friend R . . . and myself.

After a first course of the highest distinction, we were served, among other things, an enormous virgin rooster from Barbezieux,† truffled to the bursting point, and a veritable Gibraltar of Strasbourg pâté.

This dramatic appearance produced an effect on the assemblage which was very clear but is difficult to describe, almost like

---

† *Men whose word may be considered law have assured me that the flesh of such a cockerel, if not tenderer than that of a capon, is at least and very certainly of much more flavor. I have too much to do here on earth to study such a problem, which I willingly delegate to my readers; but I believe that the opinion can be accepted without question, since there is in the former of these two meats an element of sapidity which is lacking in the latter.*

A woman of great charm has told me that she recognizes gourmands by the way they pronounce the word GOOD *in their conversations:* HERE IS SOMETHING GOOD, HERE IS SOMETHING VERY GOOD, *and so on; she assures me that the real connoisseurs put into this short word an accent of conviction, of pleasure, and of enthusiasm, which people of dull palate can never hope to attain.*

the silent laugh mentioned by Cooper, and I at once saw that it was a challenge to my powers of observation.

In effect, all conversation ceased as if hearts were too full to go on; all attention was riveted on the skill of the carvers; and when the serving platters had been passed, I saw spread out in succession on every face the fire of desire, the ecstasy of enjoyment, and then the perfect peace of satisfaction.

THE TRANSLATOR'S GLOSSES

1. The Professor's startling list of the virtues possessed by a "perfect financier" has little to do with present-day standards of banking, but was perhaps influenced by his passionate loyalty to anyone coming from his part of the country: M. Felix Sibuet was a native of the Ain, as was Brillat-Savarin.

2. Here Brillat-Savarin wrote "nopces et festins," quoting an obsolete spelling used by Rabelais, and probably poking fun at the newly assumed culture of middle-class people. A hundred years later in Burgundy I heard it said of a pretentious *nouveau-riche* that he was the kind of snob who actually pronounced the *s* when he said *Mais oui*. There was knowing (and damning) laughter.

3. In Soyer's GASTRONOMIC REGENERATOR he presents with a pride which is pardonable, if almost incomprehensible to modern diners, his "most recherché" menu, which he prepared in the Reform Club in London on May 9, 1846, for ten people. It consisted of twenty-eight dishes, all of them as Lucullan as possible. Then Soyer adds wistfully: "I had also proposed the following . . . which I was unable to obtain from Paris on account of a change in the weather preventing their arrival, the articles being two dozen of ortolans; having already procured twelve of the largest and finest truffles I could obtain, it was my intention to have dug a hole in each, into which I should have placed one of the birds, and covered each with a piece of lamb's or calf's caul, then to have braised them half an hour in good

stock made from fowl and veal, with half a pint of Lachryma Christi added; then to have drained them upon a cloth, placed a border of poached forcemeat upon the dish, built the truffles in pyramid, made a purée with the truffle dug from the interior, using the stock reduced to a demi-glace and poured over, roasted the twelve remaining ortolans before a sharp fire, with which I should have garnished the whole round, and served very hot."

MEDITATION 14

ON THE
PLEASURES OF
THE TABLE

70: Man is incontestably, among the sentient creatures who inhabit the globe, the one who endures most pain.

Nature from the beginning has condemned him to misery by the nakedness of his skin, by the shape of his feet, and by that instinct for war and destruction which has always accompanied the human species wherever it has gone.

Animals have never been thus cursed, and, were it not for a few battles caused by the reproductive instinct, suffering would be absolutely unknown to the greater number of species in their natural state; whereas man, who experiences pleasure but fleetingly and with only a few of his organs, can always and in every part of his body be subjected to the most horrible pain.

This decree of fate has been made even sterner in its execution by a mass of illnesses which are the result of our social customs, so that the keenest and deepest pleasure that anyone can imagine is unable either in its intensity or its duration to compensate for the atrocious suffering which accompanies such maladies as gout, toothache, acute rheumatism, or strangury, or is caused by the deliberate punitive tortures which are customary in certain countries.

It is the basic fear of this pain which makes man throw himself, without even realizing it, toward the opposite extreme, and give himself up completely to the small number of pleasures which Nature has permitted him.

It is for the same reason that he enlarges them, perfects them, complicates them, and finally worships them, as is shown by the fact that during the days of idolatry and for a long series of centuries all the pleasures were classified as secondary gods, presided over by their superior deities.

The austerity of our new sects has destroyed all those personages; Bacchus, Venus, Comus, and Diana are nothing more than poetic memories, but the fact remains, and no matter how strict our religion may be, we still enjoy ourselves at marriages, baptisms, and even funerals.

Origin of the Pleasures of the Table

71:    Meals, in the sense which we give to this word, began with the second age-period of the human race, that is at the moment when man ceased to nourish himself on fruit alone. The preparation and the distribution of food necessarily brought the whole family together, the fathers apportioning to their children the results of the hunt, and the grown children then doing the same to their aged parents.

These gatherings, limited at first to the nearest relatives, little by little were extended to include neighbors and friends.

Later, and when the human race had spread out, the tired traveler came to join in such primitive feasts, and to recount what went on in the far countries of the world. Thus was born hospitality, with its rights sacred to all peoples, for one of the strongest of human laws is that which commands respect for the life of any man with whom one has shared bread and salt.

It is during meals that languages must have been born and perfected, whether it was because they were a constantly recurring necessity or because the relaxation which accompanies and follows a feast leads naturally to confidence and loquacity.

*   *   *

Difference between the Pleasure of Eating and the Pleasures of the Table

72: Such must have been, by the nature of things, the elements of the pleasures of the table, which should be distinguished from the pleasure of eating, their necessary antecedent.

The pleasure of eating is the actual and direct sensation of satisfying a need.

The pleasures of the table are a reflective sensation which is born from the various circumstances of place, time, things, and people who make up the surroundings of the meal.

The pleasure of eating is one we share with animals; it depends solely on hunger and on what is needed to satisfy it.

The pleasures of the table are known only to the human race; they depend on careful preparations for the serving of the meal, on the choice of place, and on the thoughtful assembling of the guests.

The pleasure of eating demands appetite, if not actual hunger; the pleasures of the table are most often independent of either one or the other.

These two states can always be observed at any of our celebrations.

During the first course, and at the beginning of the feast, everyone eats hungrily, without talking, without paying any attention to what may be going on about him, and no matter what his position or rank may be he ignores everything in order to devote himself to the great task at hand. But as these needs are satisfied, the intellect rouses itself, conversation begins, a new order of behavior asserts itself, and the man who was no more than an eater until then becomes a more or less pleasant companion, according to his natural ability.

Effects

73: The pleasures of the table do not presuppose ravishment nor ecstasy nor bliss, but they gain in duration what they lose in intensity, and are above all distinguished by their own merit of making all the others more intense for us or at least of consoling us for their loss.

The truth is that at the end of a well-savored meal both soul and body enjoy an especial well-being.

Physically, at the same time that a diner's brain awakens, his face grows animated, his color heightens, his eyes shine, and a gentle warmth creeps over his whole body.

Morally, his spirit grows more perceptive, his imagination flowers, and clever phrases fly to his lips: if La Fare and Saint-Aulaire[1] go down to posterity as witty writers, it will be because they were first and foremost delightful dinner companions.

Best of all, every modification which complete sociability has introduced among us can be found assembled around the same table: love, friendship, business, speculation, power, importunity, patronage, ambition, intrigue; and this is why conviviality is a part of every thing alive, and why it bears fruits of every flavor.

Artificial Embellishments

74:   It is as a direct result of these basic causes that all human industry has concentrated on adding to the duration and the intensity of the pleasures of the table.

Poets long ago began to complain that the throat, being too short, limited the length of the pleasure of tasting; others deplored the small capacity of the stomach; it came to the point where this organ was freed from the necessity of digesting the first course so that it could have the pleasure of holding a second one.

This was the supreme attempt to enlarge the pleasurable capacities of human taste; but if, in this case, it was impossible to break down the natural barriers, man could at least throw himself into the invention of accessories, which offered him more scope.

He ornamented his goblets and vases with flowers; he crowned his guests with them; he ate under the open sky, and in gardens and in woods and in the presence of all the wonders of Nature.

The charms of music and the sound of instruments were joined to the pleasures of the table. Thus it was that while the court of the Phaeacian king feasted, the minstrel Phemius sang of the warlike deeds of olden times.

Often dancers, wrestlers, and clowns of both sexes and in every kind of costume came to amuse the eyes of the diners without boring their palates; the most exquisite perfumes were sprayed into the air; it even happened that naked beauties acted as servant girls, so that every human sense joined in a complete pleasure.

I could cover several pages with the proof of my theory. Greek and Roman authors, and our own old writers, are there waiting to be copied; but these researches have already been made, and my easy aping of them would bring me little merit: therefore I state as a fact what other men have already proved, which is a privilege I often claim, and which the reader should be grateful for.

Eighteenth and Nineteenth Centuries

75: We have assumed as our own, then, these various ways of increasing our delights, and to them we have added all that new discoveries have uncovered for us.

Of course the delicacy of our manners could not let us accept the Roman *vomitoria*; but we have done even better, and have arrived at the same end by a path recognized by our good taste.

Such attractive dishes have been invented that they manage to revivify our appetites again and again; they are at the same time so light that they flatter the palate without overloading the stomach. Seneca would have said of them: *Nubes esculentas*.

We have thus attained to such alimentary refinement that if the pressure of private business did not force us to get up from the table, or if the need for sleep did not arise in us, the length of our meals would be practically limitless, and there would be no set way for us to determine the time we might spend between the first sip of Madeira and the last glass of punch.[2]

However, it must not be believed that all these adjuncts are indispensable to the enjoyment of the pleasures of the table. This pleasure can be savored almost to the full whenever the four following conditions are met with: food at least passable, good wine, agreeable companions, and enough time.[3]

This is why I have often wished that I could have been one of the guests at the frugal meal that Horace planned for a neighbor whom he might have invited to dine with him or for a traveller forced by bad weather to take shelter under his roof: a fine fowl, a kid (without doubt fat and good), and for dessert raisins, figs, and nuts. And joining to all this some wine pressed during the consularship of Manlius (*nata mecum consule Manlio*) and the conversation of such a sweet singer as Horace, it seems to me that I would sup in the world's best way.

> At mihi cum longum post temperus venerat hospes,
> Sive operum vacuo, longum conviva per imbrem
> Vicinus, bene erat, non piscibus urbe petitis,
> Sed pullo atque haedo, tum† pensilis uva secundas
> Et nux ornabat mensas, cum duplice ficu.

It is in the same fashion that yesterday, or even tomorrow, three pairs of friends might feast together upon a boiled leg of mutton with kidneys from Pontoise, washed down with wine from Orléans and good clear Médoc, and that having finished the evening with discussions full of warmth and gaiety they would completely have forgotten that there were other more delicate dishes and more polished cooks.

On the other hand, no matter how studied a dinner plan nor how sumptuous its adjuncts, there can be no true pleasures of the table if the wine be bad, the guests assembled without discretion, the faces gloomy, and the meal consumed with haste.

Sketch

But, the impatient reader may exclaim, how can one possibly assemble, in this year of grace 1825, a meal which will meet all the conditions necessary to attain the ultimate in the pleasures of the table?

I am about to answer that question. Draw near, Reader, and pay heed: it is Gasterea, the loveliest of the muses, who inspires me; I shall speak more clearly than an oracle, and my precepts will live throughout the centuries.

"Let the number of guests be no more than twelve, so that conversation may always remain general;

"Let them be so chosen that their professions will be varied, their tastes analogous, and that there be such points of contact

---

† *Dessert is here designated and distinguished with precision by the adverb* TUM *and by the words* SECUNDAS MENSAS.

that the odious formality of introductions will not be needed;

"Let the dining room be more than amply lighted, the linen of dazzling cleanliness, and the temperature maintained at from sixty to sixty-eight degrees Fahrenheit;

"Let the gentlemen be witty without pretension, and the ladies charming without too much coquetry;†

"Let the dishes be of exquisite quality, but limited in their number, and the wines of the first rank also, each according to its degree;

"Let the progression of the former be from the most substantial to the lightest, and of the latter from the simplest wines to the headiest;

"Let the tempo of eating be moderate, the dinner being the last affair of the day: the guests should behave like travellers who must arrive together at the same destination;

"Let the coffee be piping hot, and the liqueurs of the host's especial choice;

"Let the drawing room which awaits the diners be large enough to hold a card table for those who cannot do without it, with enough space left for after-dinner conversations;

"Let the guests be disciplined by the restraints of polite society and animated by the hope that the evening will not pass without its rewarding pleasures;

"Let the tea be not too strong, the toast artfully buttered, and the punch made with care;

"Let the leavetakings not begin before eleven o'clock, but by midnight let every guest be home and abed."

If anyone has attended a party combining all these virtues, he can boast that he has known perfection, and for each one of them which has been forgotten or ignored he will have experienced the less delight.

I have already said that the pleasures of the table, as I conceive of them, can go on for a rather long period of time; I am going to prove this now by giving a detailed and faithful account of the lengthiest meal I ever ate in my life; it is a little bonbon which I shall pop into my reader's mouth as a reward for having read me thus far with such agreeable politeness. Here it is:

---

† *I am writing this in Paris, between the Palais-Royal and the Chaussée-d'Antin.*[4]

I used to have, at the end of the Rue du Bac, a family of cousins composed of the following: Doctor Dubois, seventy-eight years old; the captain, seventy-six; their sister Jeannette, who was seventy-four. I went now and then to pay them a visit, and they always received me very graciously.

"By George!" the doctor said one day to me, standing on tip-toe to slap me on the shoulder. "For a long time now you've been boasting of your *fondues* (eggs scrambled with cheese), and you always manage to keep our mouths watering. It's time to stop all this. The captain and I are coming soon to have breakfast with you, to see what it's all about." (It was, I believe, in 1801 that he thus teased me.)

"Gladly," I replied. "You'll taste it in all its glory, for I myself will make it. Your idea is completely delightful to me. So . . . tomorrow at ten sharp, military style!" †

At the appointed hour I saw my guests arrive, freshly shaved, their hair carefully arranged and well-powdered: two little old men who were still spry and healthy.

They smiled with pleasure when they saw the table ready, spread with white linen, three places laid, and at each of them two dozen oysters and a gleaming golden lemon.

At both ends of the table rose up bottles of Sauterne, carefully wiped clean except for the corks, which indicated in no uncertain way that it was a long time that the wine had rested there.

Alas, in my life-span I have almost seen the last of those oyster breakfasts, so frequent and so gay in the old days, where the molluscs were swallowed by the thousands! [5] They have disappeared with the abbés, who never ate less than a gross apiece, and with the chevaliers, who went on eating them forever. I regret them, in a philosophical way: if time can change governments, how much more influence has it over our simple customs!

After the oysters, which were found to be deliciously fresh, grilled skewered kidneys were served, a deep pastry shell of truffled *foie gras*, and finally the *fondue*.

All its ingredients had been mixed in a casserole, which was brought to the table with an alcohol lamp. I performed on this

† *Whenever a meal is announced in this way, it must be served on the stroke of the hour: latecomers are treated as deserters.*

battlefield, and my cousins did not miss a single one of my gestures.

They exclaimed with delight on the charms of the whole procedure, and asked for my recipe, which I promised to give them, the while I told the two anecdotes on the subject which my reader will perhaps find further on.

After the *fondue* came seasonable fresh fruits and sweetmeats, a cup of real Mocha made *à la Dubelloy*, a method which was then beginning to be known, and finally two kinds of liqueurs, one sharp for refreshing the palate and the other oily for soothing it.

The breakfast being well-ended, I suggested to my guests that we take a little exercise, and that it consist of inspecting my apartment, quarters which are far from elegant but which are spacious and comfortable, and which pleased my company especially since the ceilings and gildings date from the middle of the reign of Louis XV.

I showed them the clay original of the bust of my lovely cousin Mme. Récamier by Chinard, and her portrait in miniature by Augustin; they were so delighted by these that the doctor kissed the portrait with his full fleshy lips, and the captain permitted himself to take such liberty with the statue that I slapped him away; for if all the admirers of the original did likewise, that breast so voluptuously shaped would soon be in the same state as the big toe of Saint Peter in Rome, which pilgrims have worn to a nubbin with their kisses.[6]

Then I showed them a few casts from the works of the best antique sculptors, some paintings which were not without merit, my guns, my musical instruments, and a few fine first editions, as many of them French as foreign.

In this little excursion into such varied arts they did not forget my kitchen. I showed them my economical stockpot, my roastingshell, my clockwork spit, and my steamcooker. They inspected everything with the most finicky curiosity, and were all the more astonished since in their own kitchens everything was still done as it had been during the Regency.

At the very moment we re-entered my drawing room, the clock struck two. "Bother!" the doctor exclaimed. "Here it is dinner time, and sister Jeannette will be waiting for us! We must hurry back to her. I must confess I feel no real hunger, but still I must have my bowl of soup. It is an old habit with me, and when I go for a day without taking it I have to say with Titus, *Diem perdidi.*"

"My dear doctor," I said to him, "why go so far for what is right here at hand? I'll send someone to the kitchen to give warning that you will stay awhile longer with me, and that you will give me the great pleasure of accepting a dinner toward which I know you will be charitable, since it will not have all the finish of such a meal prepared with more leisure."

A kind of oculary consultation took place at this point between the two brothers, followed by a formal acceptance. I then sent a messenger[7] posthaste to the Faubourg Saint-Germain, and exchanged a word or two with my master cook; and after a remarkably short interval, and thanks partly to his own resources and partly to the help of neighboring restaurants, he served us a very neatly turned out little dinner, and a delectable one to boot.

It gave me deep satisfaction to observe the poise and aplomb with which my two friends seated themselves, pulled nearer to the table, spread out their napkins, and prepared for action.

They were subjected to two surprises which I myself had not intended for them; for first I served them Parmesan cheese with the soup, and then I offered them a glass of dry Madeira. These were novelties but lately imported by Prince Talleyrand, the leader of all our diplomats, to whom we owe so many witticisms, so many epigrams and profundities, and the man so long followed by the public's devout attention, whether in the days of his power or of his retirement.

Dinner went off very well in both its accessory and its main parts, and my cousins reflected as much pleasure as gaiety.

Afterwards I suggested a game of piquet, which they refused; they preferred the sweet siesta, the *far niente*, of the Italians, the captain told me; and therefore we made a little circle close to the hearth.

In spite of the delights of a postprandial doze, I have always felt that nothing lends more calm pleasure to the conversation than an occupation of whatever kind, so long as it does not absorb the attention. Therefore I proposed a cup of tea.

Tea in itself was an innovation to the old die-hard patriots.

Nevertheless it was accepted. I made it before their eyes, and they drank down several cups of it with all the more pleasure since they had always before considered it a remedy.

Long practice has taught me that one pleasure leads to another, and that once headed along this path a man loses the power of refusal. Therefore it was that in an almost imperative voice I spoke of finishing the afternoon with a bowl of punch.

"But you will kill us!" the doctor said.

"Or at least make us tipsy!" the captain added.

To all this I replied only by calling vociferously for lemons, for sugar, for rum.

I concocted the punch then, and while I was busy with it, I had made for me some beautifully thin, delicately buttered, and perfectly salted slices of zwiebach (TOAST).

This time there was a little protest. My cousins assured me that they had already eaten very well indeed, and that they would not touch another thing; but since I am acquainted with the temptations of this completely simple dish, I replied with only one remark, that I hoped I had made enough of it. And sure enough, soon afterwards the captain took the last slice, and I caught him peeking to see if there were still a little more or if it was really the last. I ordered another plateful immediately.

During all this, time had passed, and my watch showed me it was past eight o'clock.

"We must get out of here!" my guests exclaimed. "We are absolutely obliged to go home and eat at least a bit of salad with our poor sister, who has not set eyes on us today!"

I had no real objection to this; faithful to the duties of hospitality when it is concerned with two such delightful old fellows, I accompanied them to their carriage, and watched them be driven away.

Someone may ask if boredom did not show itself now and then in such a long séance.

I shall reply in the negative: the attention of my guests was fixed by my making the *fondue*, by the little trip around the apartment, by a few things which were new to them in the dinner, by the tea, and above all by the punch, which they had never before tasted.

Moreover the doctor knew the genealogy and the bits of gossip of all Paris; the captain had passed part of his life in Italy, both as a soldier and as an envoy to the Parman court; I myself have traveled a great deal; we chatted without affectation, and listened to one another with delight. Not even that much is needed to make time pass with grace and rapidity.

The next morning I received a letter from the doctor; he wished to inform me that the little debauch of the night before had done them no harm at all; quite to the contrary, after the sweetest of sleeps, the two old men had arisen refreshed, feeling both able and eager to begin anew.

THE TRANSLATOR'S GLOSSES

1.   These two men, both of the nobility and of the early eighteenth century, were apparently charming fellows with a graceful hand at "madrigals and other poetical trifles."

2.   This word may come from the Hindu *panch*, meaning five, the number of essential ingredients. Or it may come from *puncheon*, an obsolete word for a large cask. It was, no matter what its origin, an important part of the eighteenth and nineteenth century vocabulary. A punch followed a good meal, or even a poor one, as the sun the stars. A punch could be hot water and brandy smoked with a ruddy poker. A punch could be a gathering of people (met to drink one!). A "company" punch would be concocted somewhat like this for a club, as Sheila Hibben records it for the Chatham Artillery of Georgia in her AMERICAN REGIONAL COOKERY:

> 1½ gallons green tea
> 2½ pounds light brown sugar
> juice 3 dozen oranges and 1½ dozen lemons
> 1 quart Gordon gin
> 1½ gallons catawba wine
> 1 quart Cognac
> ½ gallon St. Croix rum
> ½ pint Benedictine

1½ quarts rye whiskey
1 pint brandied cherries
1 case champagne

The tea, sugar, and fruit juices are well-mixed, and everything else is added except the cherries and champagne. The whole stands in a closely covered crock for one week. Just before serving, the last two ingredients are added and the whole is poured over a block of ice.

This punch has a noble background, but I feel that the Professor would have preferred a glass of hot sugared brandy with lemon.

3. In THE IRISH QUARTERLY REVIEW, Volume VIII, published in Dublin in 1858, there is what would today be called an "article" on the Professor's book, which includes translated bits from it and Dr. Richerand's preface (to the second edition), and one or two amusing lights on the Anglo-Saxon at table. The essayist approves of Brillat-Savarin's four requisites for good dining: "It is even thus that six friends would regale themselves at the present day, on a boiled leg of mutton and a kidney, washed down with good clear orleans or madoc wine, in France, or genuine port, in England, or glorious whiskey in Ireland." But as for dining out (see page 311 and the picture of a typical Paris restaurant), the poor Irishman exiled in London wails: ". . . our awful steam baths, the Strand and Fleet Street diningrooms. . . . Simpson's for example! In we rush from the roar of the Strand. A long, dark, sweltering room is before us; no bright-eyed *dame du comptoi*; no shining, flashing mirrors; no waiter to glide at your nod, hot roaring guests, shouting waiters, men in cotton coats shoving about large dishes of steaming meat on rolling tables, and you eat your dinner in an atmosphere full of gin, fat, steam, and gabble . . . and where you are choaked by foul air . . ."

4. In 1825 this was a fashionable, rich, worldly, and above all *well-bred* quarter of the city.

5. A few years after the Professor put down his pen, there appeared in England a book printed even more anonymously than the first edition of THE PHYSIOLOGY OF TASTE, called "THE OYSTER; Where, How, and When to *find, breed, cook*, and *eat* it." The pages seethe with mid-Victorian discretion, in spite of

a great many rapturous Ahs! and fashionable Alacks!: "At the period of a lady's married life when nausea is prevalent, a few fresh oysters, taken raw in their own liquor, with no addition but a little pepper, and a fairy slice of French roll or other light bread, stops the feeling of sickness, and keeps up the stamina unimpaired." It is not until we read that a mother's oyster diet will make teething much less painful for her child that we realize pregnancy is hinted at.

As for the oyster supper, which Frenchmen enjoyed even more than Englishmen, according to Anon., he says happily, "Let me sketch the scene. In the center of the table, covered with a clean white cloth up to the top hoop, stands the barrel of oysters, a kindly remembrance from a friend . . . Each gentleman at table finds an oyster-knife and clean coarse towel by the side of his plate, and he is expected to open oysters for himself and the lady seated by his side, unless she is wise enough to open them for herself. By the side of every plate is the *panis ostrearius*, the oyster-loaf made and baked purposely for the occasion, and all down the center of the table, interspersed with vases of bright holly and evergreens, are plates filled with pats of butter, or lemons cut in half, and as many vinegar and pepper castors as the establishment can furnish. As the attendance of servants at such gatherings is usually dispensed with, bottled Bass or Guinness, or any equally unsophisticated pale ale or porter, is liberally provided; and where the means allow, light continental wines . . . are placed upon the table. Of Spirits, only good English gin, genuine Schiedam, or Irish or Scotch Whiskey, are admissible . . . At some of these oyster-suppers, oysters roasted in the shell are brought in 'hot and hot,' and dishes of fried, stewed, and scalloped oysters follow each other in quick succession, and even oyster patties are sometimes introduced; but I hold up both hands against an American innovation which is creeping in, and introducing crabs and lobsters, and mixed pickles, and other foreigners into the *carte* on such an occasion."

The aftereffects of such a pleasurable bit of gluttonizing are of necessity ignored in this well-mannered little book, but with matching discretion Brillat-Savarin manages to imply them in his story of the midnight feast, on page 372, where he pulls open and then pulls tight again the "curtain of conjugal privacy."

6.   The two lusty oldsters knew beauty still (page 346), but even

if the portrait and the bust had been of a lesser goddess than la Récamier, it is probable that their reactions would have been the same: any men with their undimmed capacity for pleasure would no more quibble at the tilt of a nose or nipple than at the casserole a *fondue* bubbled in.

7.   Here the Professor uses one of his cherished words, VOLANTE, on which he so prided himself. (See page 23, and my note 5 on page 26.)

MEDITATION 15

ON HUNTING
LUNCHEONS

76:   One of the most delightful of all occasions when eating counts in the pattern of life is a hunting-luncheon; and of all such known interruptions, it is still the hunting-luncheon which can be prolonged with the least fear of boredom.

After several hours of exercise, the most vigorous hunter feels a need for rest; his face has been caressed by the early-morning breeze; his skill has served him well on occasion; the sun is about to stand at its peak in the sky; it is time for the sportsman to stop for a few hours, not because he is too tired but because instinct warns him that his activity is not limitless.

A bit of shade attracts him; the grass is soft beneath him, and the murmur of a nearby stream suggests that he leave cooling in it the flask meant for his refreshment.†

Thus seated, he pulls out with tranquil pleasure the slices of golden-crusted bread, and unwraps the cold chicken which a loving hand has tucked into his knapsack, and nearby he places

---

† I suggest to my hunting comrades that they choose white wine for their bottles; it stands up better to movement and heat, and is more exhilarating.

the chunk of Gruyère cheese or Roquefort meant for his dessert.

While he thus sets the scene, the hunter is not alone; he is accompanied by that faithful animal which Heaven itself has created for him; his crouching dog watches him with devotion; a shared occupation has broken down the barriers between them: they are two good friends, and the servant is at once happy and proud to be his master's dining companion.[1]

They feel an appetite unknown equally to the worldly, who never give hunger a chance to make itself felt, and to the pious who do not take enough exercise to arouse it.

The meal, then, is enjoyed to the full; each one has had his share; everything has come about with order and peace. Why not snatch a few moments of sleep? Noontime is meant to be an hour of repose for all the creatures of the world.

These pleasures are immeasurably heightened if several friends share them; for, in this case, a more copious feast is brought along in one of the old military cook-wagons now put to a gentler use. Everyone chatters eagerly about this chap's skill and that one's bad luck, and about the high hopes for the afternoon.

And what if watchful servants arrive, laden with those jars consecrated to Bacchus, where artificial cold chills at one time Madeira, strawberry juice, and pineapple? These are delectable liqueurs, heavenly concoctions, which make a ravishing coolness run through the veins, and lend to every sense a well-being unknown to the profane.† But this is not the whole story of such a progression of enchantments.

† *It is my friend Alexander Delessert who first put into practice this charming custom.*

We were hunting at Villeneuve under a burning sun, with the thermometer at about 90 degrees in the shade.

He had been thoughtful enough to have our footsteps through this torrid zone followed by POTOPHOROUS (*) *lackeys who carried, in their ice-filled leather buckets, everything that could be desired, whether for refreshment or for stimulation. We had but to choose, to feel revivified.*

I am tempted to believe that the application of any such fresh liquid to a parched tongue and a dried-up gullet gives rise to the most delightful sensation which anyone can experience with a clear conscience.

(*) *Monsieur Hoffman objects to this expression because of its resemblance to* POT-AU-FEU; *he wishes to substitute for it the word* OENOPHOROUS, *which is already known.*

The Ladies

77:   There are certain days when our wives, our sisters, and our pretty cousins and their equally pretty friends, are invited to share our amusements.

At the appointed hour, light carriages with prancing horses are seen approaching, laden with lovely women decked with feathers, and with flowers. The toilette of these ladies has something about it both military and coquettish; and the keen eye of the Professor manages, now and then, to catch sights for which chance alone has not been responsible.

Soon the sides of the carriages open out, and there lie all the treasures of Périgord, the marvels of Strasbourg, the dainties of Archard, and everything that can well be carried away from the most knowing culinary laboratories.

And potent champagne, which acts best when served by beauty, has not been left behind; everyone sits down on the green grass and eats, and the corks fly; we chat, we laugh, we joke in complete liberty, for the world is our dining room and the sun itself is our light. And what is more, appetite, that heaven-sent emanation, gives to this feast a liveliness unknown to tight-shut rooms, no matter how beautifully adorned they may be.

However, since everything must end, the oldest person gives the signal, and we arise. The men arm themselves with their guns, and the women with their hats. Everyone says good-bye, the carriages come up, and the beauties fly off, no more to show themselves before nightfall.

This, at least, is what I have watched in high society, where the Pactolus rolls over its golden sands;[2] but all these attributes are not indispensable.

I have hunted in the central parts of France and in its remotest country districts; I have watched charming women arrive to join us for our luncheons, young people glowing with freshness, some of them in coaches and others in simple wagons, or mounted on the modest ass which brings fortune and glory to the people of Montmorency; I have watched them be the first to laugh at the awkwardness of their conveyances; I have watched them spread out upon the grass the plates of turkey in transparent jelly, the homemade pâté, the salad waiting to be tossed in its bowl; I have watched them dance lightfootedly around the campfire built for such a picnic; I have taken part in the games and gay nonsense which are part of this gypsy feasting, and I am thoroughly convinced that there is no less charm about it for its lack of luxury, no less gaiety and pleasure.

And then, why not? Why not, as the hunting-luncheon breaks up, exchange a kiss or two with the best of the hunters, because today is his day of glory; with the duffer, because he may feel unhappy over his bad luck; with all the others, in case they be jealous? After all, it is a leave-taking, custom authorizes it, and we are permitted and even urged to profit by it!

But comrades! I warn you that sensible sportsmen will take firm aim, shoot straight, and fill the gamebags well before the arrival of the ladies: experience has shown that once they have come and gone the hunting is rarely successful.

Conjectures to explain this effect have been made to the point of exhaustion. Some men attribute it to the work of digestion, which always makes the body a little lazy; others, to the fact that their attention has been distracted and cannot be properly focused again; still others, to the intimate little conversations which may have given them a desire to return as soon as possible to the ladies.

As for ourself,

"*Whose glance can read into the heart's own depths . . .*"
we believe that it is impossible, hunters being of inflammable material and the ladies still on the safe side of forty, to avoid setting off by their very proximity some sort of vital spark which is offensive to the chaste goddess of the hunt Diana, a flash of sexual desire which makes her, for the rest of the day, curtly withdraw her favors from the culprits.

We say *for the rest of the day*, since the story of Endymion has disclosed to us that this goddess is far from being so severe after the sun has set. (See the painting by Girodet.[3])

Hunting-luncheons are virgin material, which we have done no more than lightly touch upon; they could be the object of a treatise as amusing as it would be instructive. We herewith bequeath it to whatever intelligent reader wishes to busy himself with it.

*   *   *

THE TRANSLATOR'S GLOSSES

1. The Professor is said, by at least one of the men who wrote introductions to him (Charles Monselet), to have had a little dog as his constant companion in Paris. But this somewhat sentimental picture of the hunter and his friend is the only mention Brillat-Savarin makes of the possible good feeling between two- and four-legged creatures, except for the amiable way he starts his story of traveler's luck, on page 399: "One time, mounted on my good mare *la Joie* . . ."

2. It was in the Pactolus River, in Lydia, that the accursed king Midas bathed to wash away his golden touch, and from the moment of his purification, Greek myths said, the sands of the river changed to solid gold.

3. Girodet-Trioson (1767–1824) was a noted pupil of David who won the Prix de Rome and spent the rest of his life painting large sentimental pictures of classical subjects. The one the Professor refers to is probably THE SLEEP OF ENDYMION, in the Louvre: a far from subtle reminder that inexorable Diana let herself have at least one lover.

MEDITATION 16

ON DIGESTION

78: *A man does not live on what he eats,* an old proverb says, *but on what he digests.* It follows then that it is necessary to digest in order to live; and this necessity is the basis for a law which rules both rich and poor, both king and lowly shepherd.

But how few men know what happens when they do digest! Most of them are like Monsieur Jourdain, who spoke prose without realizing it; and for such as these I shall outline here an easily read story of the process, persuaded as I am that M. Jourdain felt much happier when the philosopher had made it quite clear to him that it was indeed prose he spoke.[1]

In order to understand the whole act of digestion, it must be connected with its causes and with what follows it.

Ingestion

79: Appetite, hunger, and thirst warn us that our bodies need restorative help; and pain, that universal monitor, does not wait long to torment us, if we do not obey or are unable to.

From this come eating and drinking, which form the act of

ingestion, beginning at the moment food reaches the mouth and finishing when it enters the esophagus.†

In this journey, which is only a few inches long, a great deal takes place.

Teeth break up the solid foods, and the glands of all kinds which line the inside of the mouth moisten them. The tongue mashes and blends them; then it pushes them against the palate to press out their juice and savor it; as this takes place it brings everything together into the middle of the mouth, after which, bracing itself against the lower jaw, it curves upwards in its central part so that an inclined plane is formed toward the base, which slides the food particles to the back of the mouth. There they are received by the pharynx, which, contracting in its own turn, propels them into the esophagus, whose peristaltic action takes them as far as the stomach.

One mouthful thus cared for, another follows it; liquids which are drunk in the pauses between them follow the same path, and this process of deglutition continues until the same instinct which first invoked ingestion warns us that it is time to stop. It is rare, however, that the first signal is heeded: one of the privileges of the human race is to be able to drink without thirst and, at least in the present state of progress, our cooks know very well how to make us eat without hunger.

By a remarkable feat, every crumb of food which we swallow must escape two dangers before it reaches the stomach:

The first is that it might be caught up into the nasal passages, if the soft palate and the construction of the pharynx did not prevent it;

The second risk would be to fall into the windpipe, over the top of which all our nourishment must pass, and this could be even more serious, since the instant a foreign body falls into this pipe, a convulsive cough begins, and cannot end until the object is expelled.

But, thanks to an admirable mechanism, the glottis contracts during the act of swallowing; it is protected by the epiglottis as well, which hoods it, and we have a certain instinct which prevents us from breathing while we swallow, so that

† *The* ESOPHAGUS *is the canal which begins at the back of the windpipe and leads from the gullet to stomach; its upper end is called the* PHARYNX.

in the main it can be said that, in spite of our strange construction, our nourishment arrives safely enough in the stomach, where we lose any command over it and where digestion itself takes the helm.

The Function of the Stomach

80:   Digestion is a completely mechanical function, and its apparatus can be considered as a mill furnished with sifters destined to extract whatever foods will serve to strengthen our bodies and to reject what is left when it has been drained of its nutritive parts.

There has for a long time been argument over the manner in which digestion takes place: whether it be by the action of heat, of ripening, of fermentation, of gastric or chemical or vital dissolution, etc.

It has a little of each of these things in it; and the only trouble with the whole thing has been that a single one was blamed in each case for the result of many necessarily united causes.

Foods, in effect, arrive in the stomach impregnated with all the fluids which the mouth and esophagus furnish them, and then are penetrated by the ample gastric juice which is always present there; they are submitted for several hours to a heat of about one hundred degrees Fahrenheit; they are sifted and mixed by the organic action of the stomach, which has been excited by their presence; one acts upon another, thanks to this juxtaposition; and it is impossible to avoid fermentation, since almost everything that is edible ferments.

As a result of all these processes, the chyle[2] or fluid form of digested food develops; the first supply of any aliment in the stomach is perforce the first to be seized upon; it passes through the pyloris and descends into the intestines: another bit follows it, and so on, until there is nothing left in the stomach, which has emptied itself, it can be said, by mouthfuls and in the same way it was filled.

The pyloris is a kind of fleshy funnel, which acts as communication between the stomach and the intestines; it is so formed that food can go back through it only with the greatest of difficulty. This important part of the viscera is sometimes obstructed; death from hunger is the result, after long and hideous suffering.

The intestine which receives the food as it passes from the pyloris is the duodenum; it has been thus named because it is about twelve finger-widths in length.

Once the chyle has reached the duodenum it undergoes still another change when it is mixed with the bile and the pancreatic juices; it loses the sour greyish color it had before, turns yellow, and begins to take on that faecal odor which grows steadily stronger as it approaches the rectum. The various substances involved in this mixture act upon each other: the chyle continues to form and develop, and analogous gases are born at the same time.

The continuation of the organic impulse which drives the chyle out of the stomach pushes it toward the small intestines: there it withdraws from the solid matter and is absorbed by the organs meant to use it, so that it is carried toward the liver, where it will mingle with the bloodstream, to rectify the losses caused by the absorption of the vital organs and by breathing.

It is rather difficult to explain how the chyle, which is a white and almost tasteless and odorless liquid, can thus extract itself from a solid mass whose color, taste, and odor are necessarily very pronounced.

However it may be, this extraction of the chyle seems the true purpose of digestion, and as soon as it has blended with the bloodstream, man is made aware of it by a feeling of renewed vitality and an instinctive realization that his bodily losses have been repaired.

The digestion of liquids is much less complicated than that of solids, and can be explained in a few words.

The nutritive particles of a liquid separate themselves from it, become part of the chyle, and share all its hazardous changes.

The purely liquid part is absorbed by the sucking interior of the stomach and thrown into the bloodstream: from there it is carried by the draining arteries to the kidneys, which filter and develop it, and by means of the ureters† lead it into the bladder in the form of urine.

---

† *These ureters are two tubes of the diameter of a goose-feather quill which lead from each of the kidneys and end at the rear of the bladder.*

Once it has arrived at this last receptacle, and in spite of being held there by a sphincter muscle, the urine does not stay long; its exciting action gives rise to a need to urinate; soon a voluntary constriction forces it into the light of day, and it gushes out through those irrigation canals which everyone knows about and which we have agreed never to name.

Digestion lasts a short or a long time, following the characteristics of each person. However, it can be allotted a general period of about seven hours: a little more than three hours of work for the stomach, and the rest for the passage as far as the rectum.

By means of this explanation, which I have extracted from the best writers and have tried as politely as possible to strip of its anatomical dryness and its scientific abstractions, my readers will be able to judge fairly accurately for themselves just where the last meal they have eaten is located: during the first three hours, it will be in the stomach; later, in the intestinal tract; and, after seven or eight hours, in the rectum, waiting its turn to be expelled.

Influence of Digestion

81: Digestion is of all the bodily operations the one which has the greatest influence on the moral state of the individual.[3] This assertion will astonish nobody, and cannot be contradicted.

The simplest psychological principles teach us that the human soul is influenced only be means of the organs which are its tools and which put it in contact with the outside world; from this it follows that when these organs are badly cared for, starved, or irritated, such a state of degradation exercises an inevitable power over the sensations which are the intermediary and occasional means of intellectual activity.

Thus the customary process of digestion, and above all its results, makes us habitually sad or gay, taciturn or talkative, morose or melancholy, without our even questioning it, and especially without our being able to deny it.

Under this subject could be classified the whole civilized world, in three main categories: the regulars, the constipated, and the diarrhetic.

It is well proven that the people found in each of these divisions not only have similar natural dispositions and certain propensities in common, but that they are even alike in some ways in their manners of fulfilling the duties which chance has thrust upon them during their lifetimes.

In order to clarify my point with an example, I shall take one from the vast field of literature. I believe that men of letters more often than not owe the style in which they have chosen to write to the state of their bowels.

Following this theory, the comic poets must be found among the regulars, the tragic among the most constipated, and the elegiac and pastoral among the lax and diarrhetic: from which it follows in turn that the most tearful poet is separated from the funniest by no more than a certain degree of intestinal activity.

It was in applying this same theory to the subject of courage that someone at the court of Louis XIV cried out, during the war days when Eugene of Savoy was doing his worst to France, "Oh, if I could only loosen his bowels for eight days! That way I could soon make of him the yellowest dastard in all Europe!"

And an English general once said, "Let us be sure to hurry our soldiers into battle while they still have a bit of good beef in their bellies!"

Digestion is often accompanied by a slight chilliness among the young, and by a strong wish to sleep among the old.

In the first case it is because Nature withdraws the surface heat of the body to use it in the interior; in the second, it is the same action, which, weakened by age, is not strong enough to take care at one time of both digestion and the excitation of the senses.

In the first moments of digestion, it is dangerous to give oneself up to mental labors, and still more dangerous to abandon oneself to the frenzies of physical passion. The current which flows always into the cemeteries of Paris carries along with it every year some hundreds of men who, after having dined well and sometimes after having dined too well, have not known how to close their eyes and stop up their ears.

This observation of mine has a warning in it, even for youth which perforce will pay no heed; a bit of advice for mature men, who forget that time never stops in its flight; and a life-

and-death law for men who have stepped over the brink of fifty (ON THE WRONG SIDE FIFTY).

Some people are cantankerous as long as they are digesting: this is not the time either to propose new projects or to ask favors of them.[4]

Marshal Augereau[5] was a fine example of this; for the first hour after he had eaten he was ready to kill anyone, friend or foe.

I once heard him say that there were in the army two people whose execution could at any moment be ordered by the commander in chief, that is the chief paymaster and the chief-of-staff. Both these gentlemen were present: General Chérin replied in an obsequious but witty way, and the paymaster said nothing but probably thought none the less on it.

I was at this time attached to the Marshal's staff, and my place was always laid at his table; but I rarely sat there, because of my dislike for these chronic fits of bad temper; I was afraid that, at a word from me, he might send me to digest my meal in prison.

I have often met him since then in Paris; and as he very obligingly told me of his regret at not having seen more of me in the old days, I did not hide the reason from him. We laughed together over it, and he more or less admitted that I had not been totally mistaken.

One time when we were stationed at Offenburg,[6] a complaint was made by the staff that there was neither game nor fish to eat.

This lament was justified, for it is a maxim of warfare that the conquerors must be well-fed at the expense of the conquered. Therefore, that very day I wrote a most polite letter to the chief forester, pointing out the evil and prescribing its remedy.

The forester was a tough old soldier, tall, dry, sun-parched, who could not stand the sight of us, and who undoubtedly made us uncomfortable in the hopes that we would not take root in his land. His answer, therefore, was more or less negative and full of evasions. His keepers had fled, afraid of our soldiers; the fishermen no longer paid attention to game laws; the waters were too high, etc., etc. I made no reply to such good reasons; but I sent him ten grenadiers to be well-lodged and boarded by him until further notice.

My ruse was successful: no more than two days later, at the crack of dawn, a richly and heavily loaded wagon arrived for us; the gamekeepers had obviously come back, and the fishermen were toeing the line, for we had been brought, in game and fish, enough to treat ourselves for more than a week: deer, woodcocks, carp, pike. It was a gift from heaven.

I delivered the unhappy forester from his hostages, on receiving such an expiatory windfall. He came to see us; I talked reasonably with him; and for the rest of our stay there we could have nothing but praise for his generosity.

THE TRANSLATOR'S GLOSSES

1. M. Jourdain, the chief character in Molière's BOURGEOIS GENTILHOMME, is an old merchant who has suddenly grown rich, and who hires a string of teachers to educate him. When one of them explains to him the difference between poetry and prose, the old fellow is astonished to find that all his life he has been speaking prose without even trying to!

2. Brillat-Savarin uses the word chyle throughout this section, although according to the great Greek physician Galen, who died about 200 A.D., there is a difference between chyle and chyme. The latter comes first, and is the acid pulp made from food by gastric secretion. From this, chyle is formed by the action of bile and pancreatic juice.

3. It is all too easy to add to this true truism, to quote what one more glib or inspired human being has said about it. Disraeli, for instance, who might fall into either category, once wrote in an essay on statesmanship: "A good deal depends upon education, something upon nerves and habit, but most upon digestion."

4. An endocrinologist once told me that the best procedure

when business must be combined with eating is to watch your victim's ear lobes and feed him rare beef. When his lobes turn ruddy, make your proposition . . . and quickly!

5.   Pierre François Charles Augereau (1757–1816) was a brilliant soldier who was made both Marshal of France and Duke of Castiglione by the grateful Napoleon, but who died in disgrace as a quisling.

6.   This pretty town in the grand duchy of Baden was captured by the French in 1797.

MEDITATION 17

ON REST

82: Man is not made to enjoy an indefinite activity; Nature has shaped him for an interrupted existence, and his perceptions are bound to cease after a certain period of time. This period can be prolonged by varying the sensations which are aroused in it; but such continuity of a man's existence ends by making him crave rest. Rest leads to sleep, and sleep brings dreams.

And here we find ourselves at the final fringes of humanity: the man who sleeps is no longer a social being. Although the law still protects him, he himself is outside its control.

This is the right place for me to relate a fairly singular incident which was told to me by Dom. Duhaget, who was prior, many years ago, of the Carthusian monastery at Pierre-Châtel.

Dom. Duhaget came from a very fine Gascon family, and had served with distinction in the army: he had been a captain in the infantry for twenty years, and was a chevalier of the order of Saint-Louis. I have never known a man of deeper piety nor one whose conversation was more delightful.

"When I was Prior at . . . , before coming to Pierre-Châtel," he began his story, "we had a brother of melancholic humor and sombre character, who was known to be a sleepwalker.

"Sometimes he would leave his cell and then return to it by himself, during an attack; occasionally he would lose his way and have to be led back. Doctors were consulted, and their prescriptions were followed; finally his seizures occurred less often, and we forgot to worry about him.

"One night when I had not gone to bed at my usual hour, but was at my desk going through some papers, I heard the door of my apartment open quietly, since I almost never kept it locked, and then I saw this brother enter, in a state of complete somnambulism.

"His eyes were wide open, but fixed. He wore only the tunic in which he was supposed to sleep, and he held an enormous knife in his hand.

"He went straight to my bed, whose place in the room he knew, and it seemed as if he verified, by feeling with his hand, the fact that I was really lying there. Then he struck three such ferocious blows that after the blade had pierced the covers it buried itself deep in the mattress, or rather in the bag of straw which served as one.

"When he had first passed before me, his face was contracted and scowling, but when he had finished his stabbing he turned around, and I could see that his whole countenance had cleared and that a look of satisfaction filled it.

"The light of the two lamps which burned on my desk made no impression on his eyes; he went out as he had entered, opening and closing with caution two doors which led to my cell, and soon I made sure that he had continued directly and peaceably to his own.

"You can imagine," the prior went on, "the state I was in during this ghastly performance. I shuddered with horror to see the danger I had escaped, and gave thanks to Providence for it; but my emotion was such that I could not close my eyes for the rest of the night.

"The next day I summoned the sleepwalker, and without mincing words asked him straightway of what he had dreamed the night before.

"He seemed disturbed by my question. 'Father,' he replied, 'I had such a strange dream that I am truly ashamed to tell it to you. It may be the work of a devil, and . . .'

" 'I order you to tell it,' I said to him. 'A dream is always involuntary; it is nothing but an illusion. Speak to me frankly.'

" 'Father,' he said then, 'I had hardly gone to bed when I dreamed that you had killed my mother, that her bloody ghost had appeared to me to demand vengeance, and that at this sight I was seized with such fury that I ran to your apartment and, finding you in your bed there, I stabbed you three times. A short time later I awoke, covered with sweat, revolted by my attack on you, and then I thanked God that such a terrible crime had not really been committed . . .'

" 'It had more nearly been committed than you knew,' I said to him with a serious but unruffled air.

"Then I told him of the night's happening, and showed him the traces of the blows which he had dreamed he dealt me.

"At this sight, he threw himself at my feet, weeping help-lessly, groaning at the thought of the thing which might have happened, and begging for whatever punishment I felt I must inflict on him.

" 'No, no,' I exclaimed. 'I cannot punish you for an involun-tary act! But from now on I shall release you from assisting at any of our night-time duties, and I must warn you that your cell will be locked on you from the outside, after the evening meal, and will not be opened until it is time for you to come to low mass at daybreak.' "

If, during this incident from which the prior escaped so mirac-ulously, he had been killed, the sleepwalking monk would not have been punished by law, for it would have been involuntary murder on his part.

Time for Repose

83: The general laws imposed on the globe which we inhabit have perforce influenced our own patterns of living. The al-ternating of night and day, which happens everywhere on earth with certain variations, but in such a way that in the end the two always strike a fair balance, has established a natural time for our activity and for our repose; probably our lives would be quite different if we spent them in an endless day.

However that may be, when man has enjoyed for a certain period the full pleasures of his existence, a moment arrives when he can no longer stand them; his impressionability gradually diminishes; the most skilful attacks directed against each of his senses are futile, his organs resist what they have most ardently coveted until now, and his soul is replete: it is the time for rest.

It is needless to say that we are here considering social man, surrounded by all the resources and good things of the highest civilization, for this need for repose comes much more quickly and regularly to everyone who is subjected to the fatigue of concentrated labor in his office, in his workroom, or while travelling, at war, hunting, and so on.

Nature, that excellent mother, has added to this rest, as to all her other restorative acts, a definite and deep pleasure.

The man who is resting has a sensation of well-being as general as it is undefinable, as his arms fall to his sides under their own weight, his muscles relax, and his brain grows fresher; his senses are quiet, and his sensations vague; he desires nothing, and thinks not at all; a filmy veil lies over his eyes. A few more instants, and he will be asleep.

MEDITATION 18

ON SLEEP

84:   In spite of the fact that there are a few men so organized that it can almost be said that they never sleep, still it is a general truth that the need for sleep is as imperious as hunger and thirst. Army sentinels in the most advanced positions often fall asleep, even when they have thrown snuff into their eyes to keep them open; and Pichegru,[1] tracked by Bonaparte's police, paid 30,000 francs for one night's sleep, during which he was betrayed and taken.

Definition

85:   Sleep is that state of torpor in which man, separated from objects outside of himself by the enforced inactivity of his senses, lives only as a mechanical being.

Sleep, like the night, is preceded by its own twilight and followed by its dawn: the first comes before absolute inertia, and the second leads back to active life.

We shall try to examine these different phenomena.

From the moment sleep begins, the organs of the senses fall little by little into inaction: first taste, next sight and smell;

hearing still stands guard awhile, and touch is ever there, to warn us by means of pain of the dangers which menace the body.

Sleep is always preceded by a more or less voluptuous sensation: the body falls into it with pleasure, sure of a prompt restoration of its powers, and the mind abandons itself to it without question, confident that its means of activity will soon be refreshed.

It is because this sensation has been misinterpreted, in spite of its positive nature, that even our greatest scientists have compared sleep to death, which every living creature resists with his whole soul, and which is marked by such special symptoms that even animals are horrified by it.

Like all pleasures, sleep can become a passion: there are people who have slept away three-quarters of their lives; and like all other passions, it will produce nothing but such evil things as laziness, indolence, weakness, stupidity, and death.

The school of Salerno[2] prescribed but seven hours of sleep, without distinction of age or sex. This doctrine is too severe; something more must be allotted to children from necessity and to women from inclination; but it can be considered as certain that whenever more than ten hours are spent in bed, it is excessive.

In the first moments of the twilight of sleep, will power is still present: a man can re-awaken, and his eyes can open and still see. *Non omnibus dormio*, said Maecenas;[3] and in this state more than one husband has verified unpleasant truths. Some ideas still obtrude, but they are incoherent; faint glimmerings of reason come and go; it seems as if indefinite objects swim in the air. This state lasts only a short time; soon everything disappears, all confusion ceases, and complete sleep reigns.

And what happens now to the mind, the soul? It lives on, secretly, alone; it is like the pilot of a becalmed ship, like a mirror in the black of night, like an unplucked lute; it waits for the rebirth of excitement and life.

There are certain psychologists, however, among them Count von Redern,[4] who hold that the soul never ceases its activity; von Redern gives as proof the fact that everyone who is rudely awakened from his first sleep has the same feeling he would experience if he had been interrupted at a very serious task.

This observation is not without reason, and deserves to be verified by more attentive study.

For the rest, the state of absolute unconsciousness is fairly short (it almost never lasts more than five or six hours); little by little the bodily losses are made good; an obscure realization of existence begins to re-awaken, and the sleeper passes into the kingdom of dreams.

THE TRANSLATOR'S GLOSSES

1. Charles Pichegru (1761–1804) was a famous French general, a dauntless royalist who was condemned to Cayenne for his plottings. In 1798 he escaped, and made his way by England and Germany to Paris, to plot once more to overthrow Napoleon. He was betrayed by one of his friends, imprisoned again, and like many another dangerously opinionated patriot in the world's history, was "found strangled" one day in his cell.

2. The medical college in this Italian town was the most famous in Europe, until the fifteenth century. Its dictum was stricter than that of King George III of England, who used to say, "Six hours are enough sleep for a man, seven for a woman or child, and eight for a fool." Child and woman, I have always needed the fool's portion, but I am in noble company: George himself is reported to have snoozed many an hour upon his throne.

3. Caius Cilnius Maecenas, who died in 8 B.C., was a very wealthy and astute patron of the great poets of his time. Horace and Virgil have left loyal proofs of his generosity, and quite unaided he has bequeathed to us an amusing proof of his diplomacy: one day when the Emperor Augustus visited him, he dozed, and the ruler kissed his wife, but then when a courtier in Augustus' retinue tried to take his amorous turn, Maecenas awoke sharply from his tactful nap, and exclaimed, "I do not sleep for *everybody!*"

4.   Sigismund Ehrenreich, Count von Redern (1755–1845) was a diplomat and man of letters who became a French citizen in 1811. He was highly thought of, and until they quarrelled was the partner of Saint-Simon, the great French social philosopher.

MEDITATION 19

ON DREAMS

86: Dreams are unilateral impressions which come to the mind (that is, the soul) without the aid of exterior objects.

These phenomena, so common and at the same time so extraordinary, are still but little understood.

It is the fault of the scientists, who have not yet presented to us a sufficiently detailed study. Such an essential work is bound to come to us in time, and then man's double nature will be better understood.

In the present state of science, we can only take as a fact the assumption that there is a fluid as subtle as it is powerful, which transmits to the brain the sensations received by the senses, and that it is from the excitation caused by these impressions that ideas are born.

Absolute sleep is the result of the waste and inertia of this fluid.

It is to be concluded that the labors of digestion and of assimilation, which are far from having ceased during sleep, make up this loss, so that there is a period of time in which the individual, while possessing all that he needs to spring into action again, still is not yet influenced by exterior objects.

Then the fluid, by nature mobile, flows into the brain through the nerve channels; it creeps into the same regions and follows the same paths as in the waking state, since its track is the same; therefore it produces the same effects, but with less intensity.

The reason for this last difference seems obvious enough to me. When a waking man is impressed by an exterior object, the sensation he experiences is precise, abrupt, and inevitable; the whole sensory organ is in action. When, on the contrary, the same impression is transmitted to him while he sleeps, it is only the hindpart of the nerves which is in action; the sensation must necessarily be less vivid and less positive. To make things even more easily understood, we can say that in a waking man there is a shock from the sensation in every organ, whereas in a sleeping man there is but some slight movement in the parts nearest the brain.

It is well known, however, that in voluptuous dreams Nature attains her end almost as successfully as when man is awake. This is the direct result of differences in the organs themselves, for our genitals need only one stimulus, and each sex possesses within itself everything that is needed to complete the act it has been made for.

Research Necessary

87: When the nervous fluid is thus carried to the brain, it always flows through the channels meant to be used by one of our senses, and that is why it awakens in them certain sensations or series of ideas instead of others. So it is that we think we are seeing when the optic nerve is aroused, and are hearing when the auditory nerves are influenced, and so on; and let us remark here as a singular thing the fact that it is very rare that the sensations felt in dreams have anything to do with taste and smell: when we dream of a garden or a meadow, we see flowers without savoring their perfume; when we think we are sitting down to a feast, we see the food without tasting it.

It would be a task worthy of any scientist to try to discover why two of our senses have no influence on the soul during sleep, while the four others flourish there in almost their full power. I know of no psychologist who has bothered with this.

Let us also remark that the more hidden our affections may be which we feel while sleeping, the stronger they are. Thus, the most sensual ideas are nothing compared with the anguish we may experience if we dream of losing a beloved child, or of being condemned to hang. Anyone in a like case can awaken bathed in sweat, or all damp with tears.

Nature of Dreams

88:   No matter how fantastic may seem the ideas which come to us in dreams, we must nevertheless admit if we look closely at them that they are nothing but recollections or combinations of them. I am tempted to say that dreams are no more than the memory of the senses.

Their strangeness consists solely in the fact that the association of these ideas is an unusual one, since it is beyond the laws of chronology, of social usages, and of time; the net result, in the last analysis, is that no man has ever dreamed of what was totally unknown to him.

One need not be too astonished at the extraordinary quality of dreams if he remembers that, in a waking man, four senses stand guard and check one another reciprocally: sight, hearing, touch, and memory. In a man who sleeps, each sense stands alone, dependent on its own resources.

I am almost tempted to compare these two states of mind to a piano before which is seated a musician who, letting his fingers stray idly over the keys, draws from them some sort of remembered melody, the while he could add to it a complete harmonization if he concentrated all his forces on it. This comparison could be carried much further, with the added comment that reflection is to ideas what harmony is to sounds, and that certain ideas hold others within them, just as a primary sound contains many others which are secondary to it, etc., etc.

Dr. Gall's System

89:   In letting myself be led thus easily into a subject which holds many charms for me, I find that I have run straight into the confines of the system of Dr. Gall, who preaches and upholds his doctrine of the multiformity of the brain parts.

I should not allow myself to go any further, nor to break down the bars which I have fixed for my own good; however, out of a love for science, to which it can easily be seen I am not a stranger, I cannot help writing here two observations which I have noted with great care, and which can be known as all the more truthful since several persons among my readers are still alive to testify to them.

First Observation

There was, about 1790, in a village called Gevrin near Belley, an extremely crafty merchant; he was named Landot, and had squeezed out for himself a fairly pretty fortune.

He was, all of a sudden, struck by such a paralytic stroke that everyone believed him dying. The best doctors came to his aid, and he pulled out of it, but not without damage, for he left behind him almost all his intellectual faculties, and most important of all his memory. However, since he could still drag himself about, somehow, and was once more able to eat, he was allowed to keep the control of his properties.

When he was seen in this condition, the unfortunate people who had had dealings with him decided that it was time to take their revenge on him. On the pretext of coming to pay him a little visit, they flocked from every corner to suggest bargains, purchases, sales, exchanges, and other procedures of this kind which until then had been his stock in trade. But his adversaries soon found themselves mightily surprised, and realized that it was time to take a new view of their prey.

The cunning old fox had lost none of his commercial instincts, and the same man who often did not recognize his own servants, and even forgot his name, was always up to the minute on the price of all commodities, as well as the current value of every acre of meadow, vineyard, or woods within three leagues of him.

On these matters his judgment had stayed unclouded, and since he was less suspect as an invalid than before, the greater part of those who had hoped to best the sick merchant were caught in the traps which they themselves had set.

Second Observation

There was in Belley a certain Monsieur Chirol, who had served for a long time in the royal bodyguard, both under Louis XV and Louis XVI.

His intelligence was just sufficient for the high function to which he had devoted his life;[1] but he possessed in an extravagant degree the sense of card playing, so that he not only knew all the old-fashioned games like Spanish ombre, piquet, and whist, but also was master of every subtlety of a new one after he had held three hands of it.

Well, this M. Chirol was hit like the old merchant by a stroke of paralysis, and so hard was the blow that he fell into a state of almost complete insensibility. Two faculties alone were left to him, those of digestion and of card playing.

Every day he went to the house where for more than twenty years he had kept his place at the card table, seated himself in a corner, and stayed there motionless and dozing, without paying attention to anything that went on around him.

The minute the time came to make up a game, he was asked to join it; he always accepted, and dragged himself toward the table; and there one would have sworn that the illness which had paralyzed the greater part of his faculties had not even touched his sense of play. And only a short time before his death he gave a superlative proof of the soundness of his reputation as a card player.

We were subjected, one time in Belley, to the visit of a Parisian banker whose name was, I believe, Delins. He brought proper letters of introduction; he was a stranger and he was from Paris: this was more than enough in a little town to make us all bustle to give him a pleasant stay.

M. Delins was both gourmand and card player. On the first count we kept him busy enough by holding him for five or six hours at a time at table; on the second he was harder to amuse: he was a great lover of piquet, and spoke easily of playing with six-franc counters, much higher stakes than any we had ever contemplated in Belley.

To overcome this social danger, the townspeople formed a league in which each one took or did not take shares, according to his presentiments: some said that Parisians know a fat lot more than the provincials, and others held, on the contrary, that all citizens of that great town have a certain amount of bluff in their make-up. However that may be, the league took shape; and to whom did it confide the great task of defending the common weal? . . . To M. Chirol.

When the Parisian banker saw this enormous pale blood-less form arrive, dragging one foot behind it, to seat itself across from him, he thought at first that it was a joke; but when he watched the ghost pick up the proper cards and deal them like a professional, he began to believe that at one time his adversary might have been worthy of him.

It did not take long to convince him that the gaming instinct still existed in the old man, for not only in this hand but in a great many more M. Delins was so beaten, skinned, and plucked that when he left he owed us more than six hundred francs, which were, of course, conscientiously divided among the members of the league.

Before he left Belley M. Delins called to thank us for the cordial welcome we had given him: in spite of it he could not help protesting against the decrepit state of the adversary we had presented to him, and he assured us that he would never be able to forgive himself for having taken such a thrashing from a corpse.

Conclusion

The summing up of these two observations is an easy one: it seems plain to me that the blow which, in both these cases, almost destroyed the brain, spared that part of it which had for so long been used in the schemes of commerce and card playing; and without doubt that portion of the organ resisted the shock either because continual exercise had made it more vigorous or because the same impressions, repeated over such a period of time, had left the most profound traces upon it.

Influence of Age

90:   Age has a marked influence on the nature of dreams.
In childhood one dreams of games, gardens, flowers, green

fields and other lightsome subjects; later, of pleasures and loves, strife, marriages; later still, of established households, travels, and the favors of the highborn or their representatives; finally, of business deals and worries, of fortunes, of past pleasures and of friends long dead.

Phenomena of Dreams

91: Certain unusual phenomena sometimes accompany sleep and its dreams: a study of them would do much to advance our knowledge of the laws of human behavior,[2] and for this reason I shall put down here three observations taken from many which, during the course of a rather long life, I have had a chance to make about myself during the night's silences.

First Observation

One time I dreamed that I had discovered the secret of how to free myself from the laws of gravity, so that I could go up or down in the air with equal ease and as I wished, since it made no difference to my body.

This state was delightful to me, and probably many people have dreamed something like it; but the remarkable thing about it is that I remember explaining very clearly to myself (or so it seemed) the methods which had led me to this result, and that they seemed so simple that I was astonished that they had not already been discovered.[3]

When I awoke, this explanation had vanished completely, but its result was still clear to me; and since that time I am utterly convinced that sooner or later a greater intelligence than mine will make this discovery. In any event, it was mine first!

Second Observation

92: Only a few months ago I experienced, in my sleep, a sensation of most extraordinary pleasure. It consisted of a kind of delicious shudder, in every particle that makes up my body. It was a form of prickling numbness, full of a rare charm, which, springing from my skin, penetrated to the very marrow of my bones, from my feet to the top of my head. I seemed to see a violet flame which flickered about my brow:

Lambere flamma comas, et circum tempora pasci.

I estimate that this condition, of which I was fully conscious physically, lasted at least thirty seconds, and I awoke from it filled with an astonishment which was not without a certain amount of terror.

From this experience, which is still very clear in my memory, and from many observations which have been made of persons in ecstatic or highly nervous states, I have come to the conclusion that the limits of human pleasure have never been either understood or set, and that we do not yet comprehend what point of bliss our own bodies can reach. I can only hope that within a few more centuries the future science of physiology will learn to control these extraordinary sensations, and will be able to produce them at will, just as sleep is now caused by opium; I can only hope that our great-great-nephews will find in them some compensations for the hideous suffering to which we are all at times subjected.[4]

This idea finds some support in analogy, for I have already pointed out that the art of harmony, which today gives us such vivid, pure, and eagerly studied beauties, was totally unknown to the Romans: it is a discovery made at most five hundred years ago.

Third Observation

93: One night in the year VIII of the Republic (1800), I awakened, having gone to bed without any untoward incidents, about one o'clock, when generally I would have been in my first sleep. I found myself in a state of mental excitement which was completely extraordinary: my conceptions were vivid, my thoughts profound; the whole sphere of my intelligence seemed to have expanded. I was sitting up in bed, and my eyes seemed to see about me a pale, vague, misty light, which did not serve in any way to illuminate the objects in the room.

If I judged only by the torrent of ideas which flooded through me in rapid succession, I would have believed that this sensation lasted several hours; but, according to my clock, I am sure that it was no more than thirty minutes. I was recalled from it by an outside incident over which I had no control, and was rudely brought back to earthly matters.

In a flash the sensation of light disappeared, and I felt myself sinking; the boundaries of my intelligence shrank; in a word, I was once again what I had been the evening before. But, since I had been completely awake during this experience, my memory still held on, although by now in muted colors, to a few of the ideas which had flooded my soul.

The first ones had time itself for their subject. It seemed to me that the past, the present, and the future were identical and meant the same thing, so that it was as easy to look ahead as it was to remember what had already happened. This is all that was left to me of the first intuition, which was partly obscured by the ones that followed it.

My attention was next drawn to the senses; I classified them in their order of perfection, and having come to believe that we must have as many of them within ourselves as outside, I set myself to look for them.

I had already found three, and almost four, when I fell back to earth again:

(1) *Compassion*, which is a kind of constriction of the heart felt when we see another person's suffering;

(2) *Predilection*, which is a sentiment of preference felt not only for an object itself, but for everything connected with this object or able to remind us of it;

(3) *Sympathy*, which is also a sentiment of preference felt by two objects drawn together by it.

It might be believed that the last two sensations are one and the same, but the great difference between them is that *predilection* is not always reciprocal, whereas *sympathy* is necessarily so.

Finally, as I considered *compassion*, I was led to a conclusion which I feel is a very true one, and which I would not have thought of at another time: it is from this sensation that springs the beautiful commandment, first principle of all human law:

Ne fais pas aux autres ce que tu ne voudrais pas qu'on te fit

DO AS YOU WOULD DONE BY

Alteri ne facias quod tibi fieri non vis

So strong, in truth, is the feeling which I still remember from the state I was in for that half-hour, that I would willingly give up the rest of my life, if it were possible, for one month of such an existence.

Writers will understand this much more easily than other people, for there are few of them who have not felt, in a much less powerful degree, of course, something like it.

An author, let us say, is warmly tucked into his bed, in a horizontal position, with his head well wrapped up; he thinks of the work he has in progress, his imagination takes fire, his ideas surge, phrases follow soon behind them, and since it is impossible to write lying flat,[5] he dresses, pulls off his nightcap, and seats himself at his desk.

And then, suddenly, he is not the same; his imagination grows dull, the thread of his thoughts is broken, and all the fine phrases have fled; he is forced to search painfully for what had come so easily to him, and more often than not he must put off to another and more fortunate day the work he has attempted.

All this can easily be blamed on the effect which the change of position and temperature must have on the brain: here is a good example of the influence of a physical state upon a moral one.

I have perhaps gone too far, because of my interest in this subject; but I have finally been led to think that the exaltation of Eastern priests is partly due to the fact that as Mohammedans they always have their heads warmly covered by their turbans, and that it must be to obtain quite opposite results that the law makers for our own monks have ordered that the tops of their heads be uncovered and shaved.[6]

*   *   *

THE TRANSLATOR'S GLOSSES

1. This is one of the straight-faced remarks that make the Professor's prose a continuous delight. Innocent on the surface, and even laudatory, it is a very amusing comment on the I.Q. of the average professional guardsman, at least in Brillat-Savarin's opinion.

2. Here was another of the Professor's "words": L'ANTHRO-PONOMIE. I do not know why I reshuffled it, except that I may at this point in the translation have felt some of the exasperation which led workers like Nimmo and Bain to label such an invention "barbarous . . . atrocious. . ."

3. I think it was in THE SUN ALSO RISES that someone said, "Never be daunted in public." I made a modish law of that when I was terrified and twenty, but I can still make an old social scar twinge and shudder, remembering the day when I was about six and told three little neighbors that I would prove to them, that very afternoon, that I could fly. I had often done so: usually it was alone, but often I took a quick turn around the dark bedroom ceiling after my little sister was asleep. I knew every sensation of freedom from the laws of gravity . . . The three children stood cynically, perhaps secretly ready to be envious. I jumped from a conservatively safe fifth step. But instead of the ineffably gentle breeze which I had known would flow about my bare feet, the hard stone hit them, and the children laughed, and I managed through my shock to seem not daunted. This long afterwards I can still remember, though, how it does feel to fly. I count myself fortunate.

4. Brillat-Savarin was a strong man who lived much longer and more happily than most of his fellows, but the compassion in this sentence proves that suffering was not a stranger to him. He would indeed have made a good doctor. If he were alive today, he might well be an anesthesiologist.

5. A few people have managed to do it, and a great many more have written, and written well, in bed. It remains for some liter-

ary-minded mattress company to make a good list of them, but meanwhile the wonderful picture of Mark Twain at work can cheer the soul of authors who might otherwise take the Professor's dictum too seriously. Those snowy pillows, that snowy mop of hair, that look of purity and comfort!

6.   It was apparently impossible for the Professor to stop teasing, in a gently sardonic way which is typical of his nature as well as his period in history, the priests who had caused, and endured, so much misery in France by the beginning of the nineteenth century. When he spoke of good men he admitted them as such, but in general he had little mercy for the brotherhoods, and managed quietly to imply that thanks to their fishy diets and their cold shaved pates they were a dangerous lot.

MEDITATION 20

ON THE INFLUENCE OF DIET UPON REPOSE, SLEEP, AND DREAMS

94: When a man is resting, whether or not he may sleep or dream, he does not cease to be under the power of the laws of nutrition, and cannot escape the confines of the empire of gastronomy.

Theory and experience work together to prove that the quality and the quantity of food have a very strong influence on man's labors, his sleep, and his dreams.

Effects of Diet on Labor

95: An undernourished person cannot long stand the fatigues of protracted labor; his body becomes covered with sweat; soon his strength evaporates with it, and for him a state of repose is nothing more than the impossibility of further activity.

If it is a question of mental labor, his ideas are born without either vigor or clarity; he lacks the power to reflect on them or the judgment to analyze them; his brain exhausts itself thus futilely, and he falls asleep on the battlefield.

I have always thought that the famous suppers at Auteuil, as well as those served at Rambouillet and Soissons,[1] had a great influence on the authors of the time of Louis XIV, and the sharp-tongued Geoffroy may not have been so mistaken (if the fact were true) when he taunted the poets of the end of the eighteenth century for drinking sugar water, which he insisted was their favorite potion.

According to this theory I have looked at the works of certain authors known to have been poor and unhealthy, and I must confess that I have seen few signs of real energy in them except when they have plainly been stimulated by self-complaint, or by a feeling of envy which was often badly disguised.

On the contrary, a man who eats well and who repairs his bodily losses with wisdom and discernment can withstand more exertion than any other living creature.

On the evening of the Emperor Napoleon's departure for Boulogne, he worked steadily for more than thirty hours, both with his Council of State and with the various heads of departments, on no more than two very short meals and a few cups of coffee.[2]

Brown[3] speaks of a clerk in the British Admiralty who, having lost by accident some state papers which he alone could duplicate, spent fifty-two consecutive hours rewriting them. Never in the world would this have been possible without an appropriate diet. He carried it out in the following way: first he drank water, then ate light dishes; then he took some wine, and then concentrated broths, and finally opium.

And one time I met an official messenger whom I had known in the army, and who had just arrived from Spain, where he had been sent on an urgent mission by our government (CORREO GANANDO HORAS.—SP.);[4] he had made the trip in twelve days, stopping only four hours in Madrid; a few glasses of wine and a few cups of bouillon, and there you have all that he touched during this long series of jolting days and sleepless nights; and he added that more solid food would have made him completely incapable of continuing his journey.[5]

*   *   *

About Dreams

96:   Diet has no less influence upon sleep and dreams.

Anyone who needs to eat cannot sleep; the torment in his stomach imprisons him in a wretched wakefulness, and if perchance weakness and exhaustion force him to doze, his sleep is light, troubled, and patchy.

On the contrary, anyone who has overstepped the limits of discretion in his meal falls immediately into absolute slumber: if he dreams in it, he will not remember, because the nervous fluid will have been utterly confused in its passage along the various canals. For the same reason his awakening is rude: he returns with difficulty to his social existence, and when his sleepiness has quite disappeared he will still feel for a long time the inconveniences of digestion.

It can be stated as a general maxim that coffee repels sleep. Habit can weaken and even wipe out completely this troublesome hazard; but invariably it occurs when Europeans first drink the brew. Some foods, on the contrary, lead agreeably to sleep: among such are all those made predominantly of milk, the whole family of lettuces, poultry, the succulent purslane, orange-flower water, and above all the rennet or dessert apples, when they are eaten just before one goes to bed.[6]

Continuation

97:   Experience, based on millions of observations, has taught us that diet determines our dreams.

In general, all foods which are mildly excitant make us dream: among such are the red meats, pigeons, duck, venison, and especially hare.

This quality is also recognized in asparagus, celery, truffles, highly flavored candies, and especially vanilla.

It would be a great mistake to believe that we should banish from our tables whatever is thus troubling, for the dreams which result are in general very pleasant and light, and may prolong life even when it seems to be suspended and least real.

There are some people for whom sleep is an existence apart, a kind of prolonged novel, which is to say that their dreams have sequence to them, so that they can end one night what they had begun to dream the night before, and recognize many faces in their dreams which they have already seen there, and which they still have never beheld in actual life.

Result

98: Any man who has thought seriously about his physical existence, and who leads it according to the principles which we are here outlining, is one who prepares himself sensibly for his repose, his sleep, and his dreams.

He divides his work so that he will never overtire himself at it; he makes it lighter by giving it a certain variety, and he refreshes his taste for it by short intervals of rest which relax him without interrupting that continuity of his labors which is so often essential.

If, during the day, a longer period of rest is necessary to him, he never yields to it except in a sitting position; he refuses to go to sleep, unless he is irresistibly conquered by it, and above all he never permits himself to form the habit of nap-taking.

When night has brought with it the time of natural repose, he retires to a well-ventilated room, does not surround himself with curtains which would force him to breathe the same air a hundred times, and takes care not to close his shutters completely, so that whenever his eyes half open he may be comforted by a soft glow of light.[7]

He stretches himself out on a bed whose head is slightly raised; his pillow is of horsehair; his nightcap is of linen; his breast is not crushed under a pile of heavy blankets, but he takes care that his feet are warmly covered.

He has eaten with discernment, and has not refused whatever was either good or extra-good; he has drunk of the better and, with precaution, even the best wines. At the end of the repast he has talked more of flirtations than of politics, and he has quoted more gay songs than epigrams; he has taken a cup of coffee, if his make-up permits it, and has accepted, after a few seconds' hesitation, a tiny glass of liqueur, solely to please his palate. In everything he has shown himself as a pleasant companion, and an appreciative guest, and still he has but lightly overstepped the limits of plain thirst and hunger.

In this state he goes to bed, content with himself and his

fellows. His eyes close. He dozes through the dusk of sleep, and then for a few hours lies in complete unconsciousness.

Before long Nature has accepted its due; assimilation has made up the bodily losses. Then pleasant dreams come, to lead him into a mysterious existence; he sees people he loves, once more plays his favorite games, and finds himself transported to lands where he was happy long ago.

Finally he feels sleep withdrawing from him by degrees, and he goes back to society without once regretting the lost time, because even while he was asleep he enjoyed activity without fatigue and pleasures without fear of pain or censure.

THE TRANSLATOR'S GLOSSES

1.   These were all gathering-places of celebrated men of letters and intellectual aristocrats, from the time of Molière (1622–1673) in Auteuil through the residence in Soissons of Olympia Mancini. A general air of "plain living and high thinking" seems to have reigned in the salons of that period, but it was especially in Rambouillet, the most famous of them from 1646 until 1665, that Catherine de Vivonne-Pisani's suppers were "more renowned for their flow of reason and their feast of soul," than for their gastronomical delights.

2.   Any man must know the devil he plays with. Once he has acknowledged his respect he can as often as not emerge victor in a bout with time and sleeplessness, as did Napoleon.

The opposite of this shrewd balance is a man who in 1935 had to drive from Hollywood to New York in an impossibly short time to satisfy the impossibly long ego of his employer. Tablets of benzedrine were being sold by any druggist in those innocent days, and the man bought a bottleful, and as he grew tireder on the long, hungry, sleepless haul across Texas in his little Ford he popped pill after pill of the new drug into his mouth. The car hurtled on.

Suddenly on the flat desert he was driving through a gap, in high blue mountains, so narrow that the sides hit his car with inaudible shrieks and crashings, and then ahead of him a house floated crosswise, and a monstrous purple man with a foaming mastiff straddled the road, straining to leap.

The driver went through them as through fog, every nerve in him assaulted and outraged and shocked. He stopped the little car as best he could, and on the roadside poured a flask of water over his head, and at the next town he went to a hotel, bathed, slept, and bought a train ticket to New York, while his Ford and the half-empty bottle of pills sat in a garage.

This was, to him at least, a good example of human stupidity in not weighing the power of the stimulant against the condition of the body to be stimulated. Napoleon before Boulogne knew not only the importance of his sleeplessness to his own fate and Europe's, but the comparative strengths of his nerves and his chosen drug. The man in the Ford forgot his potentialities and weaknesses in the uncharted possibilities of a new toy.

3. Dr. Thomas Brown (1778–1820) was a professor of note at the University of Edinburgh, especially for his LECTURES ON THE PHILOSOPHY OF THE HUMAN MIND.

4. Here is another sample of the "five living languages" the Professor admitted to speaking "more or less well." For some reason he never identified Italian as such, but he was fairly meticulous about labelling Spanish and German.

5. When Lindbergh flew solo over the Atlantic Ocean in May, 1927, he took five sandwiches with him. But in the 33½ hours he was alone in his plane, he ate only one and a half of them. And two years later people in France were still shaking their heads incredulously over the freakish fact that once on the ground again he spurned the champagne that spouted in fountains in his honor, but instead had some cold milk and a roll, before he went to bed.

6. Francis Bacon once wrote: "These procure quiet sleep: violets; lettuce, especially boiled; syrup of dried roses; saffron; balm; apples, at our going to bed."

7. When I first lived in France, more than a hundred years after this sensible advice was first published, I was severely scolded for opening my windows, much less my shutters, after dark. The night air was bad, my landlady told me; it was laden with a thousand germs which could not stand sunlight and must

wait until then to pounce on me . . . It was not for many months, when I had grown to know her peculiar stinginess (and like her in proportion), that I realized she had less than no interest in what black pox filled my chamber, but that she could not stand the thought of letting good warm air escape . . . air that it cost energy and even a few sous to heat!

MEDITATION 21

ON OBESITY

99:   If I had been a graduate physician, I would first of all have written a detailed monograph on overweight; then I would have set myself up as ruler of this part of the scientific realm, to enjoy the double advantage of having the healthiest of all patients on my list, and of being besieged daily by the prettier half of the human race, for it is the life study of all women to maintain a perfect weight, neither too heavy nor too light.

What I have missed doing, another doctor will do; and if he is at one and the same time well-educated, discreet, and good-looking, I predict miracles for him.

Exoriare aliquis nostris ex ossibus haeres! [1]

While I wait for this, I can at least open up the rich vein of ore, for an article on obesity is more than proper in a work which has as its subject whatever nourishes mankind.

By *obesity* I mean that state of fatty congestion in which a person's bodily parts gradually grow larger, without his being ill, and lose their form and their original harmonious proportions.

There is one kind of obesity which centers around the belly; I have never noticed it in women: since they are generally made up of softer tissues, no parts of their bodies are spared when obesity attacks them. I call this type of fatness GASTROPHORIA, and its victims GASTROPHORES. I myself am in their company; but although I carry around with me a fairly prominent stomach, I still have well-formed lower legs, and calves as sinewy as the muscles of an Arabian steed.[2]

Nevertheless I have always looked on my paunch as a redoubtable enemy; I have conquered it and limited its outlines to the purely majestic; but in order to win the fight, I have fought hard indeed: whatever is good about the results and my present observations I owe to a thirty-year battle.

I shall begin this discussion with a condensation of more than five hundred conversations which I have held with my dinner companions who were threatened or afflicted with obesity.

Fat Man—Heavens, what delicious bread! Where do you buy it?

Myself—At Monsieur Limet's, rue de Richelieu: he is baker for Their Royal Highnesses the Duke of Orleans and the Prince of Condé: I began to go to him because he is my neighbor, and I shall continue to do so because I have already called him the best breadmaker in existence.

Fat Man—I must make a note of that; I eat a great deal of bread, and if I could get such rolls as these I'd gladly do without any others.

Another Fat Man—What on earth are you doing there? You're eating the liquid from your soup, and leaving that wonderful Carolina rice!

Myself—I am following a special diet I have prescribed for myself.

Fat Man—What a dreadful one! I love rice as much as I do thickenings, Italian pastes, and all those things: there's nothing more nourishing, nor cheaper, nor easier to prepare.

Particularly Fat Man—Will you be good enough, my dear sir, to pass me the dish of potatoes which is in front of you? At the rate they're disappearing, I'm afraid I'll miss out.

Myself—Certainly they are within reach, are they not?

Fat Man—But won't you have some too? There are enough for both of us, and after that who cares?

Myself—No, I shan't take any. I value potatoes solely as preventives of actual famine. Aside from that, I know of nothing more completely tasteless.

Fat Man—But that's gastronomical heresy! Nothing is better than potatoes; I eat them in every form, and if there happen to be any in the next part of the dinner, whether *à la Lyonnaise* or in a soufflé, I here and now declare myself for the allotting of my just share of them.

Fat Lady—It would be so very kind of you if you would bring me from the other end of the table some of those Soissons beans which I see there. . .

Myself, after having carried out the command while paraphrasing a well-known song in a low voice.—

Happy the folk of Soissons parish!
Beans on their very doorsteps flourish . . .

Fat Lady—You shouldn't joke. The whole district is made richer by them. Paris alone pays a considerable amount of money for its supply. And I must also come to the defense of those ordinary little beans now called *English:* when they are still green, they make a dish fit for the gods.

Myself—A pox on all beans! A pox even on little common English beans!

Fat Lady—And that's enough of your scorn! One might almost think that you were the sole judge of such matters!

Myself, to another Fat Lady—Permit me to congratulate you on your good health; it seems to me, Madame, that you have grown a wee bit heavier since I last had the honor to see you.

Fat Lady—I probably owe it to my new diet.

Myself—But how is that?

Fat Lady—For some time now I've made my luncheon of some good rich soup, a bowl big enough for two, and what a marvelous soup it is! A spoon could stand straight up in it!

Myself, to still another—Madame, if your glance does not deceive me, you will accept a spoonful of this charlotte? [3] I shall plunge into it in your honor.

Fat Lady—Ah, my dear sir, your eyes do indeed deceive you! I see two things I especially adore here on the table, and both of them have a French name of the masculine gender: this *gateau de riz* with its golden crust, and then this enormous *biscuit de Savoie,* for I can tell you for your records that I simply dote upon sweet cakes.

Myself, to another—While all that serious discussion is going on at the other end of the table, Madame, may I put the question to this almond tart for you?

Fat Lady—But gladly! Nothing delights me more than pastry. We have a pastry cook as one of our tenants, and between my daughter and myself, I truly believe that we eat up the price of his rent, and a little more besides.

Myself, having looked at the young lady—This diet is wonderfully becoming to you! Your charming daughter is a very beautiful creature, and more than generously equipped.

Fat Lady—Well, it is hard to believe, but some of her dearest companions sometimes tell her that she is too fat!

Myself—Perhaps they are jealous of her?

Fat Lady—That might be. Anyway, I am about to get her married, and the first baby will take care of all that . . .

And it is from such dialogues that I made clear to myself a theory which I had formed quite apart from its human connections, that the principal cause of any fatty corpulence is always a diet overloaded with starchy and farinaceous elements; it is from these conversations that I was able to prove to myself that this same diet is always followed by the same effects.

Certainly meat-eating animals never grow fat (think of the wolves, jackals, birds of prey, crows, etc.).

Herbivorous beasts seldom grow fat either, except as old age forces them into a life of greater repose; on the other hand they gain weight quickly and in any season when they are forced to eat potatoes, grains, and any kind of flour.

Obesity is never found either among savages or in those classes of society which must work in order to eat or which do not eat except to exist.

*　　　*　　　*

Causes of Obesity

100: It is easy enough to designate the causes of obesity, according to the preceding observations, which anyone can verify for himself.

The first is the natural temperament of the individual. Almost all men are born with certain predispositions which influence their physiognomy. Out of a hundred people who die from an illness of the chest, ninety have dark brown hair, long faces, and noses that come to a point. Out of a hundred fat people, ninety have short faces, round eyes, and snub noses.

It follows therefore that some people in whom the digestive forces manufacture, all things being equal, a greater supply of fat are, as it were, destined to be obese.

This physical truth, of which I am profoundly convinced, has a miserable influence on my way of looking at things, occasionally.

When a gay, rosy-cheeked girl appears in a drawing room, a little miss with roguish nose, delightful curves, plump tiny hands and feet, everyone is completely charmed by her, while I, taught by experience, see her as she will be in another ten years. I see the ravages which fatness will have wreaked on this appealing freshness, and I groan over misfortunes which have not yet come. My anticipated compassion is a painful sentiment, and furnishes one more proof among a thousand others that mankind would be much unhappier if it could see into the future.

The second principal cause of obesity lies in the starches and flours which man uses as the base of his daily nourishment. As we have already stated, all animals who live on farinaceous foods grow fat whether they will or no; man follows the common rule.

Starch produces this effect more quickly and surely when it is used with sugar: both sugar and fat contain hydrogen and both are combustible. The mixture of sugar with flour is all the more active since it intensifies the flavor, and since we seldom eat sweetened dishes before our natural hunger has been satisfied, and all that is left is that other more refined appetite which we must flatter and tempt by the subtlest tricks of art and variety.

Yeast flour is no less fattening when it is absorbed in such drinks as beer. The people who drink them habitually are the ones who develop the most marvellous bellies, and certain families in Paris who drank beer in 1817 for economy's sake, because wine was very dear then, found themselves repaid by added weight which they now find quite unwelcome.

Continuation

101: A double cause of obesity results from too much sleep combined with too little exercise.

The human body repairs many of its natural losses during sleep, and in the same way it loses little then, since its muscular action is suspended. It is necessary therefore to dispose of any superfluities by exercise; however, the more anyone sleeps, the more he limits the time in which he could be active.

In addition, long sleepers shun anything which will put them in the slightest danger of fatigue; whatever cannot be assimilated is absorbed into the circulation, and there, in an operation which Nature keeps secret from us, it takes on an additional percentage of hydrogen, fat is formed, and it is swept by the circulatory flood into all the cellular tissues.

Continuation

102: The final cause of obesity is excess, whether in eating or drinking.

It has rightly been said that one of the privileges of the human race is to eat without hunger and drink without thirst: this is naturally not an attribute of the animals, since it springs from reflection on the pleasures of the table and from the desire to prolong them.

This double penchant has been found wherever man himself exists, and it is well known that savages will eat gluttonously and drink themselves insensible whenever they have the chance to.

As for us, citizens of the old and new worlds who believe ourselves to be the finest flower of civilization, it is plain that we eat too much.

I do not say this of the small number of people who, enclosed in their own avarice or impotence, live alone and apart, the former uplifted by the thought of the money they thus save and the latter bewailing the fact that they can do no better. I do say it with firmness of all those who, everywhere about us, are time after time hosts or guests, entertaining with graciousness or accepting with pleasure; all those who, feeling no more physical hunger, eat a dish because it is attractive to them, and drink a wine merely because it is unfamiliar. I say it of them whether they sit down every day to a banquet or only celebrate on Sundays and occasionally Mondays: for in this immense majority, every single person eats and drinks too much, and enormous masses of foodstuffs and potables are absorbed every day without need.

This cause of obesity, almost always present, acts differently according to the constitution of the individual, and for people with delicate stomachs the result is not so much overweight as indigestion.

Anecdote

103: We once had before our very eyes an example of this which half of Paris knew about.

Monsieur Lang kept up one of the most brilliant houses of the city; above all his table was excellent, but his digestion was as weak as his love of good food was powerful. He was a perfect host, and ate everything with a courage worthy of a more important cause.

Everything would go well for him until he had finished his after-dinner coffee; soon, then, his stomach would rebel at the work he had inflicted on it, his suffering would begin, and the wretched gastronomer would be obliged to throw himself on a couch, where he must lie until the next morning, paying with prolonged anguish for the short pleasures he had enjoyed.

The most remarkable thing is that he never changed his habit; as long as he lived, he accepted this strange alternative, and the sufferings of one day had no influence on the delights of the next.

Among people who have strong active stomachs, any excesses of nutrition are disposed of as outlined in my preceding article: everything is digested, and whatever is not needed to repair bodily losses undergoes a chemical change and turns into fat.

Among the rest of the people there is a kind of perpetual indigestion: foods flow through them unprofitably, and those who do not understand the reason are astonished that so many good things do not produce a happier result.

It is easily apparent that I am not making an exhaustive outline of this subject: there is a mass of secondary causes of obesity which spring from our habits, professions, occupations, and pleasures, and which encourage and activate the ones I have already discussed.

I leave all this to the successor whom I have already mentioned at the beginning of the Meditation, and shall content myself with this foretaste, which is the right of anyone who first penetrates into new territory.

Intemperance has for a very long time caught the attention of observing people. Philosophers have praised its opposite, princes have made sumptuary laws, religion has preached against gourmandism; alas, we have swallowed not a bite the less, and the art of overeating grows more flourishing every day!

I shall perhaps be more fortunate than these other moralizers if I take a new tack, and expose the *physical inconveniences* of *obesity*; man's interest in his own well-being (SELF-PRESERVATION) will possibly be more influential than morality, more persuasive than sermons, and more powerful than laws, and I feel that the fair sex, at least, is quite ready to open its eyes to the truth.

Inconveniences of Obesity

104: Obesity has a distressing influence on the two sexes in that it destroys both strength and beauty.

It destroys strength, since although it adds to the weight of the body which is to be moved it does not add to the muscular power; it is still further destructive since it hinders breathing, which makes impossible any labor demanding a prolonged use of muscular force.

Overweight destroys beauty by wrecking the basic harmonies of proportion, since all parts of the body do not grow heavier in an even way.

Furthermore obesity fills up those hollows which Nature formed to add highlights and shadows: thus, nothing is commoner than to see faces which once were very interesting and which fatness has made almost insignificant.

The head of our last government, Napoleon I, could not escape this law. He grew heavier during his last campaigns; he changed from pale to pasty, and his eyes lost much of their proud luster.

Obesity brings with it a distaste for dancing, for taking walks, and for horseback riding, and an inaptitude for all those occupations and amusements which demand a little agility or skill.

It also predisposes its victims to various illnesses, such as apoplexy, dropsy, and ulcers on the legs, and makes all other afflictions more difficult to cure.

Examples of Obesity

105: I can remember only two really fat heroes, Marius and Jean Sobieski.[4]

Marius, who was very short, became as wide as he was high, and it was perhaps these fantastic proportions which so terrified the Cimbrian appointed to assassinate him.

As for the Polish king, his obesity was almost the death of him: forced to flee before a troop of Turkish cavalry, his breath soon failed him, and he would undoubtedly have been massacred if some of his aides-de-camp had not supported his fainting form upright upon his horse, while others sacrificed themselves generously to hold off the enemy.

If I am not mistaken the Duke of Vendôme,[5] that worthy son of the great Henry, was also of a remarkable corpulence. He died in a roadside tavern, abandoned by everyone, still keeping enough of his faculties about him to see one of his intimates snatch out from under him the pillow on which he lay as he breathed his last.

Books are full of examples of monstrous obesity; I shall leave them there and instead give briefly a few which I myself have known.

Monsieur Rameau, a fellow student of mine who became mayor of La Chaleur in Burgundy, was only five feet two inches tall, and weighed five hundred pounds.

The Duke of Luynes, with whom I have often sat,[6] became enormous; overweight ruined his handsome figure, and he passed the last years of his life in an almost uninterrupted doze.

But the most extraordinary case of this kind that I ever saw was a resident of NEW YORK,[7] whom many Frenchmen still living in Paris may have seen on Broadway, seated in a huge armchair whose legs could have held up a church.

Edward, as he was called, was at least five feet ten inches high, French measurement, and since fat had swollen every part of him, he was a minimum of eight feet in circumference. His fingers were like those of the Roman emperor who wore his wife's necklaces for rings; his arms and legs were tubular, as thick as a medium-sized man, and his feet were like an elephant's, half hidden by the hanging flesh of his limbs; the weight of fat had dragged down his lower eyelids, so that they were fixed in a stare; but what made him most hideous were three spheroid chins which hung on his chest for a foot or more, so that his face seemed like the capital of a wreathed pillar.

In this state Edward spent his life, seated near the window of a low room which opened onto the street, drinking from time to time a glass of ale from an immense pitcher of it which was always beside him.

Such an amazing figure could not help but be stared at, but as soon as he felt himself watched by the passersby Edward did not wait long to send them packing, by saying to them in a sepulchral voice, "WHAT HAVE YOU TO STARE LIKE WILD CATS? . . . GO YOU WAY YOU LAZY BODY . . . BE GONE YOU FOR NOTHING DOGS . . . "[8] (Qu'avez-vous a regarder d'un air effaré, comme des chats sauvages? . . . Passez votre chemin, paresseux . . . Allez-vous-en, chiens de vauriens!) and other similarly charming phrases.

I used to chat with him occasionally, since I knew him well enough to greet him by name; he insisted that he was not at all bored or unhappy, and that if death would not come to disturb him he would be delighted to sit there and wait for the end of the world.

From all that I have discussed in this chapter it is plain that if obesity is not actually a disease, it is at least a most unpleasant state of ill health, and one into which we almost always fall because of our own fault.

We can also conclude that everyone must earnestly desire

to avoid obesity, who is not already overweight, and that whoever is obese must try to escape from that state. It is to help these people that we shall now see what science, aided by common sense, can suggest as remedies.[9]

THE TRANSLATOR'S GLOSSES

1. Brillat-Savarin underlined this last word of the line from Virgil's AENEID, which he had changed to read, "There may arise some *heir* out of our bones," instead of "avenger."

2. It is impossible to know how much of this self-description is taken seriously by the Professor, especially just after he has coined the impressive word GASTROPHORIA to mean "paunchbellied"! But many otherwise humorous gentlemen fail ever to see anything amusing about their looks, and will glance at themselves in any mirror with more smugness than the world's prettiest actress feels.

3. Any delicate creamy dessert which is poured into a casserole lined with buttered bread or wafers and let chill can be called a charlotte. A good recipe to point the Professor's moral is the following, from a nineteenth century cookbook: For a half-hour work into a creamy paste one pound of blanched shaved almonds, one pound of fine sugar, and one pound of sweet fresh butter. Make a thick cream with 18 eggs, three pints of cream, one-half pound of vanilla-flavored sugar, and the necessary fine flour. Let it cool, and slowly mix into it the almond butter. Pour into a well-buttered charlotte mold lined with thin wafers, let chill twelve hours, turn out, and serve.

4. Caius Marius (150–86 B.C.) was longtime leader of the democratic party in Rome. Sobieski (1624–1696) led a victorious army against the Turks at Vienna, in 1683.

5. Louis-Joseph, duc de Vendôme (1654–1712), was not the son but the grandson, by a bastard father, of Henry IV. He can be called worthy on the strength of his fine leadership, it is true, but otherwise his character was depraved and unadmirable.

6.   Louis-Joseph-Charles-Amable, duc de Luynes (1748–1807), was one of the very few aristocrats who did not flee France during the first Revolution. He was a Member of the Constituent Assembly with Brillat-Savarin.

7.   If it were not for this preamble, preface, and/or introduction, here would be the shortest marginal gloss in all the book: "Sic!"

8.   This is perhaps the worst example of Brillat-Savarin's self-assumed role of purveyor of Yankee idiom, and in spite of the fact that several editions show the same embarrassing faults it seems most charitable, at least to one as prejudiced as I, to assume that somewhere a printer was at his most shaky.

9.   "Agayns glotonye the remedie is abstinence." Chaucer.

MEDITATION 22

PREVENTATIVE
OR CURATIVE
TREATMENT OF
OBESITY†

106: I shall begin with a story which proves that it takes real courage either to lose weight or to keep from gaining it.

M. Louis Greffulhe, who was later honored by His Majesty with the title of count, came to see me one morning, and told me he understood that I was interested in the subject of obesity, and that since he was in grave danger of it he wished my advice.

"Sir," I said to him, "since I am not a graduate doctor, I would be within my rights to refuse to counsel you. However, I am at your command, but on a single condition, that you will give me your word of honor to follow, for one month, and with the greatest fidelity, the rules of conduct which I shall prescribe for you."

---

† About twenty years ago I undertook to write a treatise EX PROFESSO on obesity. My readers will especially regret not being able to read its preface: it was in dramatic form, and in it I proved to a doctor that fever is much less dangerous than a legal trial, for the latter, after having made the plaintiff dash about, wait in court, lie, and curse his fate, after having deprived him indefinitely of repose, and of pleasure, and of money, finally finishes by making him ill and killing him with vexation. This is a fact as proper to expose as any other.

M. Greffulhe made the promise I demanded. We shook hands
on it, and the very next day I delivered to him my *fetva*,[1] the
first order of which was for him to weigh himself at the beginning and end of the treatment, so that we might have a mathematical basis on which to judge the results.

One month later M. Greffulhe returned to see me, and spoke
to me in much the following terms:

"Sir, I have followed your prescription as faithfully as if my
life depended on it, and I have verified the fact that my weight
has gone down by some three pounds, or even a little more. But,
in order to achieve this, I have been forced to submit all my
tastes and all my habits to such a violent assault, and in a word
I have suffered so much, that while I offer you all my thanks
for your excellent advice, I must renounce what good it might
do for me, and abandon myself in the future to whatever Providence has in store."

After this decision, which I did not hear without real distress,
the inevitable occurred: M. Greffulhe became more and more
obese, was the victim of all the inconveniences of extreme corpulence, and, when he was barely forty years old, died as the
result of an asthmatic condition to which he had become subject.

Generalities

107:   Any cure of obesity[2] must begin with the three following
and absolute precepts: discretion in eating, moderation in sleeping, and exercise on foot or on horseback.

Such are the first commandments which science makes to us:
nevertheless I place little faith in them, for I know both men
and things, and any such prescription which is not followed to
the letter is fairly futile.

Now in the first place it needs great strength of character for
a man to get up from the table while he is still hungry; as long
as appetite lasts, one mouthful leads to another with irresistible
attraction; and in general he eats as long as he feels the need
to, in defiance of doctors and sometimes even in imitation of
them.

As for the second prohibition, it is a painful insult to fat
people to tell them to get up early in the morning: they will
assure you that it is bad for their health; that when they arise

too soon they are worthless for the rest of the day; the women will complain of having circles under their eyes; all are quite willing to stay up late at night, but they insist on sleeping late the next morning; and there you have one more prescription to be neatly avoided.

Thirdly, horseback riding is a costly remedy, which is appropriate neither to all fortunes nor to all occupations.

Suggest to a charming fat lady that she mount a horse, and she will consent with great pleasure, but on three conditions: first, she must have a steed which is at one and the same time handsome, lively, and gentle; second, she must have a riding habit which is new and tailored in the latest style; third, she must have to accompany her a groom who is agreeable and good-looking. It is rather rare to fill all three of these requirements, so she does not ride at all.

Exercise on foot gives rise to even more objections: it is horribly tiring, and the perspiration it brings out places one in grave danger of false pleurisy; dust ruins the stockings, stones wear out the soles of dainty slippers, and the whole business is hopelessly boring. Finally if, after these various attempts, a tiny headache is felt, or an almost invisible spot shows itself on the skin, the whole system of exercise is blamed and abandoned, and the doctor fumes helplessly.

Therefore, while it is admitted that anyone who wishes to reduce his weight should eat moderately, sleep but little, and exercise as much as possible, another method must be sought to attain the same end. There is, indeed, one infallible system for keeping weight from becoming excessive, or for lessening it if it has already reached this point. This system, which is founded on the most solid precepts of both physics and chemistry, consists of a diet adapted to whatever effect is desired.

Of all medical prescriptions, diet is the most important, for it acts without cease day and night, waking and sleeping; it works anew at every meal, so that finally it influences each part of the individual. Now, an antifat diet is based on the commonest and most active cause of obesity, since, as it has already been clearly shown, it is only because of grains and starches that fatty congestion can occur, as much in man as in the animals; in regard to these latter, this effect is demonstrated every day under our very eyes, and plays a large part in the commerce of fattened beasts for our markets, and it can be deduced, as an exact consequence, that a more or less rigid abstinence from everything that is starchy or floury will lead to the lessening of weight.

"Oh Heavens!" all you readers of both sexes will cry out, "oh Heavens above! But what a wretch the Professor is! Here in a single word he forbids us everything we most love, those little white rolls from Limet, and Achard's cakes, and those cookies from . . . , and a hundred other things made with flour and butter, with flour and sugar, with flour and sugar and eggs! He doesn't even leave us potatoes, or macaroni! Who would have thought this of a lover of good food who seemed so pleasant?"

"What's this I hear?" I exclaim, putting on my severest face, which I do perhaps once a year. "Very well then; eat! Get fat! Become ugly, and thick, and asthmatic, and finally die in your own melted grease: I shall be there to watch it, and you may as well understand now that in my next edition . . . But what do I see? A single phrase has convinced you. It has terrified you, and you beseech me to hold back my lightning . . . Be reassured; I shall map out a diet for you, and prove to you that there are still a few pleasures left for you here on this earth where we live to eat.

"You love bread: very well then, you can eat it made of rye:[3] the estimable Cadet-de-Vaux[4] has preached its virtues for a long time; it is less nourishing and most important of all it is less pleasant, which perforce makes it easier to carry out the prescription! The first thing to do, you know, is to flee temptation. Remember that: it is a question of your morale.

"You love soup, so have it made *à la julienne*, with green vegetables, cabbages, and root vegetables; I must forbid you to drink it made with bread, starchy pastes, or flour.

"At the first part of the meal almost everything is proper for you to eat, with a very few exceptions such as rice with poultry and the crusts of hot pasties. Enjoy it all, but with discretion, so that later you will not find yourselves satisfying a nonexistent hunger.

"The second half of the meal will appear then, demanding a philosophical attitude on your part. Shun anything made with flour, no matter in what form it hides; do you not still have the roast, the salad, the leafy vegetables? And since you must give up a few sugary dishes, choose instead a chocolate custard or the jellies made with wine, with orange juice, and so on.

"Now comes dessert. It is a new danger for you: but if up until now you have behaved yourselves, your common sense will indeed have the upper hand. Keep away from the ends of the table (it is there that the cakes are richest);[5] ignore the biscuits and the macaroons; you still have every kind of fruit, fresh or preserved, and a dozen other things which you will know how to select if you have paid any attention to my precepts.

"After dinner I order you to drink some coffee, I permit you to have a liqueur, and I advise you to take tea and punch now and then when it is offered.

"For breakfast, you may have rye bread as always, and chocolate rather than coffee. However, I do permit rather strong *café au lait*. Absolutely no eggs. The rest you may choose for yourselves. But it is impossible to breakfast too early. When you wait too long, dinner time is there before your digestion has completed itself; you eat none the less for this; and such gobbling without appetite is one of the most important causes of obesity, since it happens so often."

Further Outline of Diet

108: Until this point I have outlined for you, like a tender and rather easy-going father, the limits of a diet which can hold back the obesity which threatens you: let us now add a few precepts against this enemy.

Every summer you must drink thirty bottles of Seltzer water, a big glass in the morning, two before luncheon, and two more on going to bed. In general drink white wines, light and acidulous ones like those of Anjou. Shun beer as if it were the plague, and eat often of radishes, fresh artichokes with a simple dressing, asparagus, celery, and cardoons. Among meats choose veal and poultry: eat only the crust of bread; whenever you are in doubt be advised by a doctor who agrees with my principles; and no matter when you may start to follow them you will soon find yourselves fresh, attractive, nimble, in good health, and ready for anything.

After having thus established yourselves, you must be shown

the pitfalls, for fear of your outdoing yourselves in a spurt of zealous enthusiasm against obesity.

The special danger which you must guard against is the habitual use of acids, which are sometimes prescribed by the ignorant and which experience has always proved to have bad results.

Dangers of Acids

109: There is current among the ladies a dreadful theory, which annually causes the deaths of many young people, that acids, and above all vinegars, are preventives of obesity.

Doubtless the continued use of acids causes a loss of weight, but only as it destroys freshness, health, and life itself; and even though lemonade be the sweetest of these acids, there are few stomachs which can long resist its attack.

The truth of what I am now saying could not possibly be made too public; there are few of my readers who could not furnish their own examples to strengthen my case, and among all such stories I prefer the following, which is in a way an intimate one.

In 1776 I was living in Dijon; I was studying law at the university there, and also taking a course in chemistry under M. Guyton de Morveau, then advocate-general, and one in practical domestic medicine under M. Maret, permanent secretary of the Academy and father of the Duke of Bassano.

I had a strong feeling of friendship for one of the loveliest people I can ever remember knowing. I say *feeling of friendship*, which is at once strictly true and very surprising, since I was at that time amply provided to cope with more demanding relationships.

This friendship, then, which must be taken for what it was and not for what it might have become,[6] had for its characteristic an intimacy which became, from its first moment, so confidential as to seem quite natural to us, with endless whisperings which did not alarm the guardian mother in the least, because they had about them a kind of innocence left over from childhood itself. Louise was a very pretty girl, I must add, and above all possessed in perfect proportions that classical plumpness which has always charmed man's eyes and added richness to his arts.

Although I was only her friend, I was far from blind to the attractions which she let be seen or merely suspected, and perhaps they may have increased somehow the chaste sentiment which I felt for her, albeit unconsciously on my part. However that may be, one night when I had looked at Louise somewhat more attentively than usual, I said to her, "My dear friend, you are not well! It seems to me that you have grown thinner!"

"Not at all," she replied with a smile that had something melancholy about it. "I feel perfectly well, and if by chance I have lost a little weight, I really would not miss it."

"Lose weight!" I said heatedly. "You have no need either to lose or to gain any! Stay the way you are, sweet enough to nibble!" and still more phrases of the same kind, which a twenty-year-old friend seems always to have in abundance.

After this conversation I watched the young girl with an interest mixed with worry, and soon I saw her face grow pale, her cheeks become hollow, and her charms dwindle. . . . Oh, what a fragile fleeting thing is beauty! Finally one night I met her at a ball, to which she had gone as usual; I made her promise that she would sit out two quadrilles; then, profiting by this stolen time, I got her to admit that, bored by the jokes of some of her friends that in another two years she would be as broad as St. Christopher, and helped by the advice of still others, she had decided to grow thinner and with this end in view had drunk a glass of vinegar every morning for one month. She added that until that moment she had told nobody of her program.

I shuddered at this confession; I understood the dangerous import of it, and the next day told the whole story to Louise's mother, who was no less alarmed than I; we met, we consulted, we prescribed. Useless attempts! Her life forces had been irremediably undermined; and from the moment the danger was suspected, there was no hope left for us.

Thus, victim of stupid advice, the lovely Louise, reduced to the shocking state caused always by consumption, went to sleep for all eternity when she was but barely eighteen years old.

She died casting saddened glances toward a future which would never exist for her; and the idea that she had, no matter how unwittingly, helped cause her own death, made it even quicker and more painful.

She was the first person I ever saw die, for she breathed her last breath in my arms, just as I lifted her up, at her request, to watch the dawn. About eight hours after her death her desolate mother begged me to go with her to pay a last visit to the mortal remains of her daughter, and we saw with astonishment that her whole face had taken on a look of radiance, almost of ecstasy, which had never before been there. It filled me with amazement: the mother drew from it a consoling augury. But it was not an unusual case: Lavater mentions it in his TREATISE ON PHYSIOG-NOMY.[7]

The Antifat Belt

110: Any antifat diet should be accompanied by a precaution which I had forgotten, and which I should have mentioned at the very beginning: it consists of wearing day and night a belt which supports the belly at the same time that it moderately confines it.

In order to understand the rightness of this, it must be remembered that the spinal column, which forms one of the sides of the intestinal cavity, is firm and inflexible; from this it follows that any excess of weight which the intestines acquire, from the instant when obesity pulls them from the proper vertical position, drags on the various envelopes which make up the walls of the belly; these, able to stretch themselves almost indefinitely,† could easily not have resilience enough to retract when the weight diminished, if they were not given some mechanical help like the belt, which by obtaining purchase on the dorsal column itself becomes its antagonist and reestablishes the proper balance. Thus this belt produces the double effect of hindering the paunch from giving way on the outside to the inner pressure of the intestines, and of lending it the necessary strength to contract again when this pressure diminishes. It must never be removed; otherwise the good done in daytime will be destroyed by the relaxation of sleep; but it is almost unnoticeable, and its wearers soon grow used to it.

The belt, which also acts as a warning sentinel by feeling

---

† *Mirabeau once said of an excessively fat man that God had created him for the sole purpose of demonstrating to what limits the human skin could stretch without bursting.*

uncomfortable when one has eaten too much, must be made with a certain care; its tightness must be both moderate and unchangeable, or in other words it must be so constructed that it grows smaller as the weight grows less.

Nobody is condemned to wear it for the rest of his life; it can be left off without harm once the desired weight has been reached and has been held static for several weeks. Naturally a sensible diet must continue to be followed. It is at least six years now that I have not worn mine.

About Quinine

111:   There is one substance which I believe to be actively anti-fat; several observations have led me to think so; however, I admit there is still room for doubt, and invite the graduate doctors to experiment further.

This substance is quinine.

Ten or twelve of my acquaintances have suffered long intermittent fevers; some of them were cured by old household remedies, powders, and so on, and others by the continued use of quinine, which never fails in its effectiveness.

All the people in the first category who were fat have regained their original corpulence; all those of the second have stayed free of their excess weight: this gives me the right to believe that it is the quinine which produced the latter result, since the only difference in the cases was the method of curing them.

Rational theory does not contradict this: on one hand the quinine, stimulating all the vital processes, can easily produce in the circulation an activity which excites and evaporates those gases otherwise destined to form fat; on the other hand it has been proved that quinine contains tannin, which can close up the cells meant, in ordinary cases, to receive fatty accumulations. It is even probable that these two effects act together and support one another.

It is according to these facts, whose truth anyone will admit, that I feel justified in advising the use of quinine to all those who wish to rid themselves of an excess of weight which has become unpleasant. Therefore, *dummodo annuerint in omni medicationis genere doctissimi Facultatis professores*, I believe that after the first month of a sensible diet, anyone who wishes to grow thinner will do well to take for the following month, every other day at seven in the morning, a glass of dry white wine in which has been dissolved about a teaspoonful of good red quinine, and that excellent results will follow. Such, then, are the means which I propose to combat an incommodity as unfortunate as it is general. I have adapted them to human weaknesses, and modified them to the social conditions under which we exist.

I have leaned heavily on the experimental truth that the severer a diet may be, the less effect it will have, since it will perforce be followed haphazardly or not at all.

Great efforts are rare; and any preacher who wishes to be followed must propose to his disciples what is easy for them, and even, if possible, what is agreeable and pleasant.

THE TRANSLATOR'S GLOSSES

1.   This is one more of the Professor's little affectations. *Fetva, fetfa, fetwa:* it is a decision given by a Mufti or a Moslem official, usually in writing.
2.   Someone wrote in a letter about Byron at Diodati, in 1816, that he was trying very hard to grow thinner, and that ". . . a thin slice of bread with tea, at breakfast, a light vegetable dinner, with a bottle or two of seltzer-water, tinged with *Vin de Grave,* and in the evening a cup of green tea without milk or sugar, formed the whole of his sustenance; the pangs of hunger he appeased by privately chewing tobacco and smoking cigars."
3.   The best bread I ever ate in my life, if bread be its staff, was what the Professor called here a *pain de seigle,* which I bought by that very name in a little shop in Dijon, a generous hundred years after his death. It was a curiosity in that so-called "gastronomical center." The second-best bread was called *pain fédéral* in Switzerland, a few years later, and was a most dark hearty loaf, good fresh and better stale. François who looked after me in a thoroughly housewifish way felt much embarrassed to have it de-

livered to my door when fine white bread went to his own wife's. It was wonderful with a smuggled cheese, called Reblochon, which came across Leman from the French Savoy in midnight boats, and was soft and ripe and mild.

4. Cadet-de-Vaux (1743–1828) was a renowned chemist who wrote several unexpectedly advanced books on public sanitation as well as dietetics.

5. According to illustrations (and the cheaper the book the more details there were), a dinner table in the Professor's day (or night) was a fairly confused thing. There was no formality of seating except for royalty or very high nobility, which must be put on one side or the other of the host. Then came the ladies. Then the men seated themselves, according to their ethical, political, or amorous slants. If the party was a giddy one and "actresses" were present, the seating was even more selective. The host and a chosen guest sat and stood at either end of the table, and tried to carve and serve. They coped with something like the following menu: two soups, two fishes, two removes, six entrées, in the first course; two roasts, two removes, and six entrées, in the second. The waiters flew around madly, for any guest could cry out, "Here, you!" The table was massed with set-pieces, goblets, and whatnots. The more pictures you look at, the crazier it gets, and a dinner party for eight at Mike Romanoff's seemed cowardly-custardy in comparison in 1947 when no living hostess dared seat mate next to reputed mate, and the blissful surcease of set-pieces was unknown, or hopefully ignored.

6. It is impossible for any woman as hopelessly attracted to Brillat-Savarin as am I, not to wonder how he managed to live 71 years as a bachelor . . . and why. Perhaps this is the secret: certainly it is the only revelation of its kind in a basically personal book. Louise, who might, he hints, have become much more than a friend to him, was to be lost forever when he was only twenty. It is a startling coincidence, I think, that the only other mention of any woman who was more than a charming dinner companion to Brillat-Savarin is in his ballade, THE DEATHBED, on page 410. "Louise must weep . . ." Was there indeed another Louise who might tend him at his last hour, or had the ghost of the pretty Dijonnaise stayed with him all his celibate years?

7. Here, at least to my loving eye, is the most intimate and

revealing moment in the book, as far as the Professor's private life goes. At the end of his story of the Foolish Virgin he almost literally says *Harrumph*, like a peppery old Englishman ashamed of the tear in his eye and the tremor in his voice, and he mentions with a surgeon's coolness one of his favorite scientific treatises and then goes resolutely into the details of his antifat belt. This may or may not be a love story, but the abrupt transition seems very emotional to me.

MEDITATION 23

ON THINNESS

Definition

112: Thinness is the state of a person whose muscular flesh, not being filled out with fat, reveals the shapes and angles of his bony structure.

Kinds

There are two kinds of thinness: the first, being the result of the basic character of the body, is accompanied by health and the complete exercise of all organic functions; the second, caused by the weakness of some organs or the faulty action of others, gives a miserable and puny look to its victims. I myself have known, in the first category, a young woman of medium height who weighed only about sixty-five pounds.

Effects of Thinness

113: It is not a great disadvantage to men to be lean; they are no less vigorous for it, and are much more active. The father of the young lady I just mentioned, although quite as thin as she, was strong enough to pick up with his teeth a heavy chair, and throw it behind him by lifting it over the top of his head.

But thinness is a horrible calamity for women: beauty to them is more than life itself, and it consists above all of the roundness of their forms and the graceful curvings of their outlines. The most artful toilette, the most inspired dressmaker, cannot disguise certain lacks, nor hide certain angles; and it is a common saying that a scrawny woman, no matter how pretty she may look, loses something of her charm with every fastening she undoes.

With sickly ladies there is no remedy for thinness, or rather it is a case for the doctors, and their treatment of it may take so long that the cure itself will arrive almost too late.

But as for women who are born thin and whose digestion is good, we cannot see why they should be any more difficult to fatten than young hens; and if it takes a little more time than with poultry, it is because human female stomachs are comparatively smaller, and cannot be submitted, as are those devoted barnyard creatures, to the same rigorous and punctually followed diet. This comparison is the most tactful one I have been able to find; I needed one, and the ladies will forgive me for it, because of my praiseworthy intentions toward them in developing this chapter.

Natural Predestination

114: Nature, so varied in her works, has moulds for thinness as well as for obesity.

People meant to be lean are built on a long scale. They have slender hands and feet, lanky legs, flat behind; their ribs show, and their noses are aquiline; they have almond-shaped eyes, wide mouths, sharp chins, and dark hair.

Such is the type in general: some parts of the body can deviate from it, but this rarely happens.

Now and then one sees a thin person who eats a great deal. All such whom I have been able to question have confessed to me that they digest badly and then . . . , which is, of course, why they continue to be scrawny.

Natural-born weaklings are of every coloring and every type of structure. They can be distinguished chiefly by the fact that they have nothing striking about them, either in their features or their figures; their eyes are lacklustre, their lips pale, and the sum total of their appearance indicates lack of energy, weakness, and something which resembles a kind of misery. One could almost say that they seem to be unfinished creatures, and that the flame of life is not yet fully lighted in them.

A Fattening Diet

115: Every thin woman wants to grow plump: that is an avowal which has been made to us a thousand times. Therefore it is in order to pay final homage to the all-powerful sex that we are going to try here to tell how to replace with living flesh those pads of silk or cotton which are displayed so profusely in novelty shops, to the obvious horror of the prudish, who pass them by with a shudder, turning away from such shadows with even more care than if it were actuality they looked upon.

With a suitably adapted diet, the usual prescriptions relative to rest and sleep can almost be ignored without endangering the net results: if you do not take any exercise, you will be inclined to grow fat; if you exercise, you will still grow fat, since you will eat more than usual. When hunger is knowingly satisfied, you not only restore what energy you have used up, but you add to what you already have, whenever there is need for it.

If you sleep a great deal, it will be fattening; if you sleep little, your digestion will take place faster and you will eat more.

The only problem, then, is to indicate to those who wish to fill out their curves what foods they must always choose for their nourishment; and this task need not be a difficult one if the various principles which we have already established are followed.

In sum, it is necessary to introduce into the stomach foods which will occupy it without tiring it, and to the assimilative powers foods they can best turn into fat.

Let us try to outline the day's fare of a sylph, whether male or female, who has been seized by the desire to materialize into solid flesh.

Basic plan. Eat plenty of bread, baked fresh each day, and take care not to discard the soft inside of the loaf.

Before eight o'clock in the morning, and in bed if that seems best, drink a bowl of soup thickened with bread or noodles, but not too much of it, so that it may be eliminated quickly; or, if you wish, take a cup of good chocolate.

At eleven, lunch on fresh eggs scrambled or fried in butter, little meat pies, chops, and whatever you wish; the main thing is that you have eggs. A cup of coffee will do no harm.

The dinner hour depends on how well your luncheon has been assimilated: we have often said that when the ingestion of one meal follows too quickly upon the digestion of another, it is, in legal terms, a form of malpractice.

After luncheon you must take a little exercise: the gentlemen, only if their professions allow it, for attention to business comes first; the ladies will go to the Bois de Boulogne, the Tuileries, their dressmakers, the shops, and finally to their friends' houses, to chat of what they have seen. We hold that such conversation is highly beneficial, because of the great pleasure which accompanies it.

At dinner take soup, meat, and fish, as much as you wish; but add to them dishes made with rice or macaroni, frosted pastries, sweet custards, creamy puddings, etc.

For dessert eat Savoy biscuits, babas, and other concoctions which are made of flour, eggs, and sugar.

This diet, although it seems very rigid, is really capable of great variety; it has place in it for the whole animal kingdom, and you must take especial care to change the use and preparation and seasoning of the different starchy foods which you will be served and which you will enliven in every possible way, so that you may avoid being surfeited by them, an event which would prove an invincible obstacle to any improvement in your appearance.

You should drink beer by preference,[1] or wines from Bordeaux or the French Midi.

Avoid all acids except in salads, which refresh the digestion.[2] Sweeten whatever fruits need it; avoid taking baths which are too cold; try to breathe from time to time the pure air of the open countryside; eat plenty of grapes in season; and do not exhaust yourselves by dancing too much at the balls.

Go to bed about eleven o'clock on ordinary days, and not later than one in the morning on special occasions.

If you follow this plan with care and determination, you will soon repair the ravages of nature; your health as well as your beauty will improve; sensual pleasure will profit from the two of them, and the professor's ears will ring agreeably to the music of grateful confidences.

We fatten sheep, calves, oxen, poultry, carp, crayfish, and oysters; and from this fact I have deduced the following general maxim: *Everything that eats can grow fat, as long as its food is sensibly and suitably chosen.*

THE TRANSLATOR'S GLOSSES

1. Love has a thinning effect upon most female silhouettes, when it is unrequited (as opposed to the fullness of its satisfaction!). A young woman in Dresden in 1903, pining for a young man in America . . . they were my parents-to-be . . . grew so bony as to be almost unstylish, and upon consulting a fashionable Scotch doctor was advised to drink all the beer she could hold, and to carry a few chocolate drops in her petticoat pocket, for between-stein nibbling. She stayed thin, the Scot and the Professor to the contrary.

2. This pretty phrase, *"la salade . . . qui réjouit le coeur,"* is often quoted and misquoted. At the expense of being thought dully practical and unpoetical, I truthfully do not think that it means that salads gladden the heart, but that they are light in the stomach and easily digested, and that they bring a feeling of easiness and comfort to the whole belly and especially to the poor overworked organ that perches on top of it, the human heart. Anything which does that is, of course, a gladsome thing.

MEDITATION 24

ON FASTING

116: Fasting is the voluntary abstinence from food for moral or religious reasons.

Even though it is contrary to one of our natural inclinations, or rather to one of our most basic needs, it is nevertheless of the greatest antiquity.

Origin of Fasting

Here is how writers explain its beginnings.

In cases of personal bereavement, they tell us, when a father, a mother, or a cherished child died in a family, the entire household grieved: there was great weeping, and the body was washed and embalmed, and then given the funeral rites proper to its social rank. At these times, the bereaved hardly dreamed of eating: they fasted without realizing that they did so.

In the same way, in public catastrophes, when there was some such affliction as an extraordinary drought, or too-heavy rains, or cruel wars, or plagues, in a word any scourge too strong for human strength and industry, men gave themselves up to lamentation, and blamed all their misery on the anger of their gods.

They bowed in humiliation, and offered up the mortifications of self-denial. Their miseries ceased, and it was easy to believe they did so because of the tears and the fasting, and to continue to rely upon such apparent remedies.

So it was that people afflicted by either private or public calamities abandoned themselves to sadness, and neglected to take any food, and it followed naturally that they came to look upon this voluntary abstinence as a religious act.

They believed that in tormenting their bodies when their souls were in distress they could stir the pity of the gods; and this idea, which took hold of all races, gave birth to public mourning, to vows, prayers, sacrifices, mortifications, and fasting.

Finally Jesus Christ, come upon earth, sanctified voluntary abstinence, and every Christian sect has adopted it, with varying numbers of self-imposed vexations.

How We Used to Fast

117: This custom of fasting, I am forced to admit, has fallen amazingly out of favor; and whether it be for the edification of the ungodly or for their conversion, I find pleasure in telling here how we used to observe it toward the middle of the eighteenth century.

On ordinary days we breakfasted before nine o'clock on bread, cheese, fruits, and sometimes cold meat or a pâté.

Between noon and one o'clock we dined on the traditional soup with boiled meat, more or less well supplemented according both to the circumstances and to our incomes.

Toward four o'clock we had a snack: this meal was light, and meant particularly for the children and those adults who prided themselves on observing the customs of their youth.

But there were also more elaborate celebrations at this time of day, beginning at five o'clock and lasting indefinitely; they were usually very gay, and ladies were marvellously fond of them; they were even held sometimes for women alone, and men were barred from them. I notice in my secret Memoirs that they were the scene of not a little scandalmongering and slanderous chitchat.

Toward eight o'clock we had a meal consisting of an entrée,

a roast, side dishes, salad, and dessert: the guests played a round of cards, and then went to their beds.

In Paris there were, as in our present time, suppers of a more elaborate kind, held after the theatre and attended, according to the circumstances, by pretty women, fashionable actresses, elegant courtesans, aristocrats, bankers, rakes, and wits.

They recounted the latest scandal, and sang the newest song; they talked of politics, literature, and the theatre, and above all they flirted.

Now let us see what our grandfathers did on fast-days.

They did not breakfast at all, and for this reason they were of course much hungrier than usual.

At the customary dinner hour they did as well as they could, but fish and vegetables are quickly digested; before five o'clock they were perishing with hunger; they looked at their watches, waited, and fumed helplessly in the very act of saving their own souls.

Toward eight o'clock there was served, not a good supper, but a collation,[1] a term straight from the cloister, where monks toward the end of the day were allowed to enjoy a glass of wine after they had assembled to discuss the lives of the church fathers.

At the collation neither butter nor eggs, nor anything that had once lived and breathed, could be served. Our forefathers, as a result, had to satisfy themselves with salads, preserves, and fruit, dishes, alas, which are far from sustaining, especially for the lusty appetites of those days: but the faithful suffered patiently for the love of God, went to their beds, and began again the next day, as long as Lent lasted.

As for those more worldly souls who enjoyed the little suppers of which I have spoken, I have been assured that they never troubled themselves with fasting, either in the Lenten season or any other.

The greatest culinary accomplishment of those far days was a collation severely apostolic which still had about it the appearance of a decent meal.

Science managed to solve this problem, thanks to the religious tolerance felt toward fish cooked *au bleu*, vegetable broths, and pastries made with oil.

A strict observance of Lent created one pleasure, also, which is unknown to us today: the end of fasting, the *de-Lenting*, at the first meal on Easter.

If we look closely at the subject, we see that our pleasures are based on the difficulties, privations, and yearnings we suffer to attain them. All of this was apparent in the act which broke the Lenten abstinence: I have watched two of my great-uncles, both of them strong levelheaded men, almost swoon with delight at that moment on Easter Sunday when they watched the carving of a ham or the first shattering of a meat pie's crust. Today, enfeebled race that we have become, we could not withstand the shock of such powerful emotions!

The Beginnings of Laxness in Fasting

118: I myself have seen the beginnings of laxness; it has crept upon us imperceptibly.

Young people up to a certain age were not forced to fast, in the old days; and pregnant women, or those who believed themselves to be so, were exempted from it because of their condition, and during Lent were served rich fare, and a nightly supper which was painfully tempting to the abstainers.

Gradually people began to convince themselves that fasting upset them, gave them headaches, kept them from sleeping. They managed to blame their abstinence for all those little miseries which afflict mankind in the Spring, such as skin eruptions, dizziness, nosebleeds, and other symptoms of purification which always indicate the reawakening of Nature. The result was that one man gave up fasting because he believed that he was ill, another because he had been so, and a third because he feared he might be, and inevitably the morning fasts and the evening collations grew rarer every day.

And that is not all: some of the winters were severe enough to arouse fears of a shortage of vegetables, and the lords of the Church themselves officially relaxed their strictures, when household providers began to complain of the high cost of meatless meals. Some of them even said that the pleasure of God could not consist in causing the ill health of his children, to which the more cynical added that Paradise could not be reached by starvation.

However, religious duty was still recognized, and for the most part any permission to break the rules of fasting was asked of the priests, who rarely refused to give it, always adding the provision that certain alms must be paid in place of the mortification of the flesh.

Finally there was the Revolution, so filling all our hearts with cares and fears and interests of another nature that there was no longer either time or excuse to go running to the priests, some of whom were hunted as enemies of the State, which still did not prevent them from treating their brother prelates as *schismatics*.

To this reason for relaxation of the rules, which happily no longer exists, there was joined another equally powerful one. Our hours for meals have changed completely: we neither eat as often nor at the same times as did our ancestors, and fasting today would need a total reorganization.

This is so true that, although my friends are among the most sensible and settled of people, and are even fairly religious, I do not believe that in some twenty-five years I have been served ten meatless meals or a single collation, *except in my own home*.

Many men might find themselves mightily embarrassed in such circumstances; but I know that Saint Paul foresaw it[2] and I take shelter under his wing.

Moreover, it would be grossly foolish to believe that intemperance has increased in this new order of things.

The number of our daily meals has grown less by almost half. Drunkenness has vanished, to reappear only among the lowest levels of society on certain feast days. There are no more orgies: a depraved sot would be ostracized anywhere. More than a third of the Parisians eat no more than a light collation in the morning, and if certain of them delight in a subtle and refined gourmandizing, I can hardly see how they should be reproached for it, since we have already proved that everyone profits from such a pleasure and that none can be impoverished by it.

Let us not end this chapter without calling attention to the new direction which the tastes of the common people have taken.

Every day thousands of men spend their evenings in the theatres or the cafés, who forty years ago would have gone to the taverns.

No doubt this new habit adds little to our national income, but it is highly advantageous from a moral point of view. At the theatre a man's ideals are uplifted; at the café he instructs himself as he reads the daily papers; and certainly he has escaped, in both places, the brawls and illnesses and general coarsening of spirit which are the inevitable result of frequenting public houses.

THE TRANSLATOR'S GLOSSES

1.   This word was in high favor, at the beginning of the twentieth century, among such small-town society reporters as worked on my father's paper. "A dainty collation was served," they would state simply, suggesting in the readers' minds a table prettily strung with garden flowers and smilax, and covered with decorated paper cups of nutmeats, and plates of homemade cakes like Lady Baltimore and angel food . . . "A great big beautiful birthday cake was the pièce-de-résistance of the collation," the aged and indomitable Minnie Brownson wrote at least once a week for thirty years, in my father's daily NEWS.
2.   This probably refers to Paul's remark, in his Epistle to Titus, "Unto the pure all things are pure."

MEDITATION 25

ON EXHAUSTION

119: By exhaustion is understood a state of weakness, of languor, and of depression brought about by preceding circumstances which make more difficult the natural bodily functions.
There are three such kinds of fatigue, not counting the one
which results from hunger.

These three are caused by muscular fatigue, by mental labors,
and by amorous excesses.

A common remedy for all three types is the immediate cessation of whatever action has brought on the condition, which if
not truly an illness is very near to one.

Treatment

120: After this first indispensable prescription, gastronomy
stands ready as always to offer its help.

To a man overcome by too prolonged muscular exercise it
suggests a good soup, plenty of wine, well-cooked meat, and
sleep.

For a scholar who has let himself be carried away by the
charms of his subject a brisk walk in the fresh air is best, to re-

vive his mind, and then a bath to soothe his tired body, and finally repose, after a little meal of poultry and leafy vegetables.

Finally we shall learn, in the following observation, what gastronomy can do for anyone who has forgotten that sensuality has its limits and physical pleasure its dangers.

A Cure Performed by the Professor

121:   I went once to pay a visit to one of my best friends (M. Rubat). I was told that he was ill, and true enough I found him in his dressing room, crouched weakly over his fire.

His looks horrified me: his face was white, his eyes burned, and his lower lip hung down so that all the teeth showed in his bottom jaw, in a way that had something hideous about it.

I inquired anxiously into the cause of this violent change. He hesitated, I insisted, and then after some resistance he said, blushing, "My dear chap, you know that my wife is jealous of me, and that this mania of hers has given me plenty of bad moments. For the past several days she has been in a really dreadful state on account of it, and it is because I tried to prove to her that she'd lost none of my love and that nobody shared my conjugal respects with her that I got myself into this condition."

"Have you forgotten, then," I asked him, "that you are forty-five years old, and that jealousy itself is an incurable illness? Don't you know that *furens quid femina possit?*" I threw a few other equally unflattering remarks at him, for I was really angry. "Look," I went on, "not only that, but your pulse is weak and thin and slow. What are you going to do about it?"

"The doctor just left," he told me. "He decided I had a nervous fever, and prescribed a bleeding for which he is at this very moment sending me a surgeon."

"A surgeon!" I cried. "Watch out, or you're a dead man! Get rid of him as if he were a murderer, and tell him that I have taken complete responsibility for you, body and soul. And by the way, does your doctor know the real cause of your exhaustion?"

"Alas, no! A foolish embarrassment kept me from telling him the whole truth about it."

"Well, we must ask him to come back. I'm going to make you a potion adapted to your condition, and while you wait for it, take this." I gave him a glass of heavily sugared water,[1] which he gulped down with the confidence of Alexander and the blind faith of a charcoal burner.[2]

Then I left him, and hurried home to concoct, prepare, and elaborate a superrestorative, whose recipe will be found in my Varieties†, with various shortcuts I made, for in such a case as my friend's a few hours of delay can cause hopeless setbacks.

I returned to his house as soon as possible, armed with my pick-me-up, and found him already looking better; the color was coming back to his cheeks, and his eyes were less brilliant, but his lip still hung down like some shocking deformity.

The doctor was not long in arriving. I told him of what I had done, and the sick man confessed to him. His professional brow wrinkled sternly at first, but soon, as he looked at both of us somewhat ironically, he said to my friend, "You ought not to be surprised that I did not suspect an illness which really does not become either your age or your build, and on your part you have been indeed too modest in hiding the cause for it, which can only do honor to your powers. I am still angry with you for having risked my prescribing what might have been a death sentence for you. Nevertheless," he added with a bow to me which I returned with compound interest, "my colleague here has pointed out the right path for you. Take his broth, no matter what he may call it, and if the fever goes down, as I think it will, breakfast tomorrow on a cup of chocolate into which you have beaten the yolks of two fresh eggs."

With these words he picked up his cane and hat and left us, and we found ourselves hard put to it not to laugh a little at his back.

Before long I had made the invalid swallow a large dose of my elixir of life. He drank it thirstily, and wanted another one, but I ordered a two hours' wait, and finally served him a second draught before I left.

The next day his fever was gone, and he was almost well. He breakfasted according to direction, continued the dosage of soup, and in another day could take up his usual pursuits; but his rebellious lip did not rise up into place again until after the third day.

† *See "Varieties," X.*

Before long this whole affair became known, and all the ladies whispered about it among themselves.

Some of them admired my friend, almost all felt sorry for him, and the gastronomical professor was praised to the skies.

THE TRANSLATOR'S GLOSSES

1. I once watched color and courage creep back into the face of a girl exhausted by childbirth, as she sipped a glass of water heavily charged with raw sugar and then plunged into the battle again.

2. This is a rare mixture of classicism and slang: Alexander the Great is supposed to have downed a weird brew handed him by his physician, after one searching look at the face of the man who was whispered to be his enemy; such blind faith in France is named for charcoal burners, or used to be, because those slow quiet men are simple-minded and will believe anything. Of such is the kingdom of Literature . . .

MEDITATION 26

ON DEATH

OMNIA MORS POSCIT; LEX EST,
NON POENA, PERIRE[1]

122:   The six most important necessities which the Creator has imposed on mankind are to be born, to move about, to eat, to sleep, to procreate, and to die.

Death is the complete interruption of sensual relations and the absolute cessation of vital action, which perforce leaves the body prey to the laws of decomposition.

These aforementioned basic needs are all of them accompanied by and made more agreeable by various sensations of pleasure, and death itself is not without enjoyment when it comes naturally, that is to say when the human body has passed through all its preordained phases of growth, maturity, old age, and decrepitude.

If I had not determined to make this a very short chapter, I would call to my aid the doctors who have watched the almost imperceptible changes which take place when living bodies change to inert matter. I would quote philosophers and kings and writers who, from the very fringes of eternity, far from being prey to pain and grief, have had cheerful thoughts which they could express with poetic charm. I would recall the reply of the dying Fontenelle, who, when he was questioned about what he felt, replied, "Nothing more than a difficulty to go on living." But I prefer only to state my personal conviction, based both on analogy and on many observations which I feel have been carefully made, and of which this is the final one:

I had a great-aunt ninety-three years old, who was dying. Although she had been bedridden for some time, she was in full possession of all her faculties, and it was impossible to guess her true condition except by the lessening of her appetite and the weakening of her voice.

She had always been very fond of me, and it was I who sat by her bed, ready to help her most tenderly, but not the least prevented by this from observing her with the philosophical eye which I have always cocked at whatever goes on around me.

"Are you there, my dear nephew?" she asked me in a barely articulated voice.

"Yes, Aunt. I shall do everything I can for you, and I feel it would do you good to take a little really fine old wine."

"Give it to me, my dear: liquid always flows downward."

I hurried to lift her up gently, and made her swallow a half glass of my best wine. She instantly grew stronger, and looking at me with eyes which had once been very beautiful she said, "Deep thanks for this last service. If ever you reach my age, you will see that death becomes a necessity, just like sleep."

These were her last words, and a half-hour later she had dozed off forever.

Dr. Richerand has described with such truth and philosophy the final changes in the human body and the last moments in the individual that my readers will thank me for making known to them the following passage:

"Here is the order in which our intellectual faculties cease and disintegrate. Reason, that attribute of which man pretends to be the sole possessor, abandons him first. At the beginning he loses the power to link his opinions sensibly and, soon after, follows his ability to compare and assemble and combine together several ideas in order to judge their net importance. It is then said that the sick man is out of his head, or that he is unreasonable or delirious. This delirium focuses usually on the thoughts which are most familiar to him, and his dominant passion is easily recognized: a miser confides the innermost secrets about his hidden gold; another man dies in the clutch of religious terror. Happy memories of the distant homeland, you, too, are reawakened in the exile, with all your charm and all your poignancy!

"After the powers of reasoning and judging, it is the faculty of associating ideas which is next struck down by the progressive destruction of death. This happens also in the state known as *swooning*, as I myself have proven. I was talking once with a friend, when I felt an insurmountable difficulty in clarifying two ideas upon whose resemblance I wished to form an opinion. I was not completely unconscious, however: I still kept my memory and my ability to feel, and could distinctly hear the people who were around me saying, *He has fainted*, and trying to bring me out of this state, *which was not without a certain pleasure.*

"The next thing to die is memory. The sick man, who even in delirium recognized the people who were near him, now does not know his close associates, and finally ignores those with whom he has lived in the greatest intimacy. Then he stops feeling anything. His senses, however, go out in a successive and set order: taste and smell give no further sign of their existence; his eyes are dimmed as by a dull cloud, and take on a sinister look; his hearing is still sensitive to both sounds and noise. This last is doubtless why the ancients, in order to assure themselves that death had actually occurred, used to shriek into the ears of their corpses. The dying man now cannot smell or taste, and he sees and hears no more. There is still left to him the sense of touch, and he moves about on his bed, stretches his arms this way and that, and changes his position constantly; he reproduces, as we have already said, the movements of a foetus who stirs in its mother's womb. The death which is about to strike him down cannot terrify him, for he has no more thoughts, and he finishes life as he began it, without any consciousness of so doing." (Richerand, Nouveaux Eléments de Physiologie, ninth edition, Volume II, page 600.)[2]

*   *   *

THE TRANSLATOR'S GLOSSES

1.   This says, "Death demands all: to die is law, not punishment."

The succinct perfundity of this undoubtedly appealed to Brillat-Savarin's orderly mind, as well as to the side of his nature which increasingly found itself preoccupied with the physical act of dying and its infinite spiritual ramifications. For many years before his death he had been known to express a fatalistic interest in the act, which at the same time had nothing morbid about it, and the song he composed (see page 410) and this present Meditation are but two proofs of his impersonal concern.

2.   It is perhaps a pity that birth and death are so little watched, in our time. I have always felt that the miracle of parturition, endured or only witnessed, makes any human being wiser and more humble. He who turns away from it is the poorer for his act. And the same may be true of death, which so seldom happens nowadays in the awesome quiet of a familiar chamber. Most of us die violently, thanks to the advances of science and warfare. If by chance we are meant to end life in our beds, we are whisked like pox victims to the nearest hospital, where we are kept as alone and unaware as possible of the approach of disintegration. Those of us who escape bombs and the mad highways have a chance to live much longer than men of the early nineteenth century, but it is hard not to agree with one good reporter of the twentieth who wrote from his cancer-tortured heart, "Science is wonderful . . . but I sometimes envy my ancestors who died too early to know how painfully life can be prolonged." For myself, I should like to die like the Professor's aunt, ancient and aware, at peace in a known room, and in the company of a loved person who was not repelled or frightened by my end. I should like my children to agree with me . . .

MEDITATION 27

PHILOSOPHICAL HISTORY OF COOKING

123: Cooking is the oldest of all arts: Adam was born hungry, and every new child, almost before he is actually in the world, utters cries which only his wet nurse's breast can quiet.

Cooking is also of all the arts the one which has done most to advance our civilization, for the needs of the kitchen were what first taught us to use fire, and it is by fire that man has tamed Nature itself.

If we take a broad view, we can count up to three different kinds of *cooking*:

The first, which applies to the preparation of food, retains its original name;

The second concerns itself with the analysis of foods and the classification of their basic elements, and it has been given the name *chemistry*;

Finally, the third, which can be called restorative cooking, is best known by the name *pharmacy*.

Even though their purposes are different, these three are alike in the way they use fire and stoves, and in the employ of corresponding kinds of vessels.

Thus, the same piece of beef which the cook turns into soup

and *pot-au-feu* the chemist will use to discover how many kinds of matter it consists of, and the pharmacist will dislodge violently from our stomachs if by chance it happens to prove indigestible.

Alimentary Progress

124: Man is an omnivorous animal: he has incisor teeth for cutting into fruits, molars for crushing seeds, and canines for tearing flesh, and of these last it has been observed that the nearer he comes to the savage state, the stronger and more prominent they will be.

It is very probable that the human race was for a long time and of necessity frugivorous:[1] man was the clumsiest of the ancient world's inhabitants, and his means of attack were extremely limited as long as he was unarmed. But the instinct for self-improvement which was a part of his nature was not long in developing; the very realization of his weakness led him to find ways of making weapons, toward which he was also pushed by the carnivorous yearnings already revealed by his canine teeth. Once armed, he made of all the creatures who surrounded him his prey and his nourishment.

This murderous instinct still exists in him: children usually kill whatever little animals are abandoned to their mercies, and would doubtless eat them if they were hungry enough.

It is not surprising that man from the beginning wanted to feed upon flesh: his stomach is too little and fruits have too few nourishing substances in them to be able to replenish sufficiently his bodily losses. He would have done better to live upon vegetables, but this diet demands culinary skills which did not develop for many centuries.

The first weapons must have been the branches of trees, and later came bows and arrows.

It is worthwhile to notice that wherever man has been discovered, in every climate, in every part of the globe, he has always been found armed with these bows and arrows. This uniformity is hard to explain. We cannot well see how the same series of ideas has occurred to individuals subjected to such differing circumstances; it must spring from a cause hidden from us by the veil of time.

Raw flesh has but one inconvenience: its viscous nature makes it stick to the teeth. Aside from this, it is not at all disagreeable to eat. It digests easily, seasoned with a little salt, and must be more nourishing thus than in any other form.

"MEIN GOD," a captain from a Croat regiment whom I had invited to dinner said to me in 1815, "all this fuss isn't necessary for a good meal! When we are in the field and are hungry we kill the first beast we come upon; we cut ourselves a good meaty slice of it, sprinkle it with some of the salt which we always carry with us in our *sabre-tasche*,† put it between our saddle and the back of the horse, and give it a good gallop. Then (and here he growled like a creature tearing meat apart with his teeth) *gnian, gnian, gnian,* we feast as well as any prince."

When sportsmen in the Dauphiné hunt in September, they too are armed with salt and with pepper. If one of them happens to bag a plump, perfect figpecker[2] he plucks it, seasons it, carries it for a time in the crown of his hat, and eats it. Such gourmands[3] insist that this is much more delicious than the bird when roasted.

It is plain that we have not completely lost our thrice-removed ancestors' predilection for raw flesh. The most fastidious palates manage to enjoy sausages from Arles and Bologna, smoked beef from Hamburg, salted anchovies and herrings, and other such delicacies which have never been near fire and which still arouse our appetites.

Discovery of Fire

125:   After a long enough time of feasting in the Croatian fashion, men discovered fire, and this was once more a thing of chance, for fire does not happen by itself: the natives of the Marianas are said not to have known that such a thing existed.

---

† *The* SABRE-TASCHE *or saber-pouch is a kind of bag protected by a shield, which hangs from the shoulder strap where the light troops wear their sabers; it plays an important role in the tales which the soldiers tell among themselves.*

Cooking

126: Once fire was recognized, man's instinct for self-improvement led him to subject meat to it, at first to dry out the flesh and finally to place it upon the embers to cook.

Meat thus treated was found to taste much better; it takes on more firmness, is chewed much more easily, and its osmazome as it browns becomes savorous and gives the flesh an aroma which has never ceased to tempt us.[4]

However, it soon became obvious that meat cooked upon live coals is not free from dirt: it always picks up little bits of ash or charcoal which are difficult to get rid of. This inconvenience was remedied by impaling the morsels of flesh on sticks which were then placed above the glowing fire, their ends resting upon stones of the proper height.

It is thus that men hit upon the various methods of grilling, which is a process as simple as it is delicious: any grilled meat has a concentrated flavor, since it is, in part at least, smoked.

Things had not progressed much further than this in Homer's day, and I hope that my readers will enjoy seeing here how Achilles entertained in his own tent three of the most important of the Greeks, of whom one was a king.

I dedicate the following excerpt to the ladies, because Archilles was the handsomest of all the Greeks, and because even his manly pride did not keep him from weeping when Briseis was torn from his arms. It is also for this reason that I shall use the elegant translation of M. Dugas-Montbel, a pleasant, charming writer who is fairly gourmand for a Greek scholar:

Majorem jam craterem, Moenetii fili, appone,
Meraci usque misce, poculum autem para unicuique;
Charissimi enim isti viri meo sub tecto.
Sic dixit: Patroclus dilecto obedivit socio;
Sed cacabum ingentem posuit ad ignis jubar;
Tergum in ipso posuit ovis et pinguis caprae.
Apposuit et suis saginati scapulum abundantem pinguedine.
Huic tenebat carnes Automedon, secabatque nobilis Achilles,
Eas quidem minute secabat, et verubus affigebat.
Ignem Moenetiades accendebat magnum, deo similis vir;
Sed postquam ignis deflagravit, et flamma extincta est,

Prunas sternens, verua desuper extendit.
Inspersit autem sale sacro, a lapidibus elevans.
At postquam assavit et in mensas culinarias fudit,
Patroclus quidem, panem accipiens, distribuit in mensas
Pulchris in canistris, sed carnem distribuit Achilles.
Ipse autem adversus sedit Ulyssi divino,
Ad parietem alterum. Diis autem sacrificare jussit
Patroclum suum socium. Is in ignem jecit libamenta.
Hi in cibos paratos appositos manus immiserunt;
Sed Postquam potus et cibi desiderium exemerunt,
Innuit Ajax Phoenici: intellexit autem divinus Ulysses,
Implensque vino poculum, propinavit Achilli,† etc.

Il. IX, 202.

"Straightway Patroclus obeys the instructions of his faithful companion. Meanwhile Achilles puts near the sparkling flame a pot which holds the shoulders of a ewe and of a fat goat, and the broad back of a succulent porker. Automedon holds this meat while the divine Achilles carves it into morsels, and sticks them through with pointed iron needles.

"Patroclus, who is himself godlike, lights a great fire. As soon as the burning wood throws out no more than a dying flame he puts over the bed of coals two long skewers upheld upon two stones, and sprinkles the sacred salt.

"When the meats are done, and when the feast is ready, Patroclus passes bread around the table in fine baskets, but Achilles himself chooses to serve the roasts. Finally he sits down facing Ulysses who is at the other end of the table, and bids his companion make the customary offering to the gods.

"Patroclus throws into the flames the first tidbits from the meal, and then everyone reaches for the feast which has been prepared and served. When they have routed thirst and hunger with the abundance of good things, Ajax signals Phoenix, and Ulysses seeing this fills his large cup with wine, and to the hero says, 'Salutations, my friend Achilles' . . ."

† *I have not used the original text, since few people would be able to follow it; instead I have decided to give the Latin version, for this more widely understood language, which follows perfectly the Greek, lends itself better to the details and to the simplicity of the heroic feast.*

Thus it was that a king, a king's son, and three Greek generals feasted right well upon bread, wine, and grilled meat.

It must be understood that if Achilles and Patroclus themselves took care of the preparations for the banquet, it was something out of the ordinary, to pay all the more homage to the distinguished guests they entertained, for ordinarily the duties of the kitchen were left to slaves and to women: Homer tells us so in the Odyssey, in singing of the feasts of the suitors.

In those days the guts of animals, stuffed with fat and blood, were highly thought of as a dish (this was nothing more than our blood pudding).[5]

Then, and doubtless for a long time before, poetry and music were considered a part of the delights of feasting. Renowned minstrels vaunted the marvels of Nature, the loves of the immortals, and the great deeds of warriors; they functioned as a kind of priesthood, and it is probable that the divine Homer himself was the pupil of some of these chosen men, for he could never have risen so high if his poetical studies had not begun early in his childhood.

Madame Dacier[6] has said that Homer never mentions boiled meat in any of his works. The Hebrews were more advanced, because of the time they spent in Egypt: they had pots which could be placed on the fire, and it is in one of these that the soup was made which Jacob sold so dearly to his brother Esau.

It is truly difficult to guess how man came to work with metals; legend has it that Tubal-Cain was the first to try it. . . .

In the present state of our knowledge, it is metals that enable us to work with other metals: we bend them with iron tongs and beat them upon the forge with iron hammers and shape them with files of steel, but I have yet to meet anyone who could explain to me how the first tongs were made, or how the first hammer was forged.

Feasts of the Orientals—of the Greeks

127: Cooking made great progress as soon as heat resistant vessels of brass or clay became common. Meats could then be seasoned and vegetables prepared; there were soups, gravies, jellies, and all such things which develop one from another.

The oldest books still remaining to us speak with high praise of the banquets of Eastern kings. It is not hard to see that rulers of lands so rich in everything, and especially in spices and perfumes, would naturally enjoy the most sumptuous of tables; but details of them are lacking. All we know is that Cadmus, who brought the art of writing to Greece, was once cook to the king of Sidon.

It was among these soft and voluptuous people that there arose the habit of placing couches around the banquet tables, and of lying upon them to eat and drink.

This refinement, which smacks of decadence, was not equally popular everywhere. Nations which made a boast of their strength and courage, and a virtue of their frugality, avoided it for a long time. It was finally adopted by the Athenians, however, and for a great many years was common throughout the civilized world.

Cooking and its amenities were in high favor among the inhabitants of Athens, an elegant people and hungry for whatever was new and exciting. Princes, rich private citizens, poets, and scholars set the example, and even the philosophers believed that they should not spurn pleasures which flowed from Nature's own breast.

From what we can read in old writings, it is plain that the feasts of the ancients were feasts indeed.

Hunting, fishing, and trade provided most of the commodities which are still considered excellent, and competition caused them to be very expensive.

All the arts combined to ornament the banquet boards, around which the guests lay upon couches richly hung with purple.

Each one strove to give even more worth to the feast by his agreeable conversation, and table talk became a science.

The minstrels' songs, which were heard toward the third part of the meal, lost their antique severity, and were no longer sung exclusively in celebration of the gods, heroes, and great historical happenings: instead they sang of friendship, and of pleasure and of love, with a grace and harmony which our own hard dry tongues can never match.

The Grecian wines, which we still find good, were studied and classified by the ancient gourmets, from the gentlest liquids to the headiest; at certain banquets the whole gamut was run, and contrary to our present-day habit, the glasses grew larger in proportion to the excellency of the wines they held.

The loveliest women came to make still more beautiful these voluptuous gatherings: dances, games, and all kinds of amusements prolonged the evening's pleasure. Sensual delight was in the very air to breathe, and more than one Aristippus who arrived under Plato's banner made his final retreat under that of Epicurus.

Scholars outdid themselves to write praises of an art which could bestow such sweet enjoyment. Plato, Athenaeus, and many others are still known to us, but alas, their works are lost! If any one of them must be singled out for our especial regret, it is the poem *Gastronomy* by Archestratus, the friend of one of the sons of Pericles.

"This great writer," said Theotimus, "travelled to the ends of the earth and the seas, to find out for himself whatever was best that came from them. He learned much in his travels, but not from the morals of the people he met, for they are unchangeable; rather he went into the workrooms where were being prepared the delicacies of their various tables, and he associated only with such men as could satisfy his curiosity. His poem is a scientific treasure-house, and every line is in itself a precept."

Such was the state of cooking in Greece;[7] it rested thus until a handful of men, who had come to settle along the banks of the Tiber, spread their domination over the neighboring people, and ended by invading the whole world.

Roman Banqueting

128:   Good living was unknown to the Romans as long as they must fight to keep their own independence or subjugate their neighbors, who were quite as badly off as they. Even their generals walked behind the plow, and lived on vegetables. Frugivorous historians never fail to laud these primitive days, when thrift was still a reigning virtue. But when the Roman conquests had spread through Africa, through Sicily, through Greece; when the conquerors had feasted upon the spoils of countries far more advanced than their own; then they brought back to Rome all the preparations that had so charmed them abroad, and everything leads us to believe that they were far from frowned upon at home.

The early Romans had sent to Athens a deputation to report back to them on the laws; they continued to go there to study literature and philosophy. And as they polished their manners, they learned the pleasures of the table: cooks came back to Rome, along with the orators and philosophers, the rhetoricians and the poets.

With time and the series of triumphs which made all the riches of the world flow into Rome, the prodigality in feasting reached almost incredible lengths.

Everything was tasted, from grasshopper to ostrich, from dormouse to wild boar;† whatever might stimulate the appetite was tried as a seasoning, and as such the cooks used substances which we cannot conceive of, like asafoetida and rue.

The whole known world was put to gastronomical use, by both soldiers and travellers. Guinea fowl and truffles were brought from Africa, and rabbits from Spain and pheasants from Greece, where they had migrated from the banks of the Phasis, and peacocks from the farthest edge of Asia.

The most important of the Romans prided themselves on their beautiful gardens, where they not only raised the fruits that had always been known, like pears, apples, figs, and grapes, but also those which had been brought in from other lands: the apricot from Armenia, the peach from Persia, the Sidonian quince, the raspberry from the deep slopes of Mount Ida, and the cherry, one of Lucullus' spoils from the kingdom of Pontus.

---

† *Glires farsi.*—*Glires isicio porcino, item pulpis ex omni glirium membro tritis, cum pipere, nucleis, lasere, liquamine, farcies glires, et sutos in tegula positos, mittes in furnum, an farsos in clibano coques.*[8]

Dormice were considered a real delicacy: sometimes scales were brought to the table to verify their weight. And there is this well-known epigram by Martial on the subject of dormice, XIII, 59.

> *Tota mihi dormitur hiems, et pinguior illo*
> *Tempore sum, quo me nil nisi somnus alit.*

Lister, sensual doctor to a very sensual queen (Queen Anne),[9] while studying the advantages of the use of scales in cooking, observed that if twelve larks do not weigh twelve ounces they are barely edible, and that they are passable if they weigh exactly twelve, but that if they weigh thirteen, they are fat and excellent.

These importations, which necessarily came about in a variety of ways, at least prove that the interest in them was general, and that every Roman felt it a glory and a duty to contribute to the pleasures of the people-sovereign.

The fish was the highest prized among all edibles. Preferences were soon established for certain kinds of it, and went so far as to be shown for certain fish caught in certain latitudes. The catch from far countries was sent back to Rome in jars filled with honey, and when the creatures were unusually large they were sold at lofty prices because of the competition among the citizens who bid for them, some of whom were wealthier than kings.

What was drunk was no less the object of earnest attention and attentive care. Wines from Greece and Sicily and Italy were the joy of Rome, and since they drew their price either from the region of their pressing or the year they had been produced, a kind of birth certificate was written on each amphora.

O nata mecum consule Manlio. HORACE.

And this was not all. Thanks to that desire to intensify sensations which we have already mentioned, the Romans did what they could to make their wines more piquant and perfumed: they steeped them with flowers and aromatics, and with drugs of various kinds, and the concoctions which contemporary authors have told us about under the name of *condita* must have scorched their tongues and violently irritated their insides.

It is thus that the Romans, so long ago, tried to find the dream of alcohol, which was not realized for another fifteen centuries or so.

But it is above all toward the appurtenances of the feasts that this monstrous luxury hurled most of its energy.

All furnishings necessary to a banquet were prepared with careful study, whether in material or workmanship. The number of courses gradually increased to twenty and more, and at each new course everything which had been used in the preceding one was removed from sight.

Slaves were especially trained to assist at each part of the ceremony of a banquet, and these ritual roles were rigorously held to. The most precious scents embalmed the air of the dining hall. A kind of herald announced the merits of such dishes as were worthy of special attention, and told of the titles which had been bestowed upon them because of their distinction: in truth, nothing was neglected which could sharpen the appetite, hold the attention, and prolong the pleasures of the table.

This sensual extravagance had also its aberrations and its perversions. Such were the feasts where the fishes and birds which were served were counted in the thousands, and the dishes which had no other merit than their exorbitant cost, like one which was made of the brains of five hundred ostriches, and another where were used the tongues of five thousand birds which had first been trained to speak.

From all this it seems to me that it is easy to understand the enormous sums Lucullus must have spent on his table and the expenses of the banquets which he gave in his Room of Apollo, where it was the rule to exhaust all known methods to flatter the sensuality of his guests.

The Second Coming of Lucullus

129: These glorious days could well come again in our own time, and to see them once more it is only necessary to produce a Lucullus for them. Let us suppose, for example, that a man known to be powerfully rich would like to celebrate a great political or financial event, and give in its honor a memorable banquet, without bothering himself in any way with what it would cost;[10]

Let us suppose that he calls on all the arts to decorate every corner of the place chosen for the festival, and that he orders his stewards to use every artifice in the feast itself and whatever is best in his cellars to refresh his guests;[11]

That he have two plays presented by the greatest actors during this luxurious occasion;

That, during the repast, music be heard, executed by the most renowned artists not only of the voice but of instruments;

That he has planned, between the dinner and the coffee, a ballet performed by everything that is lightest and loveliest among the Opera's dancers;

That the evening end with a ball attended by two hundred of the most beautiful ladies, and four hundred of the most elegant gentlemen in existence;

That the buffet be constantly replenished with whatever is known to be peerless among hot, cool, and iced drinks;

That, toward the middle of the night, an artful supper be served to give everyone new enthusiasm;

That the servants be handsome and finely uniformed, and the lighting perfect; and, to forget nothing, that the host see to it that each guest be fetched and carried in a way proper to his social importance.

Given this feast, thus well conceived and planned, thus well prepared and well executed, anyone who knows Parisian life will agree with me that the next day's reckonings would make even the cashier of Lucullus tremble.

In my exposition of what we would have to do today to imitate one of this magnificent Roman's feasts, I have given enough hints to my reader of what was necessary for the obligatory accessories of such a celebration, where there must always be actors, singers, mimes, clowns, and everything that could add to the pleasure of people who had been invited together for the sole purpose of being amused.

What was first done by the Athenians, then by the Romans, still later in our own land during the Middle Ages, and finally by us today, springs equally from the basic nature of man, who awaits with impatience the end of his life work, and from a kind of inquietude which tortures him, so long as the sum total of the life that is remaining to him is not filled to the brimming point with conscious enjoyment.

Lectisternium et Incubitatium

130:   Romans, like the Athenians, ate lying down, but they did not come to do so without following a somewhat devious route.

First of all they used couches for the sacred meals which they offered to their gods; the foremost magistrates and the most powerful citizens took up the custom, and in a short time it became general and was followed until almost the beginning of the fourth century in the Christian era.

These couches, which were at the beginning no more than a kind of bench softened with straw and covered over with skins, soon became a vital part of the luxury which crept into everything having to do with banqueting. They were constructed of the most precious woods, inlaid with ivory and gold and even gems; they were formed of cushions of incredible softness, and the covers thrown over them were encrusted with magnificent embroideries.

Guests lay upon their left sides, leaning upon that elbow; and usually one couch held three people.

This way of lying at table, which the Romans called *lectisternium:* was it more convenient, was it more comfortable than the one we have adopted, or rather resumed? I do not think so.

From a physical point of view, leaning upon one elbow demands a certain apportioning of strength in order to stay balanced, and it is not without discomfort that the weight of one part of the entire body rests upon a single joint in the arm.

There is also something to be said from a physiological viewpoint: food is put into the mouth in an unnatural way, and flows with some difficulty toward the stomach, where it collects less evenly.

The absorption of liquids, or rather the act of swallowing them, is even more difficult: it must have demanded a very special skill not to spill the wine held in those great goblets which gleamed upon the tables of the wealthy Romans, and it is doubtless during the reign of the *lectisternium* that was born the proverb which says that *there's many a slip 'twixt the cup and the lip.*

It could not have been any easier to eat decently when lying down, especially when one remembers that many of the guests wore long beards and that they all ate with their fingers, or at best a knife to carry the morsels to the mouth, since the use of forks is modern; not one was found in the ruins of Herculaneum, although many spoons were uncovered there.

It must also be assumed that there were, here and there and now and then, some assaults on common modesty, in celebrations which frequently depassed the limits of moderation, on couches where both sexes lay together and where it was not rare to see a group of slumbering guests.

Nam pransus jaceo, et satur supinus
Pertundo tunicamque, palliumque.

And thus it is man's moral sense which first protested.

As soon as the Christian faith, released from the persecutions which bloodied its cradle, had gained some power, its ministers raised their voices against the sin of intemperance. They cried out against the length of banquets, where all their precepts were violated while all the fleshly pleasures were enjoyed. Themselves pledged to an austere regimen, they placed gourmandism among the capital sins, sourly criticized the promiscuity of the sexes, and above all attacked the custom of dining upon couches, one which seemed to them the result of a shameful softness and the principal cause of all the habits they deplored.

Their doomful cry was heard; couches ceased to ornament the banquet halls, and people went back to the old way of eating in a seated position; and by a happy accident this stricture based upon morality did nothing to hinder man's enjoyment.

Poetry

131:   In the Roman period which we are discussing, convivial poetry underwent a change and took on, in the mouths of Horace, Tibullus, and other fairly contemporary writers, a languorous soft character which the Greek muses never knew.

Dulce ridentem Lalagem amabo,
  Dulce loquentem.
  HORACE.

Quaeris quot mihi basiationes
Tuae, Lesbia, sint satis superque.
  CATULLUS.

Pande, puella, pande capillulos
Flavos, lucentes ut aurum lilidum.
Pande, puella, collum candidum
Productum bene candidus humeris.
  GALLUS.[12]

Barbarian Invasion

132: The five or six hundred years which we have run through in the past few pages were happy times for cookery, as well as for those who nurtured and enjoyed it, but the arrival or rather the invasion of the Northerners changed everything, upset everything: those days of glory were followed by a long and terrible darkness.

The art of eating disappeared, at the first sight of these foreigners, with all the other arts of which it is the companion and solace. Most of the great cooks were murdered in their masters' palaces; others fled rather than prepare feasts for the oppressors of their country; the small number who remained to offer their services had the humiliation of finding them refused. Those snarling mouths, those leathery gullets, were insensible to the subtleties of refined cookery. Enormous quarters of beef and venison, quantities beyond measure of the strongest drink, were enough to charm them; and since the invaders were always armed, most of their banquets degenerated into orgies, and their dining halls often ran with blood.

However, it is in the nature of things that what is excessive does not last long. The conquerors finally grew bored with their own cruelty: they mingled with the conquered, took on a tinge of civilization, and began to know the pleasures of a social existence.

Meals showed the influence of this alleviation. Guests were invited to them less to be stuffed than to be delighted, and some even began to understand that a certain attempt was being made to please them; a more amiable pleasure affected everyone, and the duties of hospitality had something gentler about them than before.

These betterments, which emerged toward the fifth century of our era, became even stronger under Charlemagne, and we can read in his Capitularies that this great king gave his own attention to making his lands furnish their best for the fine fare of his table.

Under him and his successors, the banquet halls took on an air at once gallant and chivalrous; ladies were present to add their beauty and to distribute the prizes won in tourney, and there could be seen the pheasant with gilded claws and the spread-tailed peacock, carried to the princes' tables by page boys gaudy with gold and by lovely virgins whose innocence did not always preclude their desire to please.

It should be noticed here that this makes the third time that women, sequestered by the Greeks, the Romans, and then the Franks, were brought in again to add their beauty to the banquet hall. The Turks alone have resisted this seduction. But dreadful storms menace that unsociable race, and before another thirty years have passed the powerful voice of the cannon will have proclaimed the emancipation of their odalisks.[13]

Once this movement was inaugurated it has lasted until our own times, growing stronger with every generation.

Women, even the highest-born, busied themselves in their homes with the preparation of foods, and considered it a part of the duties of hospitality, especially as understood and practiced in France toward the end of the seventeenth century.

Under their pretty fingers some dishes suffered amazing changes; an eel grew the tongue of a serpent, a hare was served wearing cat's ears, and like whimsicalities. They made great use of the spices which the Venetians were beginning to bring from the Orient, as well as the perfumes which came from Arabia, so that now and then a fish appeared cooked in rose water.[14] Luxury at table consisted mainly in the quantity of the dishes served, and things went so far that our kings felt obliged to put a brake on them by imposing sumptuary laws. These, needless to say, met the same fate as the ones written by the Greek and Roman legislators: they were laughed at, evaded, and forgotten, and survived in books only as historical monuments.

People continued, of course, to dine as well as they could, especially in the abbeys and convents and other religious retreats, for the wealth attached to these houses was less exposed to the hazards and dangers of the civil wars which for so long have ravaged France.

Since it is very plain that Frenchwomen have always taken more or less of a hand in whatever went on in their kitchens, it must be concluded that it is due to them that our cookery has reigned supreme in Europe, mainly because it contains an immense quantity of dishes so subtle and light and tempting that only the ladies could have invented them.

I have said that our ancestors continued to dine *as well as they could*. Often they could not. The suppers of our very kings were sometimes a matter of luck, and we know that they were far from certain during the civil wars: Henry IV would have had a thin meal of it once, if he had not had the good sense to invite to his table the humble but happy owner of the only turkey in a town where the king must spend the night.

Nevertheless the science of cookery advanced little by little: the Crusaders enriched it with the shallot, plucked from the plains of Ascalon; parsley was brought from Italy; and, long before the time of Louis IX, our butchers and sausage-makers had based on their artfulness with pork the hope of making their fortunes, of which to this very day we can see memorable examples.

Pastry cooks were no less successful, and the products of their industry were an honorable part of every feast. Since before the reign of Charles IX they have been an important guild, and that ruler gave them a charter into which was written the right to make all bread used in Holy Communion.

Toward the middle of the seventeenth century, the Dutch imported coffee into Europe.† Soliman Aga, the Turkish diplomat who so flustered the hearts of our great-great-grandmothers, served them their first cups of the beverage in 1660; an American hawked it openly at the Saint-Germain Fair in 1670; and the Rue Saint-André-des-Arts had the first café decorated with mirrors and marble-topped tables, much as is the fashion today.

Sugar began to appear about then, too;‡ and Scarron,[15] when he complained that his stingy sister had made the holes

---

† *The Dutch were the first among Europeans to transplant from Arabia some coffee bushes, which they took first to Batavia, and then to their own country.*

M. de Reissout, lieutenant-general of artillery, had a root of it brought from Amsterdam and presented it to the Jardin-du-Roi; it was the first one ever seen in Paris. This plant, of which M. de Jussie has left us a description, was in 1613 one inch in diameter and five feet high: the fruit is pretty, and somewhat resembles a cherry.

‡ *No matter what Lucretius has written, the ancients did not have sugar. It is a product of art, and without crystallization the cane gives but a useless and insipid liquid.*

of her sugar sieve smaller, at least let us know that this utensil was in use in his day.

It is also in the seventeenth century that brandy began to be more commonly known. Distilling, whose basic principles had been brought back by the Crusaders, had remained a mystery known to only a few adepts. Toward the beginning of the reign of Louis XIV, stills became better understood, but it was not until Louis XV's time that brandy was really popular, and it is only a few years ago that we succeeded, after countless minute experiments, in making alcohol in a single operation.

It was still in the same period that the use of tobacco started, with the result that sugar, coffee, brandy, and tobacco, those four things so important both to trade and to national revenue, have existed as such for barely two centuries.

Periods of Louis XIV and Louis XV

133:   It was under these auspices that the period of Louis XIV began, and under his brilliant reign that the science of banqueting obeyed the instinct for progress which was advancing all the other arts.

We have not yet forgotten those feasts which attracted the whole of Europe to them, nor those tournaments where for the last time gleamed the spears so completely replaced now by our bayonets, and the knightly armor which proved such a feeble bulwark against the brutality of modern cannon.

All the tournaments ended with sumptuous banquets, which were in reality their peak, for man's constitution is such that he cannot be fully happy as long as his taste remains unsatisfied: this imperious need has even influenced our language, so that to say that something has been done with perfection, we say that it has been done with taste.

By a natural consequence, those who presided over the preparations for these great feasts became men of note, which was reasonable enough, for they needed to combine within themselves a variety of qualities: inventive genius, the knowledge of organization, a sense of proportion, the ability to search out the sources of their supplies, firmness enough to exact obedience from their helpers, and unfailing promptness in every detail, so that nothing might be late.

It was at these great festivals that were first paraded the magnificence of the *surtouts*,[16] a new art which, combining painting with sculpture, presented an attractive scene and sometimes even the correct setting for the circumstances of the banquet or of the most honored guest.

Here was indeed all that was admirable and perhaps somewhat fantastic in the cook's art! But soon less crowded gatherings and more delicate repasts began to demand from them a more thoughtful kind of attention and more exacting care.

It was in the extremely exclusive dinner parties of royalty,[17] in the apartments of the court *favorites*, and in the subtle suppers of the bankers and courtesans, that culinary artists now displayed their skill and, driven by a praiseworthy spirit of rivalry, sought to outdo one another.

Toward the end of this period, the name of any renowned chef was almost always placed next to his patron's, and the latter was proud to have it there. The twin merits of birth and skills were thus united, and the most famous historical names are linked in our cook books with recipes which they had first patronized or invented or evolved.

This partnership no longer exists: we are no less gourmands than our forebears, and indeed quite the contrary, but we pay much less attention to the name of whoever rules our kitchen regions. The gastronomical applause of tipping our heads to the left is the only sign of admiration we give to the artist who enchants us, and the restaurant chefs, which is to say the public cooks, are the only ones who are shown a recognition which immediately places them among the ranks of our great capitalists. *Utile dulci.*

It was for Louis XIV that the prickly pear, which he called *la bonne poire*, was brought from the Echelles of the Levant, and it is thanks to his old age that we now have liqueurs.

This king was at times overcome by the weakness and vital fatigue which often show themselves after the age of sixty, and various combinations of brandy with sugar and essences were made into tonics for him, which according to the usage of the day were called *potions cordiales*. And such is the origin of the art of making liqueurs.

It is noteworthy that during more or less the same period the art of cookery was flourishing in the English court. Queen

Anne was a great lover of the pleasures of the table; she did not disdain to discuss pertinent affairs with her chef, and English recipe books contain many preparations designated (AFTER QUEEN ANN'S FASHION), "according to Queen Anne's method."

Culinary science, which was stationary during the domination of Madame de Maintenon, continued its mounting progress under the Regency.

The Duke of Orléans, a sensitive witty prince and one worthy of having true friends, shared many meals with them which were as choice as they were well-planned. I have been told by unimpeachable authorities that they were especially distinguished by their extremely subtle sauces, by matelottes as delicious as if they came from the river banks, and by superbly truffled turkeys.

Truffled turkeys! ! ! Their reputation mounts almost as fast as their cost! They are like lucky stars, whose very appearance makes gourmands of every category twinkle, gleam, and caper with pleasure.[18]

The reign of Louis XV was no less happy for gastronomy. Eighteen years of peace healed painlessly the wounds made by more than sixty years of war; wealth created by industry, and either spread out by commerce or acquired by its tradesmen, made former financial inequalities disappear, and the spirit of conviviality invaded every class of society.

It is during this period † that there was generally established

---

† *According to information which I have gleaned from the inhabitants of several districts, a dinner about 1740 for ten persons would be made up as follows:*

1st course: *the bouilli (meat and its broth);*
          an entrée of veal cooked in its own juice;
          an hors d'oeuvre.
2nd course: *a turkey;*
          a plate of vegetables;
          a salad;
          a creamy pudding (sometimes).
  Dessert: *some cheese;*
          some fruit;
          a jar of preserves.

Plates were changed only three times, after the soup, at the second course, and for dessert. Coffee was very rarely served, but quite often

more orderliness in the meals, more cleanliness and elegance, and those various refinements of service which, having increased steadily until our own time, threaten now to overstep all limits and lead us to the point of ridicule.

It was during this period, too, that cooks employed in luxurious brothels and by the most fashionable kept-women outdid themselves to add to the progress of culinary science.

There are numberless facilities when it is a question of providing for a large number of people with hearty appetites: with domestic meat, wild fowl, game, and a few large orders of fish, a meal for sixty people can be turned out in no time.

But in order to gratify mouths which never open wider than a simper, to tempt vaporous nervous ladies, to awaken stomachs made of papier-mâché, to rouse thin fanciful dyspeptics in whom appetite is like a whim always on the point of vanishing: to do this takes more genius, more deep thought, and more hard work than it would to resolve one of the most difficult problems in the geometry of the Infinite.

Louis XVI

134:   Since we have now reached the reign of Louis XVI and the days of the Revolution, we shall not drag out too carefully all the details of the changes which we have witnessed, but instead be content to outline in bold strokes the various betterments which, since 1774, have come about in the science of banqueting.

These have had for their object both the natural adjuncts of the art of gastronomy and the moral and social institutions which are a part of them; and in spite of the fact that these two divisions influence each other with a continuous reciprocity, we have felt it best, for reasons of clarity, to consider them separately.

Ameliorations from the Point of View of Art

135:   All professions whose end result is to prepare or sell nourishment, like those of our cooks, caterers, and pastry-

there was a cordial made from cherries or garden pink, still something of a novelty then.

and candymakers, our grocery store owners and such, have steadily grown more numerous; and a proof that this increase has only followed a real need for it is that it has done nothing to lessen the prosperity of its practitioners.

Physics and chemistry have been called to the aid of alimentary art: leading scholars have not felt it beneath their dignity to study our basic needs, and as a result there are improvements in everything from the simple *pot-au-feu* of a working man to the most extraordinarily complex and delicate foodstuffs ever to be served from gold and crystal.

New crafts have sprung up, as, for example, that of the *petit-four* bakers, who stand somewhere between the true cake-bakers and the candymakers. They control in their profession all those preparations which blend butter with sugar, eggs, and fine flour, like sponge cakes, macaroons, decorated cakes, meringues, and comparable delicacies.

The art of preserving foods has also become a skill in itself, whose purpose is to offer us at any season of the year those aliments which are peculiar to a single one.

Horticulture has made enormous progress, and hothouses offer to our view the most exotic fruits; various new kinds of vegetables have been acquired either through breeding or importation, and among them is a kind of cantaloup which, since it produces only fine melons, give the lie daily to the old proverb.†

We have cultivated, imported, and presented in regular order the wines of every country: Madeira to make the first assault on the gullet, French wines to continue through the dinner courses, and those of Spain and Africa to crown the whole.

French cookery has appropriated many foreign dishes like curry[19] and BEEFSTEAK, and seasonings like caviar and soy,[20] and drinks like punch, negus,[21] and so on.

Coffee has become popular, in the morning as a food and

---

† *Fifty at least you'll have to try,*
  Before you find one fit to buy.

It seems that melons as we grow them today were unknown to the Romans; what they referred to as MELO and PEPO were only a kind of cucumber, which they ate with extremely spicy sauces. APICIUS, DE RE COQUINARIA.

after dinner as a stimulating and tonic drink. A great number of receptacles, utensils, and other accessories have been invented to give to a meal a more or less pronounced aspect of luxury and festivity, so that foreigners who arrive in Paris find upon our tables many objects whose names they do not know and which they are often too shy to ask about.

And from all these facts we can draw the general conclusion that, at least at this very moment of writing, everything that precedes, accompanies, or follows a banquet is treated with an orderliness, a method, and an address which shows a desire to please which should delight any guest.

Final Refinements

136:   The use of the Greek word *gastronomy* has been revived: it sounded sweetly in our French ears, and although barely understood it is but necessary to pronounce it to bring a smile of good fellowship to every face.

We have begun to separate gourmandism from voracity and gluttony. We have begun to consider it as a desirable penchant which we might even boast about as a social quality, pleasant in a host, profitable to a guest, and useful to science, and we have begun to classify gourmands with those other enthusiasts whose predilections are admitted and recognized.

A general feeling of conviviality has spread throughout all classes of society, festive gatherings have greatly increased, and every individual, as he entertains his friends, outdoes himself to offer them whatever he has chosen as the best dish served to him as a guest in social levels above his own.

As a result of the pleasure which we have come to feel in other people's company, we have evolved a new division of our time, so that we devote to business the hours between morning and nightfall, and give up the rest to the delights which accompany and follow our festivities.

We have instituted the late breakfast party, a meal which has a special character because of its traditional dishes, and the gaiety which is always a part of it, and the unconventional garb which is permissible at it.

We have in the same way invented formal teas, a type of entertainment which is really extraordinary in that it is always offered to people who have already dined well and therefore feel neither thirst nor hunger, so that its purpose is solely one of passing the time and its foundation is no more than a display of dainties.

We have, also, created political banquets, which have recurred incessantly during the past thirty years whenever it has been necessary to exercise a particular influence over a great number of individuals. It is a type of meal which demands great lavishness, to which no one pays any heed, and the enjoyment of which is only felt in retrospect.

Finally, restaurants have become a part of our life: they are completely new as an institution, something which is often forgotten, and their effect is that any fellow with three or four goldpieces in his pocket can immediately, unfailingly, and without any more bother than the mere wishing, buy himself all the earthy pleasures which his taste buds may dictate.

THE TRANSLATOR'S GLOSSES

1. This word is so Latin, and so little used, that it sounds very much like a Professorial invention. But according to the Concise Oxford Dictionary (1942), it does actually mean just what it seems to: fruit-eating.

2. Escoffier says sadly that these birds are not met with in American markets and it is therefore useless to give any recipes for them. The simplest French cook book I own says to put them plentifully upon a brochette, with a little piece of bacon between each one, and roast them over a very hot fire for eight or ten minutes. It says with gravity: "Figpeckers must never be emptied of their guts."

3. One of these may have been the Canon Charcot mentioned in "Meditation 6" (page 87), whose recipe for eating small birds continues to titillate the Professor's readers. He himself manages to endow only other people with a true taste for uncooked meat, and reports its virtues by hearsay, although a

rumor has it that he used to embarrass his legal colleagues by appearing all too often in court with a brace of wild birds tucked into his coat-tails, to hasten with his own heat their race toward that gamy disintegration known as "highness." While it cannot be thought that he prepared all high birds with the Lucullan care he prescribed for pheasant ("Varieties," XII, page 374), it is probable from his cautious approach to the subject that he preferred to let other gastronomers enjoy game in the raw, and that he at least grilled the meat he carried with such odoriferous nonchalance in his pockets.

I myself have never yet been reduced by stark hunger to the ability to tear flesh from a carcass and devour it, but a peckish gourmandism has often enabled me to relish a plate of raw beef, finely chopped, served forth with toasted sourdough bread and some watercress. And rawboned fish, cut into thin strips and marinated for an hour or two in lime or lemon juice, is finicky enough for any self-styled gourmet.

4.   One of the most overquoted things in the English language is Charles Lamb's nicely foolish story of the discovery of roast pig, and of how Bo-bo the idiot Chinese boy and his almost equally silly father kept burning down their buildings so that they might taste the poor little grilled porkers within. The Professorial word *osmazome* is never mentioned, of course, but Lamb writes: "There is no flavor comparable, I will contend, to that of the crisp, tawny, well-watched, not over-roasted *crackling*, as it is well called—the very teeth are invited to their share of the pleasure at this banquet in overcoming the coy, brittle resistance—" This plump little literary classic is as much fun to reread as some by Dickens, and is a sure proof of the connection between our sentiments and our salivary glands.

5.   *Boudin* in France is a kind of sausage, a kind of custard really. It used to be part of any Parisian Christmas Eve feast, incongruous sometimes amongst the truffles, very forthright and vulgar. I would like to taste *Kokoretzi* in Greece, any time at all but especially at Easter, when the young lambs, when there *are* any young lambs, are broiled on long pine branches over open fires and beside them spit and sizzle all the entrails, chopped and highly seasoned and either tied together or stuffed into the gut-casings. It sounds good. It sounds a little less darkly disagreeably smooth than *boudin*.

6. Anne-Lefèvre Dacier (1654–1720) was an early French bluestocking, daughter of one famous classical scholar and wife of another. She translated THE ILIAD, among many other Greek and Latin works. In ANTIQUITATES CULINARIAE, which was written and published in London in 1791 by Richard Warner, it says that Madame Dacier was mistaken, for in the Fifth Book of THE ILIAD there is a mention of boiling meat. Few readers can or will dispute this only faintly portentous point.

7. In my 1870 edition of THE PHYSIOLOGY OF TASTE there is a footnote here signed by the Marquis de Cussy, who had a rather poor opinion of the Professor's gourmandism. It is probably taken from L'ART CULINAIRE: "In spite of these successful attempts, Athens never knew *great cookery*, for the sole reason that she sacrificed too much to her love of sweet dishes and fruits and flowers; what is more, she never had the fine wheat bread of the Caesarian Romans, nor their Italian spices, nor their subtle sauces and their white Rhine wines."

8. This Apician recipe for stuffed and roasted dormice reminds me of a pleasantly drunken American called Big Boy, mentioned in LAST MAN AROUND THE WORLD by Stephen Longstreet (1941), who downed a great deal of hot wine once in China and then ate six newborn mice fried alive, thinking them some kind of crisp radish. His outlandish gourmandism was unconscious, but other men since the Romans have battened on the mouse family, as witness this quotation from the IRISH QUARTERLY REVIEW of the mid-nineteenth century: "We ourselves once betted five shillings, that a certain dear friend of ours would not eat a mouse-pie—and lost. In short, *chacun à son goût*. (He got through the task with great ease, and offered, when the pie was done, to eat a mouse roasted in the fur with butter, and oat crumb-cakes, for the same sum—but we declined indulging in any more such experiments.)"

9. This lusty and "unfeminine" ruler, reputedly an habitual tippler of champagne, could have been no more eccentric than a certain Mrs. Jeffreys, "the sister of Wilkes," as Dr. Doran tells of her in TABLE TRAITS (London, 1854). At Bath she slept the year 'round with open windows, crazy enough! A dozen clocks chimed unevenly in her chilly bedroom. And ". . . she breakfasted frugally enough on chocolate and dry toast, but proceeded daily in a sedan chair, with a bottle of Madeira at her

side, to a boarding-house to dine. She invariably sat between two gentlemen, men having more sinew in mind and body than women, and with these she shared her London Particular . . . some mighty joint that was especially well-covered with fat . . . She was served with slices of this fat, which she swallowed alternately with pieces of chalk, procured for her especial enjoyment. Neutralizing the *subacid* of the fat with the alkaline principle of the chalk, she amalgamated, diluted, and assimilated the delicious compound with half-a-dozen glasses of her delicious wine. The diet agreed well with the old lady, and she maintained that such a test authorized use."

10. Once before the First World War, Isadora Duncan gaily spent more than 200 of her Lohengrin's many thousands of dollars, to give a summer festival as she felt it should be given. It began at four in the afternoon, in the park at Versailles, where marquees filled with everything from caviar to tea cakes tempted her horde of real and self-styled friends, and where the whole Colonne orchestra, directed by Pierné, played Wagner. Then there was a magnificent banquet. It lasted until midnight, when lights sprang up everywhere in the park, and a Viennese orchestra made lively until dawn the worshippers of Siegfried and Lucullus. Duncan, gently sarcastic, wrote that if a rich man *must* spend money to entertain his friends, that was her idea of how it should be done!

11. Some time after the First World War, a financier in Paris wanted to celebrate one or another of his portentous deals, and invited ten polyglot and gastronomical colleagues to dine with him at the Ritz. "Money doesn't count," he said, handing over some twelve thousand francs. "I only want the foods and wines to be perfect . . ." And the gentlemen ate some twelve courses of Lucullan fare, floated downward on the following incredible flood: Sherry Carta Oro Viejo, Meursault Goutte d'Or 1915, Magnum de Château Léonville Barton 1878, Jeroboam de Château Lafitte 1870, Pommery 1911, Grand Chambertin 1906, Romanée 1881, Giesler 1906, Château Yquem 1869, Cognac Hennessy (Reservée Privée). This is by no means the most princely wine list to hand. But it will do.

12. There is no light Latin verse attributed to any Gallus, and I suspect this is one of the Professor's little Gallic tricks.

13. It took nearer a hundred than thirty years to emancipate

the concubines in Turkey, to unveil them and let them hold public office, and forget the blunt title they had worn, made from the Turkish words *odah*, chamber, and *liq*, function.

14. In spite of the Professor's straight face in mentioning this culinary atrocity, it manages to sound almost as funny as some of the things suggested in "women's magazines," or even in the more solemn quarterlies devoted solely to *la gourmandise*. The former lard their recipes heavily with love stories, and the latter with truffled anecdotes of gastronomical tours through France, or The Old South, or even Alaska. They both have a weakness for spices and one form or another of rose water, figuratively speaking, for they comfort uncountable hungers of the soul as well as the body.

15. Paul Scarron (1610–1660) was a writer of realistic novels and high-comedy burlesque plays. At one time he was married to the pretty woman who later became Madame de Maintenon, but perhaps a surer claim to immortality is the influence he had on Molière and Beaumarchais and many another French playwright.

16. These gastronomical pipe dreams appeared in England long before they did in France, according to the Professor's dates, and they were a necessary part of any great celebration at table. They were made, it is true, of pastry and spun sugar, but so many feathers and furbelows went into them that it was inconceivable that they be eaten . . . although it is not known what happened to them once they had been displayed at the banquet table. Many years later the Britons were more sensible, and saw to it that their great cooks made *edible* "removes," as they were called by then. Here are a few of Soyer's directions, in THE GASTRONOMIC REGENERATOR (London, 1847), for "A British Admiral's Cake": "Make a sponge-cake of twenty eggs as directed, have a tin mould in the shape of a vessel . . . (. . . 18 inches in length, 6 in breadth, and high in proportion); paper, butter, and lightly flour the interior, into which pour the mixture, which bake an hour and a half a day or two before using; mask the exterior with chocolate icing to imitate a ship, when quite dry partly empty the interior, leaving a piece across the centre, to fix the mast upon, which you have made of pâté d'office, as also the ladders, riggings, and guns; mask

the guns with chocolate icing, and form the muzzles with small rings of puff paste, place them judiciously at the sides, place the vessel upon a dish rather upon one side, lay rolls of gelée à la bacchante round, over which lay thin slices of the same to form waves, make the sails of wafer or rice-paper, fix them to the mast as if filled with wind, also have a flag made of the same and painted with a little water-colour which place at the stern; well soak the interior with wine or brandy, mixed with apricot marmalade, just before serving, and when ready fill with a delicate vanilla ice; you have previously formed some ropes of spun sugar, which affix to the rigging at the moment of serving. This dish has a pleasing effect . . ." and the directions go on and on, until finally Soyer ends by confessing: "The remains and trimmings are very good made into cabinet pudding!"

17.   The phrase *petit couvert*, which Brillat-Savarin uses here, applied only to the meals which French royalty enjoyed in complete intimacy, with a few trusted friends.

18.   In this amusing description the Professor uses one of his own words, TRIPUDIER, which has not yet shown itself in any French dictionary and is probably from the Latin *tripudiare*, to caper or dance.

19.   Here Brillat-Savarin used the word *karik*, which is to *curry* exactly what *bif-teck* is to *beef-steak* in international gastronomy. He meant the powder of bruised spices which gives even the worst curry dishes, and there are many of them, their distinctive flavor. There are almost as many recipes for the powder as there are Indians to blend it, of course. Its chief virtue, which is unknown to almost all Americans who must buy it bottled or tinned, lies in the fact that it should be ground freshly every day, but there may still be a few "peppery old colonels" in the British Empire's outposts who can follow some such recipe as this, and make it up in 2½ pound lots:

Grind in a mortar to a fine powder,
of cloves, mustard, and poppy seeds,
1 ounce each;
of cardamom, fennel, chillies, and mace,
2 ounces each;
of dry ginger and pepper,

4 ounces each;
of turmeric, cumin, and coriander seeds,
8 ounces each.

20.   This is almost surely soy sauce, a blackish liquid either thick or thin, which every cook from the old Countess Morphy to young Mrs. John Doe will admit "reigns supreme in Japan —*shoyu* . . . made from the Soya bean seeds, wheat, and pure salt, with a pleasant and distinctive flavor, unlike that of any of our European bottled sauces."

Once a cook has started to use soy, it becomes a kind of game to play, for there is perhaps no other condiment which can be added to so many things with so little potential damage, such small risk of gastronomical mayhem.

One of the best uses I have ever found for it, besides as a marinade for steaks being prepared for the barbecue, is as covering for fish which cannot be used at once and must be held over in a cold place for a day. It is patted generously onto every surface, to form an ominous dry dark skin. Then no fishy odors creep from it to other food, and when the ordinary preparation takes place there seems nothing but an added delicacy. It is mysterious.

21.   Negus is a mixture of hot water with wine, usually sherry or port, and sugar, lemon, spices. It is a pleasant tipple on a cold day, but can soon grow tiresome. I used to drink it on winter market days, in France in a small bar on the ground floor of a house named La Coupole and inevitably misnamed La Copule. If the delicate care that the barman gave to my drink was any indication of his feelings, my discreet and well-chaperoned mid-morning visits were a pleasant break in his sex-ridden routine, and the negus was a fine potion indeed.

MEDITATION 28

ON

RESTAURATEURS

137: A restaurateur is anyone whose business consists in offering to the public a repast which is always ready, and whose dishes are served in set portions at set prices, on the order of those people who wish to eat them.

The establishment itself is called a *restaurant*,[1] and he who directs it is the *restaurateur*. The list of dishes with their prices is called, quite simply, the *carte* or bill of fare, and the *carte à payer*[2] or check indicates the amount of food which has been ordered and its cost to the consumer.

There are few men among those who throng the restaurants who bother to suspect that he who first invented them must have been a genius and a profound observer of his fellows.

We shall pander to their laziness, and outline the maze of ideas which have finally resulted in this highly useful and popular institution.

Origin

138: Toward 1770, after the glorious days of Louis XIV, the skulduggeries of the Regency, and the long tranquillity of Cardinal Fleury's dominance, visitors in Paris still had very few resources properly classified as conducive to good living.

They were forced to depend on the cooking of their inn-keepers, which was generally bad. There were some hotels serving a regular dinner which, with few exceptions, offered only the strict necessities,[3] and which moreover was available only at fixed times.

It is true that there were caterers. They, however, provided not portions but whole courses, and anyone who wished to entertain a few friends must order from them well in advance. The result was that visitors who did not have the good luck to be invited to some well-ordered private home left the capital without knowing anything of the wealth and the delicacies of Parisian cookery.

A system which damaged so constantly the public interest could not last forever, and already some of the more thoughtful citizens dreamed of improvement.

At last an intelligent fellow came along who decided for himself that an active cause could not but produce its effect; that since the same needs arose every day at about the same times, hungry diners would flock to a place where they could be sure of satisfying such needs most agreeably; that, if he should cut off a chicken wing to please the first comer, there would not fail to be another arrival who would gladly accept the leg; that the carving of a slice of roast meat in the obscurity of the kitchen would not ruin the rest of the joint; that nobody minded a slight increase in cost when he had been served well, and promptly, and properly; that there would be no end to the necessarily complex arrangements if the diners were allowed to discuss the price and quality of the food they might order, but that a wide choice of dishes and a set price for each one would have the advantage of being adaptable to every purse.

This intelligent fellow considered, as well, a great many other things which are easy to guess. He became the first *restaurateur*, and created a profession which is always a successful one if he who practices it possesses sincerity, order, and skill.

* * *

Advantages of Restaurants

139:   The encouragement of this new profession, which spread from France all over Europe, is extremely advantageous to everyone, and of great scientific importance.

(1)   Thanks to it, any man can dine at the hour most convenient to him, according to the surroundings in which either his business or his pleasures have placed him.

(2)   He is sure of not spending more than the sum which he has decided upon, since he knows beforehand the price of each dish to be served to him.

(3)   Once he has fixed the limit of his expenses, he can, according to his tastes, choose a meal solid, light, or dainty; he can bathe it in the best French and foreign wines, spice it with coffee, and perfume it with the liqueurs of the Old World and the New, and without other limits than the vigor of his appetite and the capacity of his stomach. A restaurant is Paradise indeed to any gourmand.

(4)   It is, moreover, an extremely useful thing for travelers, for strangers, for those whose families are temporarily in the country, and for all those, in a word, who do not have their own kitchens or are for the time being deprived of them.

Before the period we have already mentioned (1770), rich and powerful people were almost the only ones who enjoyed two great advantages: they could travel quickly, and they were always well fed.

The advent of new public vehicles which can cover fifty leagues in twenty-four hours has eliminated the first privilege; the coming of restaurants has done away with the second, since through them good living is at the beck of any man.

If he has fifteen or twenty francs to spend, and if he can sit down at the table of a first class restaurateur, he is as well off as if he dined with a prince, or more so, for the feast at his command is quite as splendid, and since he can order any dish he wishes, he is not bothered by personal considerations or scruples.

Examination of a Restaurant

140:   The dining room of a restaurant, looked at with some care, presents to the keen eye of a philosopher a scene well worth his attention, because of the variety of human situations which it contains.

At the back is a crowd of solitary diners, who order at the top of their voices, wait impatiently, eat in a rush, pay, and get out.

There are visiting country families who, content with a frugal meal, still make it eventful by a few dishes which are unknown to them, and who seem to relish delightedly their novel surroundings.

Near them sits a married couple of Paris: it is easy to spot them by the hat and shawl hung up behind them, and plain that for a long time now they have not had much to say to each other. They have taken seats at some neighboring theatre, and I wager that one or the other of them will fall asleep in it.

Farther on are two lovers. They give themselves away by the eagerness of one, the coquetries of the other, and the gourmandism of them both. Pleasure shines in their eyes, and by the way they order their little feast their whole past together can be guessed, and their future prophesied.

In the middle of the room is a table occupied by the regular patrons, most of whom dine there at reduced rates and from a set list of dishes. They know by name all the waiters, who tip them off secretly to what is best and freshest. They sit there like a kind of stock-in-trade to the restaurateur, a center of attraction around which the other diners collect, or, to put it better, like the tame ducks which hunters in Brittany use to lure in the wild ones.

And then there are those individuals whose faces are known to everyone and whose names are never even heard. They act as if they were in their own homes, and more often than not try to pick up a little conversation with the diners nearest them. They belong to one or another of those types unique in Paris, who, having neither property nor private funds nor ambition, still manage to spend a great deal of money.

Finally there are foreigners here and there, especially Englishmen; these last stuff themselves on double portions of meat, order whatever is most costly, drink the headiest wines, and do not always leave without support.

The exactitude of this picture can be verified any day of

the week, and although it has been drawn only to stimulate our curiosity, perhaps it may also serve to point a moral lesson.

Inconveniences

141: There is no doubt that opportunity, and the all-powerful attraction of a restaurant's list of dishes, have led many diners into extravagances which were beyond their pockets. Perhaps some delicate stomachs too could trace their indigestion to this institution, and blame it for various sacrifices made willy-nilly to the least worthy of the Venuses.[4]

But what is even more ominous to the social order is that we are convinced that solitary dining strengthens egotism, and accustoms an individual to think only of himself, to cut himself off from the life around him, to rid himself of the amenities of polite intercourse; it is all too easy to distinguish those men who dine habitually in restaurants, thanks to their behavior before, and during, and after any other kind of meal at which they are guests.†

Competition

142: We have already said that the establishment of restaurants has been of great importance to the science of gastronomy.

In short, as soon as experience has proved that a highly worthy recipe for ragoût can make the fortune of its inventor, cupidity, that power of powers, fires all the imaginations and puts every cook to work.

Chemical analysis has found edible parts in substances until now judged useless; new foods have been discovered, old ones bettered, and both new and old combined in a thousand ways. Foreign inventions have been imported; the world itself has been put to use, and contributes so much to our daily fare that

---

† *Among other things, they serve themselves from any plate of food, already cut up, which is being passed, and then they put it down in front of them instead of handing it to their neighbors, whom they are not used to considering.*

in one meal we can trace a complete course of alimentary geography.

Prix-Fixe Restaurants

143: While the art of cookery thus followed an upward trend, as much in discoveries as in prices (for what is new is always dear), the same motive, that is the hope of reward, gave it a contrary movement, at least in the matter of expense.

Some of the resturateurs decided to try to wed good living to economy, and by their appealing to men of modest fortune, who are necessarily the most numerous, to assure themselves of the greatest number of patrons.

They sought out among foodstuffs of moderate cost the ones which best responded to intelligent preparation.

They discovered in butchers' meat, which is always excellent in Paris, and in sea fish which is very plentiful there,[5] an inexhaustible resource; and to complement it, fruits and vegetables which modern horticulture makes it possible to market cheaply. They calculated shrewdly the basic necessities to fill a normal stomach, and to quench an uncaptious thirst.

They observed that there are many foods which owe their high prices either to their scarcity or to the season, and which can be offered somewhat later without this pecuniary obstacle. Gradually they arrived, little by little, at such precision in their reckoning that, while still earning a profit of from twenty-five to thirty per cent, they could offer their regular customers, for two francs and even less, a sufficient dinner and one which any well-bred man would willingly enjoy, since it would cost him at least a thousand francs a month to maintain, in his own home, a table as varied and as well supplied.

The restaurant keepers, considered from this last point of view, have rendered an especial service to that significant part of the population of any large city which is made up of visitors, soldiers, and clerks, and they have been led by their shrewdness to the solution of a seemingly insoluble problem: how to live well and at the same time moderately and even cheaply.

The restaurateurs who have followed this plan have been no less well repaid than their colleagues at the other end of the scale, and have suffered fewer serious reverses; their fortunes, even if slower in coming, have been more solid, for though they made less money at one time they made it every day, and it is a mathematical truth that when an equal number of units are collected at one point, they give an equal total, whether they were brought there in dozens or one by one.

Enthusiasts have kept bright the names of many culinary artists who have shone in Paris since the beginning of the restaurants. Among them one can cite Beauvilliers, Méot, Robert, Rose, Legacque, the Véry brothers, Henneveu, and Baleine.[6]

Some of the restaurants run by these men have owed their celebrity to one special thing: the *Veau Qui Tette*, to sheep's trotters; the . . . . . to tripe served on the gridiron; the *Frères Provençeaux* to cod with garlic; *Véry* to truffled entrées; *Robert* to his dinners ordered in advance; *Baleine* to the great care he took to serve fine fish; and *Henneveu* to the mysterious little private rooms on his fourth floor.[7] But of all these gastronomical heroes, none has more right to a biographical note than Beauvilliers, whose death was announced by the newspapers in 1820.

Beauvilliers

144: Beauvilliers, who established himself toward 1782, was for more than fifteen years the most famous restaurateur of Paris.

He was the first to have an elegant dining room, handsome well-trained waiters, a fine cellar, and a superior kitchen; and when more than one of those we have just mentioned tried to equal him, he kept the upper hand with ease, since he was already so far in advance in following the progress of gastronomy.

During the two successive occupations of Paris, in 1814 and 1815, equipages of every country could be seen before his establishment: he knew personally all the foreign heads of state, and ended by speaking all their languages, at least as far as his profession demanded.

Beauvilliers published, toward the end of his life, a work in two octavo volumes called L'ART DU CUISINIER. This fruit of long experience bears the imprint of intelligent skill, and still enjoys all the esteem which was given it when it first appeared. Never before that time had cookery been discussed with so much method and precision. This book, which has appeared in several editions, made things much easier for the works which followed but never surpassed it.

Beauvilliers had a prodigious memory: he recognized and welcomed, after twenty years, people who had eaten perhaps once or twice at his restaurant. He also had, for certain cases, a method which was all his own: when he knew that a group of very wealthy people dined in one of his rooms he came up to them with an important air, bowed low, and seemed to shower them with unusual and special attentions.

He would point out a dish which was best not to try, and another one to command with all haste, and would himself order a third which nobody knew existed, at the same time calling up bottles from a cellar to which he alone held the key; in all, he showed such a friendly and agreeable manner that all these *extra* additions to the total bill seemed so many courtesies on his part. But his role of perfect host did not last long; having played it to the hilt he took his bow, and soon afterwards the swollen bill and the bitterness of paying it[8] were proof enough that the dinner had been enjoyed in a restaurant and not a private home.

Beauvilliers made and lost and remade his fortune several times, and we do not know in which of these states death surprised him; but he had such extraordinary outlets for his money that we cannot believe his beneficiaries found themselves greatly enriched by his will.

The Gastronomer in a Good Restaurant

145: It appears upon scrutinizing the bill-of-fare from each of several first class restaurants, especially those of the Véry brothers and the *Frères Provençeaux*, that a diner who has seated himself at one of such tables has at his command, as elements of his meal, at least the following things:

12 soups,
24 hors-d'oeuvres,
15 or 20 entrées of beef,
20 entrées of lamb and mutton,
30 entrées of fowl and game,
16 or 20 of veal,
12 of pastry,

20 of fish,
15 of roasts,
50 side dishes,
50 desserts.

Moreover the blissful gastronomer can drench all this with a choice of at least thirty kinds of wine, from a good Burgundy to a Cape wine or Tokay, and with twenty or thirty kinds of potent liqueurs, without counting coffee and such mixtures as punch, negus, SILLABUD,[9] and others.

Among the various parts which make up the dinner of a real gastronomer, the principal ones come from France, like butchers' meat, fowl, and fruits; some are imitated from the English, like beefsteak, the WELCHRABBET, punch, and so on; others come from Germany, like sauerkraut, Hamburg chopped beef, Black Forest fillets; still others like olla-podrida, garbanzo beans, dried Malaga grapes, pepper-cured Xerica hams, and liqueur wines from Spain; others from Italy, like macaroni, and Parmesan cheese, and Bologna sausages and polenta and sherbets, and more liqueurs; still others like dried meats and smoked eels and caviar from Russia; and others from Holland, like salt cod, cheeses, pickled herrings, curaçao and anisette; and from Asia come Indian rice, sago, curry, soy, Schiraz wine, coffee; from Africa the Cape wines; and finally from America come things like potatoes, yams, pineapples, chocolate, vanilla, sugar, and so on: all of which is ample proof of our statement, already often made, that a meal such as can be ordered in Paris is a cosmopolitan whole in which every part of the world is represented by one or many of its products.

THE TRANSLATOR'S GLOSSES

1. In 1879 Charles Monselet wrote, in one more "introduction" to the Professor's book: ". . . restaurants are multiplied to infinity. What has cookery gained? I ought rather to say what

it has lost. Nearly all the roasts are now done in the oven. An abomination!"

It is interesting to find, in a fairly thorough glance at the prefaces which have been written to THE PHYSIOLOGY OF TASTE, that almost every one bewails the present sad state of restaurant gastronomy, from Monselet through Arthur Machen, who in 1925 sang sadly: "There may be in the wilderness of London stout old taverns, chop-houses, coffee-houses, still left, where decent English food may still be obtained; but if such places exist, they must be reckoned among the many secrets of the multitudinous streets. I know them not; I cannot find them . . . Roasting is almost obsolete; and at one of the most famous 'Old English' resorts in London, where they do roast, they hang beef, veal, and lamb on one spit, and baste all three joints in the common gravy . . ."

In such good critical company I can but say: If it were only the roasts! Last night in Hollywood's best tavern, served with proper pomp, some soles *à la Meunière* were brought to me, and they were by some miracle fine fillets of true sole, and they were hot and pretty . . . and they had been dipped into an egg batter and fried in something very far removed from butter.

2. In 1853 an unremembered Paris editor of THE PHYSIOLOGY OF TASTE noted here: "This word, *carte à payer*, common from the very beginning of restaurants, has been replaced first of all by *carte*, and then by *addition*, which is most heard today." A good fifty years later Newnham-Davis wrote, in a popular and intelligent little book called THE GOURMET'S GUIDE TO EUROPE: "The payment of the *addition*—the word is slangy, but it is used even at the Café Anglais—is a disagreeable necessity . . ."

3. "The strict necessities," gastronomically, are and always have been debatable, according to the sex and surroundings and age and social position of the human being who debates. War also has its say, and many a good man who would once settle, grudgingly, for a theoretical meal of soup, bread, wine, and cheese, is now in heaven on earth to find himself face to face with any one of those four basic comforters.

4. This is a fairly complicated allusion, at least in translation. In the original it says *la Vénus infime*, the basest Venus. The English version prefaced by Arthur Machen in 1925 says, in a donnish way, "the least exalted of the Venuses." Nimmo and

Bain, much more direct in a classical way, say "Venus Cloaca."
It is possible to speculate here upon the connection between
excretory functions and various forms of love, but the simplest
conclusion is that Brillat-Savarin referred to uneasy innards
which must willy-nilly render upward or downward their sewer-
destined sacrifices.

5.   Nimmo and Bain noted in 1884: "Sea-fish is not even
now abundant in Paris, and cannot have been so in 1825, before
railways were used!" In justice to our author, however, let us
state that the ALMANACH DES GOURMANDS for 1825 also speaks
of the abundance of sea-fish in the French capital. Travelers
for many generations, though, have talked and written of the
fine fish of Paris, and probably the secret lies between the art
of preparation and the fact that the city lies where it does.
Newnham-Davis wrote, some fifty years ago: ". . . Paris—sending tentacles west to the waters where the sardines swim, and
south to the home of the lamprey, and tapping a thousand
streams from trout and tiny gudgeon and crayfish—can show
as noble a list of fishes as any city in the world."

6.   Charles Monselet wrote in 1879 that he had been told that
Brillat-Savarin was "a frequenter of the café Lemblin," and that
he always came there with a dog who was a Paris legend. This
is the only such detail of the Professor's life that I can find. As
for the Lemblin . . . ?

7.   Every city with any claim to vitality has had its good restaurateurs who capitalized more or less discreetly on the obvious
connection of the pleasures of the table and of the couch. In
1947 it was rumored that most of the better class dining rooms
in this category had been closed in New Orleans, but at least
there, as in San Francisco, memory could feed nostalgic hunger
on the recollections of Madame ***'s fourth floor, and chuckle
over the hoary remark that on the first floor you lost your purse,
on the second your reputation, on the third what my headmis-
tress used to refer to as "your underpinnings," and on the
fourth . . . ?

8.   Here Brillat-Savarin uses a phrase, *le quart d'heure de
Rabelais*, which was still recognized in France a hundred or so
years later, although in a somewhat pedagogic and self-conscious
way. It refers to the painful few minutes in which a good meal
must be paid for by the host, in any public eating place, while

his guests can sit back in easy digestive freedom, and is supposed to be so named for the time when Rabelais was caught in a tavern with no money on him. He quickly rolled up three little packets of ashes and dust, and labelled each one POISON. Then he marked one, "For the King," the second "For the King's brother," and the last "For the King's son." The landlord took one hidden peek at them, and ran for the nearest soldier. Rabelais was carted off to Paris, and there he confessed that it was the only way he could figure to escape being arrested for not paying his bill . . . and to get a free ride to the Capital! Not all postprandial reckonings are as fortunate as his.

9.   A real syllabub is to my mind cold but not thick, frothy but not cloying, and is made of light cream whipped with sherry and sugar to one instant before it curdles. Then it can be a refreshing and gently stimulating half-dessert–half-drink. But there is a wonderful recipe which is both thick and cloying, in a delightfully revolting way: 2 cups sour cream, ¾ cup medium dry sherry, ½ cup fine white sugar, peel and rind of 1 lemon. They are mixed lightly together, chilled thoroughly together, the peel and rind are removed, and the rest is whipped with a whisk-type beater until it turns thick. It must be eaten with a spoon.

MEDITATION 29

CLASSICAL GOURMANDISM IN ACTION

The Story of M. de Borose

146:   M. de Borose was born about 1780. His father was secretary to the king. He lost his parents when very young, and found himself the possessor at an early age of a fortune of some forty thousand pounds. At that time it was a pretty sum; by now it means no more than the bare pennies to prevent one's dying of hunger.

A paternal uncle supervised his education. He learned Latin, the while he felt astonished that when everything could be so well phrased in French he must learn to say the same things in another way. Nevertheless he progressed, and by the time he reached Homer he changed his first opinions, found a real pleasure in pondering on ideas so elegantly expressed, and made sincere efforts to comprehend to its depths the language used by this subtle poet.

He also learned music, and after trying several instruments he fixed on the piano. He restrained himself from diving into the infinite complexities of this musical tool,† and, adapting it to

† *The piano has been developed solely to facilitate the composition of music and to accompany singing. It has neither warmth nor expression*

his actual capacities, was content to become adept enough to accompany the songs of others.

But, in this field, he was preferred even to the professionals, for he never tried to insinuate himself into first place; he did not thrash his arms about nor roll his eyes;† and he carried out conscientiously the first duty of an accompanist, to support and make shine the person who is singing.

Thanks to his tender age he survived without accident the most terrible years of the Revolution, but finally was conscripted. He bought a man who went bravely forth to die for him, and armed with his substitute's death certificate he found himself in a comfortable position to celebrate our triumphs or deplore our reverses.

M. de Borose was of medium height, but in perfect proportions. As for his face, it was sensual, and we can give a good idea of it by saying that if we could have put him in the same room with the actors Gavaudan of the *Variétés* and Michot of the *Français*, and the vaudeville manager Désaugiers, the four of them would have seemed to be members of the same family. All in all, it was taken for granted that he was a good-looking fellow, and now and then he undoubtedly had occasion to believe so.

It was a great problem for him to choose a profession: he tried several, but since he found something inconvenient about each of them he drifted into a busy laziness, which is to say that he was always welcome in certain literary groups, that he was on the charity board of his district, and that he was a member of various philanthropic organizations; when we add to this the care of his fortune, which he managed superlatively, it is plain that he was, like any other man, kept busy by his engagements, his correspondence, and his general office work.

When he was twenty-eight, he believed that it was time for him to marry. He had no desire to see his future wife except

---

when played alone. Spaniards describe with the word BORDONEAR *the act of playing on such plucked instruments.*

† *A term in musical slang:* FAIRE LES BRAS *means to raise the elbows and shoulder blades as if one were overcome with emotion;* FAIRE LES YEUX *means to roll up the eyes as if swooning;* FAIRE DES BRIOCHES[1] *means to miss a note or an intonation.*

at table, and at his third meeting found himself sufficiently convinced that she was as pretty as she was bright and good.

The conjugal bliss of Borose was short-lived: hardly eighteen months after his marriage his wife died in childbirth, leaving him eternally regretful of this abrupt separation, and to console him a daughter whom he called Herminie, and of whom we shall speak later.

M. de Borose found pleasure enough in the various occupations he had built up for himself. Nevertheless he realized, in the long view, that even in the most exclusive gatherings there is pretension, ambition, and sometimes a little jealousy. He credited humanity itself with all these miseries, since it is never perfect, and he was not the more repelled by it; but gradually he obeyed without even realizing it the fate which was imprinted on his features, and began to make the satisfaction of his taste his principal pleasure.

He was wont to say that gastronomy is no more than appreciative reflection, applied to the science which most improves our lot.

He said with Epicurus:[†] "Is man then meant to spurn the gifts of Nature? Has he been born but to pluck the bitterest fruits? For whom do those flowers grow, that the gods make flourish at mere mortals' feet? . . . It is a way of pleasing Providence, to give ourselves up to the various delights which she suggests to us; our very needs spring from her laws, and our desires from her inspirations."

He agreed with the fat[2] professor that good things are meant for good people; otherwise one must fall back on an absurdity and believe that God created them solely for the evildoers.

Borose's first real job was with his cook, and consisted in outlining his functions in their fundamental truths.

He told him that a skilful cook, who could in theory be a scholar, was already one, always, in practice; that the manners of his profession placed him among the chemists and the biological philosophers; he even went so far as to say to him that a cook, who is responsible for the upkeep of the human mechanism, is more important than a pharmacist, who is needed but occasionally.

[†] *Alibert,* Physiologie des Passions, *volume I, page 241.*

He added, quoting from a doctor as witty as he is learned,† "The cook must understand to the full the art of modifying foodstuffs by the action of fire, which was unknown to our ancestors. This art calls forth the most erudite studies and investigations, in the present time. It needs a great deal of experimentation upon the products of the entire world in order to use skilfully the various seasonings and to disguise the unpleasantness of certain foods, to make still others more appetizing, and always to use the most appropriate ingredients. It is the European cook who outshines all others in the art of composing these marvellous mixtures."

This sermon had its proper effect, and the chef,‡ thoroughly impressed with his own importance, conducted himself from then on with a dignity worthy of his position.

A little time and thought and experience soon convinced M. de Borose that, given a fairly set number of conventional dishes, a good dinner is not much more expensive than a bad one; that it does not cost even five hundred francs more a year to drink only the best wines; and that everything depends on the will of the master, from the skilful order in his household to the enthusiasm which he instills in all those who are in his service.

The dinners of Borose, built on these fundamental points, took on a solemn and classical importance: their superb fare became famed, and it was counted a great honor to be invited to one of them, so that many people who had not yet been thus privileged boasted of their attendance.

Borose never bothered with those self-styled gastronomers who are nothing more than gluttons with bottomless bellies, and who will eat anywhere, anything, everything. He was fortunate enough to find among his friends, in the first three categories, several pleasant dinner companions who, while eating with a truly philosophical concentration and devoting all the time to this study which it demands, never let themselves forget that

† *Alibert,* Physiologie des Passions, *volume I, page 196.*
‡ *In a well-managed establishment, public or private, the cook is called the* chef. *Under him as assistants he has the entrée man, the pastry cook, the roast cook; and the scullions are the cabin boys of the kitchen, and like them they are often knocked about and often make their way upwards.*

there comes a moment when reason says to appetite: *Non procedes amplius* (Go no further, my friend).

It often happened that merchants brought foodstuffs of exceptional merit to him, which they preferred to sell him at moderate prices with the certainty that their delicacies would be consumed graciously and intelligently and be discussed in social circles, and that the reputations of their shops would thus increase and flourish.

M. de Borose's guests rarely exceeded nine in number, nor were the dishes very numerous, but the watchfulness of the host and his exquisite taste combined to make them perfect. His table invariably held whatever was the season's best, whether because of its precocity or its rareness, and the service was so carefully performed that it left nothing to desire.

The conversation during the meals was always general and lively, and often instructive, this last quality being due to a special precaution taken by Borose.

Each week a distinguished but poverty-stricken scholar, to whom a pension was paid, descended from his attic room and handed over a series of topics appropriate for discussion at table. The host took care to produce one or another of these whenever the current subjects seemed about used up, so that the conversation gathered new life and at the same time steered clear of political arguments, which are hindersome to both ingestion and digestion.

Two times a week he invited ladies to dine, and took care to arrange things so that each one would find among the guests a gentleman with eyes for none but her. This precaution added greatly to the harmony of his entertainment, for the most rigidly prudish of women cannot bear to find herself ignored in public by the opposite sex.

On these set days, and only then, a mild round of écarté was permitted, in contrast to all other times when piquet and whist were the order, both being quiet, reflective games which give proof of a good education. But more often these evenings of mixed company were spent in pleasant conversation, mixed with a few love songs which Borose accompanied with the skill we have already discussed, always attracting an applause to himself of which he was far from unconscious.

The first Monday of each month, the priest came to dine with his parishioner, and was sure of being welcomed in a thousand delightful ways. The conversation for that one occasion was a little more serious than usual, but still did not lack certain gentle pleasantries. The dear old father never missed accepting this attractive invitation, and more than once caught himself in the act of wishing that each month had four first Mondays in it.

That same day was the one set for the young Herminie to come home from Madame Migneron's,† where she was a boarding pupil: more often than not that lady accompanied her ward. Herminie grew more charming with every visit: she adored her father, and when he greeted her by kissing the forehead which she bent toward him, no human beings could have been happier than the two of them.

Borose took constant care to see that the expenses he laid out for his table had real moral value.

He dealt only with the tradespeople who were known for unfailing quality in their merchandise and moderation in their prices; he recommended them to his friends and helped them in other ways when they needed it, for it was his habit to say the men who are too anxious to make money are often careless in the methods they choose.

His wine merchant grew rich quickly enough, for Borose lauded him as innocent of adulteration, a quality which was rare even in Athens during the time of Pericles, and is far from common in our own nineteenth century.

It is rumored that it is Borose whose counsels directed the progress of Hurbain, restaurateur of the Palais-Royal, where one can find for two francs a dinner which would cost twice that anywhere else, Hurbain who is headed for a success made all the more certain by the fact that the crowds which flock to his establishment do so in direct ratio to the moderation of his prices.

What was left on Borose's table was never turned over to the discretion of his servants, who were amply repaid in other ways:

† *Madame Migneron Remy is the mistress, at Number 4 Rue de Valois, Faubourg du Roule, of a dames' school under the protection of the Duchess of Orléans. The location is superb, the establishment is run perfectly, the enrollment is very exclusive, the instructors are the best in Paris, and, what is most important to me, the tuition is so low that young ladies of even modest fortune can enjoy such unusual advantages as it offers.*

everything that still looked appetizing was commandeered by the master in person.

As a result of his position on various committees of benevolence, he knew the needs and the situations of many of his charity cases, and was sure of placing his gifts to best advanatge, so that portions of still very acceptable food arrived at poor homes from time to time, to chase hunger away and bring a little happiness: the tail of a fine pike, for instance, or the backbone of a turkey carcass, or a bit of meat or pastry.[3]

And in order to make these generosities even more important morally, he usually sent them out on a Monday morning or the day after a holiday, thus doing away with any excuse for not going to work, combatting the inconveniences of *Holy Monday*,[†] and making physical enjoyment an antidote for debauchery.

When M. de Borose discovered among the third or fourth ranks of tradesmen a really happy young married couple, whose behavior was a proof of those qualities upon which national prosperity must depend, he paid them the honor of a visit, and made a point of inviting them to dinner with him.

On the appointed day, the young woman would be sure to find herself conversing with ladies about the care of the home, and the husband with gentlemen who could disclose much about business affairs and manufacturing.

These invitations, whose motive was well recognized, ended by being a kind of accolade, and tradesmen outdid themselves to receive one.

While all these things were taking place, the little Herminie grew and developed within the protecting walls of the Rue Valois, and we owe to our readers a picture of her, as an integral part of her father's biography.

---

† *Most working men in Paris finish up their jobs on Sunday morning, turn them over to their employers, and are paid, after which they leave, to spend the rest of the day enjoying themselves.*

Monday morning they meet in groups, pool whatever money they have left, and continue to celebrate as long as the sum total permits it.

This state of affairs, which was completely usual as little as ten years ago, has been somewhat bettered by conscientious employers and by insurance companies and banking houses; but the evil is still very great, and many work hours are lost, to the profit of beer gardens, restaurants, bars, and taverns in the capital and its suburbs.

Mademoiselle Herminie de Borose is tall (five feet and one inch), and her figure has the lightness of a nymph's, and a goddess' grace.

Sole issue of a happy marriage, her health is perfect, and her physical stamina is remarkable: she fears neither storm nor burning sun, and the longest walks do not appall her.

From a distance she might be thought a brunette, but on looking more closely at her it can be seen that her hair is a dark chestnut color, and that her eyelashes are black and her eyes sky blue.

Most of her features are classically Grecian, but her nose is French, a charming little nose with such a gracious air about it that a committee of artists, after having deliberated during three whole banquets, decided that this completely Gallic type is at least as deserving as any other of being immortalized by the paint brush, the chisel, and the engraver's tool.

Miss Herminie's feet are remarkably small and well formed; the professor has so often praised and even teased her on this subject that on New Year's Day, 1825, she made a present to him, of course with the approval of her father, of a lovely little black satin slipper, which he shows to a chosen few, and which he uses to prove that intense social culture acts as much on bodies as it does on souls; he believes that a small foot, such as is so fashionable in these times, is the product of great care and breeding, and that it is almost never found among the peasant classes, and is generally the sign of a person whose ancestors have for many generations lived in ease.

When Herminie pins up the forest of her hair, and ties about her modest tunic a belt of woven ribbons, everyone finds her absolutely charming, and cannot see how flowers or pearls or diamonds could add to her beauty.

Her conversation is simple and ready, and none would suspect that she knows the works of all our best writers; but when the occasion arises she grows enthusiastic, and the wittiness of her remarks betrays her. As soon as she realizes this she blushes and lowers her eyes, and her pink cheeks prove her modesty.

Mademoiselle de Borose plays equally well on the piano and the harp, but she prefers the latter instrument for some inexplicable sentiment of enthusiasm for the heavenly instruments which angels strum, and for the golden harps so praised by Ossian.

Her voice too is of a heavenly sweetness and purity, which still does not keep her from being a little timid; nevertheless she sings without having to be begged, always permitting herself, as she begins, to look once upon her listeners so bewitchingly that she could sing completely off key, like so many others, and it would never even be noticed.

Nor does she neglect her needlework, that source of innocent pleasure which is always ready to stave off empty boredom; she sews like a fairy, and every time some fashionable new stitch appears, the head seamstress of the *Père de Famille* comes by previous arrangement to teach it to her.

Herminie's heart has not yet been assaulted, and until now her filial piety is sufficient for her happiness; but she has a veritable passion for dancing, which she loves to the point of folly.

When she takes her place in a quadrille she seems to grow two inches taller, and looks as if she would fly away; nevertheless she dances with restraint, and her steps are unpretentious. She is content to glide about lightly, with all the art of her pleasing gracious form, but occasionally she betrays her potentialities, and it is highly possible that if they were developed Madame Montessu[4] would have a veritable rival.

This bird, feet on the earth, still seems in flight.

M. de Borose, then, lived happily in the company of his charming child, whom he had by now withdrawn from her boarding school. He enjoyed a well-administrated fortune and a just renown, and saw ahead of him long years of great contentment. But all hope is treacherous, and no man can count upon the future.

About the middle of last March, M. de Borose was invited to spend a day in the country with some friends.

It was one of those days of unseasonable warmth, forerunners of the Springtime, and from beyond the horizon could be heard the muted thunderings which, the old proverb says, are the sounds of Winter breaking his own neck. They did not frighten the company, who set out upon their walk. Very soon, however, the sky grew threatening, clouds gathered, and a dreadful storm broke, with lightning and rain and hail.

Everybody dashed for cover as best he could, and wherever he might find it. M. de Borose found shelter under a poplar tree, whose lower branches bent over him as if they were a parasol.

Sinister haven! The top of the tree reached up to the clouds themselves in search of their electricity, and the rain as it flowed down the branches acted as conductor. There was the sound of a hideous explosion, and the unfortunate walker fell dead, before he could even draw breath.

Thus carried off by the kind of death which Caesar is said to have wished for, and about which he had no chance to quibble, M. de Borose was buried with the greatest pomp. His casket was followed to the cemetery of Père Lachaise by a great crowd of people in carriages and on foot; praise of him was on every tongue, and when a friend's voice pronounced over his grave a touching eulogism, it sounded an echo in the hearts of all who listened.

Herminie was prostrated by such a deep and unexpected grief: she did not have convulsions or paroxysms, nor did she try to hide from her sadness by taking to bed, but she wept for her father with such continued bitterness and abandon that her friends could but hope that the excess of her grief would in itself prove the best remedy: we mortals are not made of strong enough stuff to withstand such anguish long.

Time has worked its inevitable cure on this young heart by now. Herminie can speak of her father without dissolving in tears, but it is always with such sweet devotion, such innocent regret, with such a living affection and so meaningful an accent, that it is impossible to hear her and not share her sadness.

It will indeed be a happy man to whom Herminie gives the right to walk beside her and help her carry a wreath to their father's tomb!

In a small chapel off the nave of the church of . . . can be seen, every Sunday at the noontime Mass, a tall beautiful girl, accompanied by an aged lady. Her figure is bewitching, but a heavy veil hides her face. Nevertheless they seem to have been recognized, for about the chapel there surges a crowd of newly devout churchgoers, all of them most elegantly attired, and some of them very handsome fellows indeed.

Retinue of an Heiress

147:   One day when I was crossing from the Rue de la Paix to the Place Vendôme, I was stopped by the riding party, returning from the Bois de Boulogne, of the richest young lady of marriageable age in all Paris.

The procession was made up as follows:

(1)   The beauty herself, object of such hopes and desires, mounted on a very handsome bay, which she handled with great skill: she wore a blue habit with long skirt, and her black hat was plumed with white;

(2)   Her tutor, riding beside her, his face solemn and his very posture suggesting the gravity of his functions;

(3)   A group of twelve to fifteen suitors, each one trying to attract her attention either by his ardor, his horsemanship, or his fashionable melancholy;

(4)   An *en-cas*, beautifully turned out, in case of rain or fatigue, with a fat coachman and a jockey no bigger than my thumb;

(5)   Liveried servants of every class, dozens of them, and all prancing about.

They swept on . . . and I continued my meditations.

THE   TRANSLATOR'S   GLOSSES

1.   This slang, which was still current in 1884 when Nimmo and Bain quoted Lorédan Larchey's DICTIONNAIRE DE L'ARGOT PARISIEN, sprang from the custom in the opera of buying the little cakes called *brioches* with money collected from any artist who sang or played out of tune. Brioches are a light, pale yellow, faintly sweet kind of muffin with a characteristic blob on top, rather like a mushroom just pushing crookedly through the ground. Once eaten in Paris, they never taste as good anywhere else. The best commercial ones I ever ate were delivered every

morning about 8:57 to the Brasserie de l'Univers (or was it a café then?), across the sidewalk and past my hungry nose, from a dapper little horsedrawn wagon. That was anywhere from fifteen to fifteen hundred years ago, according to the effect upon my spirits of the weather and the daily news.

2. Here is another of Brillat-Savarin's private words, the adjective SÉBUSIEN, probably from the Latin *sebosus*, meaning stout. It might apply to Alibert (1766–1837), or it might very well describe this other Professor, who was forever wary of his silhouette, and who fought a grim but intelligent battle with overweight.

3. It is impossible for me to read this description of Borose without wondering if I only imagine that Brillat-Savarin despised him. The words seem straightforward, but I sense a hatred of the smug rich patronizing gourmand. He bought a soldier, and then he bought a scholar, one to save his life and the other to enrich it. He sent his fine scraps to the hovels and attics of *deserving* charity cases. He graciously opened social or at least commercial doors to *deserving* young married merchants. Yes, I suspect the Professor of a good bit of quiet malediction here, and the fatal stroke of lightning could not come too soon.

4. She was, obviously enough, a celebrated dancer of that day.

MEDITATION 30

BOUQUET

Gastronomical Mythology

148: Gasterea is the tenth muse: she presides over all the pleasures of taste.

She could claim to rule the world itself, which is nothing without the life in it, and that life in turn dependent upon what it eats.

She is happiest in places where the grapevine grows, where orange trees send out their perfume, where the truffle waxes and wild game and fruits may flourish.

When she condescends to appear, it is as a young girl: around her waist she winds fire colored ribands; her hair is black and her eyes are like blue sky, and her limbs are full of grace; beautiful as Venus, she is also everything that is pure loveliness.

She seldom shows herself to mortals, but her statue consoles them for her invisibility. A single sculptor has been allowed to look upon her charms, and such was the success of this god-chosen artist that whoever sees his masterpiece believes that he recognizes in it the features of whichever woman he has best loved in his life.

Among all the places where altars to Gasterea have risen, she loves this city, the world's capital, which holds the Seine between its palace steps.

Her temple rises on the famous hill to which Mars gives his name, and rests upon an immense white marble base, to which a hundred steps lead up from every side.

It is beneath this hallowed place that lie the secret cellars—kitchens where art questions nature and submits it to its unchanging laws.

It is there that air, water, iron, and fire, put into action by most cunning hands, are separated and reunited, ground and blended, to produce effects incomprehensible to the uninitiate.

It is from there, finally, that emerge, at predetermined times, those fabulous recipes whose inventors prefer to stay unnamed, since their happiness rests within themselves and their reward consists in knowing that they have pushed back the limits of human knowledge and brought new pleasures to mankind.

The temple, a unique monument of all that is simple and majestic in architecture, is supported by a hundred columns of Oriental jasper, and lighted by a dome which imitates the one of heaven itself.

We shall not give here the details of the marvels enclosed within this edifice: it will suffice to say that the carvings which ornament its pediment, as well as the bas-reliefs which encircle it, are consecrated to the memory of the men to whom we owe so much for their practical discoveries, such as the use of fire in our daily needs, the invention of the plow, and other like things.[1]

Far from the central dome, and in a sanctuary, the statue of the goddess can be seen. She leans her left hand upon an oven, and in her right holds the products most precious to her worshippers.

The crystal canopy which shelters her is held up by eight columns of the same clear mineral, and these are ceaselessly flooded by an electric flame, which seems to spread an almost celestial light within the holy place.[2]

The worship of the goddess is simple: each day at sunrise her priests come to take off the crown of flowers which ornaments her statue, place a new one on it, and sing together one of the numerous hymns by which poetry has always celebrated the countless blessings which the gods have showered upon mankind.

These priests are twelve in number, led by the oldest of them: they are chosen from the most scholarly of men, and all other things being equal the handsomest of these are the ones preferred. Their age is a question of years, and they are thus subject to the physical changes of maturity, but never to the decadence of senility, from which they are preserved by the air they breathe within the temple.

Feast days to the goddess are the same number as the days in a year, since she herself never ceases to pour out her blessings, but among these celebrations is one which is above all dedicated to her: September twenty-one, called the *gastronomical High Mass*.[3]

On this solemn day, the capital is from early morning veiled in a cloud of incense; citizens crowned with flowers throng the streets, singing the praises of Gasterea, speaking to one another with gentle affection; every heart is filled with happiness, and the air seems to vibrate with an infectious tide of friendship and love.

A part of the day is taken up with these demonstrations in the streets, and then at the traditional hour the whole mass of devotees turns toward the temple where the sacred banquet is to take place.

In the sanctuary, at the feet of the statue, a table is laid for the twelve high priests. Another table seating twelve hundred guests of both sexes has been prepared under the central dome. Every art has been called into play to decorate these two ceremonial boards, and never even in a royal palace has anything equalled their elegance.

The priests arrive, at a slow pace and with rapt countenances. They are dressed in tunics of fine white Cashmir wool, edged with incarnadine embroideries and with belts of the same color to tie up the ample folds. Their faces glow with health and good will, and after an exchange of greetings they sit down at their table.

Already servants dressed in fine linen have placed the dishes there: no ordinary preparations, meant to appease common hungers, for nothing is ever served at this august table which has not been judged worthy of it and which does not spring from a transcendental source, either through the material it contains or through the depth of skill that has composed it.

The venerable diners are more than deserving of their high functions: their calm intelligent conversation turns upon the marvels of Nature and the sublimity of Art; they eat slowly, savoring with enthusiasm; the movement of their jaws is smooth and gentle; it seems as if every bite has its own significance to them, and if it happens that one or another lets his tongue lick discreetly at his glistening lips, the cook who has made the dish then being eaten is from that moment among the immortals.

The wines, which are worthy of the feast, are poured in proper succession at set intervals by twelve maidens who have been chosen, for this single day, by a jury of painters and sculptors; they are dressed in the Greek fashion, one which flatters their beauty and does not affront their modesty.

The priests are above any affectation of hypocrisy, and do not turn away from the pretty hands which pour out the world's finest wines for them; but even as they enjoy looking at our Creator's most beautiful masterpiece they do not lose the solemnity which wisdom has engraved upon their brows: the manner in which they pay their thanks and then drink is full of this double sentiment.

Around their esoteric board can be seen a constant press of kings, princes, and famous foreigners, who have arrived for the celebration from every part of the world; they walk quietly, and watch every move that is made, for they have come to learn all that they can of the great art of good living, a difficult one of which many people are still completely ignorant.

While all this is going on in the holy of holies, a general gaiety and brilliance animates the diners around the great table under the dome.

This emotion springs mainly from the fact that no man there is seated beside the woman to whom he has already said his say: such is the will of the goddess.[4]

To the almost immeasurable table have been invited, by choice, the scholars of both sexes who have enriched gastronomy by their discoveries, the heads of households who fulfill most graciously the duties of our French hospitality, the cosmopolitans to whom society is most in debt for their pleasant or practical importations, and those generous men who nourish the unfortunate on all that is best of their own superfluous good things.

The center of the banquet table is hollow, and leaves a great space filled with a crowd of carvers and servers, who hasten here and there and to the farthest places with whatever anyone may wish to taste.

There too are displayed most advantageously everything that Nature in her prodigality has created for man's nourishment, and these richnesses are doubled a hundredfold, not only by their juxtapositions but by the changes to which the art of cookery has subjected them. This art has brought together the Old World and the New, confounded man-made boundaries, and lessened all our distances, and the perfume which rises from its knowing preparations embalms the air and fills it with a gas that is irresistibly appetizing.

Meanwhile young men, as handsome as they are well-costumed, patrol the outer circle of the table, ceaselessly presenting cups filled with the most delicious wines, which are now brilliant as red rubies and now like the more modest topaz.

From time to time skilled musicians, placed in the galleries around the dome, make the whole temple sound to the melodious accents of a harmony as simple as it is cunning.

Then heads are raised, the attention of all the diners is attracted, and for these short periods conversation ceases; it soon begins again with even more animation, as if this new gift of the gods has refreshed imaginations and given every heart a renewed capacity for gaiety.

When the pleasures of the table have taken up the time assigned to them, the band of high priests draws near, to join in the celebration, mix with the guests, and share the Mocha which even the Oriental lawgiver permits to his followers. The spicy liquor fumes in vessels of carved beaten gold, and the beautiful cup bearers from the inner sanctuary hurry among the guests with sugar to disguise its bitterness. They are charming, and yet such is the influence of the temple of Gasterea and of the air breathed in it, that not a single female heart holds any jealousy.

Finally the leader of the priests intones a hymn of gratitude; every voice joins in, and every musical instrument: this homage rises from all hearts toward the heavens, and the ritual comes to an end.

Then, finally, does the banquet for ordinary mortals begin, for there can be no veritable festivals when the people are not a part of them.

Tables which seemingly never end are set up in all the streets, in every square, and before every great building. A man can sit down wherever he may find himself: chance brings differing age and social rank and religion together, and everywhere are seen the cordial handclasp of true friendliness, and its open unsuspicious face.

In spite of the fact that the whole city is for a time no more than one great dining hall, generous private citizens have guaranteed plenty for all, while a paternal government watches with solicitude so that order may be maintained and the outer limits of sobriety not be overstepped.

Soon gay and lively music can be heard: it is time for dancing, that beloved pastime of all youthful people.

Immense ballrooms and portable outdoor floors have been prepared everywhere, and floods of every kind of refreshment.

People flock to them, some to dance and others to watch and lend encouragement. It is amusing to see more than a few old fellows, stirred by a fleeting fire of passion, offer their feeble homages to beauty; but the worship of the goddess and the significance of the festival excuse every such absurdity.

This merriment continues for many a happy hour. Pleasure is everywhere, and movement and gaiety, and it is hard to hear midnight sound the signal for repose. And nevertheless every one listens to it: the night has been spent in honest decent pleasure, and it is time now for each citizen to retire to his bed, pleased with his celebration and full of high hopes for the happenings of a year which begins under such good auspices.

THE TRANSLATOR'S GLOSSES

1. In 1947, in the workrooms of Lurçat-Aubusson where the art of tapestry weaving had sprung into new and dynamically exciting life, a tapestry of enormous size was being woven for the

Museum of the Wines of France. It was destined to be hung in the room of the Dukes of Burgundy, and to glorify their wines, as do the fifteen "ambassadors of wine" who meet there every year to dine, drink, speechify, and recite poetry in praise of that liquid which most makes glad the hearts of men.

2. This mention of *flamme électrique* so excited Nimmo and Bain in 1884 that they exclaimed with unusual abandon: "Oh, my prophetic soul, my uncle, as Shakespeare says. Electric light in 1826.—Tr." They did not allow themselves to go so far as an exclamation point, it should be noted.

3. Here the Professor, with his obvious love of exotic and romantic words, says *Halel*, which is an Arab word meaning "to pray."

4. This subtle prescription for gastronomical bliss was beautifully followed in Kansas City, Missouri, in 1947, by a group of people hopefully labelling themselves members of The Wine and Food Society. In a perfect mixture of luncheon club naïveté and what Philip Wylie might label incipient momism, the height of the celebration was, according to the news reporter, somewhat as follows: "A. D. (Bud) Eubank . . . presided at the dinner and introduced what he called 'the Eisenhower shift' . . . which preceded the third and fourth courses and consisted of each man taking his glass of wine and moving into the seat of the third man to the right of him. Thus, the women had different dinner companions for a large part of the evening, and they thought that was a bright idea. Of course, it developed that such diners as Karl K . . ., Ed M . . ., Frank W . . ., and D. D. D . . ., to mention a few, apparently couldn't count to three and invariably plopped into the wrong seat. At the beginning of the last course, Eubank announced, sternly: 'Now, home to mama.' That was the cue for the men to sit once more beside the wives they had brought, and give the correct fillip to the evening." (On rereading this simply told tale, it seems even sadder than at first, and that is saying a great deal. Perhaps it is cruel to add that "sparkling Burgundy" was being served as the gallants plopped into their new seats.)

PART II

TRANSITION

If I have been read up to this point with the attention which I have hoped for and have tried to stimulate, it has been observed that in my writing I have had a double purpose which I have never lost to view: the first part of it has been to set forth the basic theories of *gastronomy*, so that it could assume the rank among the sciences which is incontestably its own; the second, to define with precision what must be understood by *gourmandism*, and to separate from this social grace, once and for all, the gluttony and intemperance with which it has for so long and so unfortunately been linked.

This equivocation has been instigated by intolerant moralists who, led astray by their extravagant zeal, have pleased themselves to find excess where there was but an intelligent enjoyment of the earth's treasures, which were not given to us to be trampled underfoot. It has further been twisted and falsified by uncongenial grammarians, who have uttered their definitions in black incomprehension and sworn to them *in verba magistri*

It is time to wipe out such error, for by now anybody understands the word; this is so true that while everyone will admit a certain trace of gourmandism in himself and will even boast a bit of it, there is still nobody who can be accused, without insult, of being gluttonous, voracious, or intemperate.

On these two cardinal points it seems to me that what I have written up to this point is as clear as actual demonstration might be, and will suffice to persuade all those readers who are open to conviction. I could therefore lay down my pen, and consider as finished the task which I have set myself, but during the exhaustive studies I have made of subjects which are a vital part of man's existence, I have recalled many things which I should enjoy writing about: anecdotes which have certainly never yet been told, epigrams which took form before my own eyes, a few recipes of high distinction, and other such literary tidbits.

They would have broken up the main line of thought, if I had scattered them through the theoretical part of my book, but thus assembled at its end, I hope that they will be read with real pleasure, for all the while that they may be found amusing, they still offer more than a few experimental truths and useful developments.

I have wanted, too, as I have already warned, to give a little personal history which can arouse neither discussion nor commentary. I have found the reward for all my labor in this part of the book where I see myself once more among my friends. It is above all when life is about to escape our grasp that we become important to ourselves, and our intimates are a part of that final I AM.

However, I cannot hide the fact that on looking over the parts I have written about myself, I have felt a little uneasy.

These qualms are the result of my very latest readings, of personal memoirs which are by now in everybody's hands, and of the carping comments I have heard made about them.

I am afraid that some malicious soul, after a night made sleepless by his bad digestion, might say of me: "And here's a professor for you who doesn't treat himself too badly! Here's a professor who is not afraid to spend his whole time patting his own back! Here's a professor who . . . Here's a professor . . . !"

To which I can only say in advance, putting myself on guard as it were, that anyone who does not hurt his fellow men has the right to be treated with a certain amount of indulgence, and that I cannot see why I, always a stranger to any hateful sentiments, should exclude myself from my own generosity.[1]

After this response, which is indeed realistic enough, I believe that I can count on being let alone, well protected under my philosopher's hood, and those who may still plague me I shall call bad sleepers. *Bad Sleepers!* It is a new invective, for which I plan to take out a copyright, since I am the first to have discovered that it holds within it a veritable excommunication.

THE TRANSLATOR'S GLOSSES

1.   It is faintly possible that the Professor has idealized himself, but the strange fact that in a most gossipy age almost nothing was written about him adds a protective cape to his somewhat smug remark. Dr. Richerand and Balzac wrote of his kindliness and honesty with almost gushing fervor. On the other hand the waspish Marquis de Cussy in his L'ART CULINAIRE said: "Brillat-Savarin ate copiously and ill; he chose little, talked dully, had no vivacity in his looks, and was absorbed at the end of a repast." (Nimmo and Bain here note loyally: ". . . he was like the rest of the world—he had his good and his bad days.") And in 1807 the great orator and revolutionist Camille Jordan wrote to Madame de Staël from Lyons: "Say to (Madame Récamier) that I doubt not that she very cordially recommended me to her relative the judge; that I thank her heartily for her good intentions, but that never were intentions followed by less effect; that, far from finding favor in his eyes, my family have not even obtained justice at his hands, that, in the discharge of functions where it was his duty to confine himself to weighing impartially the evidence, he manifested toward us an amount of prejudice and ill-will which was the scandal of all who witnessed it." This was written by a hard-pressed patriot about a man who had already been ground fine in the mill of exile, a man who, as Balzac later wrote, did not let politics trouble his digestion . . . but even so it makes a small chink in the Professor's self-tailored armor of perfection.

VARIETIES

I. The Curé's Omelet

Everyone knows that Madame R . . .[1] has for twenty years held title without contradiction to the Parisian throne of beauty. And everyone knows that she is extremely charitable, and that at one time she was interested in almost every enterprise which had for its purpose the relief of human misery, which sometimes is much worse in this great city than anywhere else.†

Needing to confer on this subject with the curate of . . . , she went one day about five o'clock to his house, and was highly astonished to find him already at table.

The lovely resident of the Rue du Mont-Blanc believed that all Paris dined at six, and did not know that in general the ec-

---

† *Above all those are to be pitied whose needs are unsuspected; for it must be admitted in all fairness that the Parisians are generous and charitable citizens. In the Year X[2] I paid a small weekly pension to an aged nun, who lay suffering, half-paralyzed, in a sixth floor attic room. This courageous soul received enough help from her neighbors to make her life a fairly comfortable one, and to feed, besides, a lay sister who had thrown in her lot with her.*

clesiastics begin much earlier, since many of them make a light collation at night.

Madame R . . . wanted to withdraw, but the Curé insisted that she stay, perhaps because the business they were to discuss was not the kind to spoil his dinner, perhaps because a pretty woman is never a kill-joy for anyone, no matter what his state, or perhaps finally because he realized that all he needed to make a true gastronomical Elysium of his dining room was someone to talk to.

Indeed, his table was laid with an admirable elegance: an old wine gleamed in a crystal decanter; the white porcelain was of the highest quality; the plates were kept hot over boiling water; and a maid, at once canonical and neatly dressed, stood ready to follow out his orders.

The meal balanced itself between frugality and refinement. A thick crayfish soup was just being removed, and spread out upon the table were a salmon trout, an omelet,[3] and a salad.

"My dinner will prove to you what you perhaps did not realize," the priest said smilingly. "Today we must not eat meat, according to the laws of the Church." Our friend nodded agreement, but private information has it that she blushed a little, which did not prevent the Curé from continuing his repast.

He has already been served with the upper half of the trout and was in the process of enjoying it. Its sauce looked skilfully concocted, and an expression of inner bliss appeared on the pastor's face.

After this dish, he attacked the omelet, which was round and big-bellied and cooked to the exact point of perfection.

At the first touch of the spoon, the paunch let flow from the cut in it a thick juice which was as tempting to look at as to smell; the platter seemed aflood with it, and our dear Juliette admitted to herself that it made her own mouth water.

This instinctive movement on her part did not escape a priest used to observing the passions of his fellow men, and as if he were answering a question which Madame R . . . had in reality taken great care not to ask, he said, "It is a tuna omelet. My cook is a marvel with them, and few people taste them without complimenting me."

"I am not surprised," the resident of the Chaussée d'Antin

replied. "An omelet as tempting as that never appears on the tables of the laity!"

Next came the salad. (I can recommend this dish to all who have confidence in me: salad refreshes without weakening, and comforts without irritating, and I have a habit of saying that it makes us younger.)

Conversation was not interrupted by the act of dining: they talked of the business which had caused the visit, and discussed the war then raging, current happenings, the Church's hopes and expectations, and other table topics which make a bad meal pass quickly and a good meal taste even better.

Dessert arrived at its proper time. It consisted of a Septmoncel cheese, three Calville apples, and a pot of jam.

Finally the maid brought in a little round table, the kind that long ago was used for the card game of loo, upon which she placed a cup of Mocha so steaming hot and so crystal clear that its perfume filled the room.

After having SIPED[4] it (*siroté*), the Curé said grace, and remarked as he arose from the table, "I never drink strong liqueurs. They are a little extra treat which I always offer to my guests, but which I myself abstain from completely. I feel that I am thus reserving a final pleasure for my extreme old age, if the good God permits me to reach it."

While all this took place, time had sped by, and it was six o'clock. Madame R . . . hurried into her carriage, for she had invited several guests to dine with her that evening, myself among them. She arrived late, *according to her usual custom*, but at least she did arrive, finally, still full of excitement about what she had just seen and sniffed at.

There was no topic of conversation throughout our dinner but the Curé's earlier one, and especially his tuna omelet.

Madame R . . . had been especially impressed by its height and its plump shapeliness, and from all that she told us about it, we agreed unanimously that it must have been a masterpiece. Each one of us after his own fashion contributed to make a kind of sensuous equation in the discussion.

The subject of conversation finally exhausted, we went on to others and thought no more about it. As for myself, spreader of useful truths, I felt it my duty to bring out from its obscurity the recipe for a dish which I believe to be as healthful as it is pleasant. I instructed my cook to outline it for me down to the tiniest details, and I give it here with even more eagerness to those who will enjoy it, since I have not been able to find it in any cookery book.

PREPARATION OF A TUNA OMELET[5]

Take, for six people, two well-cleaned carp roes which you will blanch by plunging them for five minutes into water already boiling and lightly salted.

Have to hand a piece of fresh tuna the size of a hen's egg, to which you will add a small shallot finely minced.

Chop together the roes and the tuna so that they are well blended, toss the mixture into a casserole with an adequate lump of very good butter, and heat just until the butter is melted. This last is what gives the omelet its special savor.

Take a second good lump of butter, blend it with parsley and chives, and put it in a fish-shaped platter destined to hold the omelet; sprinkle it with the juice of a lemon, and put it over a gentle heat.

Then beat twelve eggs (the freshest are the best), and add the hot mixture of roe and tuna and mix all together thoroughly.

Make the omelet in the usual way, and take care that it is long in shape, thick enough, and soft. Slide it skilfully onto the platter which you have prepared for it, and serve it, to be eaten at once.

This dish should be reserved for especially good luncheons, and for those reunions of enthusiasts who appreciate what is served to them and eat it thoughtfully and slowly. Let it be floated downward on a fine old wine, and miracles will happen.[6]

THEORETICAL NOTES
ON THE PREPARATION OF THIS DISH

(1) The roes and tuna must be thoroughly heated in the butter, but not allowed to bubble in it, so that they do not become hard; this would keep them from blending thoroughly with the eggs.

(2) The platter must be deep, so that the sauce will collect in it and be easy to serve with a spoon.

(3) The platter must also be lightly warmed: if it were cold, the porcelain would absorb the heat of the omelet and would not leave enough in it to melt the herb butter on which the mixture rests.

II. Eggs in Meat Juice

One time I was traveling with two ladies to Melun.

We left none too early in the morning, and arrived at Montgeron with raging appetites.

They raged in vain: the inn at which we stopped, although it looked promising enough, was out of provisions, thanks to three coaches and two mail carriages which had already stopped there, whose passengers had gone through the cupboards like Egyptian locusts.

At least, so the cook told us.

Nevertheless I sighted a spit turning over the fire, laden with a very handsome leg of mutton upon which my two companions, as was natural, turned their most yearning looks.

Alas, they were wasted! The roast belonged to three Englishmen who had brought it with them, and who waited for it without impatience over their glasses of champagne (PRATING OVER A BOTTLE OF CHAMPAIN).

"But," I said to the cook with an air half-angered and half-begging, "at least could you not scramble these eggs for us in the juice from the roast? With the eggs and a cup of coffee and cream we might manage to get by."

"Gladly," he replied. "The juice of the meat is ours by public right, and I'll take care of your little suggestion this very minute." Upon which he began to break the eggs with great care.

When I saw that he was well occupied, I drew near to the hearth, and pulling from my pocket a travelling knife, I made in the forbidden roast a dozen or so deep cuts, from which the juice must drain to its last drop.

I also watched with care the concoction of the eggs, to be sure that we were cheated of nothing, and when they were perfectly cooked I myself took them to the room which had been made ready for us.

There we feasted indeed, and laughed hysterically at the

realization that we were swallowing the very essence of the roast, and leaving nothing to our English friends but the bother of chewing its worthless residue.[7]

III.   *National Victory*

While I was living in New York I used to go now and then to spend an evening in a kind of café-tavern run by a certain M. Little, where one could always find turtle soup in the morning, and all the traditional American drinks at night.

I went there most often with the Viscount de la Massue and Jean-Rodolphe Fehr, formerly a broker in Marseilles; both of them were, like myself, political exiles. I would treat them to a WELSH RABBET† which we washed down with ale or cider, and the evening would pass very pleasantly in talk of our past misfortunes, of our present pleasures, and of the hopes we had for the future.

At Little's I made the acquaintance of M. Wilkinson, a planter from Jamaica, with a man who must have been one of his friends, since he never left the other's side. This man, whose name I never knew, was one of the most extraordinary people I have ever met: he had a square face, with lively eyes which seemed to watch everything with great attention, and yet he never spoke, and his countenance stayed as expressionless as if he were blind. It was only when he heard a witty sally or a comical remark that his face would awaken, his eyes would shut, and opening a mouth as wide as the bell of a trumpet he would let out a prolonged noise which had something of real laughter about it and more of that whinnying which in England is called the HORSE LAUGH. Then he would come to order, and fall back into his usual taciturnity. The whole thing lasted about as long as a flash of lightning as it rips through the clouds. As for M. Wilkinson, who seemed to be about fifty years old, he had the manners and outward appearance of a well-bred person (OF A GENTLEMAN).

These two Englishmen were apparently very fond of our com-

---

† *The English, epigrammatically, call* WELSH RABBET (lapin gaulois) *a slice of cheese toasted on a piece of bread. Of course this preparation is not as filling as would be a rabbit, but it leads to more drinking, makes wine taste good, and has a very real place as dessert for an informal meal.*

pany, and had already shared cheerfully with us, on several occasions, the frugal supper which I offered to my friends, when one night M. Wilkinson took me to one side, and told me that he would like to make arrangements to invite the three of us to dine.

I thanked him, and believing myself to have the right, as I was obviously to be the principal guest, I accepted for my friends, and the invitation was agreed to be set for two days later at three in the afternoon.

The evening passed off as usual, but just as I was leaving the tavern, the serving man (WAITER) signaled me apart from the others and informed me that the Jamaicans had ordered a fine meal; that they had given special orders about what was to be drunk, since they regarded their invitation as a challenge to see who could drink the best; and that the man with the big mouth had said that he was confident that he alone could put the three Frenchmen under the table.

This information would have made me refuse the invitation, if I could have done so honorably, for I have always fled from such orgies; but this time it was impossible. The Englishmen would have spread the news everywhere that we had not dared present ourselves for the contest, and that their very presence had been enough to make us retreat. Therefore, in spite of being well aware of our danger, we must follow the maxim of Marshal Saxe: since the wine is drawn, we are prepared to drink it.

I was not without some anxiety, but to tell the truth, it did not have myself for its object.

I felt certain that, since I was at one and the same time younger, taller, and more active than our hosts, my constitution which had kept innocent of bacchic excess would easily triumph over those of the Englishmen, who were both of them most probably weakened by too much drinking of strong spirits.

Without doubt, I could have been proclaimed winner as I stood, over the other four contestants, but this victory, which would have been a personal one for me, would have lost much of its glory by the defeat of my two companions, who would have been carried from the field with the other losers in the ugly condition which must always follow such a failure. I wanted to spare them this affront. In a word, I wanted it to be a national rather than an individual victory. Therefore I sum-

moned Fehr and La Massue to my rooms, and made a stern
and formal speech to them to inform them of my fears. I cau-
tioned them to drink in small mouthfuls as often as they could,
to pretend to be drinking whenever I could draw the attention
of my antagonists away from them, and above all to eat slowly
and to stay somewhat hungry during the whole affair, for when
food is mixed with drink it tempers the alcoholic heat and
keeps it from mounting with all its strength into the brain;
finally we divided among us a plate of bitter almonds, which
I had heard were very valuable against the headiness of wine.

Thus armed, both physically and morally, we headed for
Little's, where we found the Jamaicans, and soon after that
dinner was served. It consisted of an enormous piece of ROST-
BEEF, a turkey cooked in its own juices, boiled root vegetables,
a salad of raw cabbage,[8] and a jam tart.

We drank *à la française*, which is to say that wine was served
from the very beginning: it was a really good claret which was
at that time even cheaper than in France, since several boat-
loads of it had arrived in succession and the last had not sold
well.

M. Wilkinson did his honors nobly, inviting us to set to,
and giving us a good example; as for his friend, he seemed to
plunge into the plate before him, said not a word, and looked
sideways about him with a faint smile.

As for me, I was proud of my two acolytes. La Massue, in
spite of being endowed by Nature with a fairly formidable appetite, nibbled at his little bites like a proper schoolmiss; Fehr
from time to time juggled several glasses of wine skilfully enough
to slip them into a beer pot at the end of the table. On my
side I stood toe to toe with the Englishmen, and the longer
the meal lasted the more confident of victory I felt.

After the claret came port, and after port madeira, to which
we confined ourselves for some time.

Then came the dessert, composed of butter, cheese, and hickory[9] and coconuts. It was the moment for the toasts: we drank
deeply to the power of kings, the liberty of the common people,
and the beauty of the ladies. We lifted our glasses, with M.
Wilkinson, to the health of his daughter Mariah, who he assured us was the loveliest creature in all the island of Jamaica.

After the wines came the SPIRITS, which is to say the rum

and brandies, the grain liquors and the raspberry liqueurs. With the spirits came the songs. I saw that we were being hard-pressed. I was afraid of these liquors, and escaped them by demanding punch, and Little himself brought us a bowl of it, doubtless ready and waiting for us, which would have held enough for forty people. In all of France we do not have containers as big as that one.[10]

This sight gave me new courage. I ate five or six slices of toast spread with delightfully fresh butter, and felt all my forces take on more life. Then I looked carefully about me, for I began to have some worries as to how this affair would end. My two friends appeared to be lasting fairly well: they drank as they cracked hickory nuts and ate them. M. Wilkinson's face was flaming red; his eyes were glazed, and he seemed stunned. His friend was as silent as ever, but his head seemed like a boiling cauldron, and his monstrous mouth protruded like a hen's behind. I saw that the dreadful climax was upon us.

Sure enough, M. Wilkinson, awakening with a shocking jump, stood up and began to thunder out the national air of *Rule Britannia*. He could go no further. His strength left him, and he fell back into his chair, and from there sagged onto the floor. His friend, seeing him in such a state, gave one of his most startling horse laughs, leaned over to help him, and fell prone.

It is impossible to express the satisfaction that this brusque dénouement brought to me, and the weight it lifted from my mind. I rushed to sound the service bell. Little came at once, and after I said the conventional phrase to him, "Please see that these gentlemen are properly taken care of," we all joined him in one last glass of punch to their health. Soon the WAITER arrived, flanked by his subordinates, and they took possession of our vanquished foes and carried them out according to the rule THE FEET FOREMOST,† the friend still maintaining his complete impassivity, and M. Wilkinson trying ceaselessly to sing the tune of *Rule Britannia*.

The next day the New York papers, which were copied successively by all those in the Union, recounted with approximate

---

† *This expression is used in English to denote any dead or drunk body which is being carried.*

truth what had happened, and since they added that the two Englishmen were sent to bed as a result of the adventure, I went to see them. I found the friend quite undone from the effects of violent indigestion, and M. Wilkinson chained to his chair by an attack of gout which our bacchic battle had probably stirred up. He seemed appreciative of my thoughtfulness, and said to me among other things, "OH! DEAR SIR, YOU ARE VERY GOOD COMPANY INDEED, BUT TOO A DRINKER FOR US." † [11]

IV. *Ablutions*

I have written that the Roman vomitoria were repellent, according to our ideas of behavior; I fear that I may have been rash in this, and must sing a recantation.

I shall explain myself:

Some forty years ago various people in high society, almost always the ladies, followed the custom of rinsing their mouths after meals.

To do this they turned their backs upon the other diners, as they were about to leave the table; a footman handed them a glass of water; they took a mouthful which they immediately spat out upon the saucer; the servant disappeared with the whole apparatus, and the operation passed almost unnoticed because of the way it was performed.

All that is changed now.

In any house that prides itself on being highly fashionable, lackeys distribute to the guests, toward the end of dessert, bowls full of cold water in each of which is placed a goblet of water that has been warmed. There, in plain sight of one another, everybody plunges his fingers into the cold water in pretense of washing them, and drinks up the heated water, with which he gargles noisily, and which he then spews out into the goblet or the bowl.[12]

I am not the only one who rebels against this new fashion, which is equally useless, indecent, and disgusting.

It is *useless*, because the mouth of anyone who knows how to eat properly is clean at the end of a meal: it has been re-

† *"Mon cher monsieur, vous êtes en vérité de très-bonne compagnie, mais vous êtes trop fort buveur pour nous."*

freshed either by fruit or by the last tastes of wine which it is the custom to drink with the dessert. As for one's hands, they should not be so used that they grow soiled, and what is more, does each guest not have a napkin to clean them with?

It is *indecent*, because it is a generally accepted principle of behavior that physical cleanliness is maintained in the privacy of the dressing room.

It is above all a disgusting innovation, because the prettiest and the freshest of mouths lose all their charms when they usurp the functions of the excretory organs: what are they then if neither fresh nor pretty? And what can we say of those hideous caverns which open only to display seemingly bottomless emptiness, if it were not for the rotting tooth stumps that occasionally rear up in them? *Proh pudor!*

Such is the ridiculous position we have been placed in by an affectation of pretentious cleanliness which has no real place in either our tastes or our morals.

When certain limits of behavior have been overstepped, it is impossible to know what will be the next move, and I cannot prophesy what new purification will be imposed upon us.

Since the first appearance of these fashionable bowls, I have invoked day and night against them. A second Jeremiah, I deplore the aberrations of high style and, made too knowing by my travels, I cannot even enter a drawing room any more without shuddering at the prospect of finding there the abominable CHAMBERPOT.†

V. *Mystification of the Professor and Defeat of a General*

A few years ago the papers announced to us the discovery of a new perfume, extracted from the *Hemerocallis*, a bulbous plant which does indeed have a very pleasant odor resembling that of jasmine.

I am deeply curious as well as something of a loiterer, and

---

† *It is well known that there were a few years ago and perhaps still are, in England, dining rooms in which one could relieve himself* (FAIRE SON PETIT TOUR) *without leaving the room: a strange custom, but one that would be fairly easy to follow in a country where the ladies retire as soon as the men begin their wine drinking.*

these two things combined to draw me as far as the Faubourg Saint-Germain, where I could find the new scent, "the nostril-sorcerer" as the Turks put it.

I was welcomed with all the honors due an enthusiast, and from the inner sanctum of a very well supplied pharmacy a little box was produced for me, thoroughly wrapped, and seeming to contain some two ounces of the rare crystallization. This politeness was recognized on my part by an expenditure of three francs, following the laws of compensation whose sphere and principles are daily enlarged by the studies of M. Azaïs.[13]

An addlepate would have torn open the package then and there, and sniffed and tasted of it. A professor behaves differently: I felt that in such a case as this the best thing to do was retire; therefore I went back to my home at my accustomed pace, and soon, tucked expectantly upon my sofa, I prepared myself to experience a new sensation.

I drew from my pocket the odorous box, and unwrapped from it the papers that still bound it. They were three different printed sheets, all discussing the Hemerocallis, its natural history, its culture, its blossom, and the unusual pleasures to be drawn from its perfume, whether it be concentrated in lozenge form, mixed with toilet preparations, or dissolved for our tables in alcoholic liqueurs or blended in frozen puddings. I read these three papers attentively: 1, to repay myself for the expenditure to which I referred higher up; 2, to prepare myself properly for the appreciation of this new treasure extracted from the vegetable kingdom.

Then I opened, with due reverence, the box which I supposed to be full of lozenges. But oh surprise, oh shock! I found, first of all, a second copy of the three advertisements, and, apparently as a secondary benefit, about two dozen of the troches whose power had led me on the long walk to our noble suburb.

First of all I tasted one, and I must be just and say that I found these little pastilles most agreeable; but this made me even more annoyed that, in spite of the outer appearance of the box, they were so few in number. The more I thought about it, really, the more puzzled I became.

I got up with the firm intention of taking the box back to its inventor, even if he kept what had been paid for it. At that moment, though, a mirror reflected back at me my greying head: I could but laugh at my own liveliness and sit down again, containing my annoyance. Plainly enough, I still feel it.

Another thing restrained me: it too concerned a pharmacist, and not four days before I had been witness to the complete imperturbability of the members of this respectable profession.

It makes one more anecdote which my readers should know: I am today (17 June 1825) in the process of storytelling, and may God preserve us from its becoming a public calamity!

Well then, I went one morning to pay a visit to my friend and fellow native of Belley, General Bouvier des Éclats.

I found him pacing his rooms in agitation, and crumpling in his hands some writing which looked to me like poetry.

"Look at this," he said, handing it to me. "Tell me your opinion of it: you are a good judge."

I took the paper, and having run through it was highly astonished to see that it was a bill for medicines: it was not my qualities as a poet that the General called upon, but my studies as an amateur pharmacist.[14]

"Well, after all, old fellow," I said as I gave him back the paper, "you know the customs of the profession to which you have entrusted yourself. It is true that they may have overstepped the limits a bit, but on the other hand why do you sport a beautifully ornamented coat, and three official decorations, and a cocked hat with tassels? There alone are three extenuating circumstances, and you are not going to be able to ignore them."

"Be quiet," he said angrily to me. "This is really a dreadful state of affairs! What is more, you are going to see my swindler. I've summoned him here, he's on his way, and you must back me up."

He was still speaking when the door opened, and we saw coming toward us a man of about fifty-five years, dressed carefully; he was tall, and walked slowly, and his whole aspect would have had an air of severity, if the set of his mouth and his eyes had not had something sardonic about it.

He drew near the fireplace, refused a chair, and I found myself witness to the following dialogue, which I have faithfully remembered.

The General—Sir, the bill which you have sent me is in very truth an apothecary's pipe dream,[15] and . . .

The Man In Black—Sir, I am not an apothecary.

The General—What are you then, Sir?

The Man In Black—Sir, I am a pharmacist.

The General—Well, Mr. Pharmacist, your messenger boy must have informed you . . .

The Man In Black—Sir, I have no messenger boy.

The General—Then who was that young fellow?

The Man In Black—Sir, it was a pupil.

The General—I was about to say, Sir, that your drugs . . .

The Man In Black—Sir, I never sell drugs.

The General—What do you sell then, Sir?

The Man In Black—Sir, I sell medicaments.

There the discussion ended. The general, embarrassed at being guilty of so many solecisms and at finding himself so ignorant of pharmaceutical terms, stuttered, forgot what he was about to say, and paid the full amount of the bill.

VI.   *The Dish of Eel* [16]

There once was, on the Rue de la Chaussée-d'Antin in Paris, a certain citizen named Briguet who, starting as a coachman, rose to be a horse dealer and ended by piling up a small fortune for himself.

He had been born at Talissieu, and when he decided to go back there he married a woman with a little money who had formerly been the cook at the establishment of Mademoiselle Thevenin, once known to all Paris as the "Ace of Spades."

The chance arose to buy a small piece of property in his native village; he took it, and installed himself there with his wife toward the end of 1791.

In those days all the priests of the diocese used to meet together once a month, at the house of each one in turn, to confer upon ecclesiastical matters. They celebrated High Mass together, discussed their business, and then dined.

Such a reunion was always referred to as *the conference*, and the priest chosen to be host for it never failed to make great preparations in order to receive his brothers worthily.

When it was the turn of the Curé of Talissieu, it happened that one of his parishioners made him a present of a magnificent eel, caught in the limpid Serans waters, and more than three feet long.

Delighted to come into possession of such a noble fish, the priest felt grave doubts that his cook would be able to treat it with the skill it deserved, and went therefore to discuss the problem with Madame Briguet. He flattered her superior culinary knowledge, and begged her to lend her artistry to a dish which would be worthy of an archbishop himself and would give the greatest splendor to his dinner party.

His amenable parishioner agreed without too much difficulty, and with all the more pleasure as she said, because she still had a little collection of various exotic spices which she used to cook with at her former employer's.

The eel was prepared with great care, and served impressively. Not only did the dish have an elegant appearance, but a most tempting odor, and once it had been tasted, there was no praise high enough for it. It vanished, sauce and all, down to the last tiny particle.

But, by the time for dessert, the worthy pastors felt themselves stirred in a most unaccustomed manner, and as a natural result of the effect of the physical state upon the moral, the conversation took on a somewhat wanton tone.

Some of the curés told high old tales of their adventures in the seminary; others teased their companions about various whispered parish scandals: in short, the table talk fixed itself permanently upon the most delightful of the seven deadly sins, and the remarkable thing was that the good men did not once realize it, so strong was the devil in them.

They broke up the banquet late, and my secret memoirs do not intrude further on their actions for that day. But at the next conference, when the curés met again, they were ashamed of what they had talked about, made their mutual apologies, and ended by blaming the whole sad business on the influence of the dish of eel. They decided that although Madame Briguet's preparation was admittedly delicious, it would not be prudent to put her artistry to a second test.

I have searched in vain for information about the spice which produced such marvellous effects, the more so since there was no complaint that it was of a burning or otherwise dangerous nature.

The artist herself confessed that her dish contained a cray-fish sauce which had been liberally peppered, but I am convinced that she did not tell all she could have.[17]

VII. *The Asparagus*

One time it was reported to Monsignor Courtois de Quincey, bishop of Belley, that an asparagus tip of incredible size had poked up its head in one of the beds of his vegetable garden.

Immediately his whole household hurried to the spot to verify the news, for even in episcopal palaces it is amusing to have something to do.

The report was found to be neither false nor exaggerated. The plant had already broken through the crust of earth, and its tip could plainly be seen. It was rounded, gleaming, and finely patterned, and gave promise of a girth greater than a handspan.

Everyone talked excitedly of this horticultural triumph, and it was agreed that to the Bishop alone belonged the right to garner it. The neighboring cutler was ordered to make immediately a knife appropriate to the great occasion.

During the following days the asparagus increased in grace and in beauty; its progress was slow but continuous, and before long its watchers could see the white part where the edible portion of this vegetable ends.

The time for harvesting thus indicated, a good dinner was first served, and the actual operation took place after a postprandial stroll.

Then it was that Bishop Courtois advanced, armed with the official knife, kneeled down solemnly, and concentrated on cutting from its root the haughty plant, while the whole episcopal entourage seethed with impatience to examine the fibers and texture of the phenomenon.

But oh surprise, oh disappointment! And oh misery! The prelate rose from his knees with empty hands . . . The famed asparagus was made of wood.

This practical joke, which was perhaps carried a little too far, was the work of Canon Rosset, a native of Saint-Claude, who had wonderful skill as a turner, and painted most admirably as well. He had made the false plant a perfect copy of reality, had buried it secretly, and then raised it a little every day in imitation of natural growth.

Bishop Courtois did not know quite how to take this mystifying prank (which indeed it was); then, seeing hilarity already spreading over the faces of his household, he smiled. His smile was followed by the general explosion of truly Homeric laughter: the evidence of the crime was borne away, without bothering about the criminal, and for that evening, at least, the carved asparagus tip was admitted to the honors of exhibition in the drawing room.

VIII. *The Trap*

The Chevalier de Langeac had a sizable fortune at one time, which melted away in the conventional extravagances expected of a man who is young, rich, and good-looking.

Finally he gathered up what was left, and with the help of a small government pension he lived a pleasant enough life in Lyons, and in the best society, for experience had taught him how to manage well.

Although he always remained charming to the ladies, he had by this time retired from active service toward them; he still enjoyed playing any and all card games with them, at which he was highly skilled, but he never risked losing his money to them, with a ruthlessness which is characteristic of a man who can no longer accept their bounties.

Gourmandism became more important to him as his other pleasures dwindled; it can be said that he made an actual profession of it, and since he was a very pleasant companion, he had more dinner invitations than he could ever accept.

Lyons is a town of good living: its location makes it rich equally in the wines of Bordeaux and Hermitage and Burgundy; game from the neighboring countryside is of the best; the finest fish in the world are brought from the lakes of Geneva and Le Bourget; and connoisseurs swoon with pleasure at the sight of the fat Bresse hens which are marketed in Lyons.

The Chevalier de Langeac, then, had his own place at the

best tables in town, and the one he enjoyed most of all was in the home of M. A . . . , a very rich banker and a distinguished connoisseur of good living. The Chevalier blamed his preference on the fact that he and the financier had gone to school together. Gossips (for they are omnipresent) attributed it to M. A . . . 's cook, who had been the favorite pupil of Ramier, a skilled caterer who flourished in those distant days.

However that may be, toward the end of the winter of 1780 the Chevalier de Langeac received a note in which M. A . . . invited him, ten days later, to supper (for they still supped then), and my secret journal assures me that he trembled with joy in concluding that such a summons made so far in advance must indicate a special occasion and a celebration of the first rank.

He presented himself on the fixed day and hour, and found ten guests assembled, all of them lovers of the pleasures of the table: the word *gastronomer* had not yet been borrowed from the Greek, or at least was not as common as it is today.

Soon a substantial meal was served; among other dishes it had an enormous sirloin in its own gravy, a richly garnished fricassee of chicken, a cut of veal that looked most promising, and a very handsome stuffed carp.

All this was appetizing and solid, but it did not measure up to what the Chevalier had hoped for after such a long-standing invitation.

Another thing surprised him: his fellow guests, all of them good trenchermen, either did not eat at all or merely nibbled. One had a headache, another suffered from a chill, a third had just come from dinner, and so it was with every one. The Chevalier marvelled inwardly at the hazards of chance which had brought together on this one night so many uncongenial dispositions, and believing himself foreordained to act for all these invalids, he fell to bravely, carved his meat precisely, and put into action all his fine powers of INTUSSUSCEPTION.[18]

The second course was no less solid than the first: a huge Crémieu turkey shared honors with a most beautiful pike *au bleu,* and they were flanked by six conventional side dishes (not counting the salad), among which a generous dish of macaroni with Parmesan was outstanding.

At the sight of all this the Chevalier felt his forces revivified, while the other diners acted as if they were at their last sighs. Stimulated by the customary shift in wines, he exulted in his companions' impotence, and toasted their health in a series of bumpers with which he washed down a generous portion of the pike, which followed in turn the second joint of the turkey.

He welcomed the side dishes in their proper order, and carried on his chosen career gloriously, deciding to limit himself at dessert to but a morsel of cheese and one glass of Malaga, for sweets had no part in his scheme of things.

It has been pointed out that he had felt two moments of astonishment during the evening: the first at noting the solidity of the fare, and the second at finding his fellow guests in such bad health. He was now to experience a third shock, and for quite another reason.

For the servants, instead of bringing in the dessert, took everything away from the table, even to the linen and silver, and then laid it a-fresh and placed upon it four new entrées, whose savory steam rose upward to the heavens.

They consisted of sweetbreads in a crayfish sauce, soft truffled roes, a larded and stuffed pike, and wings of red partridge served with a purée of mushrooms.[19]

Like Ariosto's old magician who, holding the fair Armida captive in his very arms, could make but the most impotent attempts to have her, the Chevalier was utterly crestfallen to see so many good things which he could no longer enjoy, and he began to suspect that a wicked joke was being played.

In contrast to his dejection, all the other guests seemed to feel much better than before: appetite returned to them, a slight expression of irony lurked on their lips, and now it was their turn to drink to the health of the Chevalier, whose ability to continue was exhausted.

Nonetheless he put a good face on it, and seemed to want to defy Nature herself; but at the third bite she revolted, and his stomach threatened to betray him. He was thus forced to retire from combat and, as it is phrased in musical circles, to mark time.

What must have been his feelings when a third change was made and he saw literally dozens of fine snipes brought in, gleaming with fat and lying upon their traditional rich toast;

a pheasant, rare indeed in those days, sent straight from the banks of the Seine; a fresh tuna, and pastry and side dishes which were the best that any kitchen of that ancient period could possibly offer!

He considered his position for a few minutes, and was on the point of resting, continuing, and then dying bravely on the battlefield: such, right or wrong, was the first impulse of his outraged sense of honor. But soon egotism came to his aid, and led him toward more moderate ideas.

He reflected that in such a case prudence does not indicate cowardice; that death from indigestion is always a subject of ridicule; and that the future doubtless held many compensations for his present disappointment. He took up the challenge, therefore, and tossing his napkin from him, "Sir," he said to the banker, "no man treats his friends in this manner! You have outdone your own perfidy, and I shall never see you again in my life." He had spoken; he disappeared.

His departure failed to cause much of a stir, for it was but the final proof of the success of a plot which had been laid for the sole purpose of confronting him with a good meal which he could not possibly enjoy, and all of the guests had been let into the secret.

The Chevalier, however, sulked longer than anyone believed he would. Several tactful maneuvers were necessary to bring him into the open again, but finally he emerged in time for the first figpeckers, and by the time truffles made their next appearance he had forgotten the whole affair.

IX. *The Turbot*

Discord threatened once to insinuate itself into the heart of one of the most ideal households in Paris. It was on a Saturday, the Jewish day of rest: there was question of how to cook a turbot; it was in the country, at Villecrêne.[20]

The fish, which might be said to have been torn from a much more glorious fate, was supposed to be served the next day at a gathering of pleasant people to which I too had been invited; it was as fresh and plump and gleaming as could possibly be desired, but it was so much bigger than any vessel available to cook it in that nobody knew what to do with it.

"Well, let's cut it in two," the husband said.

"How could you dare insult this poor creature so?" the wife demanded.

"But my dear, we must! There's nothing else we can do. Come on, ask for a chopper, and before you know it we'll be done with it."

"Wait a little longer, my dear. There is plenty of time. Anyway, you know that your cousin is coming. He's a professor, and is bound to know how to get us out of this mess."

"A professor! . . . get us out of this? Hah!"

And it is faithfully reported to me that the gentleman who spoke thus seemed to have very little confidence in that professor, who was, nevertheless, myself! SCHWERNOTH! [21]

The difficulty would probably have been solved in an Alexandrian manner,[22] if at that moment I had not arrived at a gallop, my nose to the wind, with the appetite which a man always has when he has been travelling, when it is seven at night, and when the odor of a good dinner greets his nostrils and invites his taste.

On my entrance I did my best to make the usual greetings; nobody answered me, since I was not even being listened to. Soon enough, however, the problem which absorbed all attention was exposed to me almost in *duo*, after which both parties fell silent as if by previous agreement. The prettier of my two relatives watched me with eyes which seemed to say, "I hope we can survive this ordeal somehow." My bearded cousin, on the contrary, had a mocking supercilious air about him, as if he were already sure that I would not be able to relieve the situation, and he kept his hand firmly on the redoubtable chopper, which had been brought at his command.

These various indications of trouble disappeared, however, to give place to a lively curiosity, when I pronounced in a grave oracular voice these solemn words: "The turbot will remain in one piece until its official presentation."

I was already confident of not having compromised myself, since I planned to cook it in the oven, but because this method presented certain difficulties I did not yet bother to discuss it. I headed silently for the kitchen, with my cousins attending me as acolytes, the rest of the household representing the faithful flock, and the cook IN FIOCCHI at the end of the procession.

The first two utensils which were shown to me were not at all practical for my purpose, but when we reached the laundry room I saw before me a copper washboiler, somewhat small but solidly fitted into its own stove. Immediately I summed up its usefulness, and turning toward my train I cried out, with that faith which can transport mountains, "Have no more fear! The turbot will be cooked whole, it will be steam-cooked, and it will be cooked here and now!"

And sure enough, although the time for dinner was well upon us, I put everyone to work without delay. While some of them lit the fire under the boiler, I evolved from a large woven hamper a kind of rigid hammock, exactly the size of the giant fish. On this hammock I had my helpers place a layer of onions, shalots, and highly flavored herbs, upon which was laid the turbot, by then well clean and dried, and properly salted. A second layer of the same herbs and vegetables was placed over it. Then the hammock was put across the boiler, which was half full of water, and the whole was covered with a small washtub around which we banked dry sand, to keep the steam from escaping too easily. Soon the water was boiling madly; steam filled the inside of the tub, which was removed at the end of a half-hour, and the hammock was taken out of the boiler with the turbot cooked to perfection, white as snow, and most agreeable to look at.

Once the operation was over, we rushed to seat ourselves at the dinner table, with appetites sharpened by the delay and by our labor and its great success. So famished were we that it took some time to reach that happy moment, so often spoken of by Homer, when the abundance and variety of the dishes had made hunger vanish.

The next day at dinner the turbot was served to the worthy guests, and all of them exclaimed at its handsome appearance.[23] And then the master of the house told, without any urging, the astonishing way we had done the cooking, and I was lauded not only for my timely inventiveness but for its results as well: after thoughtful tasting, it was unanimously agreed that the fish prepared according to my system was incomparably better than if it had been cooked in the traditional turbot pan. This decision was surprising to nobody, for it was obvious that since the fish had not been passed through boiling water, it had lost none of its basic properties, and had on the contrary absorbed all the aroma of the seasoning.

While my ears drank their fill of the compliments which were showered upon me, my eyes sought out other even more sincere ones in the visible post-mortem verdict of the guests, and I observed with secret satisfaction that General Labassée was so pleased that he smiled anew at each bite, while the curé had his throat stretched upward and his ecstatic eyes fixed upon the ceiling; I saw that of the two members of the Academy who were there with us, both of them as witty as they were gourmands, the first, M. Auger, showed the shining eyes and radiant face of an acclaimed author, while the second, M. Villemain, leaned his head with his chin tipped to the west, like a man who is listening.

All of this is useful to remember, for there are few country houses where one cannot find everything needed to set up the apparatus I used on that occasion, which one can always count on when there is the problem of cooking something that arrives unexpectedly and is bigger than ordinary.

Nonetheless, my readers would have been deprived of the recounting of this great adventure if I had not felt that it must lead to results of a more general practicability.[24]

In effect, anyone who knows the laws of Nature and the effects of steam will remember that the latter equals in temperature the liquid from which it emerges, that it can even be a few degrees hotter because of slight concentration, and that it accumulates as long as there is no vent through which it can escape.

It follows that, all things being equal, by simply adding to the capacity of the washtub which I used in my experiment, and substituting for it an empty barrel, it would be possible to steam-cook quickly and inexpensively several bushels of potatoes, root vegetables of every kind, or whatever had been piled upon the hammock and well covered with the barrel, whether it might be for men or for their animals. Furthermore, all this could be done six times faster and with six times less fuel than would be needed to bring to the boiling point a cauldron of some twenty gallons capacity.

I believe that such a simple apparatus can prove of some value wherever there may be an establishment of any size, whether in town or in the country, and this is the reason for my describing it in such a manner that anyone can understand what I have written, and profit from it.

I feel that we have not done enough about adapting the power of steam to our domestic advantage, and I very much hope that some day the bulletin of the Society of Encouragement[25] will let the farmers know that I have done what I could about it.

P.S. One day when a group of us professors assembled at Number 14, Rue de la Paix, I recounted once more the true story of the steam-cooked turbot. When I finished, the gentleman on my left turned to me, and said in a reproachful voice, "Was I not there myself? And did I not pay you just as many compliments as any of the others?"

"Certainly," I answered him. "You were sitting there right next to the curé! I meant no reproach . . . you swallowed your share nobly: please don't think that . . . I . . ."

The man who thus reminded me was M. Lorrain, of most subtle palate, a banker as pleasant as he is prudent, who has anchored safely in the harbor in order to judge more calmly the effects of the storm, and as a result of all this is deserving of mention in every respect.

X. *Some Restorative Remedies*

BY THE PROFESSOR

Improvised for the case described in Meditation 25

A

Take six large onions, three carrots, and a handful of parsley. Chop them together and throw them into a pot, where you will heat them through and brown them with a morsel of good fresh butter.

When this mixture is just right, add six ounces of sugar candy, twenty grains of powdered amber, a crust of toasted bread, and three bottles of water. Boil the whole for three-quarters of an hour, adding water as necessary so that in spite of the loss by evaporation there is always a total of three bottles of liquid.

While this goes on, kill, pluck, and clean an old rooster,

which you must then pound in a mortar, flesh and bones, with an iron pestle. Also chop two pounds of the best quality of beef.

These two kinds of meat are then mixed, and a sufficient quantity of salt and pepper is added to them.

Put them into a pot over a hot fire, so that they heat through quickly, and throw in from time to time a little fresh butter, so that the mixture will brown nicely without sticking.

When this has been accomplished, that is to say when the osmazome has taken on a dark color, the bouillon which is in the first pot is strained and added little by little to the second; when all of it has been combined, you let it boil energetically for three-quarters of an hour, always taking care to add hot water to keep the same quantity of liquid.

At the end of this time, the operation is finished, and you have a potion whose efficacy is sure as long as the invalid, no matter how undone by one or another of the causes which we have outlined, has nevertheless kept a well-functioning stomach.

To use this restorative, a cup of it is given every three hours on the first day until bedtime; the following days, a large cup in the mornings only, and the same quantity at night, until the three bottles have been emptied. The sufferer must be held to a light diet which is still nourishing, such as chicken legs, fish, ripe fruits, and preserves. It almost never happens that a new supply must be made. Toward the fourth day the invalid can take up his usual pursuits, and must admonish himself to be more prudent in the future, *if that is possible.*

By leaving out the sugar candy and the amber a soup of excellent flavor and worthy of any gathering of connoisseurs can be improvised.

The old rooster can be supplanted by four old partridges, and the beef by a morsel of mutton shank; the result will be neither less efficacious nor less agreeable.

The system of chopping the meat and letting it brown before moistening it can be used whenever you are in a great hurry. It is based on the fact that meats so treated absorb much more heat than when they are in water, and for this reason you can use this system if you must have a good rich soup without being obliged to wait five or six hours,[26] something which can often happen, especially in the country. And naturally it is understood that whoever uses this method will add that much glory to the professor's name.

B

It is a good thing for everyone to know that even if amber, considered as a perfume, can be extremely offensive to certain unbelievers with delicate nerves, it is a sovereign tonic and exhilarant[27] when taken internally. Our forefathers used it generously in their cooking, and were none the worse for it.

I know that Marshal Richelieu, of deathless memory, had a habit of sucking amber-flavored lozenges;[28] and as for myself, when I find that I have hit on one of those days when the weight of age lies heavily upon me, when I think with difficulty and feel myself oppressed by some unknown force, I stir into a good cup of chocolate a piece of amber the size of a bean, which has been pounded with some sugar, and drinking it has always helped me recover as if by magic. Thanks to this tonic the mechanics of living grow easier, my mind works quickly, and I do not suffer from the insomnia which would be the inevitable result of taking a cup of black coffee for the same purpose.

C

The first of my restoratives, called A, is meant for men of robust temperament and determination, and for all those who exhaust themselves through overexertion.

I once had occasion to invent another, much pleasanter to the taste and gentler in its action, which I prescribe for people of unstable and vacillating temperament, and for all those, in a word, who grow tired for no apparent reason. It is as follows:

Take a knuckle of veal of not less than two pounds, cut it in quarters lengthwise, flesh and bone, and brown it with four sliced onions and a handful of watercress. When it is almost cooked through, add three bottles of water, and let the whole boil for two hours, taking care to replace whatever evaporates. Here, in itself, you will have made a good bouillon of veal. Add pepper and salt in moderation.

Pound separately three old pigeons and twenty-five very fresh crayfish. Mix them well so that they may be browned as I have already outlined in Number A, and when you see that the preparation is thoroughly heated and is beginning to take on a good color, add the veal bouillon and cook rapidly for one hour. Then strain the soup which has been thus enriched, and drink it morning and night, or even better in the mornings only, two hours before breakfast. It can also be served as a delicious soup.

I was led to improvise this prescription by two writers who, seeing that my own condition was far from bad, placed their confidence in me and, as they expressed it, left everything in my lap.

They used the restorative broth as directed, and have never had reason to regret it. The poet, who before was no more than elegiac, has become romantic. The lady, who had nothing to her credit but one fairly colorless novel filled with catastrophes, has written a second one which is much better, and which ends with a happy marriage. It is plain that in both cases there has been a marked increase in creative strength, and I must confess that I feel privileged to boast a little about my part in it.

XI.   *The Pullet of Bresse*

Early in January of this current year of 1825, a young married couple named Madame and Monsieur de Versy were guests at an elaborate *full-dress*[29] oyster luncheon, and my readers know what that means.[30]

Such feasts are delightful, whether because they are composed of appetizing dishes or because of the gaiety which usually dominates them, but they have the great inconvenience of completely upsetting the rest of the day's occupations. That is what happened this time. The dinner hour arrived, and the young couple sat down at their table, but it was only a gesture. Madame swallowed a little soup, and Monsieur sipped a glass of watered wine; then a few friends came in, they all played whist for a while to pass away the evening, and finally the young couple retired to their wide bed.

About two that morning M. de Versy awoke. He was restless, and yawned and stretched so much that his wife grew worried and asked him if he felt ill. "No, my dear," he said, "but I believe I'm hungry! I was thinking of that fat Bresse pullet, so plump and pretty, that was brought in for dinner, and of what little attention we paid to it."

"If I must tell the truth, my dear, I'll confess to you that I'm as hungry as you are. Since you did actually dream of that chicken, we must have it brought up here and eat it."

"You're out of your mind! All the servants are asleep, and tomorrow everyone would laugh at us."

"Well, if all the servants are asleep, they can wake up. And nobody will laugh at us, because our friends shan't know about it. And anyway, who can tell if by morning one of us may not have died of hunger? I simply don't want to take the chance. I am going to ring for Justine."

No sooner said than done: the poor maid was roused from that deep slumber which comes to people who are nineteen and who have dined well, when they are not troubled by love.†

She appeared all tousled, her eyes half-shut, her mouth agape with yawns, and sank upon a chair with her arms dangling.

But so far everything had been easy; producing the cook was another matter. She was a true artist of the kitchen, and proportionately bad-tempered; she grumbled, whinnied, growled, roared, and snorted; finally she arose, and put her mighty bulk in motion.

While this was going on Madame de Versy slipped a jacket over her shoulders, her husband arranged himself as best he could, and Justine spread a tablecloth over the coverlet of the bed and brought the accessories indispensable to this kind of spur-of-the-moment celebration.

Everything being thus nicely arranged, the pullet arrived, and was instantly and ruthlessly demolished.

After this first refreshment, the couple divided a huge Saint-Germain pear, and a little orange preserve.

And meanwhile they had drained to the last drop a bottle of Graves, repeating over and over as they did so, and with variations, the fact that they had never had a pleasanter meal.

It ended, finally, as must everything here below. Justine picked up the tablecloth, removed the incriminating evidence, and went back to her bed. The curtain of conjugal privacy was drawn once more on the scene of such feasting.

† A PIERNA TENDIDA (SPANISH).

The next morning Madame de Versy hurried to see her friend Madame de Franval, and told her everything that had gone on, and it is to the indiscretion of this latter lady that my readers owe the present anecdote.

She never failed to remark that as Madame de Versy ended her confidence, she coughed twice and then very obviously blushed.

XII.   *The Pheasant*

The pheasant is an enigma whose secret meaning is known only to the initiate; they alone understand how to enjoy it to its full.

Every substance has its peak of deliciousness: some of them have already reached it before their full development, like capers, asparagus, young grey partridges, squab pigeons, and so on; others reach it at that precise moment when they are all that it is possible for them to be in perfection, like melons and almost all fruits, mutton, beef, venison, and red partridges; and finally still others at that point when they begin to decompose, like medlars,[31] woodcock, and above all pheasant.

This last-mentioned bird, when eaten within three days after its death, has nothing distinguishing about it. It is neither as delicate as a pullet, nor as savorous as a quail.

At its peak of ripeness, however, its flesh is tender, highly flavored, and sublime, at once like domestic fowl and like wild game.

This peak is reached when the pheasant begins to decompose; then its aroma develops, and mixes with an oil which in order to form must undergo a certain amount of fermentation, just as the oil in coffee can only be drawn out by roasting it.

The exact moment of perfection reveals itself to the uninitiate by a slight smell, and by the difference in color of the bird's belly; but the inner circle guesses it by a sort of instinct which often comes into play, and which enables a skilled roast cook, for instance, to know merely from a glance that it is time either to take a bird off the spit or to let it make a few more turns.

When the pheasant has reached this point, then, it is plucked, and not before, and it is larded carefully, with the freshest and firmest of material.

It is far from unimportant to wait until now to pluck the bird; very careful experiments have taught us that pheasants which are left in their feathers are much more savory than those which have been naked for a long time; this may be because contact with the air neutralizes certain qualities in the aroma, or because a part of the natural fluid which serves to nourish the feathers is reabsorbed and adds its flavor to the meat.

Once the bird is ready thus far, the time has come to stuff it, and in the following manner:

Bone and draw a brace of woodcock, in such a way that you have one supply of the flesh, and another of the livers and entrails.

Take the flesh and make a forcemeat of it by chopping it with some steamed beef marrow, a little scraped bacon, pepper, salt, fresh herbs, and enough fine truffles to make just the amount of stuffing needed to fill the pheasant.

You must take care not to let any of this forcemeat escape from the cavity, which is sometimes difficult when the bird is fairly high and far gone.[32] There are however various ways of doing this, among them tying a piece of bread of the proper size over the opening, to act as a kind of cork.

Prepare a slice of bread which will be about two inches bigger on every side than the bird laid lengthwise. Then take the woodcock livers and entrails, and grind them in a mortar with two large truffles, an anchovy, a little finely minced bacon, and a sizeable lump of the best fresh butter.

Spread this paste evenly on the bread slice, and place it under the pheasant, already stuffed according to the preceding description, so that it will catch every drop of juice which will appear while the bird is roasting.

When the bird is done, serve it lying gracefully upon this crisp little couch; surround it with bitter oranges, and be assured of the fortunate outcome.

This highly savorous dish should be accompanied, preferably, by a vintage Burgundy; I have reached this conclusion after a series of observations which have been more work to me than a table of logarithms.

A pheasant thus prepared is worthy of being served to angels themselves, if by chance they still roamed the earth as in the days of Lot.

But what am I saying? This has indeed already happened! Such a stuffed pheasant was prepared once, under my own eyes, by the famous chef Picard, at the chateau of La Grange, the home of my charming friend Madame de Ville-Plaine, and was brought to the table by Louis the butler, who carried it at a solemnly processional pace. It was as closely examined as one of Madame Herbault's[33] hats; it was tasted with intense concentration; and all the time the ladies' eyes shone like stars, their lips gleamed like polished coral, and their faces were ecstatic. (See "Meditation 13, On Gastronomical Tests.")

I have experimented even further: I served a similar bird to a gathering of magistrates of the Supreme Court, who understand that it is good sometimes to shed the senatorial toga, and to whom I have often proved without any difficulty that the pleasures of the table are a natural compensation for the troubles of professional life. The dean of our reunion, after a proper examination of the dish, uttered in a solemn voice the one word, *Excellent!* Every head nodded in agreement, and the verdict was unanimous.

I noticed, during this period of decision, that the nostrils of all these dignitaries were literally trembling, that their august foreheads looked as if blanketed with peaceful serenity, and that their firm honest mouths had an expression of jubilation on them, almost like a half-smile.

But such marvellous results are in the nature of things. A pheasant prepared as I have described, being already remarkably flavorsome in itself, is inundated on the outside by the savory grease of the browning bacon; inwardly it is impregnated with the odorous vapors which escape from the woodcock and the truffles. And the slice of toast underneath, so richly spread with paste, has received the triply flavored juices which seep from the roasting bird.

Thus, of all the delicious things which have been brought together, not a single droplet or crumb escapes attention, and given the excellence of the dish, I believe it worthy of the most august banquet boards.

Parve, nec invideo, sine me liber ibis in aulam.

XIII.   *Gastronomical Industry of the Exiles*

Every woman in France, as I've heard tell,
Can always cook, be it ill or well.

LA BELLE ARSÈNE, ACT III.

I have discussed in a preceding chapter the enormous benefits which France derived from gourmandism in the unusual
circumstances of 1815. This national propensity was no less
useful to the émigrés; and those among them who possessed
some talent in the art of cookery drew invaluable help from it.

When I was in Boston, for instance, I taught the restaurant
keeper Julien† how to make my *fondue*, of scrambled eggs with
cheese. This dish, new to the Americans, became so much the
rage that Julien felt obliged to reward me by sending to me in
New York the rump of one of those pretty little roebucks which
are sent down in wintertime from Canada, and which was
pronounced exquisite by the special company I invited to enjoy
it.[34]

Captain Collet, also, earned a great deal of money in New
York in 1794 and 1795 by making ices and sherbets for the
inhabitants of that commercial town.

It was the ladies, above all, who could not get enough of a
pleasure so new to them as frozen food; nothing was more
amusing than to watch the little grimaces they made while
savoring it. It was especially difficult for them to understand
how anything could stay so cold in the summer heat of ninety
degrees.

When I was in Cologne I met a gentleman from Brittany
who was doing very well for himself as owner of an eating-
house, and I could go on indefinitely, citing such examples;
but I prefer to tell, because it is more unusual, the story of a
Frenchman who grew wealthy in London because of his skill
at making salad.

He was a Limousin, and if my memory does not fail me was
named d'Aubignac or d'Albignac.

Although his spending money was greatly restricted by the

---

† *Julien was prospering in 1794. He was a clever young fellow who, according to him, had been chef to the archbishop of Bordeaux. He must
have earned a handsome fortune, if God spared him.*

bad state of his finances he still found himself, one day, dining at one of the most famous taverns in London; he was among the people who believe that a good dinner can consist of a single dish, if that dish be excellent.

While he polished off a dish of succulent ROSTBEEF, five or six young men of good family (DANDIES) were banqueting at a nearby table, and one of them got up and walked over to him, and said in a polite voice, "Mister Frenchman, it is said that your nation excels in the art of salad making; would you do us the honor of tossing one together for us?" †

D'Albignac consented, after some hesitation, asked for everything he felt he would need to make the awaited masterpiece, gave all his attention to it, and had the good luck to bring it off.

While he measured his amounts, he replied frankly to the questions that were put to him about his affairs; he said that he was an exile and admitted, not without blushing a little, that he was being helped by the British government, a confession which doubtless seemed justification enough for one of the young men to slip into his hand a note for five pounds sterling, which he accepted after a most cursory resistance.

He had given them his address; and a very short while later he was none too surprised to receive a letter begging him, in the most straightforward way, to come and concoct a salad in one of the finest homes on Grosvenor Square.

D'Albignac, beginning to sense some permanent benefit to himself, did not hesitate a minute, and arrived punctually, armed with various new seasonings which he felt were indicated to give his creations an even higher degree of perfection.

He had had the time to consider the task ahead of him; he had the good luck to succeed again, and this time received a tip which he could not have refused without being foolhardy.

The first young men for whom he had performed had, it can be assumed, praised to the point of exaggeration the merits of the salad he had tossed together for them. The second group made even more noise about it, so that d'Albignac's reputation spread at once: he was known as the FASHIONABLE SALAT-MAKER; and in this land so hungry for anything new, everyone

---

† **Word for word translation of the English compliment which must have been made on this occasion.**

with any pretensions to social importance in the capital of the three kingdoms languished for a salad made according to the French GENTLEMAN's method: I DIE FOR IT, as goes their hallowed expression.

> A nun's desire is a burning curse,
> But an English girl's burns even worse.[35]

D'Albignac, being an intelligent man, took full advantage of the adulation which was poured on him; soon he had his own carriage to transport him more quickly between the places to which he was summoned, and a servant to carry, in a fitted mahogany case, all the ingredients with which he had adorned his repertory: variously flavored vinegars, oils with or without a fruity taste, soy, caviar, truffles and anchovies, ketchup,[36] meat essences and even the yolks of eggs, which are the distinctive ingredient of mayonnaise.

Later he manufactured copies of his case, which he outfitted completely and sold by the hundreds.

Finally, thanks to following his line of endeavor with precision and wisdom, he found himself with a fortune of more than 80,000 francs, which he took back with him to France when things had become better there.

Once more in his native land, he wasted no time in making a show on the streets of Paris, but concentrated on securing his own future. He invested 60,000 francs in the public funds, which stood then at 50, and he bought for 20,000 francs a little country place in Limousin, where probably he is still living, content and happy, since he is a man who knows how to limit his desires.

These details were given to me some time ago by one of my friends who had known d'Albignac in London, and who had just seen him again after his return to Paris.

XIV. *More Memories of Exile*

THE WEAVER

In 1794 M. Rostaing† and I were in Switzerland, putting a

---

† *Baron Rostaing, my friend and relative, now commissary of stores for the army at Lyons. He is an administrator of the first rank, and has*

good face on our unhappy fortunes, and holding fast to our love for the country which was persecuting us.

We went to Mondon, where I had relatives, and were received by the Trolliet family with a kindliness which I shall always remember with emotion.

This family, one of the oldest there, has now died out, since the last heir left but one daughter, who in turn did not bear a male child.[37]

I had pointed out to me in Mondon a young French officer who had taken up the profession of weaving, and the following is how he came to such a decision.

This young man, of very good family, was passing through Mondon to rejoin Condé's army,[38] and found himself seated at table beside one of those old men blessed with a face at once sober and animated, such as artists depict in the companions of William Tell.

During dessert they talked: the officer did not hide his position, and in return received various signs of interest from his neighbor, who sympathized with him for being forced so early in life to give up everything that was dear to him, and who reminded him of the justice of Rousseau's maxim that every man should know a trade, so that he might take care of himself in adversity and be able to support himself no matter where he was. As for himself, he said that he was a weaver, a childless widower, and happy with his lot.

The conversation went no further; the next day the officer departed, and soon afterwards found himself installed in the ranks of Condé's army. But from all that was happening, both within the group and outside of it, he came easily to the conclusion that it was not by this route that he could hope to return to France. He did not have to wait long to experience some of those unpleasant shocks which are often met with by men who have no other qualifications than their enthusiasm for the royal cause,[39] and a little later he was the victim of a piece of favoritism, or some such thing, which seemed painfully unjust to him.

Then the words of the old weaver came back to him. He

---

among his papers a system of military accountancy so clear that we would do well to adopt it.

pondered on them for a time, and having made up his mind he left the army, went back to Mondon, and presented himself at the weaver's, begging to be accepted as an apprentice.

"I cannot let this chance to do a good deed escape me," the old man said. "You will eat with me. I know only one thing, and I shall teach it to you. I have only one bed, and we'll share it. You will work thus for a year, and at the end of that time you can start out for yourself, and live happily in a country where labor is honored and encouraged."

From the very next day the officer set himself to work, and succeeded so well that at the end of six months his teacher confessed to him that he had nothing more to teach him, that he felt amply repaid for the effort he had made, and that from that moment everything the young man did was for his own profit.

When I was in Mondon, the new artisan had already made enough money to buy himself a loom and a bed; he worked with an earnest attention that was remarkable, and everyone took such an interest in him that the best families in town had arranged things so that he might dine each Sunday with one or another of them in turn.

That day, then, he put on his uniform and took up his rightful position in society, and since he was most agreeable and well educated, he was made much of. But Monday he became a weaver once more and, spending his time in this double life, seemed far from discontented with his lot.

THE FAMISHED GLUTTON

To this picture of the advantages of industry I am going to compare another of a completely opposite nature.

In Lausanne I met an exile from Lyons, a big handsome fellow who, rather than go to work, had reduced himself to eating but twice a week. He would have starved to death with the best grace in the world if a kind merchant of the town had not opened an account for him at a tavern, where he could dine every Sunday and Wednesday.

The émigré would arrive on the appointed day, stuff himself to the gullet, and leave, but not without taking off with him a big piece of bread, as had been agreed upon.

He made this supplementary ration last as long as possible,

drank some water when his stomach hurt, spent part of his time stretched on his bed in a kind of daydream which was not without its own charm, and thus existed until the next meal.

He had lived in this way for some three months when I met him: he was not ill, but there was throughout his whole body such lassitude, his features were so drawn, and there was something so Hippocratic[40] about the space between his nose and his ears, that he was painful to behold.

It was astonishing to me that he would submit to such anguish rather than try to make some use of himself, and I invited him to dinner at my inn, where I shuddered to watch him gorge. But I did not ask him back, because I believe that we must stiffen ourselves before adversity, and obey, when we hear it, the sentence passed on the whole human race: *Thou must work.*

THE SILVER LION

What good dinners we had in those days in Lausanne, at the *Silver Lion!*

Averaging fifteen *batz* (2 francs 25 centimes), we were presented with three complete courses, where we would see among many other things fine game from the neighboring mountains and the excellent fish from the Lake of Geneva, and we moistened all of it, according to our own wishes and capacities, with a simple white wine as limpid as spring water, which would have made a madman drink.[41]

The head of the table was occupied by a canon from Notre-Dame in Paris (I hope that he is still living), who had made himself perfectly at home there, and before whom the headwaiter did not hesitate to place everything that was best upon the bill of fare.

He paid me the honor of recognizing me and of summoning me, as a sort of aide-de-camp, to the higher altitudes which he occupied, but I could not enjoy this advantage for long: political happenings dragged me away, and I left for the United States, where I found a haven, and work, and some peace.

STAY IN AMERICA[42]

*   *   *   *   *

*   *   *   *   *

A BATTLE

I shall end this chapter by telling of an incident in my life which proves plainly that nothing is certain in this world below, and that misery creeps up on us when we least expect it.

I was leaving for France, quitting the United States after a three years' stay, and everything had gone so well for me there that all I asked from Heaven (and it heard my prayer) in the inevitable moments of regret before a departure, was that I might be no more unhappy in the Old World than I had been in the New.

This happiness I owed principally to the fact that from the moment I arrived in America I spoke the native tongue,† I dressed like the Americans, I took care not to seem more intelligent than they, and I was pleased with whatever they did; it was thus that I paid for the hospitality I found among them by a tactfulness which I believe necessary and which I suggest to all who find themselves in the same position.

Therefore I left peacefully a country where I had lived with everyone as peacefully, and there could not have been in all creation a two-legged featherless being more filled than I was with brotherly love, when there occurred an incident quite beyond my control, which barely failed to hurl me back into a tragic series of events.

I was on a boat which would carry me from New York to Philadelphia, and here I must explain that in order to make this trip with any certainty and precision advantage must be taken of the moment when the tide goes out.

The sea was at the precise time of slack water, that is to say on the point of ebbing, and the moment of casting off had arrived, without a single sign being made that we were to set out.

There were several of us Frenchmen among the passengers, including a M. Gauthier, who must still be at this very moment in Paris: a fine chap who ruined himself trying to build *ultra*

---

† *I was seated one night at dinner beside a Creole who had lived for two years in New York, and did not know enough English to ask for bread. I admitted my astonishment. "Bah!" he said, shrugging. "Do you think I am stupid enough to bother myself to learn the language of such a loutish race?"*

vires the house which forms the southwestern corner of the palace of the Ministry of Finance.

The cause of our delay was soon discovered: two American passengers had not yet arrived, and the captain was kind enough to wait for them. This put us in danger of being held back by low tide, so that it would take us twice as long to reach our destination, for the sea waits upon no man.

Grumbling was heard at once, especially from the Frenchmen, whose passions are much livelier than those of the inhabitants of the other side of the Atlantic.

I not only took no part in it, but hardly noticed it, for my heart was full and my thoughts turned toward the fate which awaited me in France; the result was that I was uncaring of what was happening about me. Soon, however, I heard a resounding crack, and I perceived that Gauthier had given a slap that would have grounded a rhinoceros to the cheek of one of the Americans.

This violent act resulted in hideous confusion. The words *French* and *American* being yelled back and forthly angrily, the quarrel became nationalistic; there was question, no less, of throwing us Frenchmen overboard, which would have been none too easy for them, even so, for we were eight against eleven.

My outer aspect was the kind that suggested that I might make the strongest resistance to this TRANSBORDATION,[43] for I am thickset, very tall, and was then only thirty-nine years old. This was undoubtedly why the obvious ringleader of the opposing forces was pushed forward, to face me in a most menacing pose.

He was as high as a steeple, and heavy in proportion; but when I took his measure with a look that dug to the very marrow of his bones, I saw that he was of a lymphatic nature, that his face was puffy and suffused and his eyes were dull, and that his head was small, while his legs were weak as a girl's.

Mens non agitat molem, thought I to myself; let us see what stuff he's made of, and then die, if that be meant. And here word for word is what I said to him, in the manner of the Homeric heroes:

"DO YOU BELIEVE† TO BULLY ME? YOU DAMNED ROGUE.

---

† THEE *and* THOU *are not used in English, and a carter even as he showers*

BY GOD! IT WILL NOT BE SO . . . AND I'LL OVERBOARD YOU
LIKE A DEAD CAT . . . IF I FIND YOU TOO HEAVY, I'LL CLING
TO YOU WITH HANDS, LEGS, TEETH, NAILS, EVERYTHING, AND IF
I CANNOT DO BETTER, WE WILL SINK TOGETHER TO THE BOT-
TOM; MY LIFE IS NOTHING TO SEND SUCH DOG TO HELL. NOW,
JUST NOW . . ." [44]

*"Croyez-vous m'effrayer, damné coquin? . . . par Dieu! il
n'en sera rien, et je vous jetterai par-dessus le bord comme un
chat crevé. Si je vous trouve trop lourd, je m'attacherai à vous
avec les mains, avec les jambes, avec les ongles, avec les dents,
de toutes les manières, et nous irons ensemble au fond. Ma
vie n'est rien pour envoyer en enfer un chien comme vous.
Allons . . ."* †

At these words, with which my whole appearance was doubtless in accord (for I felt I possessed the strength of Hercules),
I saw my man grow shorter by an inch, while his arms fell and
his cheeks sagged inward; in a word, he gave such evident signs
of terror that a companion, probably the one who had pushed
him toward me, perceived his state and came up as if to protect
him: he did well to interpose, for I was in full cry, and the native
of the New World would have learned that men who bathe
in the waters of the Furens‡ have nerves of tempered steel.

However, more peaceful words made themselves heard from
another part of the boat: the arrival of the latecomers had
created a diversion, and it was time to hoist sail. The result
was that even as I stood ready to do battle, the confusion suddenly ceased.

---

his horse with lashes says to him: "GO, SIR, GO, SIR, I SAY (*allez, monsieur, allez, monsieur, vous dis-je*)."

† *In all countries regulated by English law, fights are inevitably preceded
by much verbal incivility, for there is a saying that* "HIGH WORDS BREAK
NO BONES (*injuries ne cassent pas les os*)." *Often the whole thing goes
no further than that, and the law is such that one hesitates to strike an
actual blow, for he who hits first is breaking the public peace, and will
always be the one who must pay the fine, no matter what the reason for
the battle.*

‡ *A limpid river whose source is above Rossillon. It flows nearby Belley, and joins the Rhone above Peyrieux. Trout from its waters have flesh
of a delicate rose color, and that of the pike is as white as ivory.* GUT!
GUT! GUT! (GERM.)

From there on things went better still; for when all was calm again, upon my going to find Gauthier to rebuke him for his hotheadedness I found him seated at table with the man he had smacked, in the presence of a ham of the most delightful appearance and a pitcher of beer as tall as my forearm is long.

XV.   *The Bundle of Asparagus*

As I strolled past the Palais-Royal, one fine day in February, I stopped before the shop of Madame Chevet, the most famous grocer in Paris, who has always paid me the honor of wishing me well; and noticing a bundle of asparagus whose thinnest stalks were thicker than my index finger, I asked her the price.

"Forty francs, Monsieur," she replied.

"They are truly handsome; but at that price there are few people beside the king and perhaps a prince or two who will be able to enjoy them."

"You are mistaken; such high quality never reaches the palace, where they want good things but not magnificent. But nonetheless my asparagus will be sold, and this is how:

"At the very moment we are speaking, there are in this city at least three hundred very rich men, bankers, capitalists, tradesmen and so on, who are kept indoors because of the gout, or the fear of catching cold, or the orders of their doctors, or for other reasons which still do not keep them from eating; they are sitting by their fires, beating their brains out to imagine something that will tempt them, and when they have exhausted themselves without thinking of a thing, they send their valets in search of it; and one of these will turn up here, notice my asparagus, and make a report on it, and the bundle will be carried off at no matter what price. Or perhaps a pretty little lady will go by with her adorer, and will say to him, 'My dear, what beautiful asparagus! Do please buy it: you know that my cook makes a perfect sauce for it!' Well, in such a case a proper lover neither refuses nor does he bargain. Or perhaps it is to pay a wager, or do honor to a baptism or a sudden rise in stocks . . . How I can tell? In a word, the most expensive merchandise sells fastest, because in Paris there are so many extraordinary events to celebrate that there are always sufficient reasons for buying it."

While we were talking, two big Englishmen who passed by arm in arm stopped in front of us, and in an instant their faces lighted with admiration. One of them seized the bundle of asparagus, without even asking the price, paid for it, tucked in under his elbow, and carried it off as he whistled GOD SAVE THE KING.

"You see, Monsieur," Madame Chevet said to me, laughing, "that was a chance just as apt to happen as the others, but I had not yet told you of it."

XVI. *About Fondue*

Fondue is a native of Switzerland. It is nothing more nor less than eggs scrambled with cheese, in certain proportions which time and experiences have set. I shall give the official recipe for it.

It is a healthful, savory, and appetizing dish, quickly prepared, and always ready to do honor to the table if unexpected guests arrive. What is more, I discuss it here solely for my own pleasure, and also because the mention of it reminds me of something which is still remembered by the old men of the district of Belley.

Toward the end of the seventeenth century, a Monsieur de Madot was appointed Bishop of Belley, and arrived there to take possession of his diocese.

Those who were in charge of receiving him and doing him the honors of his own palace had prepared a banquet worthy of the event, and had taken advantage of every resource of the old-time cookery to celebrate Monsignor's arrival.

Among the side dishes was a generous *fondue*, from which the prelate served himself without stint. But, oh surprise! Not recognizing its appearance and believing it to be a *crème*, he ate it with his spoon instead of using his fork, which from time immemorial had been the custom with this dish.

All the guests, astonished by this peculiar behavior, looked sideways at one another, with imperceptible smiles. Respect, however, stilled every tongue, for whatever a bishop from Paris does at table, especially on the day of his arrival, cannot but be well done.

News traveled fast, however, and from the next morning everybody one met would ask, "Well, and do you know how our new bishop ate his *fondue* last night?" "Of course I know! He ate it with a spoon! I have it from an eye witness . . ." and so on. The town reported the news to the country, and after three months it was public gossip throughout the diocese.

The remarkable thing about it is that this incident failed to shake the foundations of our ancestors' faith. There were some seekers after novelty who supported the cause of the spoon, but they were soon forgotten: the fork triumphed, and after more than a century one of my great-uncles was still laughing over it, and told me, with a great gust of laughter, how it was that M. de Madot had indeed one time eaten his *fondue* with a spoon.

Recipe for Fondue

As it was drawn from the papers of M. Trolliet,
bailiff of Mondon, in the Canton of Berne.[45]

Weigh the number of eggs you wish to use, according to the presumed number of your guests.

Then take a piece of good Gruyere cheese weighing one-third of this amount, and a morsel of butter weighing one-sixth of it.

You must break and beat the eggs in a casserole, after which you add the butter and the grated or minced cheese.

Put the casserole on a lively fire, and turn the contents with a spatula, until they have become properly thick and soft; add a little salt, or none at all according to whether the cheese is old or not, and a good amount of pepper, which is one of the important characteristics of this time-honored dish; serve it on a gently heated platter; call for the best wine, which will be copiously drunk, and you will see miracles.

XVII. Disappointment

Everything was quiet one day at the inn *Ecu de France*, at Bourg in Bresse, when a great rolling of wheels was heard and a superb four-horse coach, English-style, drew up to the door. It was above all remarkable because of two extremely pretty ladies' maids who snuggled on the coachman's seat, well-wrapped in a generous rug of scarlet wool, edged and embroidered in blue.

At this sight, which betokened the arrival of a British noble-man travelling by easy stages, Chicot (which was the name of the landlord) ran with his cap in hand: his wife hovered at the hotel door; the servant girls just missed breaking their necks as they tumbled down the stairs, and the stable boys appeared magically, already counting on a generous tip.

The maids were unwrapped and handed down, not without producing a few blushes for the hazards of their descent, and the coach then brought forth 1), Milord, heavy, short, red-faced and fat-bellied; 2), two young ladies,[46] lanky, pale, and red-haired; 3), Milady, who looked to be between the first and second stages of consumption.

It was this last who spoke first:

"Innkeeper," she said, "take good care of my horses; give us a room so that we may rest, and see that my maids have some refreshment; but I do not wish that all this cost more than six francs, so you must take your measures accordingly."

No sooner had this economical pronouncement been made than Chicot put on his cap again, his wife disappeared inside the hotel, and the maids went back to their duties.

Nevertheless the horses were sent to the stable, where they could read the weekly papers if they wished; the ladies were shown to a chamber (UPSTAIRS), and the servants were offered glasses and a carafe of the purest water.

But the six francs which had been insisted upon were accepted only sulkily, and as a puny compensation for the trouble caused and the hopes so well deceived.

XVIII. *Marvelous Effects of a Classical Dinner*

"Alas, what a miserable fellow I am!" remarked a gastronomer from the royal law court on the Seine. "Since I am always hoping to go back to my own estate, I have left my cook there; business keeps me in Paris, and I have given myself up to the cares of an officious old biddy whose meals really cut me to the heart. My wife is content with anything, and my children are still too ignorant to care: under-boiled beef, burned roast . . . between the pot and the spit I am starving!"

This plaint went on as he crossed at a sorry pace the Place Dauphine. Fortunately for the public weal, the professor overheard these justified lamentations, and recognized a friend in the lamenter. "You shall not starve to death, my dear chap," he said in an affectionate voice to the martyred magistrate. "No, you shall not die of a crime for which I can offer you the cure. Be good enough to come, tomorrow, to a classical dinner, in very select company. After dinner there will be a little card party which we shall arrange so that everyone will have a good time, and the evening will, like all such others, hurl itself smoothly into the chasm of the Past."

The invitation was accepted. The mysterious alchemy worked, according to the customs, rites, and ceremonies demanded of it; and since that day (June 23, 1825) the professor is happy to have saved for the good of the royal law court one of its most noble pillars.

XIX. *Effects and Dangers of Strong Liquors*

The artificial thirst of which we have already spoken ("Meditation 8"), that one which demands strong liquors for its passing satisfaction, becomes with time so intense and such a habit that those who are given up to it can not even get through a night without drinking, and are forced to arise from their beds to slake themselves.

This thirst becomes, then, a true illness, and when a man has gone that far it can be prophesied with certitude that he has not two more years to live.

I once travelled in Holland with a rich merchant from Danzig who had owned, for fifty years, the foremost retail house for brandies.

"Sir," this patriarch said to me, "there can be no question in France of the importance of the business we have carried on, from father to son, for more than a century. I have watched with close attention the men who work for me, and when they abandon themselves completely to their penchant for strong drink, all too common among the Germans, most of them meet their end in much the same manner.

"First they take only a little shot of brandy in the morning, and this quantity is enough for them for several years (what is more, this system is usual among all workmen, and the man who did not down his little glass would be ridiculed by his

comrades);[47] then they double the dose, which is to say that they
take a shot in the morning and again towards noon. They stay
at this level about two or three years; then they drink regularly
morning, noon, and at night. Soon they begin to take a drink
at no matter what time, and will have none of it unless it is
flavored with cloves; and by the time they have reached that
point they have at the most six months to live: they dry out,
fever seizes upon them, they go to the hospital, and they are
never seen again."

XX.   *The Chevaliers and the Abbots*

I have already mentioned two times these two gastronomical
categories which Time itself has done away with.[48]

Since they disappeared more than thirty years ago, the greatest
part of the present generation has never even seen them.

They will probably reappear toward the end of this century;
but since such a phenomenon demands the coincidence of a
great many future contingencies, I believe that very few men
now living will be witnesses to that palingenesis.

It is necessary then that in my role as depicter of morals I
give them the benefit of a final touch of my brush; and to
bring this about most easily I shall borrow the following passage
from an author who can refuse me nothing.[49]

"Properly, and according to custom, the title of chevalier
should only be given to persons who have been decorated with
an order, or to younger sons of titled families; but many so-called
chevaliers had found it advantageous to bestow this accolade
upon themselves,† and if by chance they were well-educated and
personable, such was the insouciant attitude of the times that
nobody bothered to question them.

"Usually they were good-looking fellows; they kept their
swords straight and their leg muscles flexed, their heads high,
their noses in the air; they were gamblers, rounders, and blus-
terers, and were essential to any reigning beauty's entourage.

"They were further distinguished by brilliant courage and an
unusual facility for finding themselves sword in hand. At times

† SELF CREATED.

all that was necessary to plunge them into a duel was to look crossways at them."

It is thus that Chevalier de S . . . , one of the best known of those days, met his end.

He had sought out an unsolicited quarrel with a young man newly arrived from Charolles, and they went to settle it behind the Chaussée-d'Antin, at that time almost entirely made up of marshes.

S . . . saw quickly enough, by the way in which the new-comer handled his weapon, that he was not dealing with a novice: nonetheless he set out dutifully to test him; but at his first thrust, the youth from Charolles parried with a stroke which was so skilful that the chevalier was dead before he hit the ground. One of his friends, witness to the duel, looked for a long time at the terrible wound and at the route which the sword had followed. Suddenly he exclaimed, as he took his departure, "What a beautiful thrust in *quarte!* What a fine wrist this young man has!" And that was to prove the dead man's only funeral oration.

At the beginning of the wars of the Revolution, most of these chevaliers enlisted in the battalions, some went into exile, and the rest disappeared. The few who have survived are still recognizable by the set of their heads; but they are thin, and they walk with difficulty: gout has them in its toils.

When there were a great many children in an aristocratic family, one of them was destined for the Church: he began by obtaining the simplest benefices, which took care of the expenses of his education; and from there he became prince, commendatory abbot, or bishop, according to the fervor of his apostolic convictions.

This was, properly speaking, the legitimate type of abbot; but there were other, false ones; and many young men who had some income, and who were none too eager to run the risks of a chevalier's life, gave themselves the title of *abbé* when they arrived in Paris.

Nothing was easier: with a slight alteration in their garb, they could suddenly appear in churchly masquerade: they were the social equals of everyone; and they were feasted, spoiled, and sought after, for no town house was without its own abbé.

They were short, thickset, chubby men, well-dressed, coaxing and agreeable, inquisitive, gourmands, quick-witted, insinuating; those who are left have run to fat, and have become devout.

There could not be a happier life than that of a rich prior or a commendatory abbot: they had money and respect, no superiors, and nothing at all to do.

The chevaliers will return again if peace lasts long enough, as one must hope it will; but unless there befalls a great change in ecclesiastical administration, the race of abbots is lost forever; there are no more *sinecures,* and we have gone back to the principles of the early Church: *beneficium propter officium.*

XXI. *Miscellanea*

"Your Honor," an old marquise of the Faubourg Saint-Germain once asked, from her end of the table to the other, "which do you prefer, a wine from Bordeaux or from Burgundy?"

"Madame," the magistrate who was thus questioned answered in a druidic tone, "that is a trial in which I so thoroughly enjoy weighing the evidence that I always put off my verdict until the next week."

A host of the Chaussée-d'Antin had an Arlesian sausage of heroic proportions presented at his table. "Please accept a slice of it," he urged the lady next to him. "Here is a piece of equipment which, I hope, implies a well-furnished establishment."

"It is truly enormous," the lady said, peering at it with lewd mischief. "What a pity that it does not resemble anything!"

It is above all people of intelligence who hold gourmandism in high esteem: the rest are incapable of an operation which is made up of a series of appreciations and judgments.

The Countess de Genlis[50] boasts, in her Memoirs, of having taught a German lady who had graciously entertained her the way of preparing up to seven delicious dishes.

It was the Count de la Place who discovered a most subtle way to serve strawberries, which consists of moistening them with the juice of a sweet orange (apple of the Hesperides).

Another scholar has improved the recipe still further, by adding the zest of the orange peel, which he obtains by rubbing it with a morsel of sugar; and he pretends to be able to prove, thanks to a scrap which escaped the flames which destroyed the library at Alexandria, that it was fruit thus seasoned which was served at the banquets on Mount Ida.

"I have no great opinion of that fellow," once said Count de M . . . , in speaking of a candidate who had just succeeded in winning a certain appointment. "He has never eaten blood sausage *à la Richelieu,* and does not even know cutlets *à la Soubise*." [51]

A heavy drinker was at dinner, and during the dessert he was offered some grapes. "Thank you very much," he said, pushing the plate to one side, "but I am not accustomed to taking my wine in capsules."

Friends were congratulating an amateur gastronomer who had just been appointed assessor of taxes at Périgueux; they dwelt on the happiness he would have, situated in the capital of good living, in the country of truffles and red partridges, of truffled stuffed turkeys, and so on and so on.

"Alas!" said with a sigh the saddened disciple of good living, "how sure can I be that anyone would survive in a country where there are no fresh seafish?"

XXII. A Day with the Monks of Saint Bernard

It was almost one o'clock in the morning: it was a fine wintery night, and we had formed in a cavalcade, not without having rendered a vigorous serenade to those town beauties who had the honor to interest us (it was about 1782).

We left Belley, and headed for Saint-Sulpice, a Bernardine abbey situated on one of the highest peaks of the district, at least five thousand feet above sea level.

I was at that time leader of a band of amateur musicians, all good companions and possessing in a strong degree the peculiar virtues which go with youth and health.

"Sir," the abbot of Saint-Sulpice had said to me one day, drawing me into a secluded window nook, "you would be very kind indeed to come with your friends and sing and play for us on the feast of Saint-Bernard; the saint himself would be even more sanctified, everyone near us would be greatly pleased, and you would have the honor of being the first disciples of Orpheus who had ever penetrated into our lofty regions."

I could not ask twice for any demand which prophesied such

a pleasant adventure: I promised to keep the engagement, and around me the whole room shook.

Annuit, et totum nutu tremefecit Olympum.[52]

All our plans were laid carefully in advance, and we left early, since we had four leagues to cover over roads capable of terrifying even those hardy travelers who have braved the heights of the mighty butte of Montmartre.[53]

The abbey was located in a valley closed to the west by the summit of the mountain, and to the east by a less lofty pinnacle.

The western peak was crowned by a pine forest, where once in a single day 37,000 trees were uprooted by a blast of wind.†

The bottom of the valley was occupied by a great meadow, where rows of beech trees hedged irregular sections, like gigantic models of those little English gardens of which we are so fond.

We arrived about daybreak, and were received by the father cellarer, whose face was quadrangular and whose nose was an obelisk.

"Sirs," the good man said, "be welcome; our holy abbot will be very happy when he knows that you have arrived; he is still sleeping, for yesterday he was very tired indeed; but you must follow me, and you will see whether or not we waited for you."

He spoke, and began to walk away, and we followed him, suspecting with good reason that he led us toward the refectory.

There all our senses were overcome by the apparition of the utmost in alluring feasts, a truly classic meal.

In the middle of a spacious table rose a pâté as big as a church; it was flanked on the north by a quarter of cold veal, on the south by an enormous ham, on the east by a monumental pat of butter, and on the west by a bushel of artichokes with pepper sauce.

Moreover, there were various kinds of fruits, and plates and napkins and knives and silverware in big baskets; and at the end of the table were lay-brothers and servants ready to serve us, albeit somewhat astonished to find themselves afoot at this hour of the morning.

† *The director of streams and forests counted them and sold them; commerce flourished because of them, as did the monks, great sums of money were put into circulation, and no man could complain of the freak storm.*

In a corner of the refectory there was a pile of more than a hundred bottles, continuously cooled by a natural spring murmuring *Evohe Bacche* as it flowed over and around them; and if the perfume of mocha did not tease our nostrils it is only because in those heroic times coffee was not drunk so early in the morning.

The reverend cellarer delighted in our astonishment for a few minutes, after which he addressed to us the following declamation, which, in our wisdom, we suspected having been prepared in advance:

"Sirs," he said, "I wish that I might keep you company; but I have not yet read my mass, and today is one of full service. I ought to invite you to partake of this food, but your age, the trip you have made, and the crisp air of our mountains will allow me to dispense with that. Accept then with pleasure what we offer in the heartiest friendship. I must leave you, and go sing my matins."

With these words he disappeared.

It was then the moment to go into action; and we attacked with an energy which bore out the three aggravating circumstances so clearly suggested by the cellarer. But what could mere puny sons of Adam do with a feast which seemed prepared for the inhabitants of Sirius[54] itself? Our efforts were futile; although we crammed ourselves to the bursting point, we left no more than imperceptible traces of our passage.

Then, well fortified until dinner time, we broke up, and I stretched out on a good bed, to doze until time for Mass, much like the hero of Rocroy and many others, who have slumbered peacefully until the moment to do battle.

I was awakened by a husky brother who almost shook my arm off, and I ran toward the church, where I found everyone at his post.

At the offertory we executed a symphony; at the elevation we sang a motet; we finished with a quartet for wind instruments. And in spite of all the jokes about music played by amateurs, my respect for truth obliges me to confess that we did a very good job indeed.

I shall remark, in this connection, that those men who are never satisfied with anything are almost always ignorant people who criticize sharply in the hope that their daring will make them seem to know many things which in reality they have not had the capacity to learn.

We accepted with benign pleasure, then, the praises which everyone showered unhesitatingly upon us, and after having received the thanks of the abbot, we went once more to the dining hall.

The dinner was served much in the style of the fifteenth century, with few side dishes and fewer superfluities; but an excellent choice of meats, and of simple hearty stews, freshly prepared and perfectly cooked, and above all of vegetables of a flavor quite unknown in the lowlands, killed any desire there might be for something not seen upon the table.

It can be gauged, moreover, what abundance reigned in this good place, by the fact that the second course offered no less than fourteen platters of roasted meats.

The dessert was especially distinguished in that it was made up in part of fruits which do not grow at such heights, and which had been brought up from the lower valleys; and the gardens of Machuraz and the Morflent, and other districts smiled on by the fiery sun god, had contributed their shares.

There was no lack of liqueurs, of course; but it was the coffee that deserves special mention.

It was limpid, odorous, and marvellously hot; the best thing about it, however, was that it was not served in those emasculated little vases which are basely called *cups* along the banks of the Seine, but in fine deep bowls into which the holy fathers plunged their full lips deeply, and then sucked up the strengthening liquid with a noise which would have done honor to two sperm whales blowing before a storm.

After the dinner we went to vespers, and between the psalms sang some anthems which I had composed expressly for that day. They were the kind of music that was common then, and I shall say nothing one way or the other about them, for fear of being either repressed by my modesty or carried away by paternal affection.

The official celebrations having ended thus, visitors from the neighborhood began to turn homeward, or to group themselves for various games and contests.

As for myself, I chose to take a walk, and having collected a few friends, I led the way across that soft thick mountain grass, which is truly worth any carpet from the Savonnerie, and breathed the pure air of those high meadows, which refreshes a man's soul and disposes his imagination to quiet thought and to romanticism.†

It was late when we returned. The abbot came up to me to wish me a good and pleasant night. "I am going to my own apartment," he told me, "and will leave the rest of the evening to you. It is not that I feel that my presence might act as a damper to our good fathers, but I want them to know clearly that they are in complete freedom tonight. We do not celebrate the feast of Saint-Bernard every day of the year; tomorrow we go back to our accustomed duties: *cras iterabimus aequor.*"

And it is true that after the departure of the abbot there was more movement in the assemblage, which became much noisier, and busy with those little jokes which are peculiar to cloisters, the kind that are almost meaningless and yet make everyone laugh without knowing why.

Toward nine o'clock supper was served, a meal skilfully and daintily prepared and several centuries removed in spirit from the noonday dinner.

We fell to with renewed appetites, and chattered and laughed and sang table songs; and one of the fathers read us some verses of his own composition, which were truly not too bad for having sprung from a shaveling.

Toward the end of the evening, someone lifted his voice to shout, "Father Cellarer, where then is that speciality of yours?" "True enough," the reverend man replied. "I'm not cellarer for nothing!"

He left for a moment, and soon came back accompanied by three serving men, the first of whom carried toast spread with excellent butter, while the other two were laden with a table bearing a huge tub of blazing brandy and sugar; it was much like our punch, which was unknown at that time.[55]

The new arrivals were hailed with noisy delight; we ate the toast, drank the heated brandy, and when the clock of the abbey struck twelve went each to his bed, to revel in the pleasures of

† *I have constantly felt this effect in the same circumstances, and am led to believe that the thinness of the air in the mountains lets come into play certain cerebral powers which are oppressed by the heaviness of the lowland atmosphere.*

a slumber justly desired, and justly earned as well, by the labors of the day.

N.B. The father cellarer so often mentioned in this truly historical narration, having become an old man, was listening to a conversation about a newly appointed abbot who arrived from Paris, and whose reputation for severity was dreaded.

"I have no worries about him in that respect," said the reverend father. "Let him be as disagreeable as he wants to, and still he'll never have the courage to take from an old man either his own corner by the hearth or his keys to the cellar."

XXIII. *Traveler's Luck*

One time, mounted on my good mare *la Joie*, I rode over the pleasant slopes of the Jura.

It was during the worst days of the Revolution, and I was on my way to Dôle, to request from Representative Prot a safe-conduct paper which would keep me from going first to prison and probably from there to the scaffold.

On my arrival at an inn in the little town or village of Mont-sous-Vaudrey, about eleven in the morning, I first saw to it that my mount was well looked after, and then, going through the kitchen, was struck by such a sight as no traveler can see without delight.

Before a lively sparkling fire turned a spit, handsomely strung with quail, truly king-like quail, and those little railbirds with green claws which are always so plump.[56] This superlative game was emitting its final delicious drops upon an immense slab of toast, whose very contours announced the fine hand of a hunter-cook; and close beside it, already prepared, could be seen one of those extremely plump young hares which Parisians do not know exist, and whose odor would be incense enough for a cathedral.

"Good!" said I to myself, revived by this fine sight. "Providence has not completely deserted me after all. Let's pluck this flower as we go by; there's always time left for us to die." [57]

Then, addressing myself to the innkeeper, who all during my examination had walked up and down the kitchen with his hands behind his gigantic back, whistling, I said: "My dear chap, what are you planning to give me that is really good, for my dinner?"

"Nothing that is not really good, sir; good bouilli, good potato soup, good shoulder of mutton, and good beans."

At this unexpected reply a shudder of disappointment ran through my whole frame; it is well-known that I never eat bouilli, since it is nothing but meat drained of its juices; potatoes and beans are obesigenous;[58] I did not feel that my teeth were steely enough to rend and tear the mutton. In other words, this menu was made especially to depress me, and once more all my miseries closed in upon me.

The innkeeper watched me slyly, and seemed to guess the reason for my despair . . .

"And precisely for whom are you holding back all this fine game?" I asked him with an air of utter exasperation.

"Alas, Sir," he replied in a sympathetic way, "I have no rights to it. It all belongs to some legal gentlemen who have been here for ten days now, giving their professional advice on an affair concerning a very rich lady; they finished their task yesterday, and are having a party to celebrate the happy event, or as we say here, to break over."

"Sir," I said to him after pondering for a few seconds, "do me the kindness to say to these gentlemen that an agreeable table companion asks, as a great favor, to be admitted to dinner with them, that he will assume his share of the expenses, and that above all he will be deeply indebted to them." I spoke: he left, and he did not return.

But soon after I saw a little fat man, fresh-cheeked, chubby, thickset and sprightly, come in and prowl about the kitchen, shift a few chairs, lift the lid of a casserole, and then disappear.

"Fine!" I said to myself. "That was the brother tyler[59] of the meeting, come to look me over!" And I began to hope once more, for experience had already taught me that my outer presence was not repulsive.[60]

Nonetheless my heart pounded as if I were a candidate being passed on by a secret jury, when the innkeeper reappeared and announced to me that the gentlemen were highly flattered by my proposal, and awaited only my coming to sit down at table.

I bounded from the room kicking my heels, received the most complimentary of welcomes, and within a few minutes had taken root . . .

What a good dinner! I shall not go into detail; but I owe

honorable mention to a chicken fricassée of great art, such as can only be found in the provinces, and so richly graced with truffles that there were enough to have revived old Tithonus[61] himself.

The roast has already been mentioned: it tasted as good as it looked, cooked to perfection, and the trouble I had experienced in getting anywhere near it added still more to its savor.

The dessert was composed of a vanilla cream, choice cheese, and excellent fruits. We bathed all this with a light rose-colored wine, and later a Hermitage, and still later a *vin de paille*[62] as soft as it was generous: the whole was crowned with unusually good coffee concocted by the sprightly tyler, who also saw to it that we did not lack for certain liqueurs from Verdun, which he abstracted from a kind of tabernacle of which he had the key.

Not only was the dinner delicious but it was very gay as well.

After having discussed with discretion the current happenings, the gentlemen fell to joking with one another in a way that let me divine something of their histories; they spoke little of the business which had brought them together; some good stories were told, some songs sung; I joined in with a few unpublished verses, and even made up one on the spot, which was according to custom loudly applauded. Here it is:

TO BE SUNG TO *Le Maréchal ferrant*:

Qu'il est doux pour les voyageurs
De trouver d'aimables buveurs:
C'est une vraie† béatitude.
Entouré d'aussi bons enfants,
Ma foi je passerai céans
Libre de toute inquietude,
 Quatre jours,
 Quinze jours,
 Trente jours,
 Une année,
Et bénirais ma destinée.[63]

If I present this verse, it is not because I think it excellent:

† *This is a mistake which we let stand out of respect for the author's text; the passage which follows the verse makes it plain, moreover, that in doing so we are carrying out his intention.*

I have written many better, thanks be to Heaven, and would have rewritten this one if I had wished to; but I preferred to leave it with its impromptu tone, so that the reader might agree with me that any man with a troop of Revolutionists at his heels who could still feel so carefree must indeed have had, and I insist upon it, the head and the heart of a true Frenchman.

We had been at table for a good four hours, and began to discuss the best way to finish off the evening: we might take a long walk to help digestion, and then on coming back to the inn play cards while we waited for supper, which would consist of a platter of trout which were being saved for us, and the still-tempting remains of our dinner.

But to all these propositions I was forced to reply with a refusal: the sun nearing the horizon warned me that I must leave. The gentlemen insisted to the very limits of politeness that I remain, and stopped only when I assured them that I was not traveling solely for my own pleasure.

My readers will already have guessed that they would not hear of my paying my share: thus it was that without any tactless questions they insisted on watching me mount my horse, and we parted with an exchange of the most amicable farewells.

If any one of those men who gave me such a heart-warming welcome still exists, and my book happens to fall into his hands, I want him to know that thirty years after that day this chapter was written with the liveliest gratitude.

One bit of luck always follows another, and my trip succeeded in a way that I had not dared hope for.

It is true that I found Representative Prot strongly prejudiced against me: he stared at me with a sinister air, and I was convinced that he was about to have me arrested; however, I got by with nothing more than my fears, and after a few explanations it seemed to me that his face softened a little.

I am not one of those people whom fright turns vengeful, and I truly believe that this was not a bad man; but he had limited capacity for his position and did not know what to do with the enormous power which had been entrusted to him: he was a child, armed with the club of Hercules.

M. Amondru, whose name I mention here with much pleasure, had in truth some difficulty in making him accept an invitation to a supper party where it was clearly said that I too would be present; he came, finally, and received me in a manner which was far from reassuring.

I was somewhat less churlishly welcomed by Madame Prot, to whom I went to present myself. The circumstances under which I arrived gave her at least some curiosity about me.

In the very first words we exchanged, she asked me if I loved music. What unexpected luck! She seemed to make it her great passion, and since I myself am a very fair musician, from that moment our two hearts beat as one.

We talked together until supper time, and were soon hand in glove. If she mentioned various works on composition, I knew them all; if she spoke of current operas, I knew them note for note; if she named any well-known composers, I usually knew them by sight. It seemed that she would never stop, for a long time had passed since she last met anyone who could discuss such things with her, which she seemed to revel in as a simple amateur, although I learned later that she had once been a singing teacher.

After supper she had her albums brought down; she sang, I sang, we sang together; never have I put more heart into anything, and never have I had more pleasure in so doing. Already M. Prot had mentioned several times that it was time to retire, but she paid no attention to him, and we were blaring like two trumpets the duet from *La Fausse Magie:*

Remember that gladsome day?

when he finally gave a peremptory order to call a halt.

We were forced to stop, for fair; but just as we parted Madame Prot said to me: "Citizen, any man who cultivates the finer things of life, as you do, cannot be a traitor to his country. I know that you have some favor to ask of my husband: you shall be granted it; I myself promise you that."

At these encouraging words I kissed her hand with all the warmth of my heart; and sure enough, early the next morning I received my letter of safe-conduct, duly signed and magnificently sealed.

Thus was accomplished the reason for my trip. I returned home with my head high: thanks to Harmony, that charming child of Heaven, my ascension to her regions was postponed for a good number of years.[64]

XXIV. Songs

My Lord, if what Cratinus says be right,
Those Verses cannot live, those lines delight,
Which Water drinkers Pen, in vain they Write.
For e'er since Bacchus did in wild design,
With Fauns and Satyrs half-mad Poets joyn,
The Muses every morning smelt of wine.
From Homer's praise his love of Wine appears,
And Ennius never dar'd to write of Wars
Till heated well, let sober dotards choose
The plodding law, but never tempt a Muse,
This Law once made, the Poets streight begin,
They drunk all night, all day they stunk of Wine:

HORACE, EPISTLE 1, 19.[65]

If I had had the time I would have made a thoughtful choice of gastronomical poems from the Greeks and Romans to our own day, and would have divided it into the proper historical periods, to demonstrate the inseparable alliance which has always existed between the arts of speaking well and eating well.

What I have not done, another will do after me.† We shall see then how the table has always given added tone to the poet's lyre, and shall have additional proof of the influence of things physical upon those purely moral.

Until toward the middle of the eighteenth century, poetry of this kind more often than not had as its subject matter the praise of Bacchus and his gifts, since to drink wine and drink it deep was the highest form of gustatory exaltation which could then be attained. However, to break the monotony and widen

† *Here, unless I am mistaken, is the third work which I have delegated to others: 1st, a Monograph on Obesity; 2nd, a theoretical and practical Treatise on Hunting Luncheons; 3rd, a chronological anthology of gastronomical Poetry.*

the boundaries a little, Venus was linked with the god, an association from which it is none too sure that the goddess profited.[66]

The discovery of the New World and the acquisitions which followed it started a whole new order of things.

Sugar, coffee, tea, chocolate, alchoholic liqueurs and all the mixtures which spring from them, have made a more composite picture of good living, in which wine plays the part of a more or less obligatory accessory, since tea can very easily replace it in the morning meal.†

Thus a much vaster world has been presented to our modern poets: they can sing of the pleasures of the table without necessarily drowning themselves in the wine barrel, and already many charming odes have celebrated the new treasures which have been added to gastronomy.

Like many another I have glanced through these works, and have delighted in the perfume of their lightsome offerings. But, the while I admired the talented resources of the stanzas, and savored their music, I felt more satisfaction than most people in seeing all these writers bow as one to my favorite principle, for most of their delightful fantasies have been composed expressly for, during, and after dining.

I devoutly hope that skilful workers will exploit the part of my domain which I abandon to them, and I content myself at this point by offering to my readers a little collection of quotations which I have chosen according to my whims, accompanied by very short annotations, so that none need rack his brains to find the reason for my preferences.

SONG
of Demochares at the Feast of Denias

This song is taken from *Travels of the Young Anacharsis*, which is reason enough for my choice.[68]

Let us drink, and let us praise Bacchus,

Bacchus who delights in our dances, who revels in our songs to

† *The English and the Dutch eat for their breakfasts bread, butter, fish, ham, and eggs, and almost never drink anything but tea.*[67]

him, who wipes out hatred and envy, and all our disappointments. He is the true father of entrancing Loves, and of seductive Graces.

So let us love, let us drink; let us praise Bacchus:

The future has not yet come; the present will soon be past; our one instant of existence is in the instant of our ecstasy.

So let us love, let us drink; let us praise Bacchus.

Made wiser by our madnesses, and richer by our pleasures, let us grind beneath our heels the world and its futile grandeurs; and in the sweet intoxication which such moments make flood through our souls,

Let us drink, and let us praise Bacchus.

(TRAVELS OF THE YOUNG ANACHARSIS IN GREECE,
VOLUME 11, CHAPTER 25.)

The next poem is by Motin,[69] who, it is said, was the first composer of drinking songs in France. It is part of the golden days of drunkenness, and has its own kind of vigor.

SONG

Tavern, I love thee more and more;
Mine every want dost thou supply;
I care not what's without thy door,
Within, there's none so rich as I:
    Thy very dishclouts are to me
    Finest of Holland napery.

When summer suns remorseless shine,
No bosky dell doth solace hold
So grateful or so fresh as thine;
And if I'd laugh at winter's cold,
    Thy meanest faggot likes me then
    More than the forest of Vincenne.

Nothing in vain I ask of thee:
I wish, and tripes turn ortolans,
I no cardoons, but roses, see,

Nor hear no strife but clinking cans:
> By inn and tavern! There's no dearth
> of paradises upon earth.

Praise Bacchus for his gift of wine,
Yea, reeling praise its potent fumes;
Sure, 'tis an essence all divine,
And whoso drinks not, yet assumes
> By grace of God the manly rank,
> Would be an angel if he drank.

Winking, the wine invites my kiss;
It drives the sadness out of me
And fills my very soul with bliss;
O ne'er were lovers fond as we:
> I ravish, then am ravished,
> I capture and am captive led.

Quart upon pint when I've sent down,
Gaily each stranger I salute;
With tingling ears and ne'er a frown
I forwards aim, and backwards shoot,
> And cut, who'd never learned to dance,
> The neatest caper in all France.

And 'tis my wish, till I be dead,
With white wine, aye, and claret too,
To keep my belly tenanted,
So they but dwell in concord due;
> For if they quarrel, I'll not pause
> But straightway cast 'em out of doors.

The next is from Racan, one of our oldest poets; it is full of
grace and philosophy, has served as a model for many other
writers, and seems much younger than its birth date proves it
to be.

TO MAYNARD[70]

Wherefore be yielding to dull care?
Let's rather drain this nectar rare

At one long draught, then call for more;
It doth in excellence precede
E'en that which the young Ganymede
Into the cup of gods doth pour.

For lo, it makes an age to be
Less than a day, and, drinking, we
Grow young again for all our years;
And every cupful drives away
One sorry dream of yesterday,
One of tomorrow's foolish fears.

Let's drink, then, Maynard: fill the bowl,
While unperceived the ages roll
Bearing us on to our last day;
All praying's vain; we may not choose,
While years, no more than rivers, use
To halt or linger by the way.

Soon shall mild Spring come o'er the scene,
And Winter's white be turned to green:
The sea hath ebb and flow: what then?
Why, nothing; once our own brief youth
Doth yield to age, 'tis simple truth
That time ne'er brings it back again.

The laws of death prevail no less
In proud imperial palaces
Than in the meanest reed-roof'd hut;
The fates apportion all our years;
The king's, the swain's, with the same shears
Each thread indifferently they cut.

They all things utterly efface,
And undo, in the briefest space,
Whate'er most painfully we've done;
Soon they'll be hailing us to drink,
Beyond the black flood's further brink,
The waters of oblivion.

The next poem was written by the professor, who has also set it to music. He has shrunk from the inconveniences of having it published, in spite of the pleasure it would give him to think of it on every piano rack, but by incredible good luck it can be sung, and *it will be sung,* to the air of the *"Vaudeville de Figaro."*

THE CHOICE OF SCIENCES

Glory let's no more pursue;
She doth sell her favors dear:
History forget we too
For a tale devoid of cheer:
Drink we like our fathers, who
Drank as much as they could hold:
Bring me wine, and wine that's old! (Repeat.)

Go thy ways, Astronomy,
Stray without me in the skies:
Chemistry, I've done with thee,
I'd be ruin'd otherwise:
Come, Gastronomy, to me,
And I'll fondly evermore
Gourmandise and thee adore! (Repeat.)

Young, I studied without cease,
Grey's my pate with studying:
All the wisdom that was Greece
Never taught me anything:
Still I toil, but toil in peace,
Learning idleness instead:
Where's the school to equal bed? (Repeat.)

Physics once were all my care;
'Twas but wasted time, for why?
All the drugs that ever were
Only help a man to die.
Now by Cookery I swear,
Which doth make us whole again:
Cooks surpass all other men! (Repeat.)

These my labors are but rude,
But, when sinks the sun to rest,
Then, lest overmuch I brood,
Love comes stealing to my breast,
And, despite the carping prude,
Love's a pretty game to play:
Come, let's to it while we may! (Repeat.)

I witnessed the actual *birth* of the following verse, which is why I *plant* it here.[71] Truffles are our current idol, and perhaps this worship suggests some doubt as to our need for it.

IMPROMPTU
*By M. B . . . De V . . . , Distinguished Amateur,
and Well-Loved Pupil of the Professor.*

Sable truffle, hail to thee!
Thou dost victory assure
(For let's not ungrateful be)
In the most delicious war;
 Thee, I say,
 To pave the way,
Providence hath surely sent
For love and bliss and all content:
 Eat we truffles every day!

I shall close with a morsel of verse which really belongs in "Meditation 26."

I should have liked to set it to music, but could never bring it off as I wished; someone else will do better with it, especially if he allows himself more leeway than I did. The accompaniment to it must be very strong, and must indicate in the second verse that the sick man is fast expiring.[72]

THE DEATHBED
Physiological Ballade

In all my senses life, alas! grows faint,
Dull is mine eye, my body hath no heat;
Louise must weep, her sorrow's past restraint,
Softly her dear hand begs my heart to beat;
I've seen my friends come, I have seen them go,

One after one, breathing a last goodbye;
Doctor, farewell; enters the priest; and so
   'Tis time to die.

Fain would I pray, my brain is void of prayers;
Speak, but my thoughts will no more spoken be:
Insistent echoings assail mine ears;
Something, I know not what, seems fluttering free.
Now all is dark; my breast upheaves to fill
With what shall feebly issue in a sigh:
'Twill wander o'er my lips, leaving them chill:
   'Tis time to die.

BY THE PROFESSOR

XXV. *Monsieur H . . . de P . . .*†

I sincerely believed that I was the first *in our time* to conceive of the idea of an Academy of Gastronomers; but I am very much afraid that I have been forestalled, as sometimes happens. How much so can be deduced from the following incident, which took place almost fifteen years ago.

President H . . . de P . . . , whose genial wit melted all the chill of old age,[73] said in 1812 in a conversation with three of the most distinguished scholars of the present epoch (M. de Laplace, M. Chaptal, and M. Berthollet): "I consider the discovery of a new dish, which excites our appetite and prolongs our pleasure, much more important than the discovery of a star. We can always see plenty of the latter.

"I shall never feel that the sciences have been adequately represented," the magistrate continued, "nor sufficiently honored, so long as I do not see a cook installed in the first ranks of the Institute."

This dear old fellow was always filled with joy when he thought of the object of my labors; he planned to write an epigraph for me, and insisted that it was not alone the *Esprit des Lois* which opened the doors of the Academy to M. de Montesquieu. It is from him that I learned that Professor Berriat Saint-Prix had written a novel, and it is he, furthermore, who

† *Henrion de Pansey.*

suggested to me the chapter in which I discussed the gastronomical activities of the émigrés. Therefore, since justice must always be done, I have composed the following quatrain, which contains both his history and his eulogy.

POEM
To Be Inscribed Beneath the Portrait of M. H . . . de P . . .

Tireless in all his learned works was he,
And his great office worthily sustain'd;
Yet the wise student still the friend remain'd,
Whose cares ne'er warped his geniality.

In 1814 President H . . . was awarded the portfolio of Justice, and the employees of this ministry still remember the reply he made to them, when they came in a body to present their initial congratulations to him.

"Sirs," he said with that paternal tone of voice which blended so well with his great stature and his advanced years, "it is probable that I shall not be with you long enough to do you any good, but at least I can assure you that I shall never do you harm."

XXVI. Useful Hints

Here my task ends; but in order to prove that I still have breath left in me, I shall proceed to kill three birds with one stone.

I shall give to my readers of every land some addresses which will be of great benefit to them; I shall bestow upon my favorite artists an order of merit which they well deserve; and I shall share with the public a faggot from my own warm fireside.

(1) Madame *Chevet*, grocery store, Palais-Royal, number 220, near the Théâtre-Français. I am more her faithful client than a heavy purchaser; our relationship dates from her first appearance on the gastronomical horizon, and she it is who had the kindness to weep once for my death, which fortunately was only a case of mistaken identity.

Madame Chevet is the undisputed intermediary between the finest provender and the great fortunes. She owes her prosperity to her professional integrity: anything that the passage of time has injured disappears from her shelves as if by magic. The nature of her business demands that she make a fairly large profit, but once the price is agreed upon, the most excellent quality is assured.

This honorable firm is to be handed on, and her daughters, hardly past infancy, are already following her principles without a false step.

Madame Chevet has agents in every country where the wishes of the most capricious gastronomer can be satisfied, and the more rivals she gains, the higher is her reputation.

(2) Monsieur *Achard*, pastry cook and confectioner, Rue de Grammont, number 9, a native of Lyons who started his business some ten years ago, built it on his reputation for his biscuits and his vanilla wafers, which for a long time have never successfully been imitated.

Everything in his shop has something delicate and tempting about it which cannot possibly be found elsewhere; the touch of common man seems completely foreign to it. It is as if these dainties sprang from some enchanted country: and since everything that is seen there disappears the same day, it could be said that *chez* Achard Tomorrow is unknown.

Almost every instant of a summer's day a fashionable carriage will draw up Rue de Grammont, usually bearing a handsome dandy[74] and a lovely befeathered lady. The former dashes into the shop, where he arms himself with a fat box of delicacies. And at his return he is greeted with an "Oh, my sweet! how good that looks!" or better: "O DEAR! HOW IT LOOKS GOOD! MY MOUTH! . . ." And quick as a wink the horse pulls away, and carries this whole pretty picture toward the Bois de Boulogne.

Gourmands are such enthusiastic and forgiving creatures that for a long time there they endured the sourness of a most disagreeable clerk. She has finally been removed; the cash desk has been reinhabited, and now the pretty little hand of Miss Anna Achard gives a new quality to concoctions which already are enough recommendation in themselves.

(3) Monsieur *Limet*, Rue de Richelieu, number 79, my neighbor and a baker to some houses of the highest rank, has also won my loyal praise.

Finding himself heir to a fairly insignificant sum, he raised it to a high degree of prosperity and reputation.

His ordinary loaves are very fine, and it would be difficult to find in a single sample of quality bread such whiteness, flavor, and delicacy as his possesses.

Foreigners, as well as visitors from the country, always find in M. Limet's shop the kind of bread they are used to; buyers come in person to him, take their turn, and often stand in line.

This success is not astonishing when it is known that M. Limet is not the slave of custom, that he tries earnestly to uncover the latest departures in his art, and that he is advised by scholars of the first rank.

XXVII. *Privations*

AN HISTORICAL ELEGY

First parents of the human race, whose feastings are historical, what did you not lose for a ruddy apple, and what would you not have given for a truffled turkey hen? But in your Earthly Paradise you had no cooks, no fine confectioners!

I weep for you!

All-powerful kings who devastated Troy, your strength is hymned from generation unto generation; but you did set a very uninviting table. You never knew, reduced as you were to ox thighs and the backs of hogs, the charms of a matelotte or the ecstasies of a chicken fricassée.

I weep for you!

Aspasia and Chloe, and all of you who, drawn by the Grecian artists, make present beauties pale, your lovely lips never savored the suave delicacy of a meringue concocted with vanilla or rose water; perhaps you never rose higher than common gingerbread.

I weep for you!

Sweet priestesses of Vesta,[75] at once weighed with so many honors and threatened with such dreadful punishment, if only you had tasted, at least, our delightful syrups, meant to refresh your souls, or our candied fruits which outbloom every season, or our fragrant creams, the marvel of our times!

I weep for you!

Roman bankers, milking all of the world's markets, never did your famous dining halls contain such jellies as our own, to delight our lazy moments, nor those many-flavored ices whose chill laughs at torrid zones.
I weep for you!

Unconquerable paladins, sung to high heaven by the prating troubadours, when you had vanquished your giants, released your captive maidens, wiped out your opposing armies, never, alas, did a sloe-eyed slave girl serve to you a sparkling cup of champagne, or a Madeiran malvoisie,[76] or a liqueur, that creation of the Golden Age. You were left to the mercies of an ale or an herb-flavored vinegar.[77]
I weep for you!

Mitred and croziered abbots, apportioners of Heaven's bliss; and you, terrible Knights Templar, who took up arms for the extermination of the Saracens: you never knew the joys of chocolate, which brings back our vigor, nor of the Arabian bean which kindles thought within us.
I weep for you!

Queenly ladies of the manor, who filled the emptiness of your masters' Crusades by elevating to your own heights your confessors and your page boys, you never shared with them the delicacies of well-made biscuits nor the delights of a macaroon.
I weep for you!

And you, finally, the gastronomers of 1825, who still find satiety at Abondance' breast, and dream of newly invented recipes, you will not live to revel in the discoveries which the sciences prepare for the year of 1900, delicacies born from the rocks, perchance, or liqueurs resulting from the pressure of a hundred different vapors;[78] you will not see the things which travelers who are not yet even born will bring from that half of the globe which still waits for our discovery, our exploration.
I weep for you!

THE TRANSLATOR'S GLOSSES

1. When the Professor wrote of his cousin-by-marriage Juliette Récamier he did so with a kind of affectionate discretion which was characteristic of him, especially in connection with women, and even more especially in connection with beautiful ones.

She, on the other hand, seems not to have mentioned him in the letters which have been saved for us. He was a favorite guest at her innumerable dinners, suppers, and soirées, but in the crush of crowned heads and assorted political, social, and sexual lions that made her one of Europe's great *salonnières*, a man as reticently unimportant as her cousin would cause very little stir.

It is known that he admired her enough to own a bust of her by Chinard, and a miniature portrait by Augustin, both of which his ancient relatives the Dubois brothers appreciated with such ageless lustiness the time Brillat-Savarin made them a *fondue* (page 188). It is known that he did not hesitate to tease her: "She came in late, as usual," he writes, and that is bold language about a beautiful woman who perhaps more than any others of her kind made great men kneel to her.

Her niece Amélie, later her adopted daughter and a relative also of Brillat-Savarin, in whose family house in Belley she probably was first presented to la Récamier, once wrote of her "imperious desire to please which she had from her birth, together with all the natural gifts which made pleasing so easy to her." This may seem an innocently sly Victorianism, an ambiguity about a famous woman who did indeed manage to puzzle the moralists of her own as well as later times. Juliette Récamier was the passionate target of too many nobly aimed arrows to remain unstung by gossip, but her cousin's quiet teasing, and the fidelity of such an austere lover as Camille Jordan, who "strove," wrote Amélie, "to counteract the influence of the intoxicating homage paid her in society," paint a truer picture of her.

Certainly her behavior was circumspect, whether seen through the eyes of her loving niece or the hurt ones of Napoleon, who repaid her for snubbing his offer of a soft bed at court by seeing to it that she became an exile. In 1875, when Miss Lyster translated Amélie's book about la Récamier, she wrote of "that most courteous and polished of *salons,* where friend and foe met on neutral ground, and antipathies were carefully concealed or ignored . . . ," and Amélie herself gave a pretty idea of the decorous tone of the famous meeting place when she wrote: "(Aunt Juliette) had early given me permission to pass the evening in the *salon,* warning me, at the same time, never to permit any man, whether young or old, to talk to me in a low voice, and, to prevent this, always to reply so as to be heard by everybody." It is easy and pleasant to dream of the beautiful room dominated by David's portrait of la Récamier and by Juliette herself on the couch under it, with the light fluty hum of conversation in the air and the little girl Amélie at her own study table in the alcove, Brillat-Savarin bending over her to help compose "An Ode To My Cat," she answering him high and clear above the hum, and her aunt smiling across at her, her aunt always kind, always tactful, always dressed in white . . .

La Récamier was "elegant, cultivated, but frivolous," some people said. She was infinitely generous of herself and her goods, a thousand others knew. She was gay, delightful, gourmande, all the friends and Brillat-Savarin too have told us . . . and only he, the country cousin, dared add gently, affectionately, "She came in late, *as usual* . . ."

2. This was 1801–1802.

3. It is interesting to speculate here upon the temperature of the famous omelet, which Brillat-Savarin says was cooked to the exact point of perfection, and which in his recipe he advises to be eaten the minute it is done. When Madame Récamier was shown into the Curé's dining room the omelet was already upon his table, and they chatted and he finished his salmon trout while it sat there steaming its precious vapors. Was there perhaps a little flame under it? That seems unlikely, especially with an omelet. We know that the plates were kept hot. But what kept the omelet so?

4. Here is one of the Professor's favorite words, both in English and French, as he himself stated on page 23 . . . and the fact

that he did not bother with another *p* in the past tense has nothing to do with his whole-hearted enjoyment of himself as a neologist.

5. English people, and Americans who consider themselves purists, at least east of the Rockies, say *tunny, tunny fish,* and even *tuna fish.* Californians invariably say *tuna.*

6. This favorite phrase of the Professor's has become almost trite in gastronomical literature, perhaps because it is so good. There is no miracle more heartening than the one which can occur whenever good people eat good food and drink good wine together.

7. This anecdote is often quoted admiringly as an example of gastronomical ingenuity. I always hated it, for it blurs my picture, undoubtedly a prejudiced one, of the fair courteous gentleman I know the Professor to have been. I think that his trick was stupid and stingy and dishonest, and it pains me.

8. Nimmo and Bain say here that the Professor referred to Cos lettuces, which were then almost unknown in France. That is quite possible: in cookery books printed in both France and England as late as 1846 there is no mention made of green salads, which have since become almost synonymous with good meals in the French style. Even in America, where Brillat-Savarin was served a raw cabbagy salad not long after the Revolution, such dishes were not the simple ones we might recognize, but intricate combinations of finely chopped and disguised "greens." The nearest thing to ours that I can find is a recipe from Common Sense, by Marion Harland, published in New York in 1871. It is called Summer Salad, and is made of lettuces, mustard leaves, water cress, radishes, and cucumbers, cut into the smallest possible pieces and tossed with a heavy dressing made with hard-boiled eggs. The whole is well mixed and then "heaped in a salad-bowl upon a lump of ice," and garnished with fennel heads and nasturtium blossoms! The only thing I can remember to compare with it is the Cobb Salad served at the Vine Street "Brown Derby" in Hollywood, a strange, soggy, and delicious mess.

9. Here Brillat-Savarin used his own phonetic spelling: YCORY.

10. The biggest punch bowl I ever saw was at the Bohemian Club in San Francisco, in 1944. It was probably silver, but I am not sure: the great wine-colored room was dark except for the

blue and yellow flames that licked up from the Gargantuan tub, and I could see nothing but the soberly gleeful, enjoyably Machiavellian face of Salvatore Lucia as he bent over his master-piece, a *Café Brûlot* for 150 people. This is his recipe, and a sure claim to immortality, if a good doctor in this world of un-good ones needs such spiritual guarantee:

The peel of 12 oranges, thinly sliced and free of white pulp
2 whole smooth-skinned oranges, studded with some of the cloves
The peel of 6 lemons, thinly sliced and free of white pulp
1 tablespoon black peppercorns
1 tablespoon whole allspice
3 crushed cardamon seeds, free of pericarp
10 vanilla beans, bisected
3 large sticks of cinnamon bark (8″ long)
120 cloves
60 cubes sugar
60 cubes rum sugar (made by adding 4 drops of Demerara rum to each cube)
1 gallon Cognac
2 gallons black coffee

Place the orange and lemon peel, spices, sugar, and rum sugar in a large bowl. Add the Cognac and let the mixture rest several hours in order to extract the aromatic substances. Hold a match under a ladle-full of the Cognac until it is warmed; then ignite the Cognac and transfer the flaming liquor to the bowl. Allow the burning to continue by ladling until the volume of the mixture is reduced by one-quarter; avoid burning the spices and fruits. Finally quench the flames by gradually adding the hot black coffee. Serve immediately in warmed demitasse cups.

11. This is a fine place to point out that not all of the amusing errors in the Professor's English were his fault. Often they can be blamed upon the French printers or copy readers: in my edition published in Paris by Garnier Frères in 1870 M. Wilkinson's apology appears as I have quoted it, but in my 1838 copy published by Charpentier it says, ". . . but tood hard a drinker for us!" Even Brillat-Savarin, so bland about speaking English like a native, would not say *tood*.

12. When my mother was a well-chaperoned young Daisy

Miller studying "voice" in Dresden, about 1902 or so, she lived in a fashionable *pension* where the other paying guests were for the most part Russians of very high birth. She remembers that they never even looked at anyone but their relatives and the servants they had brought with them, and that after every course they rinsed their mouths and spat into little bowls, and that at the end of the meal the ladies, most of them princesses and such, stood up and reached straightforwardly into secret pockets in their petticoats for fat black cigars. It is possible that Brillat-Savarin would have considered smoking at table, especially by ladies, as much an abomination as he did the spitting.

13.   Pierre Hyacinthe Azaïs (1766–1845) was a moralist and philosopher whose most important work, probably, was a treatise on the law of compensation in human destiny.

14.   Here the Professor invented another word, which I was perhaps impertinent to translate into less classical English: PHARMACONOME.

15.   The General, sarcastically, was using an idiom which is still popular in French for overcharging: *un vrai compte d'apothicaire*.

16.   The best comment on this anecdote, aside from what can be read between its lines, is in Brillat-Savarin's sixth Meditation, Section 41, a coolly mischievous dissertation on the sexual dangers of a fishy diet, and as much a part of nineteenth century thinking as an E. B. White editorial may be of the twentieth.

As for what rests between his discreet lines and phrases, the springboard into hilarious speculation lies in the fact that Madame Triguet had once been cook in the establishment of an actress known to all Paris as "The Ace of Spades." When I think of the little manuals on spices-in-the-kitchen which were sold like hot cakes to the lovelorn in those horny days, I am astonished at the simplicity of the priests of Talissieu.

17.   There is a recipe to be found in more than one French cookbook, and ascribed to more than one prominent man of letters and/or roué, which except for the mysterious spice left from the good old days in the Ace of Spade's kitchen might well be the one the priests enjoyed. Its directions are to cut the skinned eel into two-inch pieces, lard them generously with fresh truffles, and wrap them in buttered paper. They are then

to be roasted in a very hot oven for about ten minutes, taken from their wrappings, and served on a bed of crayfish tails which have been stewed in white wine and highly seasoned with cayenne. Most supposedly exciting dishes have either truffles or crayfish in them, and when both appear, coupled with the sexually significant eel, there might well be some sort of gastronomical nudging of the libido.

18.   Here is another of the Professor's quirky and somewhat outlandish inventions. It probably means "feeding power," put most bluntly.

19.   It is surprising to find recipes for this delicious dish still being printed, for it is almost extinct: the reason, to anyone who has ever tried to rub two pounds of fresh mushrooms through a sieve, is obvious.

20.   The Professor writes here of his dear friends the Richerands. It was at Villecrêne that he did much of the work on his book, as he confesses in his opening dialogue (page 6).

21.   A poll of five Germans, taken in 1947: three had never heard this expletive, one blushed faintly, and the fifth, without knowing that I quoted an author who had once been with the French Army in Germany, said that it sounded like old-fashioned soldier slang. Whatever it meant in 1825, it has a rather shocking look about it, in prose so free of exclamatory phrases.

22.   This is a typically classical allusion, made in a period when ladies and gentlemen dressed as much like the Greek gods as public morality would allow, and when Homer was read as currently as Louella Parsons is today, given a corresponding level of literacy. The Gordian knot was an intricate affair of twisted bark, which baffled everyone who hoped to untie it and become king of all Asia, until Alexander the Great arrived to sever it with one shrewd skilful blow of his sword.

23.   Here the translators Nimmo and Bain ask worriedly, "Was the turbot served up cold 'next day,' or, if not, how was it kept warm? Our author is silent on so important a subject." I think it is pretty sure that the fish was indeed served cold, whole, and noble, on a bed of fresh pretty herbs, and with perhaps a mayonnaise . . . and it is fairly sure that the Professor did not much exaggerate its goodness, although Escoffier would not agree with him that it could stand so long a wait after the cooking. He writes: "It will be found that turbot, especially when

sliced, tends to harden, crumple, and lose its flavor while cooking. It is therefore of the greatest importance that the fish should have just cooled after cooking, and that the cooking liquor (which Brillat-Savarin did not have, of course!) should have barely time to set; otherwise evil effects . . . will surely ensue." The Professor's version of a modern pressure cooker obviated such worries, it is plain, and I am surprised that Escoffier, who did not hesitate to copy almost literally the classic recipe for pheasant *à la Sainte Alliance,* passed by this fine method in favor of the tried and very untrue one of boiling *à l'Anglaise.*

24. Chinese cooks have used something like this method for many centuries, and just lately I have stood in the alley doorway of a restaurant off Portsmouth Square in San Francisco, watching a boy work a pulley delicately up and down at the Cantonese chef's signal, to cover the several dishes that steamed under the big metal bell. It was a lively scene, all hisses and white vapors. A hundred dishes must have come to perfection under that pressure in not many more minutes, and none of them stayed there more than ten or so. I ate steamed chicken, fixed into a strange beautiful mixture with datemeat, ginger, cabbage, a dozen other things. Each stood alone strongly, and the whole was mysteriously fragile.

25. The Professor's good friend Dr. Richerand, in his introduction to the second edition of THE PHYSIOLOGY OF TASTE, wrote that Brillat-Savarin was "a member of the Legion of Honor, of the Society for Encouragement of National Industry, of the Society of French Antiquarians, of the Society of Competition of Bourges, et cetera, et cetera, et cetera." He was plainly a man who, knowing the measure of his powers, used them richly and wisely, thinking of all men, and himself not the least of them.

26. This comparatively nonchalant method of making a good soup stock reminds me of Sheila Hibben's exercise in theoretical gastronomy in her KITCHEN MANUAL, which should be read at least twice a year by all modern cooks who have strayed too far from Escoffier, thanks to the tinned vagaries of both peace and war. It takes courage today to write of spending ten hours on a pot of stock, and buying four different kinds of bones (and meat) to do it. It takes a kind of courage even to *read* Mrs.

Hibben, but there is a purging excitement about it, just as there is real comedy in the picture of the affectionate and worried old lawyer dashing home to make a pot of his noted restorative broth for his friend, as he tells it on page 271, in the story of the exhausted M. Rubat.

27. The only mention I can find of the use of amber is in a recipe labelled bluntly, "Vin Aphrodisiaque," and its sounds pretty silly:

    1 ounce ginseng or mandrake
    1 ounce cinnamon bark
    1 ounce vanilla pods
    1 ounce dried rhubarb
    1 quart Chablis wine
    ⅛ ounce tincture of amber

Bruise first four ingredients in wine, and let stand for two weeks, stirring daily. Strain through fine cloth, add amber, bottle, and drink as required.

28. There are almost too many Richelieus for the translator's comfort, but I think this refers to Armand Emmanuel du Plessis, Duke of Richelieu, who was a rather hard-pressed politician before his death at the age of 56, in 1822, and who had served Russia as a soldier and governor during his years as an exile before his return to France in 1815. The note made by Nimmo and Bain about another Richelieu might as well apply to this one: ". . . he distinguished himself by his amorous and political intrigues . . ." And if my choice had not died at 56, he would qualify as well for Macaulay's description of the Richelieu who seized Minorca from the English in sight of their own squadron: ". . . an old fop who passed his life from sixteen to sixty in seducing women for whom he cared not one straw." Whichever of the sly family he was, he drew strength from his little amber lozenges!

29. Here Brillat-Savarin uses the phrase *sellé et bridé*, to mean that no expense had been spared to make the luncheon elaborate, "from soup to nuts." In this case it probably meant that oysters were served in a dozen or so ways, in the English style, or at least that many other dishes followed unlimited quantities of the live molluscs.

30.   As is so often the case in this masterpiece of discreet and classical obliquity, no more may lie here than meets the most innocent eye. On the other hand it may be the proper place for a note or two on the supposed importance of the oyster as an aphrodisiac.

This "breedy creature," as it was sometimes called in England in the eighteenth century, was most highly thought of then (as now) as a divine combination of practicability and sensuous delight. It was nourishing. It was cheap. It was a fine thing for hunters on an empty stomach. It was good for nursing children, and for growing children, and indeed for almost any sad condition inherent to mankind between the first and second childhoods. Most of all it was thought of as "celestially designed for physical regeneration, health, and vigor."

It is true that this mollusc contains a fair share of phosphorus, which according to the Professor, and many other more scientific men than he, is heating to the blood. But only the basic fact that a fresh oyster is one of the most easily digested foods in the world has kept myriad seekers of renewed virility from dying in the search. Many a man, both young and old, has downed countless slippery Dublin Powldoodies or Florida Apalachicolas in the hope that he would rise to the occasion of an imminent rendezvous with unsuspected power. Many a man has then sagged alone to bed, dragged downward by his futile gluttony.

It is astonishing that the myth still flourishes, in a dozen languages and a hundred covertly marketed books published under one variation or another of the title Cuisine d'Amour, that oysters contribute to masculine potency and even to the willingness of the ladies. Recipes for preparing them are legion, and whether they are whispered to come from the kitchen of a famed bordello, rather like the one for the Dish of Eel (page 359), or from the chef's manual of a Venetian nobleman, they usually lean heavily upon those two tried irritants, paprika and crayfish tails.

The truth of the whole hoary legend, I suspect, lies in what one nineteenth century essayist wrote in London: "The oyster, when eaten moderately . . . produces a peculiar charm and an inexplicable pleasure. After having eaten oysters we feel joyous, light, and agreeable—yes, one might say, fabulously well." In other words, they are supremely digestible! And any human being whose digestion is happy will, as the Professor has often remarked of certain gastronomical reactions, see miracles happen.

31. Medlars were called loquats, from the Japanese, when I was a child in southern California, and they were the only thing I ever stole. They always seemed to grow outside the tight-lipped houses of very cross old women who would peek at us marauders and shrill at us. There are very few of the tall dark green trees left, and most people have never tasted the beautiful voluptuous bruised fruits, nor seen the satin brown seeds, so fine to hold. The last time I saw loquats was in 1947, in the lobby of the Palace Hotel in San Francisco, many of them almost dead ripe on a long branch which was part of a decoration in the flower shop there. My early experience as a thieving gourmande warned me that they would be at their peak of decay in about six hours. That made it midnight. I asked the flower girl if the shop would be open then, and she said yes and I was there at midnight, but the fruit was gone. It smelled, she said. Of course, I cried sadly to myself, and I left with the ever-remembered perfume in my spiritual nostrils, envying her, thinking with Shakespeare, "You'll be rotten ere you be half ripe, and that's the right virtue of the medlar . . ."

32. In Colorado Springs, around 1885, there were gentlemen of every nationality who for one reason or another had plenty of money as long as they stayed there instead of in their homelands. They formed *safaris*, in their own sporting way, and in the autumns went higher than most white men had ever gone, into the great Rockies. Mounting, they killed bears, and the guides hoisted the fat furry carcasses into the tops of the tallest trees, to wait for Springtime, when the meat which had been frozen solid for months would have thawed slowly in the thin high air. Steaks from those bears are said to be the finest meat that any living man can remember . . . "high" in more ways than one, and "far gone" in a sense unknown to most game lovers.

33. This was the name of a fashionable milliner. I know nothing about her except that she made hats and turbans high off

the faces of her high-hat clients, so that their fashionably ragged "Titus" hairdos would show, and their aigrettes and bows and such.

34. Escoffier says that there is no proper roebuck in America, and that in England it is held in low esteem, being tough and of mediocre flavor. However that may be, the Professor speaks tenderly of his little Canadian creature, which was probably marinated for three or four days, roasted quickly, and served with a touch of juniper in the sauce, as was the custom then with most game . . . and is still, now and then and happily.

35. The Professor played a sly trick here with an even slyer jingle which in the original, written about 1750, said:

A maiden's lust is a burning curse,
But a nun's, in truth, is a hundred times worse.

36. Brillat-Savarin uses the word *calchup*, an unusual one in French. It, and ketchup, and catsup, probably come from the Chinese *kê-tsiap*, meaning a briny fish sauce, and I am fairly sure that what d'Albignac used in London was flavored with mushrooms or walnuts, or even elderberries or oysters, and had almost nothing in common with the unctuous scarlet liquid which *is* ketchup to every good Yankee. Here is an excellent recipe, for instance, for Oyster Catsup, which was popular with American housewives when the Professor wrote:

1 *quart oysters*
1 *tablespoon salt*
1 *teaspoon each of cayenne pepper and mace*
1 *teacupful cider vinegar*
1 *teacupful sherry*

Chop oysters and boil three minutes in own juice and the vinegar, skimming well. Strain through a haircloth, return the liquor to the fire, add wine and spices, and boil fifteen minutes. When cold, bottle and seal.

37. This name, spelled both Trollet and Trolliet, has lasted longer than many a more philoprogenitive one, for it was the old Bailiff Trollet who taught Brillat-Savarin, one deathless day, to make his first *fondue* . . . (see page 387).

38. This corps, like all hired armies, was made up of every kind of French exile, from escaped murderers to embittered dukes. One of the latter, Louis Joseph de Bourbon, Prince of Condé (1736–1818), headed it and hired it successively to Austria, Russia, and finally England, before it disbanded in 1801.

39. This is one of the very few places where an undertone of bitterness and of personal disappointment sounds through Brillat-Savarin's usual debonair attitude toward the hazards of revolution. He had as much cause as any reinstated exile to feel cynical, for he was stripped of his beloved property in Belley even to his little vineyard, but according to everyone who knew him he never complained or sulked, even with a price on his head. Dr. Richerand wrote of him, after his death, "He was forever gay, even as a poor émigré." The Professor's own attitude toward such harsh fortune is made clear in a dozen places as he discusses his fellow exiles, and never is there a hint of the snobbish martyrdom expressed, for instance, in a letter from Adrien de Montmorency to Juliette Récamier in 1812: "We must suffer, be silent, and content ourselves with our own self-respect." It is true that any kind of exile contains its own spiritual horror, and many of the sensitive intelligent people who fled France in the early part of the nineteenth century suffered deeply, no matter how handsomely they still managed to exist. But in spite of their courage, there was in their attitude a definitely morbid enjoyment which Brillat-Savarin never permitted himself. It is as clear as the contrast between their prose and his: we can read him with an undimmed enjoyment of his clarity, and find him matter-of-fact, straightforward, and cool, compared to most of his contemporaries. Madame de Staël, for example, is little read today, and would embarrass and bore most of us with an idiom which was felt to be both natural and beautiful when she wrote, as in one interminable letter to Juliette Récamier, whose husband had just gone bankrupt: "Ah, my dear Juliette, what has been my grief at the frightful news I have received! How I curse the exile which will not permit me to come to you, and press you to my heart!—May you be composed, dear friend, in the midst of these trials! Alas! neither death nor the indifference of friends menaces *you*, and these are *eternal wounds*. Adieu! dear angel, adieu!"

40. The Hippocratic mask or *facies Hippocratica* was a term still common among nineteenth century doctors, some 2200 years after the great Greek physician first used it, to identify the shrunken livid look that comes over a man's face at the approach of death.

41. I like to think this was a young Dézelay, for of all the light white wines in the world it is perhaps the most like limpid spring water, cool from the rocks. But any wine served in a Lausanne restaurant, reputable or not, would be clear, and pleasant, and easy indeed to drink . . . or so I found, a good hundred and fifty years after the Professor's stay there.

42. These orderly dots have made many people wonder. The Nimmo and Bain translation notes: "I suppose our author means to indicate that he does not wish to say anything about his stay in America . . . Accidentally he has told us some of his adventures there . . ." This seems rather foolish, for THE PHYSIOLOGY OF TASTE is one of the least *accidental* books in the world. But probably the most unperceptive criticism I have read was made in THE CORNHILL MAGAZINE in 1877, in a rather sour bad-tempered review of the book which said that the rows of dots plainly showed the boredom Brillat-Savarin had known in America, and the uncongeniality of the country! As for myself, I can see no reason for the dots, but feel that it must have amused the Professor in some way to put them there.

43. This is another of the Professor's inventions, and none too good a one, although he liked it enough to italicize it. It could possibly be a mispronunciation of the English *transportation*, used in its most strictly Latin sense.

44. This is the best example in the whole book of the Professor's naïve delight in his control of English idiom, and it would be a pity to alter one letter of it. Other translators have not agreed with my feeling: in 1884 Nimmo and Bain noted here: "(We have) taken the liberty of slightly altering a couple of the strongest and choicest English invectives, which our author uses, to prove his perfect knowledge of our language . . ." These two gentlemen were much fairer than any others of their countrymen who pretended to offer the public a sample of the old Professor's prose. *Never* was any mention made of the genetic or sexual influences of fish, truffles, oysters, and when some of the anecdotes were included at all, they were sternly altered to suit

the literary morals of Victoria's time. A review of the book in THE CORNHILL MAGAZINE in 1877 said: "Some of the stories, though they would have seemed perfectly harmless to the generation which laughed over TOM JONES, are a little too unlaced according to the ideas of the nineteenth century." And in a translation by Simpson published in New York in 1865 and called THE HANDBOOK OF DINING; *or, Corpulency and Leanness Scientifically Considered. Comprising the Art of Dining on Correct Principles Consistent with Easy Digestion, the Avoidance of Corpulency, and the Cure of Leanness; Together with Special Remarks on These Subjects. By Brillat-Savarin, Author of the "Physiologie du Goût,"* the introduction counsels: "There are a few passages somewhat free—but, gentle reader, skip them over—they are only poppies in a cornfield—dandelions on the same bank as the blue-eyed violet." No man would have appreciated this *niceness* more than the Professor.

45. This gentleman, who was so hospitable to Brillat-Savarin in exile (page 379), perhaps owes his lasting name to his recipe, since he left no other heirs. In 1934 his rule for *fondue* was given in a little book called LA BONNE CUISINE DE SUISSE ROMANDE, and in it the proportions are less euphonious but more practical (or are they?) than the Professor's: 6 eggs, 300 grams of rich grated cheese, 500 grams of fresh butter. There is no word of the pepper which is mentioned by the Frenchman as the characteristic ingredient. As an old hand at eating if not making this heavenly dish, I think Brillat-Savarin was right. I have several recipes, all from the Vaud or the Valais in Switzerland. Furthermore, almost every little café or restaurant that used to say FONDUES in the window made a perfect one, and each was subtly different from the rest. But the best ones were peppery. And the best of all, made late at night by Madame Doellanbach in Vevey, were probably more or less according to this rule, which I translate literally (for want of a better way):

For 4 people, 800 grams of very fat Jura cheese, grated or finely minced. Take a sufficiently ample earthen pot; rub its belly with a garlic clove, and put into it a piece of butter as big as a little egg. Add a small spoonful of flour, moistened in 2 or 3 décis-litres (about 5 ounces) of white wine from Neuchâtel. Let it come to the boil while working it with a wooden spoon. Add the cheese, and let it melt slowly, without ceasing to stir it. At the last moment add a small glass of kirsch, flavored with a little freshly ground pepper. Serve over a flame.

Madame Doellanbach would not make this for more than four or five people at a time. They sat around her table, behind the cash register in the alcove, and cut bread into little squares and dipped them on their forks into the gently bubbling pot. Whoever lost his bread in the mixture, or let it fall off, once twirled and coated, on the way to his mouth, must pay a round of kirsch . . . with one for the cook, of course. As the Professor said, miracles were seen . . .

46. Here Brillat-Savarin used the word *miss*, but did not italicize it as was his custom with such English terms, which had become part of the upper-class French idiom.

A hundred years later *miss* meant something prim and unattractive indeed, and I knew an old lady who had been governess for fifty years to the Burgundian aristocracy who bristled and sidled and snapped when she was so addressed. "MEEsss?" she would demand in English which had become almost unrecognizable after so long away from London. "MEEEsss?" And dutifully the greying viscount would correct himself, "Miss Lyse . . ."

47. I knew a man in good repute in French Switzerland who owned an ancient but awesome limousine (this was in about 1937) which he rented to rich tourists with himself as chauffeur; and as a sideline he ran an upstairs bar before the official opening hour for any place selling alcohol. It was a bleak small room at the top of a flight of clean stairs in the working quarter of the town. Men lined up quietly from about 6:30 in the morning, and shuffled up the stairs and through the dismal chamber and down another stair onto the street. They were most of them good men. Without a word they put a few sous (the price had not wavered much with wars and such) onto a little table by the door, were handed a small thick glass of local *schnapps*, drained it as they walked the next few paces, put it on another small table by the exit door, and went out. Nothing was said, either in the room or out of it. The liquor was almost surely untaxed and therefore contraband. The sale of it was against the law at that hour. The room was unlicensed. The men were not

supposed to drink before going to their jobs. My friend had been blandly undisturbed for many years . . .

A little fat boy used to stand on a street in St. Petersburg in 1911, and watch the workers file into another such place, owned by the government this time.

Each Russian as he came out held a little bottle of vodka with a special cork in its mouth, and with a practiced *blop* of his hand on the bottom of the flask he would push out the cork and drain down the good hot stuff.

48. See "Meditation 12," page 159, and "Varieties," VIII, page 362.

49. This generous soul was the Professor himself, quoting from his ESSAI HISTORIQUE SUR LE DUEL, which was published in 1819. In 1802 his VUES ET PROJETS D'ECONOMIE POLITIQUE appeared and then quietly disappeared, a dismal failure which may explain the hesitancy he expressed to his friend Richerand (page 6) about letting his PHYSIOLOGIE DU GOÛT see the light. When it finally was published, a few months before his death in 1826, it had been refused by Sautelet, the one editor he shyly and secretly consulted, and was brought out anonymously at his own expense. And aside from these works and, undoubtedly, some legal papers, he left nothing except the tantalizing mention, several times, of his "secret journal . . . secret memoirs . . ." Nothing vaguely like a diary by Brillat-Savarin has ever been spoken of by his friends or heirs, and it is probable that his own references to such a thing were a part of his teasing nature, his sly discreet delight in implying that he could say much more.

50. Félicité Ducrest, Countess of Genlis (1746–1830), was a popular writer who has perhaps been best, if most mercilessly described, by the two good Victorians Nimmo and Bain who had courage enough to publish an "unexpurgated" translation of Brillat-Savarin in London in 1884. They seldom lost their Olympian and calm discretion, but of the wordy countess they permitted themselves to write in a footnote here: ". . . a well-known female author of numberless novels and other works, now completely and deservedly forgotten."

51. This is a typical impasse, gastronomically, which can lead almost any amateur chef both up and down the garden path: Count M . . . may have referred to the blood pudding which modern cookery calls *boudin*, or he may have meant any of a

hundred dishes prepared with little poached dumplings which were called *boudins* by the chefs of his period; "à la Richelieu" can be simply the sauce covering the noncommittal *boudin* or it can be any of a thousand ways of serving the dish which were ascribed to or named after the Cardinal according to a cook's whim; the method probably included either and/or both lobster-coral and truffles, and could as easily have been called *à la Cardinal*. Anything labelled Soubise is somewhat easier to identify, or at least cover, with a patina of smooth onion sauce. There is a recipe in Escoffier in which a square of lamb is browned and stewed with onions, which are then put through a sieve with Bèchamel to make a Soubise, which in turn is poured over the meat. There is not a single note of wistfulness in my observation that I have never been served this dish, nor would I look down upon any candidate, political or otherwise, who was as ignorant of it as am I.

52. In the ÆNEID it says, "He nodded, and all Olympus did tremble with that nod."

53. Here is some more of the Professor's teasing: the hilly section of Paris known as Montmartre rises at most 400 feet above the level of the River Seine. Brillat-Savarin knew the place as one of ageless worship, for temples have stood on its summit since before the Druids until now when Sacré Coeur gleams there, and like all the other pilgrims he also knew the many taverns and cafés (like *Le Moulin Rouge*) where the thirsty climb toward spiritual peace could be made easier by a drink or two and a good look at the comforts of the flesh.

54. Sirius or the Dog Star is supposed to be about 8½ light years away from the Earth. For some reason its inhabitants were supposed to be at least that much hungrier than earthly inhabitants.

55. Brillat-Savarin's punch is equally unknown today, or at least is not served as it was in his time, as a matter of course in any pleasant evening. The nearest thing we have to it, except in homes at the New Year and in a few private clubs which doggedly cling to the ancient and supposedly safe patterns of their founders, is coffee mixed with flaming spirits. It is a fine comforting tipple, whether made in a little French railroad station with questionable coffee and worse rum, or at Antoine's in New Orleans with a fussier fillip of tourist-wise quality. The

best recipe for it, perhaps, and one which can be made for Lilliput or Gargantua according to your mathematical skill, is Dr. Lucia's on page 419.

56. According to Escoffier, both land- and water-rails "are prepared fresh; or, if it is thought necessary to hang them for a few days, at least they should not be allowed to get high." They are in general treated like quail . . . and there are also a few diners "who know how delicious a whole brochette of tiny fried birds may be." Such gastronomers, unconsciously or not, are why there are no more of the "black clouds of rice-birds" that once darkened Louisiana skies and lightened the fine dinner tables there: I myself was given a recipe by a very old lady from Biloxi, which started, Take 300 plump plucked birds . . .

57. Wise Solomon counselled: "Let us crown ourselves with rose-buds, before they be withered." And some two hundred years before the Professor decided much the same thing, Robert Herrick sang, in his advice to the Virgins,

> Gather ye rosebuds while ye may,
>   Old Time is still a-flying,
> And this same flower that smiles today
>   Tomorrow will be dying.

58. This is one of the most ridiculous of the Professor's inventions, OBÉSIGÈNE. It so shook the translators Nimmo and Bain that in 1884 they called it "barbarous"! Dietetically, as well as semantically, the word betrays the Professor: he watched his weight with the intense preoccupation of any movie star.

59. This is a term used especially in freemasonry, to designate the doorkeeper or watchman of secret meetings.

60. In a cheap (1 franc 10 centimes) and delightful (illustrations by Bertall) edition (Paris, 1852) of the Professor's masterpiece, there is a solid and sincere piece of hack writing by Emile de Labédollière, in a Preface which tells better than most what Brillat-Savarin seemed like to people who remembered him some twenty-five years after his death:

"Physically he was very tall, so that he had been named the drum major of the Court of Appeals. (See page 172.) Since he enjoyed lengthy meals, all the while managing to avoid indigestion and tipsiness, he had acquired a girth proportionate to his height. His fleshy face was none too expressive. His careless way of dressing, with a generous shirt collar and full trousers bagging over his shoes, gave him the appearance of an undistinguished bumpkin. Usually he preferred to listen rather than talk; he hardly seemed to come to life until the end of a good dinner, and then his conversation had the subtle effervescence of champagne which at last has been poured from its long imprisonment; but people with whom he had no close relationship state almost unanimously that he was uncommunicative, heavy, and absent-minded, and that he never unveiled in his meetings with them the classicism, the finesse, and the wide general knowledge which he proved in THE PHYSIOLOGY OF TASTE to possess."

Labédollière adds, "as for us who were not his contemporaries, we should count ourselves fortunate that he gave sparingly of himself, to pour all the treasures of his soul into the book he has left us."

61. Eos, called rosy-fingered, was the goddess of the dawn. Romans knew her as Aurora. She loved Tithonus, and had a son by him, and successfully demanded that he be made immortal. But she forgot to ask that he stay young, and when she grew tired of his creaky senile feebleness she changed him with no recorded pangs of regret into a grasshopper. It is doubtful that even the reputed powers of French truffles could have saved him from his fate.

62. This costly *vin de paille* (straw-wine) is indeed soft and generous, and also heady, made from grapes ripened slowly on straw mats.

63. The translation of this jolly song published in what is called "the Arthur Machen PHYSIOLOGY" by Peter Davies, London 1925, could probably not be much bettered:

> Oh, 'tis a pleasant thing and sweet
> When kindly folk the traveller greet,
> And merriment and wine flow free;
> With such good fellows and such cheer,
> How gladly could I tarry here,
> Secure from all anxiety,
> > Four days,
> > Fourteen days,
> > Forty days,
> > A year, nor go
> While the bless'd Fates detain'd me so!

6 . It is easy to read into this anecdote, from the first casual sentence to the last jaunty one, most of the Professor's humanly weak and wonderful traits. He manages to imply a great many things about the Prot couple. He does not *say* that they were a typical pair of newly arisen politicians in a most unsavory government, but it is plain that as a royalist or at least a federalist he despises their social crudeness. He does not *say* that Madame had bad manners, but he manages to make his boredom at her single-track conversation very evident. He does not *say* that she was a wrinkled old singing teacher, but he lets it be known that her cultured interest in "the finer things of life" once, long ago, earned a living for her. He does not *say* that he used her ruthlessly, mischievously, desperately, but the cynicism behind his bland descriptions of their two hearts beating together, of their mingled voices, of his heartfelt kiss, could be distasteful if it were not so urbane. And as for the dinner with the legal gentlemen, which gave the fortunate beginning to his trip, it is underlaid with such innate charm as to be unforgettable. It is everything admirable about a man with his back to the wall who can yet dine and drink and sing with gaiety as well as good manners. Brillat-Savarin admits as much, with the amused tolerance of an old man. He surmises that being a Frenchman did it, but there are a few like him in every country, now as then.

65. This Epistle, "To Maecenas," is from the translation printed in London in 1684. It is by Thomas Creech: "*Horatius. —Odes, satyrs, and epistles of Horace, done into English.*" It well bears out the Professor's theory that gastronomy in its ancient limited form could offer little sublimation but an alcoholic one to the men who then as now must whip themselves to find existence justifiable.

66. In Act II, Scene I of MACBETH, Shakespeare wrote about drink, "It provokes the desire, but it takes away the performance." These blunt words are etched on the hearts of many a tipsy would-be lover . . .

67. Leigh Hunt (1784–1859) wrote, about "Breakfast in Cold Weather": "Here it is, ready laid. *Imprimis*, coffee and tea; secondly, dry toast; thirdly, butter; fourthly, eggs; fifthly, ham; sixthly, something potted; seventhly, bread, salt, mustard, knives, forks, &c. One of the first things that belong to a breakfast, is a good fire. There is a delightful mixture of the lively and the snug,

in coming down to one's breakfast-room of a cold morning, and seeing everything prepared for us,—a blazing grate, a clean table-cloth and tea-things; the newly washed faces and combed heads of a set of good-humoured urchins . . ."

68.   Brillat-Savarin infers that anything from the story of the imaginary travels in Greece of the young Scythian Anacharsis will delight his readers. The book was written by Jean-Jacques Barthélemy, who died in 1795 at the age, a ripe one in those days, of 79.

69.   Very little is known about Pierre Motin, except that he flourished in the sixteenth cetury and died about 1615, and that his poems are found in every collection of that time.

70.   Maynard was a lawyer (1582–1646), and both he and the Marquis de Racan, who wrote religious and pastoral poetry, were pupils of the great poet and critic François de Malherbe.

71.   There is a complex play on words here, with *naître* and *planter,* and it becomes so weightily sesquipedalian with variations on the theme *to inseminate,* for instance, that probably the best thing is to follow the rest of the translators and scamp the issue completely!

72.   The directions for this composition, given its subject, are almost ludicrous today. But at the turn of the nineteenth century, when they were written, they were a serious and sincere expression of an amateur musician's desire to entertain his friends.

Not only was Death itself an intimate of them all, in those premortician, prehospital days when both great and small must wait for a loved one's death rattle and then close the lids, but it was considered proper and desirable for any true lady or gentleman to be able to sing, and if need be play the accompaniment, after a pleasant dinner and before the card games and the conversation.

It was the Byronic Age, and tender virgins with soft Attic curls upon their napes caroled passionately of heroes prone upon the battlefield, of noble martyred dogs, and of a babe's first lisp, as they were to do a decade or so later in the less worldly drawing rooms of America.

Brillat-Savarin may have had more than his share of philosophical detachment, but he also was a knowing observer of his times, and did not even smile at the musical histrionics he asked for as a background to his modishly moribund self-revelation. (See page 17 and page 275.)

73.   According to biographies, President Henrion de Pansey did not die until 1829, at the age of 87. Brillat-Savarin preceded him by a good three years, but could write, months before his death at 71, as a pupil might write of his mentor, with an almost protective affection. (Page 4, "Aphorism IX.")

74.   The Professor wrote here, in mild teasing, *un beau titus*, because during the Directory (1795–1799) it was the fashion for the young fops and men-about-town to wear their hair cut shaggily short, except for a few loose locks over their brows and cheeks, in imitation of the bust of the Roman Titus. Older men, more moderate, wore even shorter hair in the style called "Brutus," if they were not bewigged.

75.   The Vestal virgins were, as their name indicates, chaste Roman girls who cared for the temple of Vesta. They were high-born maidens, of almost unlimited political power, dedicated in childhood to the care of the sacred precincts and trained in obedience and virtue. After thirty years of service they could marry, but as one mid-Victorian writer stated bluntly, "by then they seldom did so." If ever they broke their vows of chastity they were condemned to be buried alive after lavish public funeral rites.

76.   In the first unabridged English translation of this book, made and published by Nimmo and Bain in 1884 in London, there is a sad note here: "I regret to say that the illustrious author speaks of *Malvoisie de Madère*. Malmsey is a wine from Candia."

This recalls another note, made in Paris in 1879 by Charles Monselet in his Preface to THE PHYSIOLOGY OF TASTE. It is somewhat smug: "I add a last note to perpetuate one of my surprises. Neither Brillat-Savarin, nor Grimod de la Reynière, nor even the Marquis de Cussy, have given a great importance to wine. It seems that they only considered it as a digestive element. Provided that it was good, they did not ask for more; and they did not make any distinctions between our innumerable brands of Burgundies and of clarets. Was the exquisite sense of this important part of taste entirely wanting to them? In this respect, at least, we are superior to them."

77.   Here for the last time the Professor refers sarcastically to "surêne herbé," which in his time was the worst thing a wine could be called. He told in a note on page 139 about the village of Suresnes that gave this vinegar its dubious renown. He mentioned it on page 41. It was indubitably a vinous insult, as he said it.

78.   "Geographical progression," as THE WORLD ALMANAC calls it, was still being made in 1900, and English, French, and Italian explorers pushed their way here and there in Africa; Sven Hedin with the blessing of the King of Norway and Sweden went on an exceedingly dangerous journey through East Turkistan; early in the year the Government of Chile dispatched a group of scientists to Southern Patagonia.

Gastronomically little is recorded of their findings, unless there is some connection between the art of dining and the discovery of many villages filled with skeletons in the country southwest of the Nile's beginning.

The consumption of champagne, in America at least, fell sharply at the turn of the century (although as one who has never seen such a moment, nor ever shall, I should think the opposite would happen: so many toasts to be drunk, and doubts to be stilled).

Coffee cost about seven cents a pound. Cheese cost nine, and butter eight. A five course table-d'hôte dinner with wine and tip could easily be found in New York for a dollar.

But Brillat-Savarin need never have wasted his tears upon his contemporaries who would not live to know the pleasures of the twentieth century table: whatever rock-borne delicacies or heady mysterious distillations may have evolved could never convince the new gastronomers that they were as well off as they would have been in 1825. They looked back longingly to the days of the Restoration, when the art of dining was not the prerogative of the overblown financiers, but the privilege of any happy human with a few francs or shillings in his pocket.

It is true that they had soft-shell crabs, which the Professor never knew. They had canvas-back ducks, and diamond-back terrapins. Still they wept, sensing that they had neither the leisure nor the instinctive simplicity for a real *fondue*.

PARTING SALUTE
TO THE
GASTRONOMERS
OF THE OLD AND NEW
WORLDS

Excellencies!

This work in which I do honor to you has for its purpose the development for all eyes of the principles of that science of which you are the bulwark and the ornament.

I send up in it, therefore, a first wafting of incense to Gastronomy, the youngest of the Immortals, who hardly before she has assumed her starry crown is taller than her sisters, like Calypso, who stood a head's height above the charming group of nymphs who crowded 'round her.

The Temple of Gastronomy, chief ornament of the capital of the world, will soon lift toward the skies its mighty porticoes; you will make it echo with your voices; you will enrich it with your talents; and when the academy promised by the oracle establishes itself on the two unshifting cornerstones of pleasure and of need, you, enlightened gourmands, you, most agreeable of table guests, will be its members and its aides.

Meanwhile, lift to high heaven your beaming visages; go forward in all your strength and mightiness; the whole edible world is open before you.

Work hard, Excellencies. Preach, for the good of your science; digest, in your own peculiar interests; and if, in the course of your labors, you happen to make some important discovery, be good enough to share it with this, the humblest of your servants!

A POSTSCRIPT
FROM THE
TRANSLATOR

I feel even more strongly than I did at the beginning of translating this book that it is a well-balanced expression of one thinking man's attitude toward life. There are few of them, in any language.

The fact that THE PHYSIOLOGY OF TASTE is about gastronomy has little, nothing really, to do with its author's innate good taste, nor with his art in making it clear upon each page. I have plumbed every word of his, and after many years of casual enjoyment and two of the most intimate kind, I have yet to find myself either bored or offended, which is more than most women can say of any relationship, whether ghostly or corporeal. For me, the Professor is a continuing delight.

I enjoy the physical picture of him, which may be wishful but is still based on a few descriptions beside his own, and a few engravings, and a few phrases like Charles Monselet's: "This figure, smiling rather than laughing, this well-lined paunch, this stylish mind and stomach . . ."

I enjoy his "stylish mind" most of all: his teasing of the priests, and his underplayed pleasure in them when they were good men of any cloth; his tenderness and irony toward pretty women, and his full fine enjoyment of them; his lusty delight in hunting, in a good row, in a cock-snoot at disaster . . . and the way he made all this plain to me, in a prose perhaps more straightforward than any that has come down to us from his verbose flighty period in French literature.

His restrained discretion, while never simpering or ridiculous, is often deliberately pedagogic. He sometimes harrumphs, tongue in cheek . . . no insignificant feat either physically or spiritually! He often plays, tongue still in cheek, the safely retired satyr . . . but never does he grow offensive or even faintly senile. Deliberately at times he outlines with mocking pedantry the A-B-C, a-b-c of a point. Never does he scorn the plodders of philosophy who have made banalities of such ways of logic. Always there is clear in everything he writes a basic humility, and that is the main reason why I think his book is one meant to last much longer than a century or so. That is why I have spent many months of my best thought and my best (my *vintage*) energy upon it.

In a Western world filled with too many books, too many human beings angry or bored enough to be voluble, it is a good thing that there are a few such distillations as this one. Brillat-Savarin spent about twenty-five years writing it. He spoke of it to almost nobody, and when finally it appeared, a few months before his death and anonymously and at his own expense, his friends were astounded that he had written it, for he had never flashed before them in its full colors the rich tapestry of his mind, but had instead woven quietly and in secret peace.

In the Professor's time it was considered the unquestioned right of any man of common sense, which he so eminently was, to choose how best he might spend his hours of creation. When young he studied war and love and politics with an ardor and directness and an unclouded simplicity impossible to our own murky days. When he grew older, and withdrew perforce from actual combat, he found himself in the happy state of being able to think, to recollect in tranquillity.

That is perhaps the greatest difference between him and us: by the time we have slugged our way as courageously as possible past the onslaughts of modern engines and bacteria and ideals we are drained and exhausted, and any one of us who reaches the age of seventy-one with serenity and a clear conscience is felt to be an unfair freak. Something must be wrong, we say resentfully; he must have cheated somewhere, taken some secret elixir.

Perhaps we can sip that potion, even vicariously, in the slow reading of a few books like this one, and can feel ourselves encouraged and renewed by the knowledge that if Brillat-Savarin could outride the wild storms of revolution and intrigue and not let them trouble his digestion, as Balzac wrote of him, so in our way can we.